VIA FOLIOS 81

A Reference Grammar of Contemporary Italian for English Speakers

Library of Congress Control Number: 2012938895

© 2013 Samuel Ghelli

All rights reserved. Parts of this book may be reprinted only by written permission from the authors, and may not be reproduced for publication in book, magazine, or electronic media of any kind, except in quotations for purposes of literary reviews by critics.

Printed in the United States.

Published by
BORDIGHERA PRESS
John D. Calandra Italian American Institute
25 W. 43rd Street, 17th Floor
New York, NY 10036

VIA FOLIOS 81
ISBN 978-1-59954-044-3

A Reference Grammar of Contemporary Italian for English Speakers

Samuel Ghelli

edited by
Zohra Saad

Bordighera Press

CONTENTS

Introduction		17
Abbreviations and Symbols		19
1.	**SPELLING AND PRONUNCIATION**	21
	1.1 The Alphabet and Its Sounds	21
	1.2 The Vowels	21
	1.3 Diphthongs and Triphthongs	22
	1.4 The Consonants	23
	1.5 Groups of Letters Making One Sound: *ch, gh, gn,* etc.	23
	1.6 Double Consonants: *tt, pp, rr,* etc.	24
	1.7 Syntactic Doubling	24
	1.8 Syllabification	25
	1.9 Stress	25
	1.10 Words Whose Meaning Changes with the Stress	26
	1.11 Written Accents	27
	1.12 Elision: *un'amica, quest'albero,* etc.	28
	1.13 Dropping One Letter or More and Using an Apostrophe: *un po', da', sta',* etc.	28
	1.14 Dropping a Final Unstressed Vowel: *signor Rossi, buon giorno,* etc.	29
	1.15 Dropping a Final Syllable: *gran giorno, fra Lorenzo, bel bambino,* etc.	29
	1.16 Punctuation	30
	1.17 Capitalization	30
2.	**ARTICLES**	31
	2.1 Gender and Number of Articles: Italian Unlike English	31
	2.2 The Indefinite Articles: *un, una,* etc.	31
	2.3 Special Uses of the Indefinite Articles	32
	2.4 The Definite Articles: *il, la,* etc.	33
	2.5 Uses of Definite Articles Unlike English	34
	2.6 Omission of Articles	35
3.	**NOUNS**	36
	3.1 Gender and Number of Nouns: Italian Unlike English	36
	3.2 Gender: General Rules Based on the Final Vowels *-o, -a, -e*	36

3.3	From Masculine to Feminine	37
3.4	Feminine Nouns in *-o*	37
3.5	Masculine Nouns in *-a* (including *-ma* and *-ta*)	38
3.6	Masculine and Feminine Nouns Ending in *-ista, -cida, -iatra, -arca*	39
3.7	Gender of Nouns Ending in *-ore, -trice, -ione, -zione, -tudine, -ie*	40
3.8	Gender of Nouns Ending in *-i* and *-u*	40
3.9	Gender of Nouns Ending in *-ò, -à, -è, -ì, -ù*	40
3.10	Gender of Foreign Nouns: *film, computer, hamburger*, etc.	41
3.11	The Most Used English Nouns in Italian	42
3.12	Abbreviated Nouns: *bici, cinema, foto*, etc.	43
3.13	Nouns Changing Meaning with Gender: *il caso/la casa, il porto/la porta*, etc.	43
3.14	Nouns with Same Form but Different Meaning: *il capitale/la capitale, il fine/la fine*, etc.	43
3.15	Nouns of Trees and Fruit: Different Genders	44
3.16	Gender of Animal Names	44
3.17	Gender of Cities, Rivers, States, etc.	44
3.18	Gender of Cars, Motorcycles, Wines, etc.	45
3.19	Compound Nouns: *capogruppo, pianoforte*, etc.	45
3.20	Gender of Compound Nouns	46
3.21	Gender of Words Other Than Nouns: Adjectives, Adverbs, etc.	46
3.22	From Singular to Plural: General Rules	46
3.23	Some Spelling Problems: *-co > -chi, -cia > -ce*, etc.	47
3.24	Singular Masculine Nouns in *-o* with Feminine Plural in *-a*	48
3.25	Some Other Irregularities: *arma > armi, uomo > uomini*, etc.	48
3.26	Nouns with Dual Plurals and Meanings: *i cigli/le ciglia , i muri/le mura*, etc.	49
3.27	Italian Singular vs. English Plural and Vice Versa: *pigiama* ('pajamas'), *capelli* ('hair'), etc.	50
3.28	The Plural of Compound Nouns	50

4. ADJECTIVES — 53

4.1	Adjectives: Italian Unlike English	53
4.2	Gender of Adjectives and Agreement with Nouns	53
4.3	Adjectives in *-co, -go, -ca* and *-ga*	54
4.4	A Few Invariable Adjectives	54
4.5	Agreement with Multiple Nouns	55
4.6	The Adjective *bello*	55
4.7	Colloquial Constructions of *bello*: *bell'e pronto, nel bel mezzo*, etc.	56
4.8	The Adjective *buono*	56
4.9	Colloquial Constructions of *buono*: *una buona mezz'ora*, etc.	57
4.10	The Adjectives *grande* and *santo*	57
4.11	Compound Adjectives	58
4.12	Compound Adjectives: Particularities	58
4.13	Position of Descriptive Adjectives	59
4.14	Adjectives of Beauty, Age, Goodness, and Size	59
4.15	Position of the Other Adjectives: *molto, due, mio*, etc.	60
4.16	Word Order in Combinations of Two or More Adjectives	60

	4.17	Adjectives Used as Nouns	61
	4.18	Adjectives with Prepositions + Infinitive	61

5. ADVERBS AND ADVERBIAL PHRASES 62

5.1	Adverbs in *-mente*: *lentamente, felicemente*, etc.	62
5.2	Adverbs with Complementary Double Forms: *certo/certamente, solo/solamente*, etc.	63
5.3	Adverbs with Distinct Double Forms: *alto* and *altamente*, *forte* and *fortemente*, etc.	63
5.4	Irregular Adverbs	64
5.5	Adverbs in *-oni* Expressing Physical Manner: *bocconi, ginocchioni*, etc.	64
5.6	Other Ways to Form Adverbs and Adverbial Expressions of Manner	65
5.7	Adverbs of Time: *oggi, adesso, sempre*, etc.	66
5.8	Adverbs of Place: *vicino, qui, là*, etc.	67
5.9	Adverbs of Quantity: *molto, nulla, poco*, etc.	68
5.10	Adverbs of Affirmation, Negation, or Doubt	69
5.11	Interrogative Adverbs: *perché, quando, come*, etc.	69
5.12	Exclamatory Adverbs: *come* and *quanto*	69
5.13	Positions of Adverbs	70

6. COMPARATIVES AND SUPERLATIVES 71

6.1	Degrees of Descriptive Adjectives	71
6.2	Degrees of Adverbs	71
6.3	Comparatives of Equality: *così ... come, tanto ... quanto*, etc.	72
6.4	Comparatives of Inequality: *più/meno ... di, più/meno ... che*, etc.	72
6.5	Sentence Comparisons	74
6.6	Relative Superlative: *il più/il meno ... di*	74
6.7	Absolute Superlative: *-issimo, molto ..., super-*, etc.	75
6.8	Irregular Comparatives and Superlatives of Adjectives: *migliore, pessimo, superiore*, etc.	76
6.9	Irregular Comparatives and Superlatives of Adverbs: *meglio, peggio, ottimamente*, etc.	77
6.10	Superlatives in *-errimo* and *-entissimo*	77
6.11	Superlatives of Nouns: *occasionissima, finalissima*, etc.	78

7. POSSESSIVES AND POSSESSIVE STRUCTURES 79

7.1	Forms of the Possessive	79
7.2	Agreement of Possessive Forms	80
7.3	Omission of the Definite Article	81
7.4	Possessives with Nouns Denoting Family Members	81
7.5	Possessives and Indefinite Articles: *un mio, un nostro, una vostra*, etc.	82
7.6	Omission of Possessives	82
7.7	Italian Equivalent of English Possessive -'s or -s'	82
7.8	Position of Possessive Adjectives	82
7.9	The Equivalent to the English 'own': *proprio*	83
7.10	The Equivalent to the English 'someone else's': *altrui*	83

8. RELATIVE PRONOUNS 84
- 8.1 Forms of the Relative Pronouns 84
- 8.2 Obligatory Use of Relative Pronouns 84
- 8.3 Uses of *che* 84
- 8.4 A Common Pitfall in the Use of *che* 85
- 8.5 *Che* and Past Participle Agreement: *La busta che è arrivata; La pizza che ho mangiato*, etc. ... 85
- 8.6 Use of *cui* 85
- 8.7 The Possessive Meaning of *il cui, la cui*, etc. 86
- 8.8 Use of *il quale, la quale, del quale*, etc. 86
- 8.9 Use of *chi* 86
- 8.10 The Forms *colui che, colei che*, and *coloro che* 87
- 8.11 The Forms of *quello che* and *ciò che* 87
- 8.12 The Relative Meaning of *quanto, quanti*, and *quante* 87

9. INTERROGATIVES 88
- 9.1 Structures of the Interrogative Sentence: Like and Unlike English 88
- 9.2 Forms and Uses of Interrogative Pronouns and Adjectives: *chi, quale*, etc. 89
- 9.3 Forms and Uses of Interrogative Adverbs: *come?, quando?*, etc. 90
- 9.4 Interrogative *se*: *Dimmi se vieni; E se fosse Marco?* 91
- 9.5 How to Answer a Question 91

10. DEMONSTRATIVES 93
- 10.1 Forms of *questo* 93
- 10.2 Forms of *quello* 94
- 10.3 The Uses of *questo* and *quello* 95
- 10.4 The Case of the Adjectives *sto, sta, sti,* and *ste* 96
- 10.5 The Particular Use of *codesto* 97
- 10.6 Equivalent Forms of *questo* and *quello*: *tale, siffatto, simile*, etc. 97
- 10.7 The pronoun *ciò* 97
- 10.8 Pronouns Referring Only to Persons: *questi, quegli, colui*, etc. 97
- 10.9 Demonstratives with Adverbs of Place: *questo qui, quello laggiù*, etc. 98
- 10.10 Demonstratives of Identity: *stesso* and *medesimo* 98

11. INDEFINITES 99
- 11.1 *Uno* and *una* 99
- 11.2 *Qualche, qualcuno,* and *qualcuna* 100
- 11.3 *Qualcosa* (or *qualche cosa*) 100
- 11.4 *Alcuno, alcuna, alcuni,* and *alcune* 101
- 11.5 *Certo, certa, certi,* and *certe* 101
- 11.6 *Tale* and *tali* 102
- 11.7 *Altro, altra, altri,* and *altre* 102
- 11.8 *Chiunque, qualunque,* and *qualsiasi* 103

11.9	*Ogni*, *ognuno*, and *ciascuno*	104
11.10	The Negative *nessuno*, *niente*, and *nulla*	104
11.11	Some Rare Forms: *alcunché*, *taluni*, *certuni*, etc.	105
11.12	*Tutto*, *tutta*, *tutti*, and *tutte*	106
11.13	The Gradation of Degrees: *poco*, *alquanto*, *parecchio*, *molto*, *tanto*, and *troppo*	106

12. NUMERALS AND NUMERAL CONSTRUCTIONS ... 107

12.1	Cardinal Numbers from 0 to 99	107
12.2	Cardinal Numbers above 100	108
12.3	Uses of Cardinal Numbers	109
12.4	Ordinal Numbers	110
12.5	Cardinals and Ordinals with Dates, Years, and Centuries	111
12.6	Numbers Expressing Time	112
12.7	Numbers Expressing Age	112
12.8	Numbers in Mathematics	112
12.9	How to Express 'half of …': *mezzo* and *la metà di …*	113
12.10	Numbers Expressing Measurements	113
12.11	Multiplicatives: *doppio*, *triplo*, etc.	113
12.12	Collective Numbers and Approximate Values: *un paio*, *una dozzina*, etc.	113
12.13	Idiomatic Uses of Some Numbers: *quattro gatti*, *due passi*, etc.	114

13. PERSONAL PRONOUNS ... 116

13.1	Subject Pronouns: *io*, *tu*, *lui*, etc.	116
13.2	Italian Equivalents of Neuter English 'it' and 'they'	118
13.3	Formal *Lei* and *Loro*	118
13.4	Use and Omission of Subject Pronouns	119
13.5	Stressed and Unstressed Object Pronouns: *me/mi*, *te/ti*, etc.	120
13.6	Direct Object Pronouns: *mi*, *me*, *lo*, *la*, etc.	121
13.7	Direct Object Pronouns and Past Participle Agreement: *L'ho mangiato / L'ho mangiata*	123
13.8	*Ecco* + Direct Object Pronouns: *eccomi*, *eccoli*, *eccovi*, etc.	124
13.9	Indirect Object Pronouns: *mi = a/per me*, *gli = a/per lui*, etc.	124
13.10	Double Object Pronouns: *melo, gliela, vele*, etc.	126
13.11	Double Object Pronouns and Past Participle Agreement: *Gliel'ho dato / Gliel'ho data*	127
13.12	Object Prepositional Pronouns: *di lui, con voi, fra noi*, etc.	127
13.13	Reflexive Pronouns: *mi, si, ci*, etc.	128
13.14	The Reflexive Pronoun *sé*	129
13.15	The Reflexive Use of *stesso*: *me stesso, loro stessi*, etc.	129
13.16	Reciprocal Pronouns: *ci, vi, si*, etc.	130

14. THE PARTICLES CI AND NE ... 131

| 14.1 | The Particle *ci* | 131 |
| 14.2 | The Locative *ci* in Combination with Direct Object Pronouns: *mi ci, ce lo*, etc. | 132 |

14.3	*Ci* and the Verb *essere*: *c'è, ci sono*, etc.	133
14.4	*Ci* in Idiomatic Expressions: *non ci casco, non c'entro,* etc.	133
14.5	*Vi* Equivalent to *ci*	134
14.6	The Particle *ne*	134
14.7	Idiomatic Uses of *ne*	135

15. PARTITIVES 137

15.1	Partitives in Italian: Like and Unlike English	137
15.2	The Partitive Article: *del, dello, della,* etc.	137
15.3	Other Partitive Expressions: *un po', qualche,* and *alcuni/alcune*	139

16. PREPOSITIONS 139

16.1	The Preposition *a*	139
16.2	The Preposition *in*	140
16.3	A Difficult Choice: *in* or *a*?	141
16.4	The preposition *da*	142
16.5	The Preposition *di*	143
16.6	The Prepositions *fra* and *tra*	144
16.7	The Preposition *con*	145
16.8	The Preposition *per*	145
16.9	The Preposition *su*	146
16.10	Articulated Prepositions and Their Uses: *del, alla, negli,* etc.	146
16.11	Other Prepositions: *dopo, eccetto, fuori,* etc.	147

17. CONNECTIVES: CONJUNCTIONS AND CONJUNCTIVE PHRASES 149

17.1	Copulative Connectives: *e, anche, inoltre,* etc.	149
17.2	Disjunctive Connectives: *o* and *oppure*	150
17.3	Adversative Connectives: *ma, però, invece,* etc.	150
17.4	Declarative Connectives: *cioè, infatti, ovvero,* etc.	151
17.5	Conclusive Connectives: *dunque, pertanto, tanto che,* etc.	151
17.6	Correlative Connectives: *e … e, o … o, ma … anche,* etc.	152
17.7	Uses of the Conjunction *che*	153
17.8	Omission of the Conjunction *che*	154
17.9	The Causal Conjunction *ché*	154
17.10	Causal Connectives: *perché, poiché, siccome,* etc.	154
17.11	Purpose Connectives: *perché, affinché, acciocché,* etc.	155
17.12	Time Connectives: *quando, mentre, dopo che,* etc.	155
17.13	Conditional Connectives: *se, semmai, qualora,* etc.	157
17.14	Concessive Connectives: *benché, sebbene, quantunque,* etc.	157
17.15	Modal Connectives: *come, comunque, quasi,* etc.	158
17.16	Connectives of Exception: *salvo che, fuorché, tranne che,* etc.	159
17.17	Restrictive Connectives: *per quanto, da quello che, a quel che,* etc.	159
17.18	Comparative Connectives: *così … come, più … che, meglio … che,* etc.	160

18. NEGATIVE STRUCTURES 161
    18.1   Structure of Negative Sentences with the Simple *non* 161
    18.2   Common Negative Phrases with *non*: *non … ancora, non … più*, etc. 162
    18.3   Negatives with Compound Tenses: *non ho mai mangiato del pesce* 162
    18.4   Negative Answers 163

19. WORD DERIVATION: PREFIXES AND SUFFIXES 164
    19.1   Word Derivation 164
    19.2   The Most Common Prefixes: *a-, dis-, inter-*, etc. 165
    19.3   The Most Common Suffixes: *-aggio, -eria, -ista*, etc. 166
    19.4   Evaluative Suffixes 168
    19.5   Diminutive and Affective Suffixes: *-ino, -etto, -ello*, etc. 168
    19.6   Augmentative Suffixes: *-one, -ona -acchione, and* acchiona 169
    19.7   Pejorative Suffixes: *accio, -astro, -uccio*, etc. 169
    19.8   The Special Cases of *patrigno, matrigna, fratellastro,* and *sorellastra* 170
    19.9   Typical Verb Suffixes: *-acchiare, -erellare, -ettare*, etc. 170

20. VERB FORMS: REGULAR AND IRREGULAR CONJUGATIONS 171
    20.1   Italian Verbs Unlike English Verbs 171
    20.2   The Three Conjugations: *-are, -ere*, and *-ire* 171
    20.3   Person, Gender, Number 172
    20.4   Moods and Tenses 172
    20.5   Transitive and Intransitive: Italian vs English 173
    20.6   The Verb *essere* 174
    20.7   The Verb *avere* 175
    20.8   Compound Tenses: *essere* or *avere*? 176
    20.9   Past Participle Agreement with *essere* and *avere* 177
    20.10   Intransitive Verbs Taking the Auxiliary *avere* 178
    20.11   Verbs with Double Auxiliaries: *essere* and *avere* 178
    20.12   The Verbs *essere* and *avere* with Modal Verbs 179
    20.13   Compound Tense Formation 179
    20.14   The First Conjugation: Verbs in *-are* 180
    20.15   Particularities of Verbs in *-care, -gare, -iare,* and *-eare* 181
    20.16   Irregular Verbs in *-are* 182
    20.17   The Second Conjugation: Verbs in *-ere* 184
    20.18   Particularities of Second Conjugation Regular Verbs 185
    20.19   Irregular Verbs in *-ere* 185
    20.20   Irregularities of the Preterite and/or Past Participle of verbs in *-ere* 189
    20.21   Verbs Without Preterite and Past Participle Forms 191
    20.22   Verbs in *-arre, -orre, -urre* 191
    20.23   The Third Conjugation: Verbs in *-ire* 195
    20.24   Verbs with *-isc-*: *finire, capire, pulire*, etc. 196
    20.25   Irregular Verbs in *-ire* 197

21. VERBS: USES OF MOODS AND TENSES 200
    21.1   The Indicative Mood 200
    21.2   Uses of the Present Indicative 200
    21.3   Italian vs English Present Progressive 201
    21.4   Uses of the Future Tense 201
    21.5   Uses of the Future Progressive 202
    21.6   Uses of the Future Perfect 202
    21.7   Uses of the Imperfect 203
    21.8   The Imperfect Progressive 204
    21.9   Uses of the Preterite 204
    21.10   Uses of the Present Perfect 204
    21.11   Preterite vs Present Perfect 205
    21.12   Uses of the Pluperfect 205
    21.13   Uses of the Preterite Perfect 206
    21.14   Combining the Imperfect and the Present Perfect 206
    21.15   The Progressive Tenses: Italian Unlike English 207
    21.16   The Subjunctive 208
    21.17   Uses of the Subjunctive in Independent Clauses 208
    21.18   The Subjunctive in Dependent *"che* Clauses" 209
    21.19   How to Use the Subjunctive Tenses in the Dependent *"che* Clauses" 211
    21.20   Omission of *che* in Dependent Subjunctive Clauses 211
    21.21   Necessity of the Subject with the Subjunctive 212
    21.22   Negative Constructions with the Subjunctive 212
    21.23   *Di* + Infinitive vs *che* + Subjunctive 212
    21.24   Indicative and Conditional Moods Instead of Subjunctive 212
    21.25   Mandatory Subjunctive After Some Conjunctions or Special Expressions: *purché, se*, etc. .. 213
    21.26   The Subjunctive in Relative Clauses: *Marco cercava chi lo aiutasse* 214
    21.27   The Subjunctive After Indefinite Adjectives and Pronouns: *Chiunque tu sia ...* 214
    21.28   The Conditional 215
    21.29   Uses of the Conditional in Independent Clauses 215
    21.30   The Conditional in Dependent Clauses 216
    21.31   Past Conditional Expressing Future 216
    21.32   The Conditional in Hypothetical Sentences 217
    21.33   Indicative, Subjunctive, and Conditional with Pronouns 217
    21.34   The Imperative 218
    21.35   The Subjects of the Imperative 218
    21.36   Negative Imperative: *non urlate, non urlare* 218
    21.37   Formal Commands and Ways to Soften the Imperative 218
    21.38   The Imperative and Pronouns: *svegliati; portamelo*, etc. 219
    21.39   Other Common Uses of the Imperative: Instructions and Conversational Expressions ... 219
    21.40   The Infinitive 220
    21.41   Agreement with the Past Infinitive: *essere partiti, averla comprata* 220
    21.42   Use of the Infinitive in Independent Clauses 220
    21.43   The Infinitive as Imperative and Instructional Form 221
    21.44   Uses of the Infinitive in Dependent Clauses: *... di fare ..., ... per essere stato ...,* etc. ... 221
    21.45   The Infinitive as a Noun: *Riposare è importante* 222

21.46	Italian Infinitive vs. English Gerund in Simultaneous Actions: *stare a …, essere a …, ect.*	223
21.47	The Infinitive with Modal Verbs	223
21.48	The Infinitive with Pronouns	223
21.49	The Gerund	224
21.50	Uses of the Gerund	224
21.51	The Agreement of the Past Gerund: *essendo arrivata, avendoli comprati*	224
21.52	Subject of the Gerund	224
21.53	Meanings of the Gerund and Its Equivalent Constructions	225
21.54	Gerund with *stare, andare,* and *venire*	225
21.55	Participle	226
21.56	Uses of the Present Participle	226
21.57	The Past Participle	226
21.58	The Past Participle Used Alone and Its Equivalent Constructions	227

22. VERBS AND PREPOSITIONS 228

22.1	Verbs and Prepositions: Italian vs English	228
22.2	Italian Verbs + Noun or Pronoun Without Prepositions	228
22.3	Italian Verbs Followed by *a* + Noun or Pronoun	229
22.4	Italian Verbs Followed by *di* + Noun or Pronoun	229
22.5	Italian Verbs Followed by *con, da, in, per,* and *su* + Noun or Pronoun	230
22.6	Verbs Requiring *a* and *di* + Infinitive	230
22.7	Nouns and Adjectives Followed by *a* or *di* + Infinite	231
22.8	Verbs Requiring *da* + Infinitive	231
22.9	Verbs Followed Directly by the Infinitive Without Prepositions	232

23. SPECIAL VERBS AND VERB CONSTRUCTIONS 233

23.1	The Passive Form	233
23.2	Alternative Auxiliaries for the Passive Form: *venire* and *andare*	234
23.3	*Si passivante: si* + 3rd Person Forms of an Active Verb	235
23.4	The Reflexive Forms: *Marco si alza presto; Io mi diverto*	236
23.5	Reciprocal Forms: *Noi ci amiamo; Loro si sposano*	237
23.6	'Reflexive' Pronominal Verbs: *arrabbiarsi, sedersi, meravigliarsi,* etc.	238
23.7	Pronominal Verbs in *-ci: capirci, volerci, starci,* etc.	239
23.8	Pronominal Verbs in *-ne: dirne, poterne, valerne,* etc.	240
23.9	Pronominal Verbs in *-cela: avercela, farcela,* and *mettercela*	240
23.10	Pronominal Verbs in *-sela: cavarsela, passarsela, prendersela,* etc.	241
23.11	Pronominal Verbs in *-cene, -cisi,* and *-sene: volercene, mettercisi, andarsene,* etc.	241
23.12	Impersonal Forms: *piove, è bello, si gioca,* etc.	242
23.13	The Impersonal *si*	243
23.14	Modal Verbs: *dovere, potere,* and *volere*	243
23.15	*Sapere* and *Conoscere*	244
23.16	Phrasal Verbs	245
23.17	Verbs Expressing a Progressive Action: *stare, andare* and *venire* + Gerund	245
23.18	Verbs Expressing an Impending Action: *stare per …, essere in procinto di …,* etc.	245

23.19	Verbs Expressing the Start of an Action: *cominciare a …, iniziare a …,* etc.	245
23.20	Verbs Expressing the Continuation of an Action: *continuare a …, seguitare a …,* etc.	246
23.21	Verbs Expressing the End of an Action: *finire di …, smetterla di …,* etc.	246
23.22	The Causative Verb *fare*: *Faccio preparare il pranzo*	247
23.23	The Causative Verb *lasciare*: *Lascia uscire il cane*	247
23.24	Verbs of Perception with the Infinitive: *ascoltare, guardare, sentire,* etc.	248
23.25	Defective Verbs: *addirsi, solere,* and *urgere*	248
23.26	Forms and Uses of *piacere*	249
23.27	Verbs Similar to *piacere*: *bastare, interessare,* etc.	250
23.28	The Case of "Computer" Verbs: *chattare, bannare, zippare,* etc.	251
23.29	Hypothetical Constructions	251

Bibliography 255
Index 257

Introduction

The purpose of this book is to provide detailed grammatical explanations, a pronunciation guide using English as a reference, notes on usage, and on fading and emerging linguistic trends, all based on contemporary Italian. It is especially centered on English speakers learning Italian as a foreign language but will make a great reference book for teachers seeking explanations on discrete grammatical points or examples of use as well.

The rationale for focusing on grammar is that most books of Italian available to learners across the United States are based on the communicative language methodology, which alone is not sufficient to equip students of Italian with the systemic knowledge needed to become independent learners capable of making strides in their language study on their own. Also, it has been proven that grammar helps to learn a language more quickly and more efficiently and Italian language books based on the communicative approach tend to leave out important structures or provide haphazard rules of grammar and usage that confuse more than help English speakers to learn Italian. To this end, a large portion of the book relates to verbs and verb usage. Being the driving force of a language, verbs, especially Italian ones, can be the most difficult part for English speakers to learn. To make the task of mastering these verbs attainable, the most useful irregular verbs are conjugated next to the regular ones.

One of the noteworthy features of this book is that unlike most grammar reference books, which address the more advanced language learner, often glossing over or simply excluding basic points, this book is different. It is designed as an accessible tool and adjunct for all English speakers learning Italian, regardless of their level of competence. Hence, beginners who need to check article usage in Italian will find this book useful as will the more sophisticated learners checking more refined points of grammar or usage.

Another useful feature is that this book adopts the "compare and contrast" approach, aiming to accurately describe and explain elements of Italian that differ from English without belaboring similarities in grammar between the two languages since these tend not to present problems for learners. As a reference grammar, this book facilitates 'reference' in the sense that it offers a clear and concise explanation of Italian language rules of writing and speaking, taking great care to provide brief and concrete examples of every point mentioned with an English translation.

Likewise, tables are used wherever possible to display information in a visually and readily accessible format.

Zohra Saad

Abbreviations and Symbols

Below is a list in alphabetical order of the abbreviations for the grammatical terms used in this book, particularly in tables: **adj.** (adjective), **adv.** (adverb), **art.** (article), **cond.** (conditional), **conj.** (conjunction), **cons.** (consonant), **f.** (feminine gender), **form.** (formal), **indic.** (indicative), **invar.** (invariable), **m.** (masculine gender), **neg.** (negative), **obj.** (object), **part.** (participle), **pers.** (person), **pl.** (plural), **prep.** (preposition), **pron.** (pronoun), **refl.** (reflexive), **sing.** (singular), **subj.** (subjunctive).

Next is a list of the symbols used in this book with an explanation of their function:

'...' Single quotation marks are used to enclose the English translation of Italian examples, always written in italic: *questa automobile* ('this car');

(...) In addition to their regular use, parentheses are used to enclose the English equivalent of Italian words and phrases: *Anna ha i suoi giocattoli* ('Anna has her toys');

[...] Square brackets are used to enclose a word that can be omitted *Il presidente, [a] cui è stata fatta domanda, non ha ancora risposto* ('The president, to whom the application was presented, has not answered yet');

[=...] Square brackets with an equals symbol inside are used to enclose an equivalent expression: *Non è timido, parla con chicchessia* [= *chiunque*] ('He's not shy; he talks to anyone');

= An equals sign indicates words and phrases that are equivalent (*mi = a/per me*);

\> and < Right and left angled brackets indicate word derivation (*dici > di'*; *mo' < modo*) or word transformation (*l'amico > gli amici*);

\+ A plus sign indicates word combination: *a + pena > appena* ('just');

\- A hyphen is used to separate elements of a word, prefixes (*super-*), suffixes (*-ino*), etc.;

/ A slash is used to divide words (*anche/pure*), phrases (*il dentista/la denstista*), and vowels (*amato/a*) without a space separating them, or sentences (*Mi voglio alzare presto / Voglio alzarmi presto*) with a space in between;

_ An underscore is used to indicate (when necessary) a stressed vowel: *c_a_ntano* ('they sing').

N.B. An **English translation** is always given, except: a) where the Italian words are simply used to show spelling and pronunciations rules; b) in case of proper nouns (*Marco*, *Roma*, etc.); c) in all cases where Italian and English are perfectly equivalent (*bar*, *film*, etc.); and d) when the meaning of the Italian word is transparent because of its English origin (*downloadare*, *twittare*, etc.).

1. Spelling and Pronunciation

1.1 The Alphabet and Its Sounds

Italian is the easiest language to pronounce because the correspondence between letters and sounds is almost absolute. In fact, one letter mostly stands for one sound and vice versa. This means that an Italian word is, by and large, pronounced the way it is written. It is worth noting that there are some problematic areas, especially where the pronunciation is not necessarily indicated by the spelling (the open or closed sounds of *e* and *o*, the double pronunciation of *s* and *z*, and a few more cases), although a foreign learner of Italian should not be too concerned about these because even Italians will pronounce the words differently, depending on the region where they grow up.

The Italian alphabet consists of twenty-one letters, plus five (*j, k, w, x, y*) that are found in words of foreign language origin. Every letter is pronounced except *h*, which is always silent. The table below lists all the letters of the Italian alphabet with their names and keys indicating the proper way to pronounce them:

Letters	Sounds	Letters	Sounds	Letters	Sounds
a	a	*l*	elle	*u*	u
b	bi	*m*	emme	*v*	vu
c	ci	*n*	enne	*z*	zeta
d	di	*o*	o	....	....
e	e	*p*	pi	*j*	i lunga
f	effe	*q*	cu	*k*	kappa
g	gi	*r*	erre	*w*	vu doppia
h	h	*s*	esse	*x*	iks
i	i	*t*	ti	*y*	i greca or ipsilon

1.2 The Vowels

Italian vowels are always pronounced very clearly. Although they are represented by only five letters (*a, e, i, o, u*), they correspond to seven sounds. Indeed, if *a, i,* and *u* are always pronounced the same way, *e* and *o*, on the other hand, have two different sounds each, open or closed. The vowels and their pronunciation are as follows:

- *a* is always pronounced like 'a' in the word 'cat' or 'o' in 'mouse';

- *i* is always pronounced like 'ea' in the word 'tea', 'eo' in 'people' or 'ee' in 'feet';
- *u* is always pronounced like 'u' in the word 'rule' or 'oo' in 'cool';
- *e* has two sounds. It can be pronounced open like 'e' in the word 'met' or closed like 'a' in the word 'may'. This distinction is not reflected in spelling except in the case of the verb è ('is'), which is open, and words ending in é (*perché, benché, affinché*) always pronounced closed;
- *o* has two sounds. It can be pronounced open like 'o' in the word 'dog' or closed like 'o' in the word 'row'. This distinction, as for the vowel *e*, is not reflected in spelling except in those words ending in ò (*lavorerò, però, ciò*), which are always pronounced open.

A foreign learner should not be too concerned about the distinction between *e* and *o*, open or closed, because a different pronunciation does not in general hinder comprehension of a word. Even Italians, except Tuscans, pronounce these vowels in different ways: the predominant tendency is to use more closed sounds in the North and more open ones in the South. However, it is important to keep in mind just a few cases, where the different and distinct pronunciation of *e* and *o* change the meaning of the words:

Open *e* (as in 'pen')	Closed *e* (as in 'fair')
l*e*gge ('he/she reads')	l*e*gge ('law')
p*e*sca ('peach')	p*e*sca ('fishing')
v*e*nti ('winds')	v*e*nti ('twenty')

Open *o* (as in 'dog')	Closed *o* (as in 'blow')
c*o*lto ('picked')	c*o*lto ('educated')
b*o*tte ('blows')	b*o*tte ('cask')
v*o*lto ('turned')	v*o*lto ('face')

1.3 Diphthongs and Triphthongs

Diphthongs and triphthongs are respectively a sequence of two and three vowels fused together to produce a single sound. A diphthong is formed when an unstressed *i* or *u* is combined with *a, e,* or *o*. The *i* and *u* can come before the vowels *a, e, o* (*quando, piede, uomo*) or follow them (*mai, vorrei, cui, pseudonimo*).

Triphthongs are relatively rare but exist, nonetheless. They are usually formed by the combination of diphthongs followed by an unstressed *i* (*miei, guai, cucchiai*).

> **N.B.** Numerous Italian words contain a series of three vowels that are not triphthongs but simply sequences of a vowel and a diphthong (*gennaio, noia*). When four vowels are combined together, they form sequences of two diphthongs (*gioia, guaio*).

1.4 The Consonants

Italian has fewer consonants than English because the letters *j*, *k*, *w*, *x*, and *y* do not occur in native words but appear in some foreign and international loanwords. Given the fact that a larger number of English words are becoming part of Italian, the presence of these letters is more pervasive. The Italian consonants are:

- ***b, d, f, l, m, n, p, t, v***, which are pronounced as in English;
- ***c*** before the vowels *a, o, u* (*casa, arco, cubo*) and before consonants, including the silent *h*, (*credere, chiesa*) is pronounced like 'c' in the word 'cat'; when *c* occurs before *e* and *i* (*centro, baci*), it is pronounced like 'ch' in the word 'check';
- ***g*** is pronounced like 'g' in the word 'golf' when it occurs before *a, o, u* (*gatto, lago, gusto*), before the consonants *h, m, r* (*ghiro, pragmatico, grazie*), and before *la, le, lo, lu* (*glaciale, globo, glutine*); when *g* occurs before *e* and *i* (*gelato, girare*), it is pronounced like 'g' in the word 'gel';
- ***h*** is always silent. It is used in writing to distinguish between homophones (*hanno* 'they have', *anno* 'year') or appears in some loanwords (*hotel, hamburger*);
- ***q*** is only used in combination with *u* followed by another vowel (*quadro, questo*), a combination that is always pronounced like 'qu' in the English word 'question';
- ***r*** is undoubtedly the Italian sound that is the most difficult for the majority of English speakers. It can be produced by vibrating the tip of the tongue against the roof of the mouth, just behind the teeth. Even if the Italian *r* doesn't really have a close English equivalent, it can be pronounced approximately like 'rr' in the word 'arrive';
- ***s*** has two sounds: unvoiced, like 's' in the word 'say', and voiced, like 's' in the word 'rose'. When *s* is placed before vowels or the consonants *c, f, p, q, s, t*, it is unvoiced (*buonasera, scuola*); but if *s* is placed before *b, d, g, l, m, n, r, v*, it is voiced (*sbaglio, risvegliare*);
- ***z*** has two sounds: unvoiced (*terzo*), pronounced like 'ts' in the word 'bets', and voiced (*pranzo*), pronounced like 'ds' in the word 'beds'. A clear standard rule does not exist in Italian; however, there is a tendency to pronounce *z* unvoiced when it is at the beginning of a word. Learners of Italian should not be concerned about this difference because it is subject to regional variation and it makes little difference in everyday language.

1.5 Groups of Letters Making One Sound: ch, gh, gn, etc.

There are groups of two or more letters that produce only one sound:

- ***ch*** before *e* and *i* (*amiche, chiesa*) is pronounced like 'k' in the word 'key';
- ***gh*** before *e* and *i* (*spaghetti, funghi*) is pronounced like 'g' in the word 'golf';
- ***ci*** before *a, o*, and *u* (*ciao, ciocco, ciurma*) is pronounced like 'ch' in the word 'check';
- ***gi*** before *a, o*, and *u* (*giallo, giorno, giusto*) is pronounced like 'j' in the word 'job';
- ***qu*** (*quadro, questo, squillo*) is pronounced like 'qu' in the word 'question';

- **gn** (*lavagna, sogno, montagne*) is pronounced approximately like 'ni' in the word 'onion';
- **gli** (*figli, famiglia, biglietto*) is pronounced approximately like 'll' in the word 'million';
- **sc** before *e* and *i* (*scena, fascia*) is pronounced like 'sh' in the word 'fish'; when *sc* occurs before *a*, *o*, and *u* (*scarpe, disco, scuola*), it is pronounced like 'sk' in the word 'skate'.

1.6 Double Consonants: tt, pp, rr, etc.

Many Italian words have double consonants that can occur in any part of the word, but never in initial or final positions. These double consonants are pronounced much more forcefully than single ones, and they sound stronger than their English counterparts. The contiguous double 's' in 'bus stop' can approximately produce the sound of double consonants in Italian.

In Italian, all consonants except *h* can be doubled. They are usually followed by a vowel (*affetto, bella*) but can also, in some cases, be followed by the consonant *r* (*labbra, attraversare*). The letter *q* is never doubled except in the word *soqquadro* ('upside down') but is often combined with the letter *c* (*acqua, acquistare*). The letter *z* when followed by *i* + vowel is never doubled except in just a few words: *pazzia* ('madness'), *razzia* ('raid'), *corazziere* ('cuirassier').

It is important to pronounce and spell double consonants correctly because in Italian there are word pairs whose meaning changes depending on whether a particular consonant is doubled or not:

Single consonant	Double consonant
ano ('anus')	*anno* ('year')
casa ('house')	*cassa* ('crate')
eco ('echo')	*ecco* ('here we/there they go')
gramo ('wretched')	*grammo* ('gram')
nono ('ninth')	*nonno* ('grandfather')
note ('notes')	*notte* ('night')
pala ('shovel')	*palla* ('ball')
papa ('pope')	*pappa* ('bread soup')
pena ('pain')	*penna* ('pen')
rosa ('rose' or 'pink')	*rossa* ('red')
sera ('evening')	*serra* ('greenhouse')
sete ('thirst')	*sette* ('seven')

1.7 Syntactic Doubling

Most Italians pronounce such expressions as *è bello, a casa, ma dove* as one word and pronounce as double the initial consonant of the second word (-*bb*-, -*cc*-, -*dd*- in the examples above). This linguistic aspect, known as syntactic doubling, is standard native pronunciation in Central and Southern Italy but not in the Northern part.

In standard Italian, syntactic doubling occurs after the following words:

- all monosyllabic words carrying an accent like *è, là, dà, sì*;
- many monosyllabic words without an accent like *e, o, a, da, fra, tra, ma, che, chi, se, me, sa, so, sto, sta, do, fu, fa, ho, ha, qua, qui, sci, re, blu, tre*;
- some words like *come, dove, qualche, sopra*.

Syntactic doubling is an oral phenomenon that is not reflected in spelling unless a new word is produced by the fusion of the two. Below are listed the most common words usually spelled with two consonants in contemporary italian. The words from which the combination resulted are given as well:

*a + pena > **appena*** ('just')
*chi + sa > **chissà*** ('who knows')
*da + capo > **daccapo*** ('from the beginning')
*e + pure > **eppure*** ('nevertheless')
*fra + tanto > **frattanto*** ('in the meantime')
*ma + che > **macché*** ('of course not')
*se + no > **sennò*** ('otherwise')
*se + pure > **seppure*** ('though')

1.8 Syllabification

When at the end of a line a word needs to be divided, a hyphen is inserted between the syllables according to accepted rules. English learners of Italian need to pay attention to Italian syllabification because it is quite different from that of English. Considering that every syllable must contain a vowel, we can summarize a few rules as follows:

- a single consonant goes with the vowel following it (*ca-sa, ge-la-to*);
- double consonants, including *cq*, are divided (*tet-to, ac-qua*);
- two consonants, the first of which is *l, m, n,* or *r*, are divided (*cam-po, al-ber-go*); otherwise, a combination of two consonants belongs to the following syllable (*ma-dre, sa-cro*);
- a group *s* + consonant is never divided (*mo-stro, a-scolta*);
- a group of three consonants is divided between the first and the second consonant (*sem-pre, sor-pre-sa*), except the ones starting with *s* (*mo-stro, a-spra*)
- an initial and single vowel is a syllable by itself (*a-ma, e-co*);
- two vowels are divided (*le-one, re-ame*);
- diphthongs and triphthongs (see 1.3) are never divided (*pie-di, a-iuo-la*), but when *i* or *u* is stressed, the diphthong is divided in two (*vi-a, pa-ura*).

1.9 Stress

In all Italian words with two or more syllables, one syllable always gets more stress than the others. The primary stress (indicated in the following Italian words by the underlined vowel) can fall on any one of the last four syllables of a word. It is not always easy for foreign learners to pronounce a word correctly because the position of the stress (especially in proper nouns or in loanwords) is often unpredictable. However, **in most Italian words the stress falls on the penultimate syllable** as in *casa, amico, uscire,* and so on.

Listed below are a few practical and useful rules that can help to identify the stress and teach to pronounce words correctly when the stress falls on syllables other than the penultimate ones:

- are **stressed on the last syllable** all words that carry a written accent on the last vowel (*città, gioventù, canterò, così, caffè*). This is the only case where the spelling helps;
- are **stressed on the third to last syllable**
    - all words ending in *-agine* (*immagine*), *-aggine* (*goffaggine*), *-igine* (*origine*), *-iggine* (*fuliggine*), *-edine* (*acredine*), *-udine* (*abitudine*), *-abile* (*adattabile*), *-evole* (*amorevole*), *-ibile* (*risibile*), *-aceo* (*violaceo*), *-etico* (*atletico*), *-ognolo* (*amarognolo*) *-oide* (*pazzoide*), *-obile* (*mobile*);
    - all the compound words with the second element ending in *-cefalo* (*acefalo*), *-crate* (*burocrate*), *-crono* (*sincrono*), *-dromo* (*autodromo*), *-fago* (*esofago*), *-filo* (*cinofilo*), *-fobo* (*idrofobo*), *-fono* (*microfono*), *-geno* (*ossigeno*), *-grafo* (*fotografo*), *-logo* (*biologo*), *-mane* (*piromane*), *-metro* (*termometro*), *-ttero* (*elicottero*);
    - almost all the infinitive forms of verbs in *-ere* like *leggere, scrivere, correre* (but not *avere* and *vedere*);
    - the third person plural forms in *-ano, -ono, -ino, -ero* of all verbs (*cantano, leggono, parlino, arriverebbero*);
    - the first person plural forms of the imperfect subjunctive ending in *-ssimo* (*parlassimo, leggessimo, partissimo*);
    - the third person singular forms of the present of a few verbs in *-are* like *esamina, litiga, telefona*;
- are **stressed on the fourth to last syllable** third person plural forms of verbs such as *esaminano, litigano, telefonano* whose third person singular forms are stressed on the third to the last syllable (*esamina, litiga, telefona*).

When a pronoun is attached to the end of a verb, the position of the stress does not change: *parla + mi > parlami, andiamo + ci > andiamoci.*

> **N.B.** Learners of Italian should remember that it is always a smart choice to stress the penultimate syllable when they cannot predict the position of the stress.

1.10 Words Whose Meaning Changes with the Stress

In Italian the stress is only spelled (see 1.11) when it is carried by the last vowel (*città, gioventù, caffè*), so there are a few words that can have the same spelling but a different meaning based on the position of the stress. When spoken, the meaning of such words may be distinguished through different pronunciations, but when written, their meaning can only be inferred through the context in which they occur. Below is a list of the most significant words in this category with the stressed vowel underlined.

The noun **a<u>n</u>cora** ('anchor')	The adv. **anc<u>o</u>ra** ('still', 'again', 'yet')
The verb **c<u>a</u>pitano** ('they happen')	The noun **capit<u>a</u>no** ('captain')
The verb **des<u>i</u>deri** ('you desire')	The noun **desid<u>e</u>ri** ('desires')
The verb **l<u>e</u>ggere** ('to read')	The adj. **legg<u>e</u>re** ('light')
The noun **pr<u>i</u>ncipi** ('princes')	The noun **princ<u>i</u>pi** ('principles', 'values')
The adv. **s<u>u</u>bito** ('right away')	The verb **sub<u>i</u>to** ('undergone')
The verb **vi<u>o</u>la** ('he/she/it violates')	The adj. **vi<u>o</u>la** ('purple')

> **N.B.** In these particular cases it is also possible (but rare) to indicate the stress with a written accent in order to avoid confusion. Notice the difference between *i prìncipi di Spagna* ('the princes of Spain') and *i sani princìpi* ('the high principles').

1.11 Written Accents

In writing it is mandatory to mark the accent only in two cases:

- in all polysyllabic words stressed on the last vowel (*città, così, trentatré*);
- in monosyllabic words that could be confused with other words with the same spelling but a different meaning. They are listed in the following table:

With the accent	Without the accent
The verb **dà** ('gives')	The prep. **da** ('from', 'by')
The verb **è** ('is')	The conj. **e** ('and')
The adv. **là** ('there')	The art. **la** ('the') and pron. **la** ('her', 'it')
The adv. **lì** ('there')	The pron. **li** ('them')
The neg. conj. **né** ('neither ... nor')	The pron. **ne** ('of it') or the adv. **ne** ('from here/there')
The refl. pron. **sé** ('oneself')	The conj. **se** ('if') and the refl. pron. **se** ('oneself') followed by *lo, la, li, ne*, and the adj. *stesso*
The adv. **sì** ('yes')	The personal pron. **si** ('oneself') or the impersonal particle **si** ('one')
The noun **tè** ('tea')	The personal pron. **te** ('you')

> **N.B.** It is a very common mistake, even for Italians, to put an accent on some monosyllabic words that do not have one. Keep in mind that *fa* ('he/she/it makes'; 'he/she/it does'), *do* ('I give'), *qui* ('here'), *qua* ('here'), *sta* ('he/she/it stays'), *sto* ('I stay'), and *su* ('on') must be written without an accent. Another frequent mistake is to write the phrase *un po'* ('a little') with an accent mark instead of the correct apostrophe.

1.12 Elision: un'amica, quest'albero, *etc.*

Elision is the omission of a vowel in between two words. In Italian the final vowel of a word can be dropped when it is followed by another word beginning with a vowel. Note that this can also happen when the second word begins with *h* followed by a vowel (*hai, hotel*) because the Italian *h* is always silent. This linking, very frequent in spoken language, makes pronunciation more fluid. In written language **elision must always be indicated by an apostrophe ('), replacing the dropped vowel**. This happens in the following cases:

- with singular articles *una* (*un'arancia*), *lo* and *la* (*l'amico, l'isola*), and their corresponding articulated prepositions *allo* (*all'olio*), *della* (*dell'acqua*), *nello* (*nell'albergo*), etc.;
- with the singular forms *questo* (*quest'uomo*), *questa* (*quest'amica*), *quello* (*quell'albero*) and *quella* (*quell'arancia*);
- with *ci* before the verb *essere* (*c'è, c'erano*);
- with the singular *bello* (*bell'appartamento*) and *bella* (*bell'abitudine*);
- with the singular *santo* (*sant'Antonio*) and *santa* (*sant'Agata*);
- in a series of expressions like *a quattr'occhi, mezz'ora, tutt'e due, d'oro, d'argento*.

Elision must always be avoided in the following cases:

- with the plural article *le* (*le amiche*) and *gli* (*gli uomini*), except before *i* (*gl'inglesi*) where eilision is allowed;
- with the plural pronouns *li* (*li ascolto*) and *le* (*le ordino*);
- with *ci* before *a* (*ci amate*), *o* (*ci offrono*), *u* (*ci urta*), and *h* (*ci ha detto*);
- with *da* (*da Antonio*) except in expressions like *d'accordo, d'ora in poi, d'ora in avanti*.

> **N.B.** Apart from the cases where elision must be avoided, it is optional (*mi ama* or *m'ama, lo ha visto* or *l'ha visto*. Sometimes even *una* and *la* can be written without the elision (*una amica, la amica*), especially in formal writing.

1.13 Dropping One Letter or More and Using an Apostrophe: un po', da', sta', *etc.*

Dropping one or more letters from the end of a word, especially an unstressed vowel, is usual but not mandatory. As is illustrated in the cases listed below, an apostrophe must replace the dropped vowel:

- with the 2nd pers. sing. imperative of the verbs *andare* (*vai* > **va'**), *dare* (*dai* > **da'**), *dire* (*dici* > **di'**), *fare* (*fai* > **fa'**), and *stare* (*stai* > **sta'**);
- with **po'** (< *poco*) and **mo'** (< *modo*) in the expressions *un po'* ('a little') and the colloquial *a mo' di* ... ('like ...').

1.14 Dropping a Final Unstressed Vowel: signor Rossi, buon giorno, *etc.*

Dropping a final unstressed vowel is quite frequent in Italian. This happens in words in which the consonant before the final vowel is *l, n, m,* or *r* but never in words that are the last in a sentence: for example, it is possible to drop the *e* from *difficile* in a sentence like *È stata una diffícil scelta* but not in *È stata una scelta difficile* (both meaning 'It was a difficult choice').

Dropping the final unstressed vowel is possible with infinitive forms (*cantar, veder, partir*), especially in poetry and song lyrics, with the first and third person plural of verbs (*noi cantiam, loro vedon, noi partiam*), and with expressions like *ben fatto* ('well-done'), *ben detto* ('well-said'), *man mano* and *pian piano* (both meaning 'little by little'), *il fior fior della gioventù* ('the best of youth').

However, dropping a final unstressed vowel is mandatory in the following cases:

- with an infinitive form combining with an unstressed pronoun (see 21.52) as in *mangiarla, vederti, andarci*;
- with the word *signore* ('Mister') and the professions *dottore* ('doctor'), *ingegnere* ('engineer'), *professore* ('professor'), *ragioniere* ('accountant') when followed by a last name (*signor Rossi, ingegner Biondi, professor Vettori*);
- with the adjectives ending in *-uno* (*buono, alcuno, qualcuno, nessuno*) in front of words that require the article *un* (see 4.8) as in *buon giorno, alcun uomo, nessun amico*.

> **N.B. *Qual è* or *qual'è*?** The case is somewhat problematic as even native Italians make mistakes writing *qual'è*. Keep in mind that the word *quale*, when followed by another word, is spelled *qual* without the apostrophe. In fact, it's not an example of elision (see 1.12), but a simple dropping of the vowel *e*. For this reason, *qual* can be used before vowels (*qual è, qual amico*) as well as before consonants (*qual città, qual fiore*).

1.15 Dropping a Final Syllable: gran giorno, fra Lorenzo, bel bambino, *etc.*

Dropping a whole syllable from the end of a word is not frequent in Italian. It is optional with the adjective *grande* (*gran giorno, gran signori*), with the word *frate* when it is followed by a proper noun (*fra Giovanni, fra Cristoforo*), and with the third person plural forms of the verbs *andare* (*vanno > van*), *dare* (*danno > dan*), *fare* (*fanno > fan*), and *stare* (*stanno > stan*), especially in poetry and song lyrics.

However, it is mandatory with *bello* (see 4.6) and *quello* (see 10.3) in front of words that would require the article *il* (see 2.4) as in *bel bambino, quel signore*, and with *santo* (see 4.10) in front of words that would require *un* (*san Francesco*). The word *santo* is also written *san* in front of proper nouns that begin with *z* (*san Zaccaria, san Zeno*).

1.16 Punctuation

Italian punctuation uses the same marks as English and works broadly the same as in English. However, a comma is not used in front of the conjunction *e* (*Voi, loro e noi* 'You, they, and we') and sometimes can be omitted in a list of words (*Mangio pasta carne formaggio e frutta* 'I eat pasta, meat, cheese, and fruit'). Furthermore, English learners should be aware that a comma is an acceptable way of separating two independent clauses. Where English would write 'I haven't seen Carla; I think she is in Milan', Italian accepts *Non ho visto Carla, penso sia a Milano*.

A point of note to keep in mind is that Italian places punctuation marks outside of quotation marks not inside. For example, a sentence like "I always eat ice-cream." would be written in Italian with the period outside of the quotations marks: "*Mangio sempre il gelato*".

1.17 Capitalization

Many words that are capitalized in English are not in Italian. Unlike English, Italian does not capitalize, unless beginning a sentence:

- names of days (*lunedì, martedì*) and months (*gennaio, febbraio*);
- points of the compass (*nord, sud, est, ovest*);
- languages (*l'italiano, il francese*);
- adjectives indicating nationalities and origins (*italiano, siciliano, romano*);
- the pronoun *io* (*io sono, io mangio*).

Below are other cases where Italian differs somewhat from English:

- titles of books, movies, articles, and songs only have the first letter capitalized (*Il visconte dimezzato, Cinema paradiso, Con te partirò*);
- titles of newspapers can be capitalized as in English (*Il Corriere della Sera, La Gazzetta dello Sport*) or have only the first letter capitalized (*Il corriere della sera, La gazzetta dello sport*);
- names of organizations and abbreviations usually have only the first letter capitalized (*Società editrice fiorentina, Fiat*);
- streets, highways and roads, when accompanied by a proper noun, can be or not be capitalized (*via Aurelia* or *Via Aurelia, viale Matteotti* or *Viale Matteotti*);
- formal pronouns (see 13.3) are usually capitalized by convention as much as to avoid possible ambiguity with the informal forms (*Signora Rossi, Lei è molto gentile; Professore, La ringrazio sinceramente*).

N.B. In Italian when the name of a population is capitalized, it usually refers to the ancient population. For example, *Romani* applies to the old Romans while *romani* pertains to the contemporary inhabitants of Rome.

2. ARTICLES

> **Articles:** An article is a word that precedes a noun (*Marco è un amico* 'Marco is a friend') or an adjective describing the noun (*Marco è un buon amico* 'Marco is a good friend') in order to indicate the type of reference being made by the noun. There are two types of articles: indefinite, as in the examples above, where the article simply refers to an object or a person in a non-specific way, and definite, if the article is used to restrict and specify the meaning of a noun (*Il cane abbaia* 'The dog is barking').

2.1 Gender and Number of Articles: Italian Unlike English

Although there are many correspondences between Italian and English articles, there are differences as well. The Italian indefinite articles (*un, uno, una, un'*) correspond to the English 'a' and 'an', while the definite articles (*il, lo, la,* etc.) correspond to the English 'the'. Italian articles, unlike English ones, have a gender and a number associated with them and always agree with the noun they precede: *il ragazzo e la ragazza* ('the boy and the girl'), *i ragazzi e le ragazze* ('the boys and the girls').

When an Italian noun has the same form regardless of gender or number, the article is often the only way to distinguish between masculine and feminine, singular and plural forms: *il/la giornalista* ('male/female journalist'), *la/le città* ('city/cities').

2.2 The Indefinite Articles: un, una, etc.

The Italian indefinite articles corresponding to the English 'a' or 'an' are used only with singular nouns. These articles take two forms in both the masculine and feminine because they not only agree with the gender of the noun they precede but also vary depending on the initial letter(s) of that noun:

Masculine	Feminine
uno	una
un	un'

- ***uno*** is used with masculine nouns beginning with: ***z*** (*uno zaino*, 'a backpack', *uno zio* 'an uncle'), the group ***s + consonant*** (*uno squalo* 'a shark', *uno stadio* 'a stadium'), the group ***gn*** (*uno gnomo* 'a goblin', *uno gnocco* 'a potato dumpling'), the group ***ps*** (*uno psicologo* 'a psychologist', *uno psichiatra* 'a psychiatrist'), and **foreign words** that start with ***x*** (*uno xilofono* 'a xylophone'), ***y*** (*uno yogurt*), ***sh*** (*uno show*), and ***ch*** (*uno chef*);
- ***un*** is used with **all other masculine nouns:** *un amico* ('a friend'), *un gatto* ('a cat'), *un treno* ('a train');
- ***una*** is used with feminine nouns beginning with **consonants:** *una casa* ('a house'), *una sera* ('an evening');
- ***un'*** is used with feminine nouns beginning with **vowels:** *un'amica* ('a girlfriend'), un'ora ('an hour').

When a descriptive or possessive adjective occurs before a noun (see 7.5), the indefinite article must precede this adjective. In such cases, the article keeps the same gender but may change its form depending on the initial letter of the adjective. For example, if adjectives such as *buono* ('good') or *mio* ('my') are placed in front of *zio* in the phrase *uno zio* ('an uncle'), *uno* will be replaced by *un* because *buono* and *mio* start with a consonant other than *z*. The phrases respectively become *un buono zio* ('a good uncle') and *un mio zio* ('one of my uncles').

> **N.B.** The feminine article *una* can at times, though rarely, be used instead of the elided equivalent *un'*, especially in formal writing (see 1.12).

2.3 Special Uses of the Indefinite Articles

Sometimes the indefinite article can occur before a noun that does not usually take one to give the noun a special meaning.

- With **nouns expressing emotions or physical feelings** the article acts as an intensifier. In this case the article is close in meaning to 'so' in informal English. Note the difference between *Ho sete* ('I am thirsty') and *Ho una sete!* ('I'm so thirsty!') or *Ho avuto paura* ('I was afraid') and *Ho avuto una paura ...* ('I was so afraid ...'). The latter constructions are usually followed by expressions like *... che non ti dico* ('... that I can't even describe the feeling') or *... che è impossibile da immaginare* ('... that it is unimaginable').
- With **proper nouns** the article indicates 'someone like' if the person is famous (*Ci vorrebbe un Einstein a risolvere questo problema* 'It would take an Einstein to solve this problem') or 'someone called' if the person is unknown (*È arrivato un Mazzetti* 'Someone called Mazzetti arrived'). Sometimes the article before a proper noun can also indicate a person in a particular condition (*Non credevano di trovare un Nicoletti in così grande forma* 'They did not think they would find Nicoletti in such good shape') or an object directly related to that person as in the expressions *un Michelangelo, un Leonardo da Vinci,* where the article *un* means 'a work by the artist' as 'a' does in the English expressions 'a Renoir', 'a Picasso'.

- With **numbers** (only the sing. and m. *un* can be used in this case) the article means 'about', 'more or less' (*'C'erano un duecento persone allo spettacolo* 'There were about two hundred people at the show').

2.4 The Definite Articles: il, la, *etc.*

The Italian definite articles correspond to the English 'the'. These articles, unlike their English counterparts, vary according to the gender, number, and initial letter(s) of the noun they precede:

Singular Masculine	Plural Masculine	Singular Feminine	Plural Feminine
il >	*i*	*la* >	*le*
lo >	*gli*	*l'* >	*le*
l' >	*gli*		

- *lo*, like *uno*, is used for masculine nouns beginning with: **z** (*lo zaino* 'the backpack', *lo zio* 'the uncle'), the group **s + consonant** (*lo squalo* 'the shark', *lo stadio* 'the stadium'), the group **gn** (*lo gnomo* 'the goblin', *lo gnocco* 'the potato dumpling'), the group **ps** (*lo psicologo* 'the psychologist', *lo psichiatra* 'the psychiatrist'), **foreign words** that start with **x** (*lo xilofono* 'the xylophone'), **y** (*lo yogurt*), **sh** (*lo show*), and **ch** (*lo chef*);
- *il* is used with singular masculine nouns beginning with **all the other consonants** except the ones already discussed above: *il gatto* ('the cat'), *il treno* ('the train');
- *l'* is used with singular masculine and feminine nouns beginning with **vowels** or **h**: *l'amico* ('the friend'), *l'erba* ('the grass'), *l'hotel*;
- *gli* replaces the masculine *lo* in the plural: *lo zio* > *gli zii* ('the uncles'), *lo stadio* > *gli stadi* ('the stadiums'); it also replaces *l'*: *l' amico* > *gli amici* ('the friends'), *l'hotel* > *gli hotel*;
- *i* replaces the masculine *il* in the plural: *il gatto* > *i gatti* ('the cats'), *il treno* > *i treni* ('the trains');
- *le* replaces the feminine *la* in the plural: *la casa* > *le case* ('the houses'), *la stazione* > *le stazioni* ('the stations'); and it also replaces *l'*: *l'amica* > *le amiche* ('the girlfriends'), *l'oca* > *le oche* ('the geese').

The placement of a descriptive or possessive adjective before a noun (see 7.1) may result in a change in the definite article which now must precede the adjective. Although the gender remains the same since the adjective agrees in gender with the noun it modifies, its form may change because the article must take into consideration the initial letter of the adjective, not the noun. For example, if the adjective *nuova* ('new') or *mia* ('my') is placed in front of *auto* in the phrase *l'auto* ('the car'), the article *l'* will be replaced by *la* because *nuova* and *mia*, contrary to *auto*, start with a consonant. The phrase, thus, becomes *la nuova auto* ('the new car') or *la mia auto* ('my car').

> **N.B.** The word *dei* ('gods'), plural of *dio* (see 3.25), takes *gli* instead of the regular *i*.

2.5 Uses of Definite Articles Unlike English

There are many correspondences in the way Italian and English use the definite article, but in several instances Italian requires the definite article where English uses an indefinite one or omits the article altogether. Unlike English, Italian uses the definite article before:

- **plural nouns indicating an entire species or a category**: *Gli animali sono innocenti* ('Animals are innocent'), *Le stelle sono belle* ('Stars are beautiful'). This is the case of *uomini* ('men') and *donne* ('women') when referring to humankind: *Gli uomini e le donne sono uguali* ('Men and women are equal');
- **nouns indicating abstract concepts**: *La dignità è un valore assoluto* ('Dignity is an absolute value'), *Apprezzo la sincerità* ('I value sincerity');
- **nouns indicating substances and minerals**: *L'acqua fa bene al corpo* ('Water is good for the body'), *L'oro è prezioso* ('Gold is precious');
- **possessive adjectives and pronouns**: *il mio libro e il tuo* ('my book and yours'), *i miei cugini* ('my cousins'); but never with singular nouns denoting family members (see 7.4): *mio cugino* ('my cousin'), *mia sorella* ('my sister');
- **names of countries, regions, and continents** (*l'Italia, il Veneto, l'America*), but never with *Israele, Cuba, Santo Domingo,* and a few more;
- **a few names of cities** such as the foreign *Il Cairo, La Mecca, L'Avana,* and the Italian *L'Aquila, La Spezia*;
- **last names referring to women** (*la Rossi, la Bindi*) but not usually when referring to men;
- **last names indicating the entire family** (*i Verdi, gli Angelo*), in which case the article is always plural and masculine;
- **nicknames** of famous people indicating their place of origin such as *il Caravaggio, il Perugino* or popular nicknames such as *il Freddo* ('the Cold'), *il Sorcio* ('the Rat'). When the nickname is an adjective that follows the first name, the article precedes the adjective as in *Lorenzo il Magnifico* ('Lorenzo the Magnificent'), *Ivan il Terribile* ('Ivan the Terrible');
- **titles**: *il signore Bianchi* ('Mr. Bianchi'), *la dottoressa Allegri* ('Doctor Allegri'). However, the article is not used when addressing someone directly: *Buongiorno, Signora Rossi* ('Good morning, Mrs. Rossi');
- **names of languages**: *l'italiano* ('Italian'), *lo spagnolo* ('Spanish'); but never if the language indicates a subject or a course of study (*Il lunedì ho italiano* 'On Monday I have Italian') and after the preposition *in* (*Parliamo in inglese* 'Let's speak English');
- **names of days** to indicate habitual actions: *il lunedì* ('every Monday'), *il martedì* ('every Tuesday'); but never when refering to a specific day: *Martedì vado a Roma* ('I am going to Rome this Tuesday').

In Italian the definite article is always used between the adjective **tutto** ('all') and the noun (see also 11.12) that it modifies (*tutto il giorno* 'all day', *tutti gli studenti* 'all students'), while in English 'the' is only used if the noun is followed by a phrase or a clause ('all the dishes in the sink', 'all the books that I bought'). It should be noted that the article is omitted in Italian when *tutto* is followed by an adjective, in which case it means 'completely': *Questo libro è tutto rotto* ('This book is completely damaged').

2.6 Omission of Articles

The indefinite and definite articles **must sometimes be omitted**. This happens especially with:

- **adverbial expressions formed with prepositions** like *senza paura* ('with no fear'), *in ritardo* ('late'), *di fretta* ('hastily'), *con coraggio* ('boldly');
- **expressions formed by some verb + noun constructions** like *avere ragione* ('to be right'), *avere sete* ('to be thirsty'), *cambiare scuola* ('to change schools'), *cercare lavoro* ('to look for a job'), *dare ragione* ('to agree'), *dare torto* ('to disagree'), *fare paura* ('to scare');
- **exclamations formed by adjectives + nouns** like *Povero ragazzo!* ('Poor boy!'), *Bella giornata!* ('What a nice day!');
- **interrogative**, **demonstrative**, and **indefinite adjectives** as in the following question and answer sequence that makes use of all three: *Quale libro vuoi? – Voglio questo libro o nessun libro* ('Which book do you want? – I want this book or no book');
- the expression ***giocare a*** followed by names of sports or games like *giocare a calcio* ('to play soccer'), *giocare a carte* (to play cards');
- **idiomatic expressions** like *non chiudere occhio* ('not to sleep a wink'), *non muovere dito* ('not to lift a finger');
- **proverbs** like *Can che abbaia non morde* ('His bark is worse than his bite'), *Tra moglie e marito non mettere il dito* ('Don't get between the tree and the bark', literally 'Don't interfere between a wife and a husband');
- **pairs of same category nouns** coordinated by *e* like *Padre e figlio sono identici* ('Father and son look alike'), *Italiani e americani sono amici* ('Italians and Americans are friends').

3. NOUNS

> **Nouns:** Nouns are words used to name people (*sorella* 'sister'), animals (*gatto* 'cat'), things (*penna* 'pen'), geographical places (*city* 'città'), different events (*pioggia* 'rain'), feelings (*amore* 'love'), and other abstract ideas (*libertà* 'freedom'). When a noun indicates a particular person (*Maria* 'Mary') or a geographical place (*Firenze* 'Florence'), it is called a proper noun and must be capitalized.

3.1 Gender and Number of Nouns: Italian Unlike English

Gender in English is extremely simple. The vast majority of English nouns are classed as neuter ('house', 'pen', 'table'), while nouns that have a natural gender ('man', 'woman', 'boy', 'girl') are either masculine or feminine. However, it is possible sometimes to use the gender when referring to ships, pets, etc. In any case, the gender of nouns in English only affects the personal pronouns ('he', 'she', 'it', 'him'), or the possessive adjectives and pronouns ('his', 'her', and 'its') that can be used with them.

Unlike English, Italian assigns gender to all nouns: nouns are either masculine or feminine, and never neuter. This means that, in addition, to the natural gender (*uomo* 'man', *donna* 'woman', *ragazzo* 'boy', *ragazza* 'girl'), Italian has a grammatical gender that is related more to the form and sound of the noun than to its meaning. For example, nouns such as *libro* ('book'), *albero* ('tree'), *fiume* ('river') are masculine by convention and nouns such as *penna* ('pen'), *casa* ('house'), *notte* ('night') are feminine for the same reason. The last vowel of the nouns usually gives an indication of the gender in most cases (see 3.2).

With regard to number, Italian works exactly as English does, in the sense that the singular form is used to refer to one element (*un bambino* 'a boy', *una ragazza* 'a girl', *uno studente* 'a student') and the plural form to two or more (*due bambini* 'two boys', *dieci ragazze* 'ten girls', *molti studenti* 'many students'). It remains, however, that Italian has more forms because the distinction between masculine and feminine is marked in the singular as well as in the plural.

3.2 Gender: General Rules Based on the Final Vowels -o, -a, -e

The gender of Italian nouns is usually indicated by the vowel at the end of the singular form. Based on this, we can generalize that nouns are:

- **almost always masculine** if they end in *-o*: *quaderno* ('notebook'), *cielo* ('sky'), *zio* ('uncle');

- **almost always feminine** if they end in **-a**: *lavagna* ('blackboard'), *casa* ('house'), *zia* ('aunt');
- **either masculine or feminine** if they end in **-e**. Unless dealing with special endings such as *-ore, -trice, -zione* (see 3.7), the gender of which is predictable, there is no alternative than learning the gender of these words one by one: *dente* m. ('tooth'), *mese* m. ('month'), *notte* f. ('night'), *gente* f. ('people').

3.3 From Masculine to Feminine

The majority of nouns denoting a person or an animal have the same roots for masculine and feminine but different endings. The table below indicates how masculine nouns change into their feminine equivalents. Next to each noun will be placed its masculine or feminine article to make the gender immediately clear, especially when some confusion is possible as in, for example, *cantante* (it can be either male or female 'singer') or *poeta* (masculine word ending in *-a*).

Masculine nouns ending in	have their feminine in
-o (*il bambino* 'boy', *l'avvocato* 'lawyer')	**-a** (*la bambina*), or **-essa** (*l'avvocatessa*)
-a (*il collega* 'colleague', *il poeta* 'poet')	**-a** (*la collega*) or **-essa** (*la poetessa*)
-e (*il signore* 'gentleman', *lo studente* 'student', *il cantante* 'singer')	**-a** (*la signora*), **-essa** (*la studentessa*), or **-e** (*la cantante*)
-tore (*l'attore* 'actor')	**-trice** (*l'attrice*)
-sore (*il professore* 'professor')	**-essa** (*la professoressa*)

3.4 Feminine Nouns in -o

Although most nouns ending in *-o* are masculine, a few of them are feminine. This is the case of:

- *mano* ('hand'), *radio, libido, dinamo* ('dynamo'), *eco* ('echo'), and both *meglio* ('better') and *peggio* ('worse') when used as nouns in expressions such as *avere la meglio* ('to win') or *avere la peggio* ('to lose');
- compound words formed with *palla* ('ball') such as *pallacanestro* ('basketball'), and *pallavolo* ('volleyball');
- abbreviated forms of feminine nouns (see 3.12) such as *foto* (< *fotografia* 'photography'), *auto* (< *automobile* 'car'), *metro* (< *metropolitana* 'subway') and *moto* (< *motocicletta* 'motorcycle');
- nouns indicating opera singers such as *contralto, mezzosoprano* and *soprano*, which are used exclusively for women;
- personal nouns of Greek origin: *Aletto, Calipso, Ero* and *Saffo*.

> **N.B.** Remember that the feminine *eco* ('echo') becomes masculine in the plural *echi* ('echoes') and *metro* ('subway') and *radio* ('radio') mean respectively 'meter' and 'radium' if used in the masculine.

3.5 Masculine Nouns in -a (including -ma and -ta)

Although most nouns ending in *-a* are feminine, it is not too rare to find masculine nouns in *-a,* as in the following:

- all nouns of **Greek origin ending in -ma** such as *clima* ('climate') and *problema* ('problem'). An English speaker can easily predict the gender in the case of *-ma* by following this practical rule: if the Italian word in *-ma* has an obvious English equivalent (*aroma* 'aroma', *dogma* 'dogma', *problema* 'problem'), the Italian word is masculine; otherwise, it is feminine (*lacrima* 'tear', *anima* 'soul');
- a few nouns of **Greek origin ending in -ta** such as *asceta* ('ascetic'), *delta* and *pianeta* ('planet');
- nouns of other **foreign origins** such as *karma, nirvana,* and *yoga*;
- nouns indicating **male persons** such as *poeta* ('poet'), *papa* ('pope'), and *duca* ('duke') that have feminine equivalents (*poetessa, papessa, duchessa*), but also nouns such as *boia* ('executioner'), *messia* ('messiah'), and *scriba* ('scribe') because they refer to positions originally held by men;
- some **animal** nouns such as *gorilla, panda,* and *puma*;
- some **proper names** of wine (*Barbera, Marsala*), cheese (*gorgonzola, groviera*), or objects (*mitra* 'machine gun', *insetticida* 'insecticide');
- some **names of countries** such as *Canada, Guatemala, Nicaragua, Panama,* and *Venezuela*;
- some **compound nouns** such as *dopobarba* ('after-shave'), *guardaroba* ('wardrobe'), and *scioglilingua* ('tongue-twister');
- a few **personal names** such as *Andrea, Luca,* and *Nicola*;
- some nouns of **dialectal origin** with a negative connotation such as *bauscia* ('boaster'), *capoccia* ('ringleader'), and *pirla* ('dumb').

Below is a complete list of masculine nouns ending in *-a* sorted by alphabetic order:

abracadabra ('hocus-pocus')	*caccia* ('fighter aircraft')	*cruciverba* ('crosswords')
aforisma ('aphorism')	*camerata* ('comrade')	*dada* ('dadaist')
amalgama ('amalgam')	*capolinea* ('terminal')	*delta* ('delta')
arciduca ('archduke')	*carcinoma* ('carcinoma')	*diadema* ('diadem')
aroma ('aroma')	*carisma* ('charisma')	*diaframma* ('diaphragm')
asceta ('ascetic')	*carovita* ('cost of living')	*dilemma* ('dilemma')
assioma ('axiom')	*cataclisma* ('cataclysm')	*diploma* ('diploma')
automa ('automaton')	*cavalcavia* ('overpass')	*dogma* ('dogma')
bagnasciuga ('waterline')	*cinema* ('cinema')	*doposcuola* ('after school')
bagnomaria ('bain-marie')	*clima* ('climate')	*dormiveglia* ('slumber')
barbanera ('man with black beard')	*cobra* ('cobra snake')	*dramma* ('drama')
barbarossa ('man with red beard')	*colera* ('cholera')	*duca* ('duke')
barbera ('a kind of wine')	*coma* ('coma')	*elettrocardiogramma* ('electrocardiogram')
battistrada ('outrider')	*comma* ('paragraph')	*ematoma* ('hematoma')
boa ('boa snake')	*crocevia* ('cross-road')	*emblema* ('emblem')
boia ('executioner')	*cromosoma* ('chromosome')	*encefalogramma* ('encephalogram')

enfisema ('emphysema')	morfema ('morpheme')	profeta ('prophet')
enigma ('enigma')	panama ('straw hand-plaited hat')	programma ('program')
entroterra ('hinterland')	panda ('panda')	promemoria ('memorandum')
enzima ('enzyme')	panorama ('panorama')	puma ('puma')
fantasma ('ghost')	papa ('pope')	retrobottega ('backshop')
fibroma ('fibroma')	parabrezza ('windshield')	retroterra ('hinterland')
fonema ('phoneme')	paradigma ('paradigm')	schema ('scheme')
geometra ('surveyor')	parapiglia ('bustle')	scioglilingua ('tongue twister')
gerarca ('hierarch')	parapioggia ('umbrella')	scisma ('schism')
germicida ('germicide')	parassita ('parasite')	sistema ('system')
gesuita ('Jesuit')	passamontagna ('woolen hood')	sofisma ('sophism')
glaucoma ('glaucoma')	patema ('anxiety')	sosia ('look-alike')
gorgonzola ('gorgonzola cheese')	patriarca ('patriarch')	spermicida ('spermicide')
gorilla ('gorilla')	pentagramma ('pentagram')	stemma ('coat of arms')
grana ('grana cheese')	pianeta ('planet')	stratagemma ('stratagem')
guardaroba ('wardrobe')	pigia pigia ('great turmoil')	telegramma ('telegram')
idioma ('idiom')	pigiama ('pajamas')	tema ('theme')
lama ('lama' or 'Buddhist monk')	pilota ('pilot')	teorema ('theorem')
lemma ('headword')	pirata ('pirate')	toccasana ('cure-all')
madera ('madeira wine')	plasma ('plasma')	trauma ('trauma')
magma ('magma')	poema ('poem')	vaglia ('money order')
marasma ('slump')	poeta ('poet')	valpolicella ('valpolicella wine')
marsala ('marsala wine')	portafortuna ('amulet')	voltafaccia ('turnabout')
messia ('messiah')	prisma ('prism')	voltagabbana ('turncoat')
miasma ('miasma')	problema ('problem')	
monarca ('monarch')	proclama ('proclamation')	

N.B. Most of these nouns form their plural in *-i*: *il problema* > *i problemi* ('problems'), *il poeta* > *i poeti* ('poets'). Some of them are invariable: *il gorilla* > *i gorilla*, *lo scioglilingua* > *gli scioglilingua* ('tongue-twisters'). Remember that *lama, grana,* and *caccia* mean respectively 'blade', 'trouble', and 'hunting', if used in the feminine.

3.6 Masculine and Feminine Nouns Ending in -ista, -cida, -iatra, -arca

Some nouns in *-a* can be either masculine or feminine depending on whether they name a male or a female person. This category includes:

- nouns ending in **-ista**: *il concertista/la concertista* ('concert performer'), *il dentista/la dentista* ('dentist');

- nouns ending in **-cida**: *il fratricida/la fratricida* ('fratricide'), *il suicida/la suicida* ('suicide');
- nouns ending in **-iatra**: *il pediatra/la pediatra* ('pediatrician'), *lo psichiatra/la psichiatra* ('psychiatrist');
- nouns ending in **-arca**: *il gerarca/la gerarca* ('hierarch'), *il monarca/la monarca* ('monarch');
- other nouns in **-a**: *l'atleta/l'atleta* ('athlete'), *il collega/la collega* ('colleague'), *il pirata/la pirata* ('pirate').

3.7 Gender of Nouns Ending in -ore, -trice, -ione, -zione, -tudine, -ie

Nouns ending in *-e* can be either masculine or feminine (see 3.3). Although there is no systematic way to determine the gender of such nouns, there are some practical rules that help to predict the gender:

- **masculine** for nouns ending in **-ore** such as *professore* ('professor'), *attore* ('actor'), and *fiore* ('flower');
- **masculine** for nouns ending in **-one** such as *campione* ('champion'), *padrone* ('owner'), and *milione* ('million');
- **feminine** for nouns ending in **-trice** such as *attrice* ('actress'), *affettatrice* ('cutter'), and *istruttrice* ('instructress');
- **feminine** for nouns ending in **-zione, -sione, -gione** such as *stazione* ('station'), *occasione* ('occasion'), and *regione* ('region');
- **feminine** for nouns ending in **-tudine** such as *abitudine* ('habit'), *gratitudine* ('gratitude'), and *moltitudine* ('multitude');
- **feminine** for nouns ending in **-ie** such as *calvizie* ('baldness'), *serie* ('series'), and *canizie* ('white hair').

3.8 Gender of Nouns Ending in -i and -u

In Italian, nouns ending in *-i* (for *ì*, see 3.9) such as *analisi* ('analysis'), *oasi* ('oasis'), and *crisi* ('crisis') are not numerous. They are usually feminine with the following masculine exceptions: *brindisi* ('drinking toast'), *bisturi* ('scalpel'), *safari*, *bonsai*, and *bikini*.

There are no Italian nouns ending in *-u* (for *ù*, see 3.9), except the masculine *menu* (also written *menù*), *guru*, and the feminine *gru* ('crane').

3.9 Gender of Nouns Ending in -ò, -à, -è, -ì, -ù

Some Italian nouns are stressed on the last vowel and carry an accent mark. In this case there are some practical and useful rules to predict the gender:

- **masculine** for nouns ending in **-ò** such as *falò* ('bonfire'), *comò* ('chest of drawers'), and *casinò* ('casino');

- **feminine** for nouns ending in **-à** such as *città* ('city'), *verità* ('truth'), and *età* ('age'); but *papà* ('dad'), *baccalà* ('dried salted cod'), *sofà* ('sofa'), and *ultrà* ('rowdy supporter') are masculine;
- **masculine** for nouns ending in **-è** such as *caffè* ('coffee'), *bebè* ('baby'), and *pancarrè* ('sandwich loaf');
- **masculine** for nouns ending in **-ì** such as *lunedì* ('Monday'), *mezzodì* ('noon'), and *colibrì*, ('humming bird'); but *pipì* ('pee') is feminine;
- **feminine** for nouns ending in **-ù** such as *gioventù* ('youth'), *virtù* ('virtue'), and *tribù* ('tribe'); but *bambù* ('bamboo'), *caucciù* ('rubber'), *tabù* ('taboo'), *tutù* ('tutu'), and *tiramisù* ('tiramisu') are masculine.

3.10 Gender of Foreign Nouns: film, computer, hamburger, *etc.*

Italian has integrated a lot of foreign nouns into its vocabulary. Italian (unlike French, for example) tends not to translate new words that indicate something originally not Italian (*bar, bloc-notes, computer, mouse*) but accepts them in their original form. They are easy to identify since most of them end with consonants. Today the number of these words is constantly increasing, especially words coming from English: in some way we could say that an English speaking person knows a great number of Italian words without ever having studied Italian (see 3.11). The majority of these words are related to new concepts or products in the fields of science, technology, and economy, but there has recently been a growing tendency in Italy to accept even words for which there are Italian equivalents. It is the case of *fashion* for *moda*, *meeting* for *riunione*, *party* for *festa*, just to mention a few.

All the foreign words from languages that distinguish between masculine and feminine retain the original gender: for example, the French masculine 'cabaret' is masculine in Italian, too (*il cabaret*), and the Spanish feminine 'siesta' is also feminine in Italian (*la siesta*).

It is entirely different for nouns from languages that do not have gender, like English, from which come most loanwords in contemporary Italian. In this case it is important to keep in mind the following:

- **most English nouns are masculine** in Italian: *il bar, il benefit, l'hamburger, il film*;
- **a few nouns have become feminine** based on the gender of the Italian equivalent. For example, *connection* is feminine because its Italian equivalent is the feminine *connessione*, while *show* is masculine because its Italian equivalent *spettacolo* is masculine;
- **nouns are masculine when they denote males and feminine when they refer to females:** *il boyfriend, la cheerleader, la hostess, lo steward, la miss, la top-model*;
- **nouns indicating positions or professions can be used as masculine or feminine** depending on the gender of the person holding that position: *il manager/la manager, il talent-scout/la talent-scout, il personal trainer/la personal trainer*;
- the word ***e-mail*** can be used as either masculine or feminine: *un e-mail/un'e-mail*.

3.11 The Most Used English Nouns in Italian

Italian has integrated a lot of English nouns into its vocabulary, accepting them in their original form. Below are the most significant nouns in this category:

assist	fashion	OK
authority	fast food	outing
background	fiction	outlet
backstage	file	party
band	fitness	PC
banner	flash	pool
best seller	footing	pop
blitz	gay	pressing
boss	gossip	provider
box	hacker	puzzle
break	hardware	rapper
brochure	home	relax
browser	home page	reporter
card	internet	rock
casual	jazz	server
channel	jogging	sexy
chart	killer	shampoo
chat	leader	shock
chip	link	show
clown	live	slide
club	location	smoking
cocktail	magazine	spam
computer	manager	speaker
corner	marketing	stage
database	master	stretching
decoder	match	team
default	media	tennis
design	meeting	toner
designer	mixer	topic
devolution	mobbing	trash
dispenser	mouse	tutor
display	network	webcam
DVD	news	weekend
editor	non-stop	wrestling
fantasy	offside	zoom

3.12 Abbreviated Nouns: bici, cinema, foto, *etc.*

In Italian, abbreviated nouns retain the gender of the words from which they are derived and maintain the same form in the singular and in the plural: in this case the article makes the number clear. The most important words of this kind are:

- **auto** ('car') from *automobile*: *l'auto/le auto*;
- **bici** ('bike') from *bicicletta*: *la bici/le bici*;
- **cinema** ('cinema') from *cinematografo*: *il cinema/i cinema*;
- **foto** ('photo') from *fotografia*: *la foto/le foto*;
- **info** ('information') from *informazione*: *l'info/le info*;
- **metro** ('subway') from *metropolitana*: *la metro/le metro*;
- **moto** ('motorbike') from *motocicletta*: *la moto/le moto*.

3.13 Nouns Changing Meaning with Gender: il caso/la casa, il porto/la porta, *etc.*

A few Italian words end in a different vowel depending on whether they are masculine or feminine. They constitute different nouns and have different meanings. Below are the most significant nouns in this category:

Masculine	Feminine
banco ('desk')	*banca* ('bank')
busto ('bust')	*busta* ('envelope')
caso ('case')	*casa* ('house')
gambo ('stem')	*gamba* ('leg')
manico ('handle')	*manica* ('sleeve')
panno ('cloth')	*panna* ('cream')
pianto ('crying')	*pianta* ('plant')
porto ('harbor')	*porta* ('door')
suolo ('ground')	*suola* ('sole')
tappo ('corker')	*tappa* ('stage')

3.14 Nouns with Same Form but Different Meaning: il capitale/la capitale, il fine/la fine, *etc.*

There are a few nouns in Italian that are identical in form but different in meaning depending on whether they are used as masculine or feminine. Below are the most significant nouns of this kind:

Masculine	Feminine
il capitale ('possessions')	*la capitale* ('capital city')
il fine ('purpose')	*la fine* ('end')
il fronte ('front')	*la fronte* ('forehead')

3.15 Nouns of Trees and Fruit: Different Genders

A group of words that change meaning with gender are those pertaining to trees and their fruit. Often, but not always, the tree name is masculine while the fruit is feminine:

Tree Masculine	Fruit Feminine
l'arancio ('orange tree')	*l'arancia* ('orange')
il banano ('banana tree')	*la banana* ('banana')
il castagno ('chestnut tree")	*la castagna* ('chestnut')
il ciliegio ('cherry tree')	*la ciliegia* ('cherry')
il melo ('apple tree')	*la mela* ('apple')
il noce ('walnut tree')	*la noce* ('walnut')
l'olivo ('olive tree')	*l'oliva* ('olive')

N.B. *Il limone* ('lemon') and *il fico* ('fig') indicate both the tree and the fruit.

3.16 Gender of Animal Names

Names of animals with both masculine and feminine forms such as *gatto* ('male cat')/*gatta* ('female cat'), *leone* ('male lion')/*leonessa* ('female lion') are relatively rare in Italian. Most of them have only one form and so one grammatical gender: *canarino* m. ('canary'), *farfalla* f. ('butterfly'), *serpente* m. ('snake'). In this case, Italian, like English, marks the difference by adding the word *maschio* ('male') or *femmina* ('female'): *il falco maschio* ('the male hawk')/*il falco femmina* ('the female hawk'), *la scimmia maschio* ('the male monkey')/*la scimmia femmina* ('the female monkey').

3.17 Gender of Cities, Rivers, States, etc.

Proper names represent unique entities and for this reason, in Italian as in English, are usually capitalized (see 1.17). The gender of these names can easily be predicted based on the gender of the noun denoting the class of entities to which they refer. For example, names such as *Milano* and *Firenze* are feminine because they refer to the feminine noun *città* ('city'), while *Po* and *Tevere* are masculine because they refer to the masculine noun *fiume* ('river'). Below are listed all the classes with their gender; however, there are always some exceptions:

- **names of cities** are feminine, but *Cairo* is masculine and must always be accompanied by the masculine article *il* (*Il Cairo*) to mark its gender;
- **names of regions** (*la Campania, la Toscana, la Sicilia*) are usually feminine, but *il Piemonte, il Friuli, il Lazio, il Molise,* and *il Veneto* are masculine;
- **names of continents and states** are usually feminine (*l'Europa, l'America, la Germania*), but *il Sud Africa, il Belgio, il Giappone, il Perù, lo Zambia, il Colorado,* and *gli Stati Uniti* are masculine;

- **names of mountains** are masculine (*il Cervino, l'Himalaya, gli Appennini*), but names of chains of mountains (*le Alpi, le Dolomiti, le Ande, la Sila*) are usually feminine;
- **names of rivers** are masculine (*l'Hudson, il Tamigi, il Tevere*), but *la Senna, la Vistola,* and a few more are feminine;
- **names of lakes, seas and oceans** are masculine (*il Garda*, il *Mediterraneo, il Pacifico*).

3.18 Gender of Cars, Motorcycles, Wines, etc.

The gender of these names can easily be predicted based on the gender of the noun denoting the class of entities to which they refer. Below are listed all the classes with their gender; however, there are some exceptions:

- **names of cars** are feminine (*la Ferrari, la Lamborghini, la Chrysler*) because they refer to the feminine noun *automobile* ('car');
- **names of motorcycles** are feminine (*la Ducati, la Honda, l'Harley*) because they refer to the feminine noun *motocicletta* ('motorcycle');
- **names of wines** are usually masculine (*il Barbera, il Chianti, il Montalcino*) because they refer to the masculine noun *vino* ('wine'), but *la Malvasia* and *la Vernaccia* are feminine;
- **names of beers** are feminine (*la Moretti, la Peroni, la Budweiser*) because they refer to the feminine noun *birra* ('beer');
- **names of cheeses** are usually masculine (*il brie, il grana, il gorgonzola*) because they refer to the masculine noun *formaggio* ('cheese'), but most names of cheese ending in *-a* are femine (*la ricotta, la fontina, la mozzarella*);
- **names of sports teams** are usually feminine (*la Juventus, la Fiorentina, la Benetton*) because they refer to the feminine noun *squadra* ('team'), but are masculine when the name of the team is the same as that of the city it represents in order to distinguish between the two (*il Venezia, il Torino, il Barcellona*)with the exception of *la Roma* f.

3.19 Compound Nouns: capogruppo, pianoforte, *etc.*

Italian, more than English, has a great number of nouns formed by a combination of two (or more) different words: for example, the word *capofamiglia* ('head of household') results from the combination of *capo* ('head') + *famiglia* ('family'), as *capodanno* ('New Year's Day') results from the combination of *capo* ('head') + *di* ('of') + anno ('year'). These nouns can be formed in a variety of ways:

- **noun + noun**: *capostazione* ('stationmaster'), *ferrovia* ('railway');
- **noun + adjective**: *cassaforte* ('strong box'), *terremoto* ('earthquake');
- **adjective + noun**: *altopiano* ('highland'), *mezzanotte* ('midnight');
- **adjective + adjective**: *agrodolce* ('sweet and sour'), *pianoforte* ('piano');
- **verb + noun**: *asciugamano* ('towel'), *salvagente* ('life jacket');
- **verb + verb**: *dormiveglia* ('drowsiness'), *lasciapassare* ('pass');
- **preposition + noun**: *senzatetto* ('homeless'), *sottopassaggio* ('underpass');

- **adverb + verb**: *benestare* ('approval'), *malessere* ('indisposition');
- **adverb + noun or adjective**: *menomazione* ('impairment'), *malfermo* ('unsteady');
- **noun + preposition + noun**: *capodanno* ('New Year's Day'), *ficodindia* ('cactus pear').

3.20 Gender of Compound Nouns

Compound nouns are **generally masculine** regardless of their final vowel: *il sottopassaggio* ('underpass'), *il cruciverba* ('crosswords'), *il cacciavite* ('screwdriver'), *il tiramisù* ('tiramisu'). However, they are feminine in the following cases:

- when referring to a female: *la capocuoco* ('female chef'), *la prestanome* ('female figurehead');
- when formed by two feminine nouns: *la calzamaglia* ('pantyhose'), *la madrelingua* ('mother tongue');
- when formed by a feminine noun + adjective and vice versa: *la cassaforte* ('strong box'), *la belladonna* ('deadly nightshade').

> **N.B.** Although a few nouns formed by adverbs or prepositions + feminine nouns are feminine (*la retromarcia* 'reverse gear', *la sottoveste* 'petticoat'), most remain masculine (*il retrobottega* 'backshop', *il sottoscala* 'cupboard under the stairs').

3.21 Gender of Words Other Than Nouns: Adjectives, Adverbs, etc.

When words other than nouns function as nouns, their gender is **always masculine**. This is the case of some:

- **adjectives** such as *il giallo* ('yellow'), *il vero* ('the truth'), *il brutto* ('the ugly'): *Non dichiarare il falso* ('Don't make a false statement');
- **adverbs** such as *il bene e il male* ('good and evil'), *il peggio* ('the worst'): *Il peggio deve ancora arrivare* ('The worst is yet to come');
- **infinitive forms of verbs** such as *l'amare* ('the act of loving'), *il dormire* ('the act of sleeping'), *il mangiare* ('the act of eating'): *Il gioire per una vittoria* ('The act of rejoicing for a victory');
- **conjunctions** such as *il quando* ('the when'), *il come* ('the how'), *il perché* ('the reason why'): *Mi rifuto di discutere il perché e il percome della mia decisione* ('I refuse to discuss the whys and wherefores of my decision');
- **words that describe sounds** such as *il drin drin* ('the ting-a-ling'), *il tic* ('the click'), *il bum* ('the boom'): *È stato un don di una campana* ('It was a bell ding').

3.22 From Singular to Plural: General Rules

Generally, the plural of nouns is derived according to the following rules:

- **singular masculine nouns ending in -o have their plural in -i**: *il bambino > i bambini* ('kids'), *il quaderno > i quaderni* ('notebooks');
- **singular masculine nouns ending in -a have their plural in -i**: *il problema > i problemi* ('problems'), *il poeta > i poeti* ('poets');
- **singular feminine nouns ending in -a have their plural in -e**: *la ragazza > le ragazze* ('girls'), *la penna > le penne* ('pens');
- **singular feminine nouns ending in -o maintain the same form in the plural**: *la radio > le radio* ('radios'), *la dinamo > le dinamo* ('dynamos'); in this case the article makes the number clear. *La mano > le mani* ('hands'), *l'eco > gli echi* 'echoes' (the latter also changing gender) are exceptions to this rule;
- **singular nouns ending in -e have their plural in -i**: *il leone > i leoni* ('lions'), *la notte > le notti* ('nights');
- **singular nouns ending in -i maintain the same form in the plural**: *l'analisi > le analisi* ('analyses'), *la crisi > le crisi* ('crises'); in this case the article makes the number clear;
- **singular nouns ending in -u maintain the same form in the plural**: *il menu > i menu* ('menus'), *la gru > le gru* ('cranes'); in this case the article makes the number clear;
- **singular nouns ending in a stressed vowel (-ò, -à, -è, -ì, -ù) maintain the same form in the plural**: *il falò > i falò* ('bonfires'), *la città > le città* ('cities'), *il caffè > i caffè* ('coffees'), *il lunedì > i lunedì* ('Mondays'), *la virtù > le virtù* ('virtues'); in this case also the article makes the number clear;
- **singular nouns ending in -ie** (for *-cie, -gie,* and *-glie,* see 3.23) **maintain the same form in the plural**: *la barbarie > le barbarie* ('barbarism'), *la carie > le carie* ('cavities'); in this case the article makes the number clear;
- **singular nouns formed by one syllable maintain the same form in the plural**: *il re > i re* ('kings'), *lo sci > gli sci* ('skies'); again the article makes the number clear;
- **singular nouns ending in consonants maintain the same form in the plural**: *lo sport > gli sport* ('sports'), *l'autobus > gli autobus* ('buses'); the article makes the number clear;
- **abbreviated nouns** (see 3.12) **maintain the same form in the plural**: *la bici > le bici* ('bikes'), *il cinema > i cinema* ('movie theaters'); the article makes the number clear.

3.23 Some Spelling Problems: -co > -chi, -cia > -ce, etc.

Although the nouns belonging to the following categories form their plural according to the general rules (3.22), they usually acquire or lose a letter before the vowel forming the plural:

- most masculine nouns ending in **-co, -go** acquire an *h* between *c* or *g* and their plural ending *i* (*banco > banchi* 'desks', *intrigo > intrighi* 'intrigues'), but nouns that are stressed on the third to last syllable do not (*medico > medici* 'doctors', *sociologo > sociologi* 'sociologists'). However, there are exceptions to this rule. In fact, a few plural nouns that should have the *h* don't have it: *amico > amici* ('friends'), *nemico > nemici* ('enemies'), *porco > porci* ('pigs'), *greco > greci* ('Greeks'); others that should be spelled without *h* because

they are stressed on the third to the last syllable do have it: *incarico > incarichi* ('roles'), *obbligo > obblighi* ('commitments');
- all feminine nouns ending in **-ca** and **-ga** acquire an *h* between *c* or *g* and their plural ending *e*: *barca > barche* ('boats'), *bottega > botteghe* ('stores');
- masculine nouns ending in **-io** maintain the *i* in the plural if the *i* is stressed as in *zio > zii* ('uncles'), and *fruscio > fruscii* ('whirs'), but they lose it when the *i* is not stressed as in *bacio > baci* ('kisses'), and *viaggio > viaggi* ('travels');
- feminine nouns ending in **-ia** always maintain the *i*, whether stressed as in *ferrovia > ferrovie* ('railroads') and in *zia > zie* ('aunts'), or unstressed as in *bestia > bestie* ('beasts') and in *reliquia > reliquie* ('relics');
- feminine nouns ending in **-cia** and **-gia** maintain the *i*, if not stressed, in the plural (*-cie*, *-gie*) when *c* and *g* are preceded by a vowel as in *camicia > camicie* ('shirts') and in *ciliegia > ciliegie* ('cherries'); on the contrary, they lose the *i* (*-ce*, *-ge*) when *c* and *g* are preceded by a consonant as in *arancia > arance* ('oranges') and in *pioggia > piogge* ('rains');
- feminine nouns ending in **-cie**, **-gie**, and **-glie** lose the *i* in the plural as in *superficie > superfici* ('surfaces'), *effigie > effigi* ('effigies'), and in *moglie > mogli* ('wives').

3.24 Singular Masculine Nouns in -o *with Feminine Plural in* -a

Several singular **masculine nouns in -o have a feminine plural in -a.** Below is a list of the most significant:

il centinaio > le centinaia ('a hundred or so')
il migliaio > le migliaia ('a thousand or so')
il miglio > le miglia ('miles')
il paio > le paia ('pairs')
il riso > le risa ('smiles')
l'uovo > le uova ('eggs')
il centinaio > le centinaia ('a hundred or so')
il migliaio > le migliaia ('a thousand or so')

In several cases, in addition to the feminine plural in *-a*, there are accepted regional masculine plurals (but the feminine plural in *-a* is always preferable) in *-i* like *il grido > le grida/i gridi* ('shouts') and *il lenzuolo > le lenzuola/i lenzuoli* ('sheets'). Most of these nouns denote body parts: *il dito > le dita/i diti* ('fingers'), *il ginocchio > le ginocchia/i ginocchi* ('knees'), *il labbro > le labra/i labbri* ('lips'). Sometimes the two forms are not interchangeable but have a different meaning (see 3.26).

3.25 Some Other Irregularities: arma > armi, uomo > uomini, *etc.*

Nouns that do not follow the above plural rules (see 3.22, 3.23, 3.24) are considered 'irregular':

- two feminine nouns with a singular in -*a* form their plural in -*i*: *l'arma* > *le armi* ('weapons'), *l'ala* > *le ali* ('wings');
- some masculine nouns with a singular in -*a* maintain the same form in the plural. In this case the article makes the number clear: *il delta* > *i delta* ('deltas'), *il sosia* > *i sosia* ('look-alikes');
- three masculine nouns with variant singular and plural roots form their plural in the following way: *il dio* > *gli dei* ('gods'), *l'uomo* > *gli uomini* ('men'), and *il bue* > *i buoi* ('oxen');
- the number *mille* ('one thousand') has the plural form *-mila* (see also 12.2): *duemila* ('two thousand'), *tremila* ('three thousand');
- the singular masculine *il carcere* ('jail') has the feminine plural *le carceri*;
- the singular masculine *il rene* ('kidney') has the feminine plural *le reni*;
- the singular feminine *l'eco* ('echo') has the masculine plural *gli echi*.

3.26 Nouns with Dual Plurals and Meanings: i cigli/le ciglia, i muri/le mura, *etc.*

There are several singular masculine nouns that have two plurals, one masculine and one feminine, each with a different meaning. English speakers should not be too concerned about these because even Italians are often unaware of the rules and use them interchangeably. However, it is useful to note the following nouns:

- *il braccio* ('arm') > *i bracci/le braccia*: the masculine plural *i bracci* is used to denote mechanical arms (*i bracci della gru* 'the crane arms'), while the feminine *le braccia* refers to human arms (*le braccia di una donna* 'the arms of a woman');
- *il ciglio* ('eyelash' or 'edge') > *i cigli/le ciglia*: the masculine *i cigli* is used to indicate the borders, the edges of the road (*i cigli della strada* 'roadsides'), while the feminine *le ciglia* means 'eyelashes', (*ciglia false* 'false eyelashes');
- *il dito* ('finger') > *i diti/le dita*: the masculine *i diti* is used when the fingers are considered separately (*i diti anulari* 'ring fingers'), while the feminine *le dita* is used to indicate the fingers of the hand as a whole (*incrociare le dita* 'to keep one's fingers crossed');
- *il fondamento* ('foundation') > *i fondamenti/le fondamenta*: the masculine *i fondamenti* denotes the fundamentals of something (*i fondamenti della musica* 'the fundamentals of music'), while the feminine *le fondamenta* is used to denote the foundations of buildings (*gettare le fondamenta* 'to lay the foundation');
- *il gesto* ('gesture') > *i gesti/le gesta*: the masculine *i gesti* is used to denote physical gestures (*gesti inappropriati* 'inappropriate gestures'), while the feminine *le gesta* means 'deeds' (*gesta eroiche* 'heroic deeds');
- *il membro* ('member' or 'limb') > *i membri/le membra*: the masculine *i membri* refers to the members of something (*membri della famiglia* 'family members'), while the feminine *le membra* denotes the human limbs (*membra pesanti* 'heavy limbs');
- *il muro* ('wall') > *i muri/le mura*: the masculine *i muri* refers to the walls of a room or a building (*i muri portanti* 'bearing walls'), while the feminine *le mura* denotes the walls of a town or a city (*fuori dalle mura* 'outside of the city walls').

3.27 Italian Singular vs. English Plural and Vice Versa: pigiama *('pajamas'),* capelli *('hair'),* etc.

In Italian as in English there are nouns used only in the singular or in the plural, but a one-to-one correspondence in number between the two languages does not always occur. If, for example, words like *pantaloni* ('pants') and *forbici* ('scissors') do not create problems because they are plural in both Italian and English, other words require much more attention since they can be singular in one language but plural in the other or vice versa. This is especially the case of collective nouns that indicate a group of objects, people, or animals. The most significant differences between the two languages are listed below.

Nouns treated as **singular in Italian but plural in English**:

- ***bestiame*** ('cattle'): *Il bestiame è al pascolo* ('The cattle are out to pasture');
- ***gente*** ('people'): *La gente italiana è allegra* ('Italian people are cheerful');
- ***merce*** ('goods'): *Questa è merce rubata* ('These are stolen goods');
- ***pigiama*** ('pajamas'): *Il mio pigiama è nuovo* ('My pajamas are new');
- ***polizia*** ('police'): *La polizia aiuta i cittadini* ('Police help citizens').

Nouns treated as **plural in Italian but singular in English**:

- ***bagagli*** ('luggage'): *I bagagli sono pesanti* ('The luggage is heavy');
- ***capelli*** ('hair'): *I miei capelli sono lunghi* ('My hair is long');
- ***lavori domestici*** ('housework'): *I lavori domestici stancano* ('Housework is tiring');
- ***soldi*** ('money'): *I soldi non fanno felici* ('Money doesn't buy happiness')
- ***notizie*** ('news'): *Le belle notizie fanno piacere* ('Good news is pleasant')
- ***spaghetti*** ('spaghetti'): *Gli spaghetti sono buoni* ('Spaghetti is good').

> **N.B.** The Italian noun ***famiglia*** is always treated as singular (*La mia famiglia è matta* 'My family is crazy') whereas the English word 'family' can be used as a plural when it indicates the members of the family ('My family are crazy').

3.28 The Plural of Compound Nouns

Compound nouns (see 3.19) form their plural in different ways depending on the words from which they are formed. The most important cases are indicated below:

- **noun + noun**: when the compound is formed by two nouns, only the second noun is made plural as in *l'arcobaleno > gli arcobaleni* ('rainbows'), *la banconota > le banconote* ('bills');
- ***capo* + noun**: compounds with the prefix *capo* ('head') do not always behave in the same way. If *capo*, meaning **'he who heads something'**, is combined with a collective noun like *squadra* ('team') or *gruppo* ('group'), only *capo* is made plural as in *il caposquadra > i capisquadra* ('team leaders'), *il capogruppo > i capigruppo* ('group leaders'). On the contrary,

if the second word indicates only one person like *cuoco*, or *redattore*, it is the one that is made plural as in *il capocuoco > i capocuochi* ('chefs'), *il caporedattore > i caporedattori* ('managing editors'). If the word *capo*, meaning **'she who heads something'**, is combined with a collective noun like *squadra* ('team') or *gruppo* ('group'), the word maintains the same form in the plural. In this case the article makes the number clear as in *la caposquadra > le caposquadra* ('female team leaders'), *la capogruppo > le capogruppo* ('female group leaders'). However, if the second word indicates only one person like *cuoca*, or *redattrice*, it is the one that is made plural as in *la capocuoco > le capocuoche* ('female chefs'), *la caporedattrice > le caporedattrici* ('female managing editors'). The last case to keep in mind is when the word *capo* means **'the beginning or the prominence of something'**. Here the second noun is made plural as in *il capodanno > i capodanni* ('New Year's Days'), and *il capolavoro > i capolavori* ('masterpieces');

- **noun + adjective**: such compounds usually make both parts plural as in *la cassaforte > le casseforti* ('strong boxes'), *il terremoto > i terremoti* ('earthquakes'), but there are also a few exceptions like *il palcoscenico > i palcoscenici* ('stages'), *la roccaforte > le roccaforti* ('bastions');

- **adjective + masculine noun**: in words of this category the noun is usually the one made plural as in *il francobollo > i francobolli* ('stamps'), *il mezzogiorno > i mezzogiorni* ('middays'), but there are a few exceptions as well like *l'altopiano > gli altipiani* ('highlands'), *il purosangue > i purosangue* ('purebreds');

- **adjective + feminine noun**: these types of compounds make both parts plural as in *la malasorte > le malesorti* ('misfortunes'), *la falsariga > le falserighe* ('patterns');

- **adjective + adjective**: in compounds of this type, only the second adjective is made plural as in *il chiaroscuro > i chiaroscuri* ('chiaroscuros'), *il pianoforte > i pianoforti* ('pianos');

- **verb + plural noun**: such compounds maintain the same form in the plural. In this case the article makes the number clear as in *il cavatappi > i cavatappi* ('corkscrews'), *il portaombrelli > i portaombrelli* ('umbrella stands');

- **verb + singular masculine noun**: in compounds of this type, only the second part is made plural as in *il passaporto > i passaporti* ('passports'), *il salvagente > i salvagenti* ('life jackets'), but there are exceptions like *il prestanome > i prestanome* ('figureheads'), *lo spartitraffico > gli spartitraffico* ('traffic islands');

- **verb + singular feminine noun**: such compounds maintain the same form in the plural. In this case the article makes the number clear as in *l'aspirapolvere > gli aspirapolvere* ('vacuum cleaners'), *il portalampada > i portalampada* ('lamp sockets');

- **verb + verb**: compounds of this type maintain the same form in the plural. Here too the article makes the number clear as in *il dormiveglia > i dormiveglia* ('states of being drowsy'), *il lasciapassare > i lasciapassare* ('passes');

- **preposition + noun**: such nouns form their plural in two ways depending on the gender of the whole compound and the gender of its noun part. If both have the same gender, only the noun part is made plural: for example, the compound *il soprannome* is masculine as is *nome*, so its plural is *i soprannomi* ('nicknames'); if, on the other hand, the compound has a different gender from its noun part, it maintains the same form in the plural: for example, the compound *il retrobottega* is masculine, but *la bottega* is feminine, so the plural is *i retrobottega* ('backshops');

- **adverb + verb**: when an adverb and a verb combine, the resulting compound maintains the same form in the plural. Here again the article makes the number clear as in *il benestare > i benestare* ('approvals'), *il malessere > i malessere* ('states of being indisposed');
- **adverb + noun or adjective**: words of this kind make the second part plural as in *la menomazione > le menomazioni* ('impairments'), *il malfermo > i malfermi* ('those who are unsteady');
- **noun + preposition + noun**: such compounds form their plural by making plural either the second word as in *il pomodoro > i pomodori* ('tomatoes') or sometimes the first word as in *il ficodindia > i fichidindia* ('cactus pears').

4. ADJECTIVES

> **Adjectives**: An adjective is a word that describes or gives information about nouns or pronouns. There are different types of adjectives in Italian as well as in English. They can be descriptive (*un grande appartamento* 'a big apartment'), indefinite (*molti studenti* 'many students'), numeric (*due parole* 'two words'), possessive (*mio padre* 'my father'), interrogative (*Quali libri preferisci?* 'Which books do you prefer?'), exclamatory (*Quale follia!* 'What foolishness!'), demonstrative (*questa casa* 'this house') or they can express a relation to a certain thing or category of things (*carriera accademica* 'academic career').
>
> **N.B.** This chapter mainly discusses descriptive adjectives and adjectives of relation. All the others will be covered in detail in the next chapters together with their equivalent pronouns (see chapters 7, 9, 10, 11, 12).

4.1 Adjectives: Italian Unlike English

In English the form of an adjective is invariable regardless of the noun it modifies. In Italian, instead, an adjective always agrees in gender (*piccolo palazzo* 'a small building', *piccola casa* 'a small house') and number (*piccoli appartamenti* 'small apartments', *piccole ville* 'small villas') with the noun it modifies.

A descriptive adjective is usually placed after the noun and not before it as in English: *una borsa rossa* ('a red bag'), *un'auto veloce* ('a fast car').

4.2 Gender of Adjectives and Agreement with Nouns

Since in Italian an adjective always agrees with the noun it modifies, the adjective has an invariable part (the stem) and endings that vary according to gender and number. Based on the number and form of the endings, Italian adjectives can be divided into three classes.

1. The **first class** includes adjectives with **four endings**: masculine singular -**o**, masculine plural -**i**, feminine singular -**a**, and feminine plural -**e**:

	Sing.	Pl.
Masc.	-*o*: uomo **allegro** ('cheerful man')	-*i*: uomini **allegri** ('cheerful men')
Fem.	-*a*: donna **allegra** ('cheerful woman')	-*e*: donne **allegre** ('cheerful women')

2. The **second class** includes adjectives with **two endings**: masculine and feminine singular -*e*, and masculine and feminine plural -*i*:

	Sing.	Pl.
Masc.	-*e*: *uomo felice* ('happy man')	-*i*: *uomini felici* ('happy men')
Fem.	-*e*: *donna felice* ('happy woman')	-*i*: *donne felici* ('happy women')

3. The **third class** includes adjectives with **three endings**: masculine and feminine singular -*a*, masculine plural -*i*, and feminine plural -*e*. Included in this class are all adjectives ending in -*ista*, -*cida*, and -*ita*:

	Sing.	Pl.
Masc.	-*a*: *uomo ottimista* 'optimistic man'	-*i*: *uomini ottimisti* 'optimistic men'
Fem.	-*a*: *donna ottimista* 'optimistic woman'	-*e*: *donne ottimiste* 'optimistic women'

4.3 Adjectives in -co, -go, -ca *and* -ga

While adjectives ending in -**go** always form the plural in -*ghi* (*spazio largo* > *spazi larghi* 'large spaces'), adjectives in -**ca** always in -*che* (*formula chimica* > *formule chimiche* 'chemical formulas') and in -**ga** always in -*ghe* (*risposta vaga* > *risposte vaghe* 'vague answers'), **adjectives ending in -*co* present a few particularities in the masculine plural:**

- adjectives in **consonant + *co*** have the plural in -*chi*: *cappotto bianco* > *cappotti bianchi* ('white coats'), *bambino stanco* > *bambini stanchi* ('tired kids');
- adjectives in -***ico*** have the plural in -*ici*: *uccello acquatico* > *uccelli acquatici* ('water birds'), *locale pubblico* > *locali pubblici* ('public places'); but *carico* ('loaded') and its opposite *scarico* ('unloaded'), as well as *antico* ('ancient') have the plural in -*ichi*: *treno carico/scarico* > *treni carichi/scarichi* ('loaded/unloaded trains'), *tempo antico* > *tempi antichi* ('ancient times');
- adjectives in -***iaco*** have the plural in -*iaci*: *studente austriaco* > *studenti austriaci* ('Austrian students'), *paesaggio idilliaco* > *paesaggi idilliaci* ('idyllic landscapes'); but *ubriaco* ('drunk') has its plural in -*chi*: *uomo ubriaco* > *uomini ubriachi* ('drunken men').

4.4 A Few Invariable Adjectives

Some adjectives, against the rules, maintain the same form for masculine and feminine, for singular and plural. This group includes:

- the **colors** *amaranto* ('reddish purple'), *blu* ('blue'), *rosa* ('pink'), *lilla* ('lilac'), and *viola* ('purple'): *camicia blu* ('blue shirt'), *pantaloni rosa* ('pink pants'), *scarpe viola* ('purple shoes'). The color *marrone* ('brown') and *arancione* ('orange'), originally invariable, tend to be regu-

lar and have the plural in -*i* according to the rules of the second class of adjectives (see 4.2). All adjectives formed by **color + noun** such as *verde bottiglia* ('bottle-green'), *giallo ocra* ('earth-yellow'), *rosso porpora* ('purple-red') are also invariable;
- a few **adjectives ending in -*i*** such as *pari* ('even') and *dispari* ('odd'): *numeri pari e dispari* ('even and odd numbers');
- all **foreign adjectives** such as *chic, hippy, snob*;
- the adjective ***arrosto*** ('roasted'): *peperoni arrosto* ('roasted peppers'), *castagne arrosto* ('roasted chestnuts');
- a few **adverbial adjectives** (adjectives functioning as adverbs) such as *perbene* ('well-behaved') and *ammodo* ('respectable'): *ragazzi perbene* ('well-behaved kids'), *persone ammodo* ('respectable people').

4.5 Agreement with Multiple Nouns

When an adjective qualifies two or more nouns, a few rules must be kept in mind, especially in the case of nouns of different genders:

- if the nouns are **all masculine**, the adjective takes the masculine plural form: *Ho incontrato un amico e un professore americani* ('I met an American friend and an American professor');
- if the nouns are **all feminine**, the adjective takes the feminine plural form: *Ho un'automobile e una casa nuove* ('I have a new house and a new car');
- if the nouns (masculine or feminine) are part of a **homogeneous series** like *vino e formaggio* ('wine and cheese'), *storia e filosofia* ('history and philosophy'), the adjective keeps the singular form: *il salame e il prosciutto italiano* ('Italian salami and prosciutto'), *l'arte e la letteratura classica* ('classical art and literature');
- if the nouns are of a **different gender,** the adjective takes the plural masculine form: *un divano e una poltrona nuovi* ('a new sofa and armchair'). It is always possible, of course, to repeat the adjective next to each noun, in which case the adjectives agree respectively with the noun they modify: *un divano nuovo e una poltrona nuova* ('a new sofa and a new armchair').

4.6 The Adjective bello

The adjective ***bello*** ('beautiful'), when placed before a noun, follows a pattern similar to that of the definite article (see 2.4). The complete form *bello* can be used only before singular masculine nouns beginning with *z, ps, gn* (*bello zaffiro* 'beautiful sapphire') or with the group *s* + consonant (*bello scherzo* 'nice joke'), or with foreign words that start with *x, y, sh,* and *ch* (*bello show* 'beautiful show'). The feminine ***bella*** can be used only before singular feminine nouns beginning with a consonant (*bella ragazza* 'beautiful girl'). In all other cases, the adjective takes variant forms:

- **bel** is used before singular masculine nouns beginning with consonants other than those mentioned above and *h*: *bel gatto* ('beautiful cat'), *bel ragazzo* ('beautiful boy');
- **bell'** is used before singular masculine and feminine nouns beginning with vowels or *h*: *bell'amico* ('beautiful friend'), *bell'avventura* ('beautiful adventure'), *bell'hotel* ('beautiful hotel');
- **begli,** plural of *bello* and the masculine *bell'*, is used before plural masculine nouns beginning with *z*, *ps*, *gn* (*begli zaffiri* 'beautiful sapphires'), with the group *s* + consonant (*begli scherzi* 'nice jokes'), with foreign words that start with *x*, *y*, *sh*, and *ch* (*begli show* 'beautiful shows'), and with vowels or *h* (*begli amici* 'beautiful friends', *begli hotel* 'beautiful hotels');
- **bei**, plural of *bel*, is used before plural masculine nouns beginning with consonants other than those mentioned above or *h*: *bei gatti* ('beautiful cats'), *bei ragazzi* ('beautiful boys');
- **belle,** plural of *bella* and the feminine *bell'*, is used before all plural feminine nouns: *belle ragazze* ('beautiful girls'), *belle avventure* ('beautiful adventures').

> **N.B.** The feminine *bella*, can sometimes be used instead of the elided equivalent *bell'*, especially in formal writing: *Vorrei ringraziarla per la bella esperienza* ('I would like to thank you for the beautiful experience').

4.7 Colloquial Constructions of bello: bell'e pronto, nel bel mezzo, etc.

The adjective *bello* also has particular constructions when used in a colloquial context:

- **bell'e + past participle** indicates a completed action: *Siamo in ritardo, lo spettacolo a quest'ora è bell'e finito* ('We are late, the show is over by now');
- **bell'e pronto** is frequently used to emphasize the idea that someone or something is 'ready'. Being an adjective, *pronto* always agrees with the noun it modifies: *Possiamo andare, noi siamo bell'e pronti* ('We can go; we are ready'), *Venite. La cena è bell'e pronta* ('Come. Dinner is ready');
- **bello + adjective or noun** can be used to emphasize a negative concept with the sarcastic meaning of 'really': *Sei un bello zotico* ('You really are a boor');
- **nel bel mezzo** indicates an action that happens right in the middle of something: *Sono arrivato nel bel mezzo della lezione* ('I arrived right in the middle of the lecture').

4.8 The Adjective buono

The singular forms of the indefinite adjective **buono**, when placed before a noun, follow a pattern similar to those of the indefinite article (see 2.2):

- ***buono*** is used for masculine nouns beginning with *z, ps, gn* (*buono zio*, 'good uncle'), with the group *s* + consonant (*buono studente* 'good student'), with foreign words starting with *x, y, sh*, and *ch* (*buono chef* 'good chef');
- ***buon*** is used before all other masculine nouns: *buon amico* ('good friend'), *buon libro* ('good book');
- ***buona*** is used before feminine nouns beginning with consonants: *buona cena* ('good dinner'), *buona sera* ('good evening');
- ***buon'*** is used before feminine nouns beginning with vowels (*buon'amica* 'good girlfriend', *buon'arancia* 'good orange').

> **N.B.** The feminine *buona* can sometimes be used instead of the elided equivalent *buon'*, especially in formal writing: *Questo saggio dimostra buona immaginazione* ('This essay demonstrates good imagination').

4.9 Colloquial Constructions of buono: *una buona mezz'ora, etc.*

Like *bello*, the adjective *buono* can have particular constructions when used in a colloquial context:

- **indefinite article + *buono* + noun** is used to emphasize completeness in measures of time, space, and quantity: *Ho atteso una buon'ora* ('I waited a full hour'), *È lungo un buon metro* ('It is a full meter').

4.10 The Adjectives grande *and* santo

The adjective ***grande*** may present optional variant forms when placed before a singular noun. In this case, *grande* means 'great' more than 'big' (see 4.14):

- ***gran*** may be used instead of *grande* before any singular masculine or feminine nouns beginning with consonants: *gran personaggio* ('great character'), *gran signora* ('great lady'); but the form *grande* is usually preferred to *gran* before masculine nouns beginning with *z, ps, gn,* with the group *s* + consonant, or with foreign words that start with *x, y, sh* and *ch*: *grande studente* ('great student), *grande chef* ('great chef');
- ***grand'*** may be used before any singular masculine or feminine nouns beginning with vowels: *grand'uomo* ('great man'), *grand'avventura* ('great adventure').

Likewise, the adjective ***santo*** ('saint') may present variant forms when placed before a singular noun:

- **san** is used before names of male saints beginning with consonants (*san Giuseppe, san Francesco*); but the form *santo* is usually preferred when the name starts with *z*, or *s* + consonant: *santo Zaccaria, santo Stefano*;
- **sant'** is used before names of male and female saints beginning with vowels: *sant'Antonio, sant'Anna*.

4.11 Compound Adjectives

Some Italian adjectives are formed by the combination of two elements. They can be made up of:

- **two adjectives**: *dolce + amaro > dolceamaro* ('bittersweet'), *agro + dolce > agrodolce* ('sweet and sour');
- **prefix + adjective**: *auto + sufficiente > autosufficiente* ('self-sufficient'), *anti + aderente > antiaderente* ('nonstick');

All these compound adjectives form their feminine and plural regularly (see 4.2) by changing only the ending of the second element: *dolceamaro > dolceamara, autosufficiente > autosufficienti*.

4.12 Compound Adjectives: Particularities

Although most compound adjectives are written as one word (*sordomuto* 'deaf-mute', *onnipotente* 'all-powerful'), when indicating ethnicity they can be hyphenated: *italoamericano* or *italo-americano* ('Italian-American'). In adjectives of ethnicity, in Italian as in English, the first element is usually modified: *africano* ('African') > *afro-* (*afroamericano* 'African-American'), *inglese* ('English') > *anglo-* (*anglofrancese* 'Anglo-French'). All of them form their singular feminine and their plural by changing the second element only: *ragazzo italoamericano > ragazza italoamericana* ('Italoamerican girl') > *ragazze italoamericane* ('Italoamerican girls').

Compound adjectives whose first element ends in **-ale**, drop the vowel *e*: *nazionale + comunista > nazionalcomunista* ('National Communist'), *liberale + socialista > liberalsocialista* ('Liberal Socialist').

Adjectives composed of **color + noun** such as *verde bottiglia* ('bottle-green'), *giallo ocra* ('earth-yellow') are always written as two words, and they maintain the same form for masculine and feminine, singular and plural (see 4.4): *un'auto giallo ocra > due auto giallo ocra* ('two earth-yellow cars').

The adjective **mezzo** ('half') can also be used as the first element of compound adjectives, which are always written as two words: *mezzo vuoto* ('half-empty'), *mezzo matto* ('half-mad'). Adjectives formed with *mezzo* can regularly make the feminine and the plural by changing only the ending of the second element: *una bottiglia mezzo piena* ('a half-empty bottle'), *due ragazzi mezzo matti* ('two half-mad boys'), or by changing both elements: *una bottiglia mezza piena* ('a half-empty bottle'), *due ragazzi mezzi matti* ('two half-mad boys').

4.13 Position of Descriptive Adjectives

If in English the position of adjectives does not change, in the sense that the adjective always precedes the noun it modifies ('the red car'), except when used after linking verbs ('the car is red'), in Italian things are somewhat more complex. While Italian **adjectives indicating colors or ethnicity always follow the noun they modify** (*capelli neri* 'black hair', *un film italiano* 'an Italian film'), **other descriptive adjectives may come either before or after the noun.** If in most cases the position does not alter the meaning (*un felice pensiero* and *un pensiero felice* 'a happy thought' are, for example, perfectly interchangeable), in other cases (see 4.14) the position affects the meaning: *una brutta persona* means 'a bad person' while *una persona brutta* means 'an ugly person'.

All **adjectives modified** by a suffix (*una casa piccolina* 'a very small house') or preceded by an adverb (*una persona veramente buona* 'a really good person'), or followed by a preposition (*un bicchiere pieno di acqua* 'a glass full of water') always come after the nouns they modify.

There are many adjectives (**adjectives of relation**) that do not exactly describe a quality of the noun to which they refer, but rather indicate a state of relating to or pertaining to a certain thing or category of things. In modern Italian these adjectives always follow, without exception, the noun they modify: *legge federale* ('federal law'), *la luce solare* ('sunlight').

4.14 Adjectives of Beauty, Age, Goodness, and Size

In some cases, changing the position of an adjective combined with a specific noun completely changes its meaning. This occurs especially with adjectives of beauty, age, goodness, and size ("**BAGS**" adjectives). When placed before a noun, the adjective is used figuratively (expressing subjectivity, opinion, emotion) but when placed after the noun, it is used literally. Here are the most significant cases:

Adjectives	Before	After
bello	*un bel problema* ('a big problem')	*un problema bello* ('a nice problem')
brutto	*una brutta persona* ('a bad person')	*una persona brutta* ('an ugly person')
nuovo	*un nuovo libro* ('another book')	*un libro nuovo* ('a new book')
vecchio	*un vecchio amico* ('an old friend')	*un amico vecchio* ('a friend who is old')
buono	*buona gente* ('simple people')	*gente buona* ('good people')
bravo	*un bravo ragazzo* ('a good boy')	*un ragazzo bravo* ('a boy good at something')
povero	*un povero studente* ('an unlucky student')	*uno studente povero* ('a student without money')
grande	*una grande persona* ('a great person')	*una persona grande* ('a big person')
piccolo	*un piccolo uomo* ('a mean man')	*un uomo piccolo* ('a small/short man')
alto	*un alto ufficiale* ('an important officer')	*un ufficiale alto* ('a tall officer')

The adjective ***caro*** can also be considered part of this category. When it modifies nouns denoting people or abstract elements, *caro* means respectively 'dear' and 'nice' and always comes before the noun: *una cara persona* ('a dear person'), *un caro pensiero* ('a nice thought'); however, when it modifies nouns denoting objects, it means 'expensive' instead and always follows the noun: *un appartamento caro* ('an expensive apartment'), *un'auto cara* ('an expensive car').

4.15 Position of the Other Adjectives: molto, due, mio, *etc.*

All adjectives other than the descriptive ones normally precede the noun they modify. This is the case of:

- **indefinite** adjectives such as *molto* ('much'), *troppo* ('too much'), *poco* ('little'): *Ho bevuto troppa acqua* ('I drank too much water'), *Ho pochi minuti* ('I have a few minutes');
- **numeric** adjectives such as *due* ('two'), *terzo* ('third'), *decimo* ('tenth'): *Dimmi due parole* ('Tell me two words'), *È la terza strada a destra* ('It is the third street on the right');
- **possessive** adjectives such as *mio* ('my'), *loro* ('their'), *nostro* ('our'): *Parlo con mio fratello* ('I am talking with my brother'), *Luca ha venduto i suoi libri* ('Luca sold his books');
- **interrogative** adjectives such as *quale* ('which') and *quanto* ('how much'): *Quale libro preferisci?* ('Which book do you prefer?'), *Quanto tempo hai per me?* ('How much time do you have for me?');
- **exclamatory** adjectives such as *quale* and *quanto* ('what a/an ...'): *Quale onore!* ('What an honor!'), *Quanta gioia!* ('What a joy!')
- **demonstrative** adjectives such as *questo* ('this') and *quello* ('that'): *Mi piace questa casa* ('I like this house'), *Quelle finestre sono nuove* ('Those windows are new').

A few adjectives such as **diverso** and **vario** ('several' or 'different') express an indeterminate number when preceding a plural noun (*diversi impegni* 'several commitments', *varie funzioni* 'several functions') but mean 'a different kind' when following it (*impegni diversi* 'different commitments', *funzioni varie* 'different functions'). The same is true of **certo** ('certain' or 'sure'), which placed before a noun expresses an indeterminate quantity (*una certa cosa* 'a certain thing') but expresses certainty when placed after the noun (*una cosa certa* 'a sure thing').

4.16 Word Order in Combinations of Two or More Adjectives

Keeping in mind that adjectives of color and ethnicity and adjectives of relation (see 4.13) must always follow the noun, English speakers should know that the order of adjectives in Italian is usually the same as in English. The position of adjectives of different categories in a sentence or noun phrase can be represented by the following sequence translating the English phrase 'These three beautiful presidential red Italian cars':

demonstrative	numeric	descriptive	noun	of relation	ethnicity	color
Queste	tre	belle	auto	presidenziali	italiane	rosse

4.17 Adjectives Used as Nouns

Adjectives are often used as nouns. This happens when the nouns they modify are omitted or simply replaced by the adjective. They are always preceded by either a definite article (*I giovani sono ottimisti* 'The young are optimistic') or an indefinite one (*Conosco un tedesco* 'I know a German guy'). Specific cases of this kind are:

- the plural masculine of **adjectives indicating an entire category of people**: *Non sopporto gli arroganti* ('I can't stand the arrogant'); *gli arroganti,* like its English equivalent, stands for all arrogant people;
- the plural **adjectives of ethnicity**: *gli americani* ('the Americans'), *i francesi* ('the French'). Adjectives of ethnicity used in their singular form denote one person out of the entire population if they are preceded by an indefinite article (*Ho conosciuto un algerino* 'I met an Algerian') or languages if they are preceded by a definite article (*Parlo il francese* 'I speak French');
- singular masculine **adjectives of color**: *Il verde ti sta bene* ('You look good in green'), *Mi piace il blu* ('I like blue'). When used in their plural masculine forms, they can indicate the members of a political side or party (*i rossi* 'the reds' equivalent to *i comunisti* 'the communists'), the players or fans of a team (*i viola* 'the purples' equivalent to 'players or fans of *Fiorentina*', team of Florence), or the human race (*i bianchi* 'white people');
- singular masculine **adjectives indicating abstract concepts** that replace nouns expressing the same idea. For example, in the sentence *Il vero verrà presto scoperto* ('The truth will soon come out'), the adjective *vero* ('true') replaces the noun *verità* ('truth'). The most common adjectives of this kind are *il bello* for *la bellezza* ('beauty'), *il buono* for *la bontà* ('goodness'), *il giusto* for *la giustizia* ('fairness').

4.18 Adjectives with Prepositions + Infinitive

An adjective followed by a preposition can introduce a subordinate clause with the verb in the infinitive form: *Sono contento di parlarti* ('I am happy to talk with you'). Although the English structure generally corresponds to the Italian one (*Sono felice di partire* 'I am happy to leave), it is sometimes possible to have the gerund instead of the infinitive in English: *Mi sento colpevole per essere in ritardo* ('I feel guilty for being late').

5. ADVERBS AND ADVERBIAL PHRASES

> **Adverbs:** An adverb is a word that modifies a verb, an adjective, or another adverb. An adverb can indicate manner (*veramente* 'truly'), time (*poi* 'then'), place (*lontano* 'far'), and quantity ('molto'); there also are adverbs of affirmation, negation, or doubt (*sì* 'yes', *no* 'no', *forse* 'maybe'), interrogative (*perché* 'why') and exclamatory (*come* 'how'). While some adverbs can easily be identified by their characteristic suffix *-mente* (equivalent to the '-ly' form in English), most of them must be identified by the grammatical relationships within the sentence or clause as a whole. Because they are invariable, adverbs do not change according to gender or number, but they accept comparative and superlative forms (see 6.2).

5.1 Adverbs in -mente: lentamente, felicemente, *etc.*

The most common type of Italian adverbs denoting manner end in *-mente*, equivalent to the '-ly' form in English. They are simply formed by adding the suffix *-mente* to the feminine form of the corresponding adjective:

Adjective m. >	Adjective f. >	Adverb
vero 'true'	*vera* 'true'	*veramente* 'truly'
felice 'happy'	*felice* 'happy'	*felicemente* 'happily'

If the adjective ends in *-le* or *-re* preceded by a vowel, the final *-e* is dropped in front of *-mente*:

Adjective >	>	Adverb
naturale 'natural'	*natural*	*naturalmente* 'naturally'
regolare 'regular'	*regolar*	*regolarmente* 'regularly'

Four adverbs have special forms that deviate from the above rules: *leggero* > **leggermente** ('lightly'), *violento* > **violentemente** ('violently)', *altro* > **altrimenti** ('otherwise'), and *pari* > **parimenti** ('likewise').

Like the English suffix '-ly', the Italian adverbial suffix *-mente* can never be added to adjectives denoting color or ethnicity.

5.2 Adverbs with Complementary Double Forms: certo/certamente, solo/solamente, *etc.*
Besides the forms in -*mente*, some adverbs accept the form of the masculine singular adjective. In some cases, the two forms are perfectly interchangeable:

- **certo/certamente** ('certainly', 'for sure'): *Così facendo, non sei certo/certamente di aiuto* ('In doing so, you're certainly not helping'); when *certo* is used as adverb, it is preferably preceded by the preposition *di*: *Di certo Marco non verrà* ('Marco is definitely not coming');
- **chiaro/chiaramente** ('clearly'): *Parla chiaro/chiaramente, non ti capisco* ('Speak clearly; I don't understand you');
- **solo/solamente** ('only'): *Loro non vengono, vengo solo/solamente io* ('They are not coming; I am the only one coming'); Italian in this case presents a third adverb, **soltanto**, formed from the same root and having the same meaning: *Ho comprato soltanto un paio di scarpe* ('I only bought a pair of shoes');
- **veloce/velocemente** ('fast'): *Corri veloce/velocemente* ('Run fast').

5.3 Adverbs with Distinct Double Forms: alto *and* altamente, forte *and* fortemente, *etc.*
In other cases Italian differentiates between the form in -*mente* and the form of the adverb corresponding to the adjective:

- **alto** ('high'), **altamente** ('highly'). *Alto* indicates a high position (*Le aquile volano alto* 'Eagles fly high') and can sometimes be preceded by the preposition *in* (*Guarda in alto* 'Look up'); in contrast, the form *altamente* is an adverb of manner meaning 'highly', 'greatly', or 'extremely'; it always combines with an adjective with which it forms the superlative degree: *La situazione è altamente pericolosa* ('The situation is extremely dangerous');
- **basso** ('low'), **bassamente** ('basely'). The form *basso* is similar to *alto* in that it indicates a low position (*Certi aerei volano basso* 'Certain airplanes fly low') and can sometimes be preceded by the preposition *in* (*Guarda in basso* 'Look down'). In Italian the expression *cadere in basso* has the figurative meaning of 'to degrade oneself': *Sei proprio caduto in basso!* ('You couldn't get any lower!'). The form *bassamente* always carries a moral connotation of baseness: *Agisci bassamente* ('You are acting despicably');
- **forte** ('loud', 'hard'), **fortemente** ('strongly'). The form *forte* adds intensity to an action (*Non puoi parlare così forte* 'You can't speak so loud', *Se corri forte arrivi primo*, 'If you run hard, you will arrive first') while *fortemente* intensifies an adjective with which it forms the superlative degree: *Sono fortemente contrario a questa idea* ('I am strongly against this idea');
- **giusto** ('exactly') **giustamente** ('rightly'). *Giusto* is the form used to express precision in time, place, or in measure: *Sono arrivato giusto dieci minuti fa* ('I arrived just ten minutes ago'), *Il pacco pesa giusto un chilo* ('The package weighs exactly one kilo'); on the other hand, the adverb *giustamente* expresses the rightness of an action: *Riceverai quello che giustamente meriti* ('You will get what you rightly deserve');
- **lontano** ('far'), **lontanamente** ('vaguely', 'remotely'). *Lontano* always expresses distance (*Vivo lontano da tutti* 'I live far from everybody') while *lontanamente* suggests the idea

of vagueness of an action (*Mi ricordo lontanamente di te* 'I vaguely remember you') or its carelessness (*Non mi interessa lontanamente quello che fai* 'I couldn't care less what you do'); to emphasize the carelessness, the word *neppure* ('not even') often occurs together with *lontanamente*: *Non ci penso neppure lontanamente* ('I wouldn't give it so much as a thought');

- **proprio** ('really') **propriamente** ('properly'). *Proprio* is used to intensify the concept expressed by an adjective (*Sei proprio vigliacco* 'You are really cowardly'), a noun (*Ho proprio bisogno di una macchina* 'I really need a car'), or another adverb (*Hai fatto proprio bene* 'You did really well'), while *propriamente* expresses the correctness and appropriateness of an action (*Lo studente si esprime propriamente* 'The student expresses himself properly').

5.4 Irregular Adverbs

The adverbs below have corresponding adjective forms, but they are not easily traced back to the original adjective bases. They must be memorized as new words:

Adjective >	Adverbs
buono ('good')	**bene** ('well')
cattivo ('bad')	**male** ('badly')
migliore ('better')	**meglio** ('better')
peggiore ('worse')	**peggio** ('worse')

Other adverbs do not derive from any adjective. They are special adverbs of time, place, quantity, and so on, examined in the following paragraphs.

5.5 Adverbs in -oni *Expressing Physical Manner:* bocconi, ginocchioni, etc.

A few adverbs expressing physical manner are formed by adding *-oni* to the root of a noun indicating a body part or to a verb indicating movement. They are typical of an informal register and usually convey clumsiness: *Non camminare strasciconi* ('Do not walk dragging along'). Most of them can be, and usually are, preceded by the preposition *a*: *Non vedo niente, vado a tentoni* ('I can't see anything; I am groping around'). Below is a list of the most significant of them with their English equivalents:

Nouns or Verbs >	Adverbs
bocca ('mouth')	**bocconi** ('facing down')
cavalcare ('to ride')	**cavalcioni** ('astride')
carpire ('to grab')	**carponi** ('on hands and knees')
ciondolo ('pendant')	**ciondoloni** ('with legs dangling')
ginocchio ('knee')	**ginocchioni** ('kneeling')
strascicare ('to drag')	**strasciconi** ('dragging along')
tentare ('to try')	**tentoni** ('gropingly')
zoppicare ('to limp')	**zoppiconi** ('limpingly')

5.6 Other Ways to Form Adverbs and Adverbial Expressions of Manner

Many adverbs or adverbial expressions are formed with more than one word (sometimes written as one word). This is usually done through the **combination of a preposition (simple or articulated) and a noun or an adjective**. Below are the most common of these, listed by the preposition that governs them:

- **a**: *almeno* ('at least'), *a stento* ('hardly'), *appena* ('just'), *a momenti* ('almost'), *appieno* ('completely'), *a precipizio* ('headlong'). Particular attention must be paid to the combination **alla + adjective or noun**, which is extremely frequent in Italian. It can indicate a way of being or acting (*all'antica* 'old-fashioned way', *alla buona* 'down-home', *alla giornata* 'hand-to-mouth'), or the origin or characteristic of a dish (*alla parmigiana*, 'from Parma', *alla fiorentina* 'florentine style'). Very common also is the expression **alla maniera di + noun,** which can describe a way of acting (*alla maniera di un amico* 'in a friendly way', *alla maniera degli italiani* 'as the Italians do') or be equivalent to 'in the style of' when followed by a proper noun (*alla maniera di Michelangelo* 'in the style of Michelangelo')
- **di**: *di fretta* ('rushing'), *di continuo* ('continuously'), *di solito* ('usually'), *di sicuro* ('certainly'), *di rado* ('rarely'), *di nascosto* ('secretly'), *di nuovo* ('again'), *di proposito* ('on purpose'), *di giorno* ('in the daytime'), *di notte* ('at night');
- **in**: *in cambio* ('in exchange'), *in breve* ('in brief'), *in alto* ('upwards'), *in basso* ('downwards'), *in grande* ('in a big way'), *in segreto* ('in secret'), *in privato* ('in private'), *in fretta* ('rushing'). Very common is also the expression **in maniera + adjective**, or the equivalent **in modo + adjective,** which indicate an adverb of manner: *in maniera rapida/in modo rapido* ('in a fast way'), *in maniera elegante/in modo elegante* ('elegantly');
- **per**: *per caso* ('by chance'), *per davvero* ('truly'), *per gradi* ('little by little');
- **con**: *con sforzo* ('with effort'), *con cura* ('carefully'), *con prudenza* ('prudently'), and so on. Adverbial phrases of manner with **con + noun** are exceedingly frequent in Italian and possible with almost all nouns. Similar constructions exist in English as well, but Italian makes much more use of them;
- **senza**: *senza fatica* ('easily'), *senza indugio* ('without delay'), *senza attenzione* ('absentmindedly'), and so on. Also the construction **senza + noun** is very frequent in Italian as an adverbial phrase of manner.

Other adverbial expressions of manner can be produced by a **repetition** of a noun (*passo passo* 'step by step', *man mano* 'little by little'), an adjective (*zitto zitto* 'without making oneself noticed', *bel bello* 'unexpectedly'), an adverb (*così così* 'so-so', *quasi quasi* 'very nearly'), or an adverbial phrase (*a poco a poco* 'little by little', *a corpo a corpo* 'hand-to-hand').

Certain expressions like *un sacco, un monte, un mucchio* all mean 'a lot' and have a specific **colloquial connotation**: *Ci siamo diverti un sacco alla tua festa* ('We had a lot of fun at your party'). The common expression **a mo' di + noun**, typical of an informal register, is equivalent to *come fosse* ('as if'): *Hai preso la mia casa a mo' di* [= *come fosse*] *un albergo* ('You are acting as if my house was a hotel').

5.7 Adverbs of Time: oggi, adesso, sempre, *etc.*

Adverbs of time tell when an action happens, how long it lasts, and how often it happens. Many Italian adverbs of time have an English equivalent, and they can be easily learned by English speaking learners. This is the case of *oggi* ('today'), *domani* ('tomorrow'), *ieri* ('yesterday'), *appena* ('just'), *già* ('already'), *ora* and *adesso* (both meaning 'now'), *spesso* ('often'), and so on. However, other adverbs can create some problems because they can have more than one English equivalent, depending on the context in which they are used. Below are indicated the most common Italian adverbs of this kind:

- ***allora*** means 'then' in the sense of 'at that time'*: Allora il computer non esisteva* ('The computer did not exist at that time'), *Allora ero più felice* ('I was happier then'). When *allora* is combined with the preposition *da*, it means 'ever since' in affirmative sentences (*Viviamo insieme da allora* 'We have been living together ever since') or simply 'since' in negative ones (*Non l'ho più visto da allora* 'I haven't seen him since'). *Allora* is often preceded by *proprio* (*Proprio allora lo vidi* 'I saw him right then'), or *solo* (*Solo allora si presentarono* 'Only then did they introduce themselves');
- ***poi*** means 'then' but in the sense of 'after that time'. It is also used to indicate a sequence of actions in time: *Mangio, poi vengo con te* ('I eat, then I come with you'). It can always be replaced by *dopo* (*Mangio, dopo vengo con te* 'I eat, then I come with you') and is often used in combination with *prima* 'first' (*Prima studio, poi esco* 'I study first, then I go out');
- ***ancora*** corresponds to different meanings in English. It means 'still' in affirmative sentences (*Sono ancora qui* 'I am still here') and 'not yet' in negative ones (*Non ho ancora mangiato* 'I have not eaten yet'). But *ancora* can also indicate the repetition of an action. In this case it is equivalent to the English 'again': *Mangi ancora?* ('Are you still eating?');
- ***sempre*** can mean 'always' as in *Ho sempre voluto un cane* ('I have always wanted a dog') but also 'still' as in *Lavoro sempre qui* ('I am still working here'), in which case *sempre* can be replaced by *ancora* without changing the meaning of the sentence: *Lavoro ancora qui*. When *sempre* is preceded by the preposition *per*, it is equivalent to the English 'forever' (*Ti amerò per sempre* 'I will love you forever');
- ***mai*** is generally used in negative sentences and can be translated with 'never' *Non sono mai stato a Roma* ('I have never been to Rome'). In affirmative sentences *mai* translates into the English 'ever': *Verrai mai a trovarmi?* ('Will you ever come to visit me?');
- ***qualche volta***, ***certe volte***, ***talvolta***, ***a volte*** are interchangeable and translate all into the English 'sometimes': *Qualche volta sono stanco* ('Sometimes I am tired'), *A volte vorrei vivere in un'altra città* ('Sometimes I wish I lived in a different city');
- ***ogni tanto*** and ***di quando in quando*** can replace the above adverbials and translate into 'sometimes' even though literally they mean 'every so often' and 'from time to time' respectively: *Ogni tanto vado allo stadio* ('Every so often I go to the stadium'), *Di quando in quando mangio la pizza* ('From time to time I eat pizza');
- ***prima*** can mean 'before' (*Prima non ti avevo visto* 'I had not seen you before') or 'first' when indicating the order of actions (*Prima leggi bene questo, poi puoi parlare* 'First read

it carefully, then you can talk'). It is useful to remember that *prima* is always equivalent to the English 'before' when it is followed by the preposition *di* (*Partono prima di maggio* 'They will leave before May', *Prima di uscire prendi l'ombrello* 'Before you go out, take the umbrella') or by the conjunction *che* (*Prima che tu arrivi la cena sarà pronta* 'Dinner will be ready before you arrive');

- **dopo** can be 'then', 'after', or 'later'. It indicates an action that comes after another: *Prima riposati un po', dopo lavora* ('First rest a little, then work'). It is often replaced by *poi* without changing the meaning of the sentence: *Prima riposati un po', poi lavora* ('First rest a little, then work'). Unlike *prima*, the adverb *dopo* is not followed by the preposition *di*, but it can be followed by *che* introducing another clause: *Dopo che abbiamo visitato Roma, siamo andati a Firenze* ('After we visited Rome, we went to Florence'). This construction can always be replaced by *dopo* + past infinitive: *Dopo aver visitato Roma, siamo andati a Firenze* ('After having visited Rome, we went to Florence').

5.8 Adverbs of Place: vicino, qui, là, etc.

A location can be expressed by a prepositional phrase (*Siamo a Roma* 'We are in Rome', *Il giornale è sul tavolo* 'The newspaper is on the table') or by adverbs. A lot of place adverbs have the same form as prepositions (*Vieni dentro* 'Come inside', *Io vado sotto* 'I go below'); also, they can occur with other adverbs (*qui sopra* 'above here', *là davanti* 'there ahead'). Below is a list of the most common of them and a sample of their use:

Adverbs	Examples
dentro ('inside')	*Vieni dentro* ('Come inside')
fuori ('outside')	*Vai fuori* ('Go outside')
avanti ('ahead')	*Andiamo avanti* ('Let's move ahead')
davanti ('in front')	*Posso sedere davanti?* ('Can I sit in the front?')
dietro ('behind')	*Stai dietro* ('Stay behind')
lontano ('far away')	*Abito lontano* ('I live far away')
vicino ('outside')	*Vieni vicino* ('Come close')
sotto ('below')	*Che cosa è successo sotto?* ('What happened below?')
sopra ('above')	*Vai due metri sopra* ('Go two meters above')
a destra ('on the right')	*Mettiti a destra* ('Put yourself on the right')
a sinistra ('on the left')	*Stai a sinistra* ('Stay on the left')

In addition, the above adverbs with the same form as prepositions, there are other adverbs of place extensively used in Italian:

- **qui** or **qua** (both meaning 'here') indicates proximity to the speaker or writer: *Vieni qui* ('Come here'), *Mi vedi? Sono qua* ('Can you see me? I am here'). *Qua* can combine with *su* and *giù* to form the single word adverbs *quassù* ('up here') and *quaggiù* ('down here').

While *qui* and *qua* preceded by the preposition *da* indicate **provenance** (*Parto da qui* 'I leave from here'), preceded by the prepositions *di* or *per* they indicate **passage through** (*Passa di/per qui* 'Pass through here');

- **lì** or **là** (both meaning 'there') indicates distance from the speaker or writer: *Il mio libro è lì* ('My book is there'), *Vai là* ('Go there'). *Là* is often combined with *su* and *giù* to form the single word adverbs *lassù* ('up there') and *laggiù* ('down there'). When *lì* and *là* are preceded by the preposition *da*, they indicate **provenance** (*Sono arrivato da là* 'I arrived from there') while when preceded by the prepositions *di* and *per*, they indicate **passage through** (*Andiamo di/per là* 'Let's go through there');
- **su** ('up'), **giù** ('down'), **avanti** ('forward', 'ahead'), **indietro** ('back') all indicate direction: *Guarda su/giù* ('Look up/down'), *Vai avanti/indietro* ('Go ahead/back'). *Su* and *giù* can also refer to 'upstairs' and 'downstairs' when the location is clear from the context: *La mamma non è in cucina, forse è su* ('Mom is not in the kitchen; maybe she is upstairs'). Both adverbs are often used metaphorically to indicate good or bad emotional or physical states. A phrase like *Mi sento su* is equivalent to *Sono contento* ('I am happy'), or *Sto bene* ('I feel happy') just as the opposite *Mi sento giù* means *Sono un po' triste* ('I am a little sad'), or *Sto male* ('I don't feel well'). *Su*, as an interjection, also means 'come on': *Su, ragazzi, state attenti* ('Come on, kids; pay attention'). *Avanti*, as an interjection, can be used with the meaning of 'come on': *Avanti, ragazzi, non perdete tempo* ('Come on, kids; don't waste time');
- **ovunque**, **dovunque** (both meaning 'anywhere'): *Ovunque tu sia, fammi sapere* ('Anywhere you are, let me know');
- **dappertutto** ('everywhere'): *Pietro porta il suo libro dappetutto* ('Peter takes his book everywhere');
- **altrove** ('elsewhere'): *Compra questo altrove, se qui non ti piace* ('Buy this elsewhere if you don't like it here').

5.9 Adverbs of Quantity: molto, nulla, poco, *etc.*

Adverbs of quantity answer the question 'how much', so they indicate measure or quantity. Most of them (*molto, poco, troppo, parecchio*, and *tanto*) have the same form as indefinite adjectives and pronouns (see 11.14), but as adverbs they are invariable. Note, for example, the difference between the use of *molto* as adjective ('a lot of') and as adverb ('a lot', 'very'): *Marta ha mangiato molta cioccolata* ('Marta ate a lot of chocolate'), *Marta ha mangiato molto* ('Marta ate a lot'), and *Marta è molto golosa* ('Marta is very greedy'). In the first sentence the adjective *molta* agrees with the noun *cioccolata*, while in the second and third ones *molto* is an adverb and so invariable.

Below is a list of the most significant adverbs of quantity with a sample of their use:

Adverbs	Examples
molto ('very', 'a lot')	*Giovanni studia molto* ('Giovanni studies a lot')
poco ('not much', 'little')	*Franco lavora poco* ('Franco works little')
abbastanza ('enough')	*Maria dorme abbastanza* ('Maria sleeps enough')
assai ('very', 'a lot')	*Luca mangia assai* ('Luca eats a lot')

troppo ('too much')	*Anna parla troppo* ('Anna talks too much')
niente ('at all')	*Non mi importa niente* ('I don't care at all')
parecchio ('very', 'a lot')	*Questo mi piace parecchio* ('I like it a lot')
affatto ('at all')	*Non ci credo affatto* ('I don't believe it at all')
tanto ('very', 'a lot')	*Mi piace tanto viaggiare* ('I like to travel a lot')
quasi ('almost')	*Sono quasi arrivato* ('I am almost there')
[di] più ('more')	*Alberto, studia di più!* ('Alberto, study more!')
[di] meno ('less')	*Marta, mangia meno* ('Marta, eat less')

N.B. Although *molto*, *tanto*, and *parecchio* are interchangeable, *molto* occurs more frequently than the others. *Assai* can substitute for *molto*, but it is rare in contemporary Italian and confined mostly to the South of Italy.

5.10 Adverbs of Affirmation, Negation, or Doubt

In Italian, the most common way to affirm, negate, or express a doubt is by using respectively the adverbs *sì* ('yes'), *no* ('no'), and *forse* ('maybe'), beside which, as in English, are other frequent adverbs: *assolutamente* ('absolutely'), *probabilmente* ('probably'), *davvero* ('indeed'), *nemmeno* ('not even'), and so on.

5.11 Interrogative Adverbs: perché, quando, come, *etc.*

If 'yes' or 'no' questions usually lead to simple 'yes' or 'no' answers, questions introduced by the interrogative adverbs *come* ('how'), *dove* ('where'), *perché* ('why'), *quando* ('where'), and *quanto* ('how much') elicit more information. In Italian, as in English, they are placed at the beginning of direct (*Come stai oggi?* 'How are you today?') and indirect questions (*Voglio sapere dove è mia sorella* 'I want to know where my sister is').

Note that the Italian *perché*, unlike the English 'why', can be used both in a question in which it means 'why' and in the corresponding answer in which it means 'because': *Perché non stai attento? – Perché sono stanco* ('Why don't you pay attention? – Because I am tired').

When *quanto* precedes an adverb of time, it simply means 'how': *Quanto spesso vai al cinema?* ('How often do you go to the movies?').

5.12 Exclamatory Adverbs: come *and* quanto

The most common words for exclamation in Italian are *come* and *quanto*, both of which are equivalent to the English 'how': *Come sei carino!* ('How nice you are!') *Quanto sei forte!* ('How strong you are!'). They are used at the beginning of the exclamatory sentence.

5.13 Positions of Adverbs

Unlike English, Italian is more flexible as to the position of adverbs in a sentence. Most Italian adverbs can occur in three main positions without changing the meaning of the sentence:

- **right after the verb**: *Ho suonato raramente la chitarra* ('I have rarely played the guitar'), *Telefono spesso in Italia* ('I often call Italy');
- **following the object**: *Ho suonato la chitarra raramente* ('I have rarely played the guitar'), *Telefono in Italia spesso* ('I often call Italy');
- **between an auxiliary or modal verb and the following past participle, infinite, or gerund**: *Ho raramente suonato la chitarra* ('I have rarely played the guitar'), *Marco deve spesso viaggiare* ('Marco must travel often'), *Sto seriamente pensando a questo* ('I am seriously thinking about it').

There are just a few exceptions to the above rules:

- **interrogative and exclamatory adverbs** must always be placed at the beginning of the sentence: *Quando arriverai?* ('When are you coming?'), *Quanto sono felice!* ('How happy I am!');
- **adverbs of quantity** must always be placed after simple, compound verbs, the infinitive, and the gerund: *Dormo molto* ('I sleep a lot'), *Ho mangiato troppo* ('I ate too much'), *Voglio viaggiare tanto* ('I want to travel a lot'), *Studiando poco, non passerai l'esame* ('If you study little, you will not pass the exam'). When they modify an adjective or another adverb, they always precede them: *Maria è stata molto brava* ('Maria was very good'), *Noi andiamo molto spesso al cinema* ('We go very often to the movies');
- **adverbs of time** indicating when an action occurs, such as *oggi* ('today'), *domani* ('tomorrow'), *ieri* ('yesterday'), are preferably placed at the beginning of the sentence as in English: *Oggi, ho letto un libro* ('Today I have read a book'), *Domani verrò a trovarti* ('Tomorrow I will come to see you'). At the end of the sentence is a further option, even though less common, but no other positions are possible: *Ho letto un libro oggi* ('I read a book today'), *Verrò a trovarti domani* ('I will come to see you tomorrow');
- ***bene*** ('well'), ***meglio*** ('better'), ***male*** ('badly'), and ***peggio*** ('worse') always occur after the verb: *Ho dormito bene* ('I slept well'), *Mi sento meglio* ('I feel better'). If these adverbs occur with a noun, they either precede or follow it: *Ho fatto bene l'esame* or *Ho fatto l'esame bene* ('I did well on the exam').

6. COMPARATIVES AND SUPERLATIVES

> **Degrees**: Adjectives and adverbs often have forms that express degrees of comparison. When an adjective and an adverb simply describe a quality (*attento* 'careful') or a manner (*attentamente* 'carefully'), they are considered in their positive forms. The comparative and superlative forms indicate instead a greater/lesser or the maximum degree of a quality (*più/meno/molto attento* 'more/less/very careful') or manner (*più/meno/molto attentamente* 'more/less/very carefully').

6.1 Degrees of Descriptive Adjectives

The degrees of an adjective are known as the positive, the comparative, and the superlative:

- **positive degree**: the adjective expresses a quality of a person, an animal, or a thing, but does not give any indication of the intensity of the quality, nor does it compare it to that of another person, animal, or thing: *Sono felice* ('I am happy');
- **comparative degree**: the quality of a person, an animal, or a thing expressed by an adjective is compared with the same quality in another person, animal, or thing: *Giovanni è più alto di Marco* ('Giovanni is taller than Marco'). Also two qualities of the same person, animal, or thing can be compared: *Giovanni è più intelligente che simpatico* ('Giovanni is more intelligent than he is nice');
- **superlative degree**: the adjective expresses the highest or lowest degree of a quality of a person, an animal, or a thing. The superlative can be relative when it expresses the highest or lowest degree of quality of a person, an animal, or a thing within a group: *Giovanna è la più bella di tutte le sue amiche* ('Giovanna is the most beautiful of all the girlfriends'); or it can be absolute, without any comparison to another person, animal, or thing: *Anna è bellissima* ('Anna is very beautiful').

6.2 Degrees of Adverbs

Like adjectives, adverbs have three degrees of comparison: positive, comparative, and superlative. This is especially the case of adverbs of time, place, and manner:

- **positive degree**: the adverb is expressed in its basic form to show how one thing is done and does not indicate any comparison: *Mario canta divinamente* ('Mario sings divinely');

- **comparative degree**: the adverb is used to show how one thing is done equally, with more or less intensity in comparison to two elements: *Tu mangi molto come me* ('You eat as much as I do'), *Tu esci più/meno spesso di me* ('You go out more/less often than I do');
- **superlative degree**: the adverb is used to show how one thing is done in its highest degree without any comparison (absolute superlative): *Lui guida attentissimamente* ('He drives very carefully'); or it is used to compare three or more persons or things (relative superlative): *Lui guida più attentamente di tutti* ('He drives the most carefully of all').

6.3 Comparatives of Equality: così ... come, tanto ... quanto, *etc.*

When the nouns, pronouns, adjectives, and infinitive verbs being compared have equal characteristics, a comparative construction of equality is used. The following constructions are used in Italian:

- **[*così*] + adjective or adverb + *come*** ('as ... as'): *Il mio appartamento è [così] grande come il tuo* ('My apartment is as big as yours'), *Tu canti [così] bene come tua sorella* ('You sing as well as your sister');
- **[*tanto*] + adjective or adverb + *quanto*** ('as ... as'): *Il mio appartamento è [tanto] grande quanto il tuo* ('My apartment is as big as yours'), *Tu canti [tanto] bene quanto tua sorella* ('You sing as well as your sister').

As the examples above show, *così* and *tanto* are usually omitted, especially in spoken Italian. Note that *tanto* and *quanto* are used here as adverbs, so they maintain the same form regardless of the gender of the noun and the pronoun.

Comparatives of equality can also be used with nouns. The following structure is used in this case:

- ***tanto* + noun + *quanto*** ('as much/many ... as'): *Io ho tanta forza quanta ne hai tu* ('I have as much strength as you'), *In casa ci sono tanti quadri quanti libri* ('There are as many paintings as books at home').

It is important to note that *tanto* and *quanto* vary according to their function in the sentence. In the earlier examples, *tanto* and *quanto* were used as adverbs, so they were invariable; however, in this instance, they are used as adjectives, so they must agree with the noun they refer to: the singular feminine *forza* in the first example, and the plural masculine *quadri* and *libri* in the second one.

6.4 Comparatives of Inequality: più/meno ... di, più/meno ... che, *etc.*

When the nouns, pronouns, adjectives, and infinitive verbs being compared have differing degrees of a quality, a comparison of inequality is used. Two situations are possible: the first element of the comparison can present more or less quality than the second one. In structures using the comparatives of inequality, the second element of the comparison is introduced by the preposition *di* (or its contraction with an article where necessary), equivalent to the English 'than'. The following constructions are used in Italian:

- ***più* + adjective or adverb + *di*** ('more/-er ... than'): *Marco è più intelligente di suo fratello* ('Marco is more intelligent than his brother'), *La mia bici è più nuova della tua* ('My bike is newer than yours'), *Noi usciamo più spesso di voi* ('We go out more often than you do');
- ***meno* + adjective or adverb + *di*** ('less ... than'): *Marco è meno intelligente di suo fratello* ('Marco is less intelligent than his brother'), *La mia bici è meno nuova della tua* ('My bike is less new than yours'), *Noi usciamo meno spesso di voi* ('We go out less often than you do').

As in English, the comparative construction with *meno* is not very common in contemporary Italian, especially when an adjective with an opposite meaning can be used together with *più*. Let's take the example *La mia bici è meno nuova della tua* ('My bike is less new than yours'): to express the same meaning, Italians prefer to say and write *La mia bici è più vecchia della tua* ('My bike is older than yours').

Comparatives of inequality can also be used to compare the quantity or number of something expressed by a noun. The constructions remain the same:

- ***più* + noun + *di*** ('more ... than'): *Io ho più libri di te* ('I have more books than you');
- ***meno* + noun + *di*** ('less ... than'): *Io ho meno libri di te* ('I have less books than you').

Più and *meno* can directly precede the preposition *di* when a number follows the preposition:

più di ('more than'): *La biblioteca contiene più di centomila libri* ('The library contains more than one hundred thousand books');
meno di ('less than'): *Non posso entrare, ho meno di diciotto anni* ('I can't go in; I am less than eighteen years old').

Che replaces *di* when two words of the same category (nouns, adjectives, or infinitives) are compared in the same person, animal, or thing:

- ***più/meno* + noun + *che* + noun**: *Mangio più/meno pesce che carne* ('I eat more/less fish than meat');
- ***più/meno* + adjective + *che* + adjective**: *Giovanni è più/meno intelligente che simpatico* ('Giovanni is more/less intelligent than he is nice');
- ***più/meno* + infinitive + *che* + infinitive**: *Mi piace più/meno correre che nuotare* ('I like running more/less than swimming').

Che replaces *di* also when the second element of comparison is preceded by a preposition: *Sono più bravo in inglese che in matematica* ('I am better at English than at mathematics').

6.5 Sentence Comparisons

It is possible to compare two nouns, pronouns, adjectives, or infinitive verbs, but it is also possible to compare two clauses.

In **comparatives of equality**, the first part of the comparison can contain ***così*** or ***tanto*** (though not mandatory), while the second part is introduced by ***come*** or ***quanto*** plus a conjugated verb, giving a construction equivalent to the English 'as much/as many ... as': *Sono stato [così] felice come immaginavo* ('I was as happy as I imagined I would be'), *Ho mangiato [tanto] quanto avresti mangiato tu* ('I ate as much as you would have').

In **comparatives of inequality**, words like ***più*** ('more'), ***meglio*** ('better'), ***peggio*** ('worse'), or ***meno*** ('less') combine with ***che***, ***di quanto***, ***di quello che***, ***di come*** (all equivalent to 'than') plus a conjugated verb: *Ho studiato più di quello che credi* ('I studied more than you think'), *La festa è andata meglio di quanto non avessi mai potuto immaginare* ('The party was better than I could have ever imagined'). The comparative of inequality can also be expressed by ***più che***, ***piuttosto che***, ***piuttosto di***, or simply by ***che*** (all equivalent to the English 'rather than') plus an infinitive verb: *Guardo un film in TV piuttosto che uscire* ('I'd rather watch a movie on TV than go out'), *Ho deciso di scriverti più che chiamarti* ('I decided to write rather than call you').

6.6 Relative Superlative: il più/il meno ... di

If the comparative structure involves two elements (*Giovanni è più alto di Marco* 'Giovanni is taller than Marco'), the relative superlative expresses the highest or lowest degree of quality of a person, an animal, or a thing within a group: *Giovanni è il più alto della classe* ('Giovanni is the tallest of the class'). As in English, this construction designates 'the most' or 'the least' and is formed simply by using a definite article in front of *più* or *meno*. The preposition *di* (or its contraction with an article where necessary), equivalent to the English 'of', introduces the second element (in this case a group of persons, animals, or things) when expressed. The following constructions are used in Italian:

- **definite article + *più* + adjective + *di*** ('the most/-est ... of'): *Giovanna è la più bella di tutte le sue amiche* ('Giovanna is the most beautiful of all the girlfriends');
- **definite article + *meno* + adjective + *di*** ('the least/-est ... of'): *Mario è il meno competitivo della classe* ('Mario is the least competitive of the class').

The prepositions *fra* or its equivalent *tra* (both meaning 'among') can replace *di* when introducing the second element: *Il cane è il più fedele fra/tra [= di] tutti gli animali* ('The dog is the most faithful among all animals').

The relative superlative can also have the following structure when the second element is implied rather than clearly expressed:

- **definite article + noun + *più/meno* + adjective** ('the most/the least/-est ...'): *Lorenzo è lo studente più bravo* ('Lorenzo is the best student'). In this example, the second element implies something similar to *fra gli altri studenti* ('among the other students').

In case of the relative superlative of an adverb, the article in front of *più* or *meno* is usually omitted unless the adjective *possibile* ('possible') is added to the adverb. In this case the article must be *il*:

- ***più/meno* + adverb + *di*** ('the most/the least/-est ...'): *Lei ha risposto più gentilmente di tutti* ('She answered the kindliest of all');
- ***il* + *più/meno* + adverb + *possibile*** ('as ... as possible'): *Sono arrivato il più presto possibile* ('I arrived as soon as possible').

6.7 Absolute Superlative: -issimo, molto ..., super-, *etc.*

The absolute superlative expresses the highest degree of quality (positive or negative) of a person, animal, or thing without any comparison to another person, animal, or thing. It conveys the meaning of the English 'most', 'very', 'extremely', and so on. Using a variety of constructions, Italian expresses this degree by:

- dropping the last vowel of the adjective and adding the suffix *-issimo*, *-issima*, *-issimi*, or *-issime*, depending on the gender and number of the noun. The absolute superlative always agrees with the noun it modifies: *La giraffa è altissima* ('The giraffe is very tall'), *Conosco studenti intelligentissimi* ('I know very intelligent students'). This form is the most used in contemporary Italian;
- simply adding adverbs such as ***molto*** ('very'), ***veramente*** ('really'), ***incredibilmente*** ('incredibly') in front of the adjective: *Sono molto felice di vederti* ('I am very happy to see you'), *Siamo veramente stanchi* ('We are really tired');
- adding special prefixes such as ***iper-*** (*iperattivo* 'very active'), ***stra-*** (*straricco* 'very rich'), ***super-*** (*superaffollato* 'very crowded') to the adjective;
- **repeating the adjective**: *Matteo è un ragazzo magro magro* ('Matteo is very slim'). This construction is typical of colloquial Italian and is only possible with a few adjectives, usually expressing measures such as *grande grande* ('very big'), and *piccolo piccolo* ('very small');
- **adding another adjective or a special phrase** to the adjective. The following constructions are typical of an informal register: *pieno zeppo* ('crammed full'), *ricco sfondato* ('filthy rich'), *stanco morto* ('dead-tired'), *ubriaco fradicio* ('dead-drunk'). Particularly colorful are the following phrases that express specific aspects of the Italian culture: *buono come il pane* (literally 'as good as bread' equivalent to 'very good'), *sordo come una campana* (literally 'as deaf as a bell' equivalent to 'very deaf'), *pazzo come un cavallo* (literally 'as crazy as a horse' equivalent to 'very crazy');
- adding the suffix *-one* to the adjective. This construction, typical of colloquial Italian, contains a touch of irony and is used only in reference to people. It is especially used with *bello > bellone* ('very beautiful'), *grasso > grassone* ('very fat'), *ricco > riccone* ('very rich'), and a few more.

The absolute superlative of **adverbs** is obtained by dropping the last vowel of the word and adding the suffix *-issimo*: *presto > prestissimo* ('very soon') or for adverbs ending in *-mente* by dropping the last vowel of the original adjective form and adding the suffix *-issimamente* to it: *velocemente > veloce > velocissimamente* ('very fast'). In colloquial Italian the suffix *-one* is acceptable with the adverb *bene* ('well') to give it a superlative meaning: *È andata benone* ('It went very well').

6.8 Irregular Comparatives and Superlatives of Adjectives: migliore, pessimo, superiore, *etc.*

The adjectives **buono** ('good'), **grande** ('big'), and **alto** ('high' or 'tall') with their three corresponding opposites **cattivo** ('bad'), **piccolo** ('small' or 'little'), and **basso** ('low' or 'short') have irregular comparative and superlative forms in addition to the regular ones. Below is a useful table where the irregular forms are indicated in bold next to the regular ones:

Adjective	Comparative	Relative Superlative	Absolute Superlative
buono ('good')	*più buono*/**migliore** ('better')	*il più buono*/**il migliore** ('the best')	*molto buono*/*buonissimo*/**ottimo** ('very good')
cattivo ('bad')	*più cattivo*/**peggiore** ('worse')	*il più cattivo*/**il peggiore** ('the worst')	*molto cattivo*/*cattivissimo*/**pessimo** ('very bad')
grande ('big', 'great')	*più grande*/**maggiore** ('bigger')	*il più grande*/**il maggiore** ('the biggest')	*molto grande*/*grandissimo*/**massimo** ('very big')
piccolo ('small', 'little')	*più piccolo*/**minore** ('smaller')	*il più piccolo*/**il minore** ('the smallest')	*molto piccolo*/*piccolissimo*/**minimo** ('very small')
alto ('high', 'tall')	*più alto*/**superiore** ('higher')	*il più alto*/**il superiore** ('the highest')	*molto alto*/*altissimo*/**supremo** ('very high')
basso ('low', 'short')	*più basso*/**inferiore** ('lower')	*il più piccolo*/**il minore** ('the lowest')	*molto basso*/*bassissimo*/**infimo** ('very low')

Irregular forms are generally used:

- to indicate **abstract qualities and values**: *È necessario maggiore impegno* ('More commitment is necessary'), *Tu sei un ottimo esempio per tutti noi* ('You are an excellent example to all of us');
- with **technical and scientific language**: *Il deficit è stato inferiore alle attese* ('The deficit was lower than projected'), *Indica l'angolo minore di questo triangolo* ('Indicate the smallest angle of this triangle');
- with some **special expressions or phrases** like *sommo poeta* ('supreme poet'), *sommo pontefice* ('the Pope'), *comandante supremo* ('commander-in-chief'), *andare per la maggiore* ('to be trendy').

Particular attention must be paid to the comparative forms **maggiore** and **minore**. They can also be used in Italian to mean 'older' and 'younger' in age: *mio fratello maggiore* ('my older brother'), *mia sorella minore* ('my younger sister'). As in English, *minore*, used as a noun, can replace *minorenne* ('underage'): *Vietato ai minori* [= *minorenni*] ('Minors are not allowed'). **Inferiore** and **superiore** are also used to indicate the floor of a building: *piano inferiore/superiore* ('lower/upper floor').

6.9 Irregular Comparatives and Superlatives of Adverbs: meglio, peggio, ottimamente, *etc.*

Like adjectives, some adverbs also present irregularities in comparative and superlative forms. Unlike adjectives, adverbs have only a few regular forms existing side by side with the irregular ones. Below is a useful table where the irregular forms are displayed in bold:

Adverb	Comparative	Absolute Superlative
bene ('well')	**meglio** ('better')	*molto bene, benissimo*/**ottimamente** ('very well')
male ('badly')	**peggio** ('worse')	*molto male, malissimo*/**pessimamente** ('very badly')
molto ('much', 'a lot')	*[di]* **più** ('more')	*moltissimo* ('very much')
poco ('little')	*[di]* **meno** ('less')	*molto poco, pochissimo* ('very little')

The preposition **di** in front of the comparative *più* and *meno* is typical of the colloquial register and is usually omitted, as the square brackets in the table indicate.

The article **il** must precede *meglio* and *peggio* when they are followed by the adjective *possibile* ('possible'): *Voi mangiate il meglio/il peggio possibile* ('You eat as well/bad as possible'). The article *il* is also mandatory in front of *meglio* and *peggio* when they are used as nouns to mean 'the best thing' or 'the worst thing': *Il meglio/peggio deve ancora venire* ('The best/worst is yet to come').

6.10 Superlatives in -errimo *and* -entissimo

Five adjectives have their absolute superlative in *-errimo* instead of in *-issimo*:

Adjective	Absolute Superlative
acre ('acrid')	**acerrimo** ('very acrid')
celebre ('famous')	**celeberrimo** ('very famous')
integro ('integral')	**integerrimo** ('very integral')
misero ('poor')	**miserrimo** ('very poor')
salubre ('healthy')	**saluberrimo** ('very healthy')

In addition to *miserrimo* and *saluberrimo*, the forms *miserissimo* and *salubrissimo* are also possible, especially in spoken Italian.

Four other adjectives have their superlative in *-entissimo*:

Adjective	Absolute Superlative
benefico ('beneficent')	**benificentissimo** ('very beneficent')
benevolo ('benevolent')	**benevolentissimo** ('very benevolent')
malevolo ('malevolent')	**malevolentissimo** ('very malevolent')
munifico ('munificent')	**munificentissimo** ('very munificent')

Forms in *-errimo* and *-entissimo* are typical of the formal register and are rarely used in spoken Italian where placing adverbs such as *molto* ('very') or *veramente* ('really') in front of the adjective is preferable: *Tu sei molto benevolo con tutti* ('You are very benevolent to everybody'), *Il tuo atteggiamento è veramente malevolo* ('Your attitude is really malevolent').

6.11 Superlatives of Nouns: occasionissima, finalissima, *etc.*

The endings *-issimo/-issima* and their plural *-issimi/-issime* are a peculiarity of the superlative of adjectives, but it is possible to add them to nouns. These forms are typical of an informal register and are often used to express greatness, tongue-in-cheek: *affarissimo* ('a great deal'), *occasionissima* ('a great opportunity'), *offertissima* ('a great offer'), and so on. When the meaning is more equivalent to the English 'the ultimate' or 'the top', these superlative forms can also be found in more formal Italian: *Oggi si gioca la finalissima* ('The grand finale will be played today'), *Ecco le ultimissime dal mondo* ('Here is the latest news from the world').

7. Possessives and Possessive Structures

> **Possessives:** Possessive adjectives and pronouns constitute words that denote ownership (*la mia auto* 'my car') or relationship (*mia mamma* 'my mom'). Possessive adjectives are always followed by the noun they qualify (*la mia penna* 'my pen', *tuo padre* 'your father') while the pronouns are used on their own (*Non ho bisogno di una nuova auto. La mia funziona ancora benissimo* 'I don't need a new car. Mine still runs very well').

7.1 Forms of the Possessive

Unlike English ones, Italian possessive adjectives and pronouns are identical in form: *mio* is 'my' but also 'mine', *tuo* is 'your' but also 'yours'. All possessives are formed, like regular adjectives, with four endings (see 4.2) except in the plural masculine *miei, tuoi, suoi,* and the invariable *loro*. Unlike English, Italian uses the definite article, with few exceptions (see 7.3), as part of the possessive constructions. The table below indicates possessive adjectives and pronouns in Italian:

Possessor	Masc. Sing.	Fem. Sing.	Masc. Plur.	Fem. Plur.
io ('I')	*il mio*	*la mia*	*i miei*	*le mie*
tu ('you')	*il tuo*	*la tua*	*i tuoi*	*le tue*
lui ('he')/*lei* ('she')	*il suo*	*la sua*	*i suoi*	*le sue*
Lei ('you' sing. formal)	*il Suo*	*la Sua*	*i Suoi*	*le Sue*
noi ('we')	*il nostro*	*la nostra*	*i nostri*	*le nostre*
voi ('you' pl.)	*il vostro*	*la vostra*	*i vostri*	*le vostre*
loro ('they')	*il loro*	*la loro*	*i loro*	*le loro*
Loro ('you' pl. formal)	*il Loro*	*la Loro*	*i Loro*	*le Loro*

> **N.B.** Unlike English, Italian also has formal possessives corresponding to the formal person *Lei*: *Signora, ecco il Suo biglietto* ('Madam, here is your ticket'). The formal possessives for the formal *Loro*, used as a second plural person (see 13.3), are nowadays really rare. However, these forms are identical to the forms of *loro*, written capitalized: *Vengano; ora possono ritirare il Loro premio* ('Come; now you can take your prize').

7.2 Agreement of Possessive Forms

Possessive forms always agree both in gender and number with the object possessed (*la mia penna* 'my pen') or with the noun indicating the relationship (*i miei fratelli* 'my brothers'). Some problems for an English speaker can arise with the third person possessives. Unlike English possessive adjectives or pronouns, the Italian *suo, sua, suoi,* and *sue* do not agree with the gender and number of the possessor, but with the gender and number of the noun they modify or replace. This means that the forms 'his', 'her', and 'its', can be translated as *suo, sua, suoi,* or *sue* depending, not on the owner but on the object possessed or person in case of relationship. For example, the Italian equivalent of:

1. 'his' in 'Mario has his + noun'
2. 'her' in 'Anna has her + noun'
3. 'its' in 'The dog has its + noun'

can be any one of *suo, sua, suoi,* or *sue* because they do not agree with 'Mario', 'Anna', or the 'dog' but with the gender and number of the 'noun'. Therefore, if the noun is a masculine and singular word like *giocattolo* ('toy') in all three cases the Italian equivalent will be *suo* regardless of the gender of the owner:

1. *Mario ha il suo giocattolo* ('Mario has his toy')
2. *Anna ha il suo giocattolo* ('Anna has her toy')
3. *Il cane ha il suo giocattolo* ('The dog has its toy')

In case of a singular feminine word like *tazza* ('bowl'), the possessive will instead be *sua*:

1. *Mario ha la sua tazza* ('Mario has his bowl')
2. *Anna ha la sua tazza* ('Anna has her bowl')
3. *Il cane ha la sua tazza* ('The dog has its bowl')

When the word is a plural masculine noun like *giocattoli* ('toys'), the possessive will always be *suoi*:

1. *Mario ha i suoi giocattoli* ('Mario has his toys')
2. *Anna ha i suoi giocattoli* ('Anna has her toys')
3. *Il cane ha i suoi giocattoli* ('The dog has its toys')

When the word is a plural feminine noun like *tazze* ('bowls'), the possessive will always be *sue*:

1. *Mario ha le sue tazze* ('Mario has his bowls')
2. *Anna ha le sue tazze* ('Anna has her bowls')
3. *Il cane ha le sue tazze* ('The dog has its bowls')

Since the possessive never reveals the gender of the possessor, when the possessor cannot be inferred from the context, there is possibility for ambiguity. For example, in a sentence like *Ho lavato il suo piatto*, the possessive *suo* can be 'his', 'her', or 'its' ('I washed his/her/its plate'). In these cases, to avoid any ambiguity, Italian uses the phrases *di lui* (literally 'of him'), *di lei* (literally 'of her'), or replaces the possessive with the structure *di* + possessor (*di Mario* 'Mario's', *di Anna* 'Anna's', *del cane* 'the dog's').

7.3 Omission of the Definite Article

In Italian the article is an integral part of the possessive constructions but is not always used. This always occurs with:

- **unmodified singular family members** (see also 7.4): *mio padre* ('my father'), *mia sorella* ('my sister');
- **invocations**: *Tesoro mio!* ('Sweetheart!'), *Figli miei!* ('My sons!'), where the possessive follows the noun;
- **demonstratives**: *questo mio libro* ('this book of mine'), *queste tue amiche* ('these girlfriends of yours');
- **common expressions**: *a mio vantaggio* ('in my favor'), *in mio potere* ('in my power'), *a mia insaputa* ('unbeknown to me').

The article is also preferably omitted with **forms of the verb *essere*** ('to be') when a possessive pronoun directly follows the verb: *Questi sono miei* ('These are mine'), *È tuo?* ('Is it yours?'). However, it is used for emphasis or when clarification is necessary: *Questi sono i miei, non i tuoi* ('These are mine, not yours').

7.4 Possessives with Nouns Denoting Family Members

The definite article, which is always used with the possessive before plural family members (*le mie sorelle* 'my sisters', *i miei zii* 'my uncles'), is **generally omitted with possessive adjectives preceding singular family members** (*mia sorella* 'my sister', *mio zio* 'my uncle'), but preferably used with *papà, babbo* (both meaning 'dad'), and *mamma* ('mom'). However, the article must be used:

- if the singular forms are **modified** by adjectives (*la mia bella sorella* 'my beautiful sister'), suffixes (*il mio fratellino* 'my little brother'), or prefixes (*la mia ex moglie* 'my ex-wife');
- with ***loro*** (*la loro sorella*, 'their sister', *il loro fratello* 'their brother');
- with the **obsolete words** (see 19.8) *matrigna* ('stepmother'), *patrigno* ('stepfather'), *fratellastro* ('stepbrother'), and *sorellastra* ('stepsister'): *La mia matrigna è di Venezia* ('My stepmother is from Venice'), *Il nostro fratellastro vive in Australia* ('Our stepbrother lives in Australia').

> **N.B. a.** In contemporary Italian, the words *matrigna, patrigno, fratellastro,* and *sorellastra* are not used anymore because of their original negative connotations (see also 19.8). They are usually replaced by constructions like *la moglie di mio padre* ('my father's wife'), *il marito di mia madre* ('my mother's husband'), and so on. **b.** The plural masculine forms *i miei, i tuoi,* and *i suoi* are often used on their own in colloquial Italian to refer to parents or close relatives: *I miei stanno benissimo* ('My parents are very well').

7.5 Possessives and Indefinite Articles: un mio, un nostro, una vostra, *etc.*

When the possessive is preceded by an indefinite article (*un* and *una*) instead of a definite one, the Italian construction is equivalent to the English 'one of': *un mio studente* ('a student of mine'), *una loro amica* ('a girlfriend of theirs').

7.6 Omission of Possessives

The use of possessives is definitively less extensive in Italian than in English. When the context makes the ownership or the relationship clear, a simple article is used where in English a possessive is required: *Giovanna e i genitori* ('Giovanna and her parents'), *Mi fa male un piede* ('My foot hurts'). The addition of a possessive in such cases would sound unnecessary or redundant.

7.7 Italian Equivalent of English Possessive -'s or -s'

The English endings -'s or -s' indicating possession or relationship are simply expressed in Italian by the preposition *di* or its articulated forms such as *del, dello, della*: *Gli occhi di Marco* ('Marco's eyes'), *I giochi dei ragazzi* ('Kids' toys').

When the English construction -'s refers specifically to someone's place, it is expressed in Italian by the preposition *da* and its articulated forms such as *dal, dallo, dalla* (see 16.4): *Sono da Maria* ('I am at Maria's'), *Vado dal dottore* ('I am going to the doctor's').

7.8 Position of Possessive Adjectives

A possessive adjective usually precedes the noun it qualifies (*il mio quaderno* 'my notebook', *la mia auto* 'my car'), but sometimes it can be placed after the noun. In this case the idea of ownership or relationship is emphasized. Note, for example, the difference between *Questo è il mio ufficio* and *Questo è l'ufficio mio*; if both can be translated as 'This is my office', in the first sentence the possessive simply states a fact while in the second one it puts emphasis on the fact that the office is 'mine', and not 'somebody else's'.

This particular construction with the noun preceding the possessive adjective is typical of **invocations** such as *Figlio mio!* ('My son!'), *Bella mia!* ('My beauty!'), *Amici miei!* ('My friends!'). It is also found in common expressions such as *a casa mia* ('at my house'), *per colpa tua* ('your fault'), *per merito nostro* ('our merit'), *di testa sua* ('in his own way'), *in vita mia* ('in my life'), *da parte nostra* ('from our side'), and *affari loro* ('their business').

When a possessive adjective is combined with other adjectives, its position is regulated as indicated below:

- **descriptive adjectives follow the possessives** and agree with them in gender and number: *la mia bella casa* ('my beautiful house'), *i tuoi cari amici* ('your dear friends');
- **demonstrative adjectives precede the possessives** and agree with them in gender and number: *questo mio computer* ('this computer of mine'), *questa tua matita* ('this pencil of yours');
- **indefinite adjectives always precede the possessives**, but the latter can change position: *qualche mio amico/qualche amico mio* ('some friends of mine');
- **numerical adjectives always precede the possessives**, but also in this case their position is flexible: *due miei amici/due amici miei* ('two friends of mine').

7.9 The Equivalent to the English 'own': proprio

The word *proprio* can function as an adverb with several meanings ('just', 'really') but can also be used as a possessive intensifier ('own') when it is combined with other possessives: *il mio proprio* ('my own'), *la tua propria* ('your own'). Unlike the English 'own', *proprio* can be a possessive in itself and so be used on its own. In this case, it can only mean 'his own', 'her own', 'its own', or 'their own': *Marco pensa solo al proprio interesse* ('Marco only thinks of his own interest'), *Ognuno ha le proprie colpe* ('Each person has his/her own faults').

As a possessive intensifier or possessive on its own, *proprio* (as seen in the examples above) always agrees with the item possessed.

7.10 The Equivalent to the English 'someone else's': altrui

The adjective *altrui* is invariable and equivalent to the English phrases 'other people's', 'another person's', and 'of others'. It is generally used in elevated register, never in colloquial Italian. *Altrui* usually follows the noun (*la proprietà altrui* 'other people's property', *in casa altrui* 'in someone else's house'), but it can also precede it. In the latter case, *altrui* is always combined with an article (*l'altrui proprietà* 'other people's property'), or with an articulated preposition (*nell'altrui casa* 'in someone else's house').

8. RELATIVE PRONOUNS

> **Relative Pronouns:** A relative pronoun ('that', 'which', 'who', 'whom', and 'whose') introduces a subordinate clause, giving additional information about a preceding noun, pronoun, or a verb phrase. A relative pronoun can be found only in sentences with more than one clause where it acts as the subject (*Lo studente che frequenta la mia lezione è bravissimo* 'The student who is attending my class is very good') or the object of the relative clause (*Lo studente a cui parlo non mi ascolta* 'The student to whom I am speaking is not listening to me').

8.1 Forms of the Relative Pronouns

Italian has two invariable relative pronouns *che* and *cui* and a variable one *quale* (and its pl. *quali*) that agrees in number and gender with its antecedent and is always preceded by a definite article or an articulated preposition. All these forms translate into the English 'that', 'which', 'who', 'whom', and 'whose'. Beside these, there is the double pronoun *chi* ('he/him who', 'she/her who', 'people who') that does not require an antecedent and is used only for people.

Relative Pronouns
che
cui preceded by a preposition (*a, di, da, con, in, tra, verso*, etc.)
quale and *quali,* preceded by an article (*il, la, lo, la,* etc.) or articulated preposition (*del, alla, dagli,* etc.)
chi (used only for people)

8.2 Obligatory Use of Relative Pronouns

Unlike English, Italian cannot omit relative pronouns in object position. If, for example, in English it is possible to say either 'The book that I read is interesting' or 'The book I read is interesting', in Italian it is obligatory to use the relative pronoun *che*: *Il libro che leggo è interessante*.

8.3 Uses of che

The pronoun ***che*** is invariable and corresponds to 'who', 'whom', 'that', 'which'. It can refer to people, animals, or things, function as subject of the verb (*Il bambino che gioca è mio figlio*

'The little boy who is playing is my son') or direct object (*Il bambino che tu vedi è mio figlio* 'The little boy whom you see is my son') because Italian, unlike English, has only one form for both the subject 'who' and the object 'whom.'

Che can be preceded by the article *il* ('the'), in which case **il che** does not refer to a noun or a pronoun but to the whole preceding clause and is equivalent to the English 'which': *Non posso venire, il che mi dispiace molto* ('I can't come, which makes me really sorry').

Che can also be preceded by a simple preposition (***a che***, ***con che***, ***da che***, etc.) or preposition combined with the article *il* (**al che**, **con il che**, **dal che**, etc.): *Sei caldo, dal che capisco che sei malato* ('You feel hot, from which I understand you are sick').

8.4 A Common Pitfall in the Use of che

As mentioned above, *che* only functions as subject or direct object of the verb, but in popular spoken Italian, it is possible to find *che* used as an indirect object replacing the appropriate grammatical construction **preposition + *cui*** (see 8.6). However, cases like *Lo studente che* [= *a cui*] *ho dato il libro è mio amico* ('The student to whom I gave the book is my friend') and *È una persona che* [= *di cui*] *non ricordo il nome* ('He is a person whose name I can't remember') must be avoided since they are still considered mistakes, even if they are commonly found in spoken Italian.

8.5 Che *and Past Participle Agreement:* La busta che è arrivata; La pizza che ho mangiato, *etc.*

When the pronoun *che* precedes a verb conjugated with *essere* ('to be'), the past participle must always agree in gender and number with the noun to which *che* refers. For example, in a sentence like *Ho ritirato la scatola che è arrivata ieri* ('I picked up the package that arrived yesterday') the past participle *arrivata* agrees with the singular feminine noun *scatola*.

On the contrary, agreement with a past participle conjugated with *avere* ('to have') is obsolete, so it is recommended to keep the original form in -*o*: *La storia che avete raccontato è molto interessante* ('The story you told is really interesting'). In this example, the form *raccontata*, in agreement with the feminine *storia,* is possible but sounds antiquated in contemporary Italian.

8.6 Use of cui

The pronoun ***cui*** is a variant of *che* and must be preceded by a preposition. If *che* functions as subject or direct object, *cui* functions as indirect object or prepositional object depending on the preposition preceding it. It is equivalent to the English 'to which', 'with whom', and other relative phrases formed with prepositions: *Giovanni è l'amico con cui sono andato in Italia* ('Giovanni is the friend with whom I went to Italy'), *Il film di cui ti ho parlato ieri è molto interessante* ('The movie, I was telling you about yesterday, is really interesting').

The pronoun *cui* can be used by itself in formal and bureaucratic style to replace *a cui*: *Il presidente, cui* [= *a cui*] *è stata fatta domanda, non ha ancora risposto* ('The president, to whom the application was presented, has not answered yet').

8.7 The Possessive Meaning of il cui, la cui, *etc.*

When *cui* is preceded by a definite article and followed directly by a noun (**article + *cui* + noun**), it is equivalent to 'whose' and 'of which' and expresses possession. In a clause like *Lo studente il cui professore è partito ...* ('The student whose professor has left ...') *il cui professore* means the 'student's professor', as in *Il ragazzo la cui sorella conosco ...* ('The boy whose sister I know ...') *la cui sorella* means the 'boy's sister'. The article preceding *cui* always agrees in gender and number with the noun following it: in the first example, *il* agrees with the singular masculine *professore* while in the second one, *la* agrees with the singular feminine *sorella*.

8.8 Use of il quale, la quale, del quale, *etc.*

The singular pronouns ***il quale***, ***la quale*** and the plural ***i quali*** and ***le quali*** can always replace *che*: *L'uomo il quale* [= *che*] *ha parlato ...* ('The man who talked ...'), *Le studentesse le quali* [= *che*] *conoscete ...* ('The students whom you know ...'). Unlike the invariable *che*, these forms agree with the nouns they refer to, so they are used in particular to make the antecedent clear when some ambiguity is possible. For example, in a sentence like *Lapo doveva incontrare suo fratello e le sue sorelle, le quali lo avevano invitato alla festa* ('Lapo had to meet his brother and his sisters who invited him to the party') *le quali* makes clear that the sisters, not the brother, invited *Lapo*. The use of *che* in this context would blur any distinction between the brother and the sisters.

When *il quale, la quale, i quali,* and *le quali* are combined with a preposition, they can replace the phrase preposition + *cui*: *Le amiche con le quali* [= *con cui*] *vado in vacanza ...* ('The girlfriends with whom I am going on vacation ...'), *Lo studente al quale* [= *a cui*] *ho dato un buon voto ...* ('The student to whom I gave a good grade ...').

> **N.B.** Even if *quale* can replace the forms *che* or *cui*, it is important to keep in mind that contemporary Italian favors the use of these two invariable pronouns, unless there is ambiguity.

8.9 Use of chi

The relative pronoun ***chi,*** unlike the other previously studied, **refers only to people** and does not require an antecedent, a noun to refer to. *Chi* is considered a double pronoun referring usually to unspecified people and approximately meaning 'the person who/whom', 'those who/whom': *Chi non studia non passa l'esame* ('The person who does not study does not pass the exam'), *Non parlo a chi non dice la verità* ('I don't talk to those who do not tell the truth'). *Chi* must always be used with a singular form of the verb even when it has a plural meaning: *Chi verrà, riceverà un premio* ('Those who come, will receive a prize').

The relative pronoun *chi* is **typical of proverbs**: *Chi dorme non piglia pesci* ('The person who sleeps won't get fish'), *Chi la fa l'aspetti* ('He who wrongs someone has to expect something in retaliation'), *Chi fa da sé fa per tre* ('He who works by himself does the work of three people').

Chi can also be translated with the English 'whomever': *Assumi chi vuoi. Tu sei il capo* ('Hire whomever you want. You are the boss').

The construction **chi di/fra + noi/voi/loro** can also be used as a relative phrase to indicate 'the person(s) of/among us/you/they who': *Chi di voi mi tradisce, pagherà* ('Those of you who betray me will pay').

When *chi* is used in a correlative construction (**chi ... chi**), it is equivalent to the English 'some people ... others': *C'è chi è onesto e chi ruba* ('Some people are honest; others steal').

8.10 *The Forms* colui che, colei che, *and* coloro che

The double forms, like the singular masculine **colui che** ('he/him who/whom'), the feminine **colei che** ('she/her who/whom'), and their plural **coloro che** ('they/them who/whom'), can always replace the invariable pronoun *chi* (see 8.9): *Colui che [= Chi] non studia non passa l'esame* ('The person who does not study does not pass the exam'), *Non parlo a coloro che non dicono [= a chi non dice] la verità* ('I do not talk to those who do not tell the truth'). These forms are typical of a more formal register, so *chi* is preferred in normal writing and conversation.

8.11 *The Forms of* quello che *and* ciò che

If *colui che*, *colei che*, and *coloro che* can be used for people only, **quello che**, **quella che** (both meaning 'that which', 'what') and their plural **quelli che**, **quelle che** (both meaning 'those which', 'what') refer preferably to things: *Quello che ho visto è un buon film* ('What I have seen is a good movie'), *Quelle che abbiamo comprato sono scarpe italiane* ('What we have bought are Italian shoes'). In contemporary Italian, especially in informal usage, these forms are frequently employed for people as well: *Quelli che non hanno il permesso non possono entrare* ('Those people who do not have a permit, cannot enter').

The invariable form **ciò che** can replace all of the above when referring to an unspecified thing, but its meaning is always singular: *Ciò che [= quello che] ho visto è interessante* ('What I have seen is interesting'), *Ciò che [= quello che] abbiamo comprato non mi piace più* ('That which we bought, I don't like anymore').

8.12 *The Relative Meaning of* quanto, quanti, *and* quante

The singular **quanto**, as a relative pronoun, corresponds to *quello che* and is equivalent to the English 'what', 'that which': *Quanto [= quello che] hai fatto è sciocco* ('What you did is stupid'). The plural masculine **quanti** and the feminine **quante** can be considered the plural of *chi* or the equivalent of *coloro che* and mean 'the people who/whom': *Quanti [= Coloro che] hanno il biglietto possono entrare* ('The people who have a ticket can enter'). In the case of the feminine *quante*, English must specify that 'the people who/whom' are female: *Quante [= Coloro che] parteciperanno all'evento, riceveranno un profumo in omaggio* ('Those women who are going to take part in the event, will receive a free perfume').

9. Interrogatives

> **Interrogative sentences**: An interrogative sentence is a sentence that asks a question. In Italian, as in English, there are two kinds of interrogative sentences: direct and indirect. The direct sentence occurs alone, asks a question directly, and always ends with a question mark: *Che cosa mangiamo oggi?* ('What are we eating today?'). In contrast, the indirect interrogative cannot occur independently but is always introduced by verbs such as *chiedere* ('to ask'), *dire* ('to tell'), *sapere* ('to know'): *Ditemi che cosa mangiamo oggi* ('Tell me what we are eating today'). Indirect questions do not end with a question mark but with a period.

9.1 Structures of the Interrogative Sentence: Like and Unlike English

Whereas an English interrogative sentence normally changes the word order of an affirmative sentence ('You are happy' > 'Are you happy?') or is introduced by the auxiliary 'do', 'does', 'did', 'can', will', etc. ('You like ice cream' > 'Do you like ice cream?'), the structure of the sentence does not generally change in Italian but simply acquires a question mark (*Sei felice* > *Sei felice?*; *Ti piace il gelato* > *Ti piace il gelato?*). This is especially true with questions requiring a *sì* ('yes') or *no* ('no') answer as in the above examples. In these cases, the subject can be placed after the verb simply to add emphasis, not to form the question: *Tu hai preso l'ombrello?* ('Did you take the umbrella?'), *Hai preso tu l'ombrello?* ('Is it you who took the umbrella?').

In open-ended questions, which require more than a 'yes' or 'no' answer and start with *chi* ('who'), *come* ('how'), *dove* ('where'), etc., the subject must follow the verb: *Chi sei tu?* ('Who are you?'), *Dove hanno mangiato i tuoi amici?* ('Where did your friends eat?').

As is sometimes the case in English, especially in a colloquial register, a statement can be turned into a question simply by adding expressions like *vero* ('right'), or *non è vero* ('isn't it') at the end of it: *Siete italiani, vero?* ('You are Italians, right?'), *Tu hai un fratello, non è vero?* ('You have a brother, don't you?').

Unlike English, which allows a preposition to be stranded, Italian always maintains an introductory preposition in an interrogative sentence in its initial position: *A che cosa lavori?* ('At what are you working?' / 'What are you working at?'), *Con chi hai cenato* ('With whom did you have dinner?' / 'Whom did you have dinner with?').

N.B. If in written Italian the question mark denotes the interrogative nature of the sentence, in spoken Italian, in contrast to English, only the rising intonation at the end of the sentence indicates the interrogative nature of the sentence.

9.2 Forms and Uses of Interrogative Pronouns and Adjectives: chi, quale, *etc.*
Below is the complete list of the interrogative pronouns and adjectives:

	M. Sing.	F. Sing.	M. Pl.	F. Pl.	English Equivalent
Pron. (invar.)	*chi*	*chi*	*chi*	*chi*	('who', 'whom')
Pron. and Adj. (invar.)	*che cosa/cosa*	*che cosa/cosa*	*che cosa/cosa*	*che cosa/cosa*	('what')
Pron. and Adj. (invar.)	*che*	*che*	*che*	*che*	('what', 'which', 'what kind of')
Pron. and Adj.	*quale*	*quale*	*quali*	*quali*	('which one', 'which ones')
Pron. and Adj.	*quanto*	*quanta*	*quanti*	*quante*	('how much', 'how many')

- **chi** is invariable and refers exclusively to people: *Chi sei?* ('Who are you?'), *Chi vi ha chiamato?* ('Who called you?'). The gender and number of the pronoun *chi* is usually recognized in context: *Chi è quella ragazza?* ('Who is that girl?') *Chi sono loro?* ('Who are they?'). If the structure calls for the use of a preposition, that preposition always precedes *chi*: *Di chi parli?* ('About whom are you talking?'), *Con chi andrai allo stadio?* ('With whom will you go to the stadium?'). *Chi* frequently combines with the verb *sapere* ('to know') to express doubt. In this case, the structure *chi + sa* can be written as two separate words or form a stressed contracted word: *Chi sa?/Chissà?* ('Who knows?');
- **che cosa** and **cosa** are used to indicate things. When they function as pronouns, they all mean 'what' and are interchangeable: *Che cosa/Cosa vuoi?* ('What do you want?'). When it is followed by a vowel, *cosa* can optionally lose the letter *a* and take an apostrophe: *Che cos'è?* ('What is it?') *Cos'ascolti?* ('What are you listening to?'). Like the English 'what', *che cosa* and *cosa* can be used on their own to indicate that one is not sure what was said and is asking for repetition: *Che cosa/Cosa?* ('What?');
- **che** can always replace *che cosa* or *cosa*: *Che* [= *Che cosa/Cosa*] *leggi?* ('What are you reading?'). Moreover, as an adjective meaning 'which' in English, *che* can be used instead of *quale, quali* (see below), but being an invariable form, unlike them, it can be used indifferently for all genders and numbers: *Che* [= *quale*] *libro vuoi?* ('Which book do you want?'), *Che* [= *quali*] *pantaloni metti questa sera?* ('Which pants are you wearing tonight?'). Also, as interrogative adjective, *che* often implies 'what kind of': *Che macchina guidi?* ('What kind of car do you drive?'), *Che cibo preferite?* ('What kind of food do you prefer?');
- **quale** and **quali** are used to indicate people, animals, or things and are used when the answer involves a choice between two or more alternatives: *Quale film guardi oggi* ('Which

film are you going to watch today?'), *Quali scarpe metti per l'occasione?* ('Which shoes are you wearing for the occasion?'). *Quale* and *quali* correspond not only to the English 'which' or 'which one(s)' but also to 'what' when one requests information such as a name, telephone number, address, and so on. In this case, *quale* doesn't call for a choice but an unequivocal answer: *Qual è il tuo numero di telefono?* ('What is your phone number?'). *Quale* can optionally drop the final *e* before any word without taking an apostrophe (see 1.14). If this use is rare (but possible) before a consonant (*qual libro* 'which book'), it is quite frequent, especially in spoken Italian, before nouns starting with vowels (*qual auto* 'which car', *qual uomo* 'which man'), and almost constant with the verbal forms *è*, and *era*: *Qual è casa tua?* ('Which one is your house?'), *Qual era il vostro posto* ('Which one was your place?');

- **quanto**, **quanta**, **quanti**, and **quante** are used to indicate a quantity (*Quanto pane vuoi?* 'How much bread do you want?') or a number (*Quanti siete?* 'How many are you?') with people, animals, or things.

> **N.B.** Remember that all the interrogative pronouns and adjectives, when governed by a preposition, are always preceded by that preposition because in Italian, in contrast to English, a sentence cannot end with a preposition: *Di chi parli?* ('About whom are you talking? / Whom are you talking about?').

9.3 Forms and Uses of Interrogative Adverbs: come?, quando?, *etc.*

Interrogative adverbs are invariable and introduce questions about manner, time, place, purpose, quantity, measure, and value. Below is a list of the Italian interrogative adverbs and examples of their use:

Interrogative adverbs	Examples
come ('how')	*Come stai?* ('How are you?')
dove ('where')	*Dove abitate?* ('Where do you live?')
quando ('when')	*Quando hai l'esame?* ('When is your exam?')
quanto ('how much', 'how long')	*Quanto costano le mele?* ('How much are the apples?') *Quanto dura il film?* ('How long is the movie?')
perché ('why')	*Perché non mangi?* ('Why aren't you eating?')

- **come** and **dove** drop the *e* and take an apostrophe before forms of the verb *essere* ('to be') beginning in *e-* (*è*, *era*, and *erano*): *Dov'è il libro?* ('Where is the book?'), *Com'era il film?* ('How was the movie?'). Interrogative expressions like *in che/quale modo, in che/quale maniera* can replace *come*: *In che modo* [= *come*] *sei venuto?* ('How did you get here?'), *In quale maniera* [= *come*] *ti vesti?* ('What are you going to wear?'). Interrogative expressions like *in quale luogo, in quale posto* can replace *dove*: *In quale luogo* [= *dove*] *abiti?* ('Where do you live?'), *In quale posto* [= *dove*] *lo incontri?* ('Where are you meeting him?').

- ***quando*** drops the *o* and takes an apostrophe when it is followed by the form *è* ('is') of the verb *essere*. This is the case of the colloquial expression ***quand'è che* + verb**, which imparts a bitter tone to the question: *Quand'è che arrivi?* ('When is it that you came?').
- ***quanto*** is invariable and expresses quantity and measure when it is used as an adverb meaning 'how much'. However, when combined with another adverb (*Quanto lentamente parli?* 'How slowly do you speak?') or with an adjective (*Quanto difficile è l'esame?* 'How difficult is the exam?'), it means simply 'how'.
- ***perché*** can be used to introduce a question, an answer, or to make a statement, so it is equivalent to 'why' and 'because' in English. Adverbial expressions like *per quale motivo*, *per quale ragione* can replace the interrogative *perché*: *Per quale ragione* [= *perché*] *sei venuto?* ('Why did you come here?'), *Per quale motivo* [= *perché*] *non parli?* ('Why don't you talk?').

All the interrogative adverbs can be followed by the word **mai,** which serves to reinforce them, impart a bitter tone to the question, and express surprise or incredulity: *Come mai non mangi?* ('How come you're not eating?'), *Dove mai ti eri nascosto?* ('Wherever were you hiding?').

Except for *come* and *perché*, all the interrogative adverbs, can be preceded by a **preposition** to form adverbial expressions such as *da dove* ('from where'), *per quanto* ('for how long'), and so on: *Da dove venite?* ('Where are you coming from?'), *Per quanto ti devo aspettare?* ('How long do I have to wait for you?').

9.4 Interrogative se: Dimmi se vieni; E se fosse Marco?

The interrogative *se*, equivalent to 'whether' or 'if', is generally used, as in English, in indirect interrogative sentences: *Dimmi se vieni* ('Tell me if you're coming'), *Ti chiedo se sei stanco* ('I am asking you if you are tired'). However, in colloquial Italian *se* can introduce a direct question when one uses the previous question as part of one's answer. For example, in the sentence *Se ho studiato per l'esame? Certamente!* ('Did I study for the exam? Sure!'), *se* is placed in front of a question that rephrases the original one *Hai studiato per l'esame?* ('Have you studied for the exam?').

Se can also be found in direct questions formed with the subjunctive (see 21.17). In this case, the interrogative *se* expresses doubt and conjecture and is frequently preceded by the conjunction *e* (see also 23.29): *E se fossero ancora vivi?* ('What if they were still alive?'), *E se non avessimo scelta?* ('What if we had no choice?').

9.5 How to Answer a Question

In Italian one answers a question exactly as one would in English, with a simple *sì* ('yes') or *no* ('no'), isolated or accompanied by additional information: *Sei Giacomo? – Sì, sono Giacomo* ('Are you Giacomo? – Yes, I am Giacomo'). If the answer is negative, the word *no* must be followed by *non* which then precedes the verb: *Sei Giacomo? – No, non sono Giacomo* ('Are you Giacomo? – No, I am not Giacomo').

As in English, *sì* and *no* can be replaced by adverbs like *certo* ('sure'), *affatto* ('at all'), *assolutamente* ('absolutely'), and in colloquial Italian, especially among young people, *sì* is increasingly replaced by *esatto* ('correct') and *okay*, English word completely integrated into Italian.

In case of doubt or uncertainty, when the answer is in between *sì* and *no*, Italians use expressions like *forse* ('maybe'), *chissà* ('who knows'), *può darsi* ('it could be'), *probabilmente* ('probably').

When a question doesn't require a simple 'yes' or 'no' answer, but a specification of *chi* ('who'), *come* ('how'), *dove* ('where') and so on, the answer provides the information with a simple declarative sentence: *Come stai? – Sto bene* ('How are you? – I am well'), *Dove vai in vacanza? – Vado in Italia* ('Where are you going on vacation? – I am going to Italy').

If the answer is unknown, the common way of replying to the question is *Non lo so* ('I do not know').

10. Demonstratives

> **Demonstratives**: Demonstrative adjectives and pronouns (*questo* 'this', *quello* 'that', etc.) are used in both English and Italian to indicate the position of specific items in space or time, in relation to the speaker or writer, or based on the opposition proximity/distance: *Questa casa è nuova, quella invece è vecchia* ('This house is new; that one, on the other hand, is old').

10.1 Forms of questo

Following is a table with the forms of the demonstrative *questo*:

	Masculine	Feminine
this	questo quest'	questa quest'
these	questi	queste

Whereas the demonstrative pronouns equivalent to 'this' and 'these' have respectively only two forms each, one for the masculine and one for the feminine (*questo*, *questi*, and *questa*, *queste*), on the contrary the adjectives present a number of variants depending on the noun that follows:

- **questo** is used in front of singular masculine nouns or adjectives starting with a consonant: *questo cane* ('this dog'), *questo libro* ('this book');
- **questa** is used in front of singular feminine nouns or adjectives starting with a consonant: *questa donna* ('this woman'), *questa bottiglia* ('this bottle');
- **quest'** is used in front of singular masculine and feminine nouns or adjectives starting with a vowel: *quest'uomo* ('this man'), *quest'amica* ('this girlfriend');
- **questi** and **queste** are used respectively in front of all masculine and feminine plurals: *questi libri* ('these books'), *questi uomini* ('these men'), *queste automobili* ('these cars'), *queste amiche* ('these girlfriends').

> **N.B.** The elision (see 1.12) of the last vowel of *questo* and *questa* (*quest'*) in front of a noun or an adjective starting with a vowel is grammatically optional but rather common in contemporary Italian. The forms *questo* and *questa* can still be found instead of their elided equivalents, especially in formal writing: *Questo oggetto è stato rinvenuto* ('This object was revealed'), *Questa esperienza è necessaria* ('This experience is necessary').

10.2 Forms of quello

Following is a table with the forms of the demonstrative *quello*:

	Masculine	Feminine
that	quello quel quell'	quella quell'
those	quelli quei quegli	quelle

The demonstrative pronouns equivalent to 'that' and 'those' have respectively two forms each, one for the masculine and one for the feminine (*quello*, *quelli* and *quella*, *quelle*), while the adjectives present a number of variants depending on the noun that follows. The adjective forms *quel*, *quello*, *quell'*, *quelli*, *quei*, *quegli*, *quella*, and *quelle* follow a pattern similar to that of the definite article (see 2.4):

- the **masculine** forms **quel** (sing.) and **quei** (pl.) are used in front of nouns or adjectives starting with a consonant (*quel gatto* 'that cat', *quei ragazzi* 'those boys') unless the nouns or adjectives start with *s* + consonant, *z*, *ps*, *x*, *y*, *sh*, and *ch*. In these cases, **quello** (sing.) and **quegli** (pl.) occur: *quello studente* ('that student'), *quegli zaini* ('those backpacks'). The forms **quell'** (sing.) and **quegli** (pl.) are used in front of vowels or *h*, which is always silent in Italian: *quell'amico* ('that friend'), *quell'hotel* ('that hotel'), *quegli alberi* ('those trees');
- the **feminine** form **quella** (sing.) is used in front of nouns or adjectives starting with a consonant (*quella ragazza* 'that girl', *quella stazione* 'that station') while **quell'** (sing.) is used in front of nouns or adjectives starting with a vowel: *quell'automobile* ('that car'), *quell'oca* ('that goose'). There is only one feminine plural form **quelle**, occuring indistinctly in front of all plural nouns and adjectives: *quelle amiche* ('those girlfriends'), *quelle belle mele* ('those beautiful apples').

> **N.B.** While with *questo* and *questa* the elision (1.12) of the last vowel is optional, with *quello* and *quella* it is the norm when they occur in front of a noun or an adjective starting with a vowel or the letter *h*.

10.3 The Uses of *questo* and *quello*

The demonstrative *questo* and its related forms are equivalent in large part to the English 'this' or 'these' and indicate items that the speaker or writer considers close, while *quello* and its related forms mean 'that' or 'those' and indicate items that are considered far from the speaker or writer. The distance can refer to space (*Prendi questo libro* 'Take this book') or time (*Che belli quegli anni!* 'What beautiful years, those years!'). Unlike most Italian adjectives, **demonstratives always precede the noun they modify.** When used alone, they function as pronouns and agree with the noun they refer to. In a sentence like *Non voglio queste scarpe, ma quelle* ('I don't want these shoes but those') *quelle* refers back to *scarpe* and so agrees with it.

In addition to the above uses, *questo, quello,* and their related forms can have other particular uses:

- whereas the pronouns *lui*, *lei*, and *loro* are used in Italian to refer to persons, *questo* and *quello* represent the non-person or neuter pronoun. In this case, they are the **English equivalents of 'it' and 'they'**: *Ho comprato un dizionario nuovo; questo mi è costato 100 euro* ('I bought a new dictionary; it cost me 100 euros'), *Mio fratello ha due moto e queste sono velocissime* ('My brother has two motorcycles, and they are very fast'). Sometimes, in a colloquial register, they can even indicate persons, but this use is impolite and a little rude, especially when they are combined with the locative *qui* ('here'), *lì*, or *là* (both meaning 'there'): *Questo qui non ha nessuna idea* ('This person doesn't have any idea'), *Quello lì è molto antipatico* ('That person is very unpleasant');
- as pronouns *questo* and *quello*, used alone, correspond to the Italian expression **questa cosa** or **quella cosa** to indicate a generic thing or fact and not to refer to a specific item. In these cases, they can be translated in English by adding 'matter': *Questo è difficile* ('This is a difficult matter');
- **quello** means **'the same'** in particular contexts where adverbs of time such as *sempre* ('always'), *non ... più* ('not ... anymore') occur: *Giovanni non è più quello* ('Giovanni is not the same anymore'), *Niente è cambiato, la situazione è sempre quella* ('Nothing has changed; the situation is still the same');
- *questa* can appear **in exclamations** with an ironic meaning: *Questa è bella!* ('That's just great!'), *Questa poi!* ('This too!');
- the structure **questa di** + **noun** is equivalent to the English 'all this about': *Questa dei soldi da restituire è una cosa strana* ('All this about the money to give back is weird');

- when **questo** (rarely *questi*) **and *quello* are used together**, they can mean 'the former' and 'the latter': *Dante e Leopardi sono due poeti italiani; questo è di Recanati, quello è di Firenze,* ('Dante and Leopardi are two Italian poets; the former is from Florence, the latter is from Recanati');
- ***quest'ultimo, quest'ultima, questi ultimi,*** and ***queste ultime*** are used in Italian to indicate the last item in a list: *Ho visto Marco, Giovanni, Antonio e Carlo. Quest'ultimo è appena tornato da New York* ('I saw Marco, Giovanni, Antonio, and Carlo. The latter had just come back from New York');
- *questo* and *quello* can **denote positive or negative characteristics** when these can be easily inferred from the context. In a sentence like *Con questa squadra si può vincere tutto* ('With this team we can win it all'), the adjective *questa* carries the meaning 'so strong'. In contrast, in *Con quel carattere finirai male* ('With that character you will come to no good'), the adjective *quello* carries the meaning 'so bad';
- *quello, quella, quelli,* and *quelle* can be **followed by an adjective** only. In these cases, they are equivalent to the English 'the … one', and 'the … ones': *Non ascolto musica classica, ma quella leggera* ('I don't listen to classical music but to the pop one');
- *quello, quella, quelli,* and *quelle* when **followed by the relative pronoun *che*, or *cui*** correspond to the English 'the one(s) who', 'the one(s) that': *Grazie per il libro. È quello che volevo* ('Thank you for the book. It is the one I wanted');
- the structure ***in quel di* + name of a city or town** can sometimes be used to indicate 'the area in which': *Giovanni è nato a Campi, in quel di Firenze* ('Giovanni was born in Campi, in the Florence region'). However this structure is rare in comtemporary Italian.
- ***in quel di* + name of month** can sometimes be used to indicate a generic time in that month: *Lui arrivò in quel di marzo* ('He arrived one day in March'). However this phrase, as the previous one, is extremely rare in contemporary Italian.
- ***per questo*** is equivalent to the English 'that's why' or 'for this reason': *Stavo male, per questo non sono venuto* ('I wasn't feeling well; that's why I did not come');
- the expressions ***questo sì*, *questo no***, and ***quello sì*, *quello no*** can be used alone to affirm or deny something and can be translated with the English 'that's true' and 'that's wrong': *Hai rubato un libro? – Questo sì, ma nient'altro* ('Did you steal a book? – That's true, but nothing else').

10.4 The Case of the Adjectives sto, sta, sti, and ste

The adjective *questo* can be shortened into **sto,** often spelled *'sto*. Likewise, *questa* becomes **sta** (*'sta*), *questi* changes into **sti** (*'sti*), and *queste* is turned in **ste** (*'ste*). These forms are typical of informal speech: *'Sti ragazzi sono proprio cafoni* ('These kids are really gross'). For this reason, it is always better to avoid using such contractions in formal contexts and in written Italian, except for *stamattina* or the equivalent *stamani* ('this morning'), *stasera* ('this evening'), *stanotte* ('tonight'), and *stavolta* ('this time'), where they form one word with the noun that follows them.

10.5 The Particular Use of codesto

Besides *questo* and *quello*, Italian also has the demonstrative *codesto*, which doesn't have a direct English equivalent. **Codesto, codesta** and their plural **codesti, codeste** indicate something that is close to the addressee but far from the speaker and can always be translated in English with 'that' or 'those': *Potresti passarmi codesto libro, per favore?* ('Could you pass me that book, please?'), *Codeste sedie sono davvero belle* ('Those chairs are really beautiful').

The use of these demonstratives is, nowadays, restricted to Tuscany and to bureaucratic writing; otherwise, they are always replaced by *quello* and its related forms.

10.6 Equivalent Forms of questo and quello: tale, siffatto, simile, etc.

The words **simile, tale, siffatto, cosifatto** can all substitute for *questo* ('this') or *quello* ('that') in formal contexts, especially in written Italian: *In siffatta* [= *questa/quella*] *situazione, avrei agito diversamente* ('In this/that situation, I would have acted differently').

Simile and **tale** + noun can also be translated into English by the structure 'such a + noun': *Non voglio un simile problema* ('I do not want such a problem').

10.7 The pronoun ciò

The pronoun **ciò** ('this', 'that') can replace the singular form of the pronouns *questo* and *quello*: *Volevo vedere il film, ma ciò* [= *questo/quello*] *non è stato possibile* ('I wanted to watch the movie, but that was not possible'). *Ciò* is invariable and can be used as a subject (*Ciò non è facile* 'This is not easy') or as an object (*Parlami di ciò* 'Tell me about that'). If the use of *ciò* by itself is occasional, combined with the relative pronoun *che*, it is rather frequent. The structure **ciò che** is equivalent to the English 'what': *Ciò che hai detto è interessante* ('What you said is interesting').

10.8 Pronouns Referring Only to Persons: questi, quegli, colui, etc.

The following pronouns refer to persons only, never to animals or things. Nowadays, they are used only in a formal context and in written language. In English they are generally conveyed with 'he', 'she', and 'they'.

- **questi** ('he') can be used only as a singular and masculine subject: *Ho visto l'avvocato. Questi mi ha detto di presentarmi in tribunale* ('I saw the lawyer. He told me to appear in court');
- **quegli** ('he') can be used only as a singular and masculine subject: *Marco ha parlato con il medico. Quegli gli ha detto che va tutto bene* ('Marco spoke with the doctor. He said that everything is fine');
- **costui** ('he') and its related forms **costei** ('she') and **costoro** ('they') can be used as subjects or non-subjects: *Costui parla troppo* ('He talks to much'), *Conosci Francesca? Che cosa pensi*

di costei? ('Do you know Francesca? What do you think of her?'). In spoken language, *costui* and its related forms do not refer to somebody mentioned before but rather denote a pejorative nuance about a person: *Ma che cosa dice costui?* ('Just what is that person saying?');

- **colui** ('he'), **colei** ('she'), and **coloro** ('they') generally combine with the relative pronoun *che*, meaning 'the person who' and 'those who': *Colui/Colei che lo desidera, entri* ('The person who wants can come in now'), *Per coloro che fanno domanda sarà offerto un premio* ('A prize will be given to those who apply').

10.9 Demonstratives with Adverbs of Place: questo qui, quello laggiù, *etc.*

In colloquial Italian, demonstrative pronouns are often combined with locative adverbs such as *qui* ('here'), *là* ('there'), *laggiù* ('over there') to point out a person, an animal, or a thing: *Che bel palazzo quello laggiù* ('What a nice building that is, over there'), *Questa qui è la mia nuova auto* ('This here is my new car').

10.10 Demonstratives of Identity: stesso *and* medesimo

The demonstrative adjectives and pronouns **stesso** and **medesimo** (*medesimo* being less frequent) are used in Italian to mark identity and correspond to the English 'same': *Abitiamo nella stessa città* ('We live in the same city'), *Ho incontrato la medesima persona che avevo visto ieri* ('I met the same person I saw yesterday').

Stesso (but not *medesimo*) can sometimes be used as an intensifier to emphasize the identity of somebody or something. In this case, *stesso* can be replaced by words like *proprio* or *in persona*, corresponding to the English structure 'the ...-self'. Hence, in *Oggi, il presidente stesso ha annunciato il taglio dei finanziamenti* ('Today, the president himself announced financial cuts'), the expression *il presidente stesso* can be replaced by *proprio il presidente* or *il presidente in persona*.

11. INDEFINITES

> **Indefinites**: Indefinite adjectives and pronouns are words that can refer to a quantity, quality, or identity in a non-specific way. In Italian as in English, indefinite adjectives always precede the nouns they modify (*Ho mangiato molta cioccolata* 'I ate a lot of chocolate') and indefinite pronouns are used in place of nouns, usually to avoid repeating the nouns (*Gli studenti sono in classe. Alcuni non hanno portato i compiti* 'The students are in class. Some of them did not bring in their homework'). Most of the indefinites, like other adjectives and pronouns, agree in gender and number with the nouns they modify or replace (see examples above). However, there exist, even in Italian, particular cases of invariable indefinites (*Ogni uomo ed ogni donna dovrebbe saperlo* 'Every man and every woman should know it').

11.1 Uno *and* una

The **pronouns *uno*** and ***una*** are equivalent to the English 'one.' They usually stand for *una persona* ('someone') and are used:

- to indicate someone unknown: *Ho parlato con uno e mi ha detto che il negozio oggi è chiuso* ('I spoke with someone who told me that the store is closed today');
- to indicate an indefinite subject in an impersonal sentence. In this case, the pronoun *uno* (not *una*) substitutes for the more common impersonal *si* (see 23.13) and always takes a singular verb: *Uno [= Si] mangia bene in questo ristorante* ('One eats well in this restaurant');
- combined with a relative pronoun in constructions such as *uno che* ('someone who'), *uno di cui* ('one of whom'), *uno con il quale* ('someone with whom'): *Ho visto uno che credevo di conoscere e l'ho salutato* ('I saw someone I thought I knew, and I said hello to him');
- followed by the preposition *di* or its articulated forms (*del, della, degli*, etc.) to indicate 'one of', 'one among': *Uno di noi verrà a trovarti* ('One of us will come to visit you').

As **adjectives, *uno*** and ***una*** are often used in exclamatory sentences meaning *così grande* or *così bello*, which are equivalent to the English 'so' or 'such a ...': *Ho una paura!* ('I am so afraid'), *È stata una festa!* ('It was such a party!'). When *una* is combined with the word *figura* ('impression'), it always means *così brutta* ('such a bad ...'): *Ho fatto una figura!* ('I made such a bad impression!'). Such indefinite constructions are sometimes followed by a clause beginning with *che* ('that') to indicate the consequence of the expressed condition: *Ho una sete che potrei bere l'intero mare* ('I am so thirsty that I could drink the entire sea').

> **N.B.** The indefinites *uno* and *una*, like all the singular indefinites formed with them (*qualcuno, nessuna, alcuno*, etc.), follow a pattern similar to that of the indefinite article (see 2.2): *nessun gatto* ('no cat'), *alcun amico* ('no friend').

11.2 Qualche, qualcuno, *and* qualcuna

Qualche (see also 15.3) is equivalent to the English 'some' or 'a few' and indicates an unspecified quantity. It is an adjective only and is always followed by a singular noun, even if the meaning is plural: *qualche amico* ('some friends'), *qualche cartolina* ('some postcards'). It is invariable and used with either masculine or feminine nouns: *qualche ragazzo* ('some boys'), *qualche ragazza* ('some girls').

In some instances, the indefinite article *un* or *una*, placed in front of *qualche*, adds vagueness to the resulting constructions, which can be equivalent to the English 'some': *Abbiamo un qualche dubbio in proposito* ('We have some doubts about it'), *Ho una qualche esperienza* ('I have some experience').

Qualcuno and **qualcuna**, which are the equivalent pronouns of the adjective *qualche*, are used only in the singular and indicate an indefinite person: *C'è qualcuno in casa?* ('Is anybody at home?'), *Hai visto qualcuna che ti è simpatica?* ('Did you see anyone you like?'); or an indefinite quantity or number of something: *Quante belle matite! Ne vorrei qualcuna* ('So many beautiful pencils! I would like some'). In colloquial Italian, *qualcuno* can always be replaced by the word *nessuno* in interrogative sentences (see 11.10): *Hai visto nessuno [= qualcuno]?* ('Did you see anybody?').

11.3 Qualcosa *(or* qualche cosa*)*

Qualcosa ('something'), or the less common equivalent **qualche cosa**, indicates an indefinite thing. Despite its form, *qualcosa* is masculine, an important detail to keep in mind when considering agreement as can be seen from the use of the masculine *cambiato* and *un* (the indefinite article intensifying the sense of vagueness) in the following examples: *Qualcosa è cambiato* ('Something has changed'), *C'è un qualcosa che non mi piace* ('There is something I do not like').

When *qualcosa* occurs with an adjective, Italian requires the insertion of the preposition *di* in between. The adjective, for reasons of agreement, must always be singular and masculine: *qualcosa di buono* ('something good'), *qualcosa di bello* ('something beautiful'). *Qualcos'altro* ('something else') can be considered an exception to this rule even though the construction *qualcosa d'altro* is possible, too.

Qualcosa can, in colloquial contexts, be replaced by *una cosa* ('a thing') when, and only when, the speaker or the writer knows what this 'thing' is. One can say or write, for example,

Ho comprato una cosa per te ('I bought something for you') using *una cosa* instead of *qualcosa*, but never *Mi hai comprato una cosa?*, because whoever is saying or writing this question does not have any idea what that thing is. *Qualcosa* is necessary in the last example: *Mi hai comprato qualcosa?* ('Did you buy something for me?'). In colloquial Italian, *qualcosa* can always be replaced by the word *niente* or *nulla* in interrogative sentences (see 11.10): *Vuoi niente/nulla [= qualcosa] da mangiare?* ('Do you want something to eat?').

11.4 Alcuno, alcuna, alcuni, *and* alcune

The singular adjective and pronoun forms **alcuno** and **alcuna** are quite rare in Italian. When they occur, they always appear in negative constructions and are equivalent to *nessuno* and *nessuna* ('not any …', 'no …', 'nobody'): *Non ho alcuna [= nessuna] notizia di Marco* ('I do not have any news about Marco').

The plural forms **alcuni** and **alcune** are much more frequent. As adjectives, they correspond to the English 'some' or 'a few' (see also 15.3) and can replace the singular form *qualche* (see 11.2): *Ho incontrato alcuni studenti [= qualche studente]* ('I met some students'), *Ho mangiato alcune fragole [= qualche fragola]* ('I ate some strawberries'). When used as pronouns, they are equivalent in meaning to the singular *qualcuno, qualcuna* (see 11.2): *Alcuni dicono [= qualcuno dice] che sei un bravo ragazzo* ('Some say that you are a good boy'.)

Alcuni and *alcune* are frequently used in combination with *altri* and *altre* ('other', 'others'): *Alcuni uomini sono onesti, altri no* ('Some men are honest, others not'). It must be noted that *alcuni* and *alcune* are considered more formal than *qualche, qualcuno,* and *qualcuna* and generally limited to written language.

11.5 Certo, certa, certi, *and* certe

Certo can function as an adjective as well as a pronoun. As an **adjective**, when it is preceded by the indefinite article (*un certo, una certa*) and followed by a word indicating people, it refers to an indeterminate person and corresponds to *un tale* and *una tale* both meaning 'a certain' (see 11.6): *Un certo [= un tale] Sig. Rossi ha chiamato* ('A certain Mr. Rossi called'), *Una certa [= una tale] attrice sarà alla festa* ('A certain actress will be at the party'). Similarly, when followed by a word indicating a thing, *un certo* denotes the same indeterminate value: *So che abita in una certa strada* ('I know he lives on a certain street'); but not if the word is an abstract noun, in which case *certo* means 'some': *Ho avuto un certo successo* ('I had some success').

Certo is often employed in special constructions that one may find helpful to remember: *per un certo periodo* ('for a while'), *in un certo modo* ('in a way'), *fino a un certo punto* ('up to a certain point'), *un certo non so che* ('a certain something'), *una certa somma di* ('a certain amount of').

Furthermore, as an adjective *certo* can substitute for the singular *qualche* (see 11.2), meaning 'some' or 'a few': *Certe ragazze non erano [= Qualche ragazza non era] in classe* ('A few girls were not in class'). Sometimes, *certo* is used to denote a negative value, something not really acceptable. In this case, it means 'such': *Non sopporto certi comportamenti* ('I can't stand such behavior'), *Certe cose non si fanno* ('Such things can't be done').

As a **pronoun**, *certo* can only be used in its plural forms *certi* and *certe*, which are respectively equivalent to *alcuni* and *alcune* ('someone'): *Certi [= alcuni] parlano bene di te* ('Someone speaks well of you').

> **N.B.** It is important not to confuse *certo* ('some') as indefinite adjective with *certo* ('sure') as descriptive adjective. While the former always precedes the noun it modifies, the latter always follows it. Note the difference between these two sentences: *Ho una certa idea* ('I have some idea') and *Ho un'idea certa* ('I have a precise idea').

11.6 Tale *and* tali

Tale and its plural **tali** function either as adjectives or as pronouns and indicate absolute or relative indeterminateness in identity in certain instances. If preceded by an indefinite article (*un tale, una tale*), the indeterminateness is absolute; if, on the other hand, they are preceded by a definite article (*il tale, la tale, i tali, le tali*) or the demonstrative *quello* (*quel tale, quella tale, quei tali, quelle tali*) then the indeterminateness is relative. Note the difference between these two sentences: *Ho incontrato un tale Sig. Rossi* ('I met a certain Mr. Rossi') and *Ho incontrato il/quel tale Sig. Rossi* ('I met that certain Mr. Rossi'). In the first sentence, *un tale* underscores the fact that Mr. Rossi is completely unknown to the speaker or writer, while in the second sentence *il/quel tale* shows that Mr. Rossi is more or less known.

Tale and *tali* have other meanings also. Indeed, they can:

- correspond to the English **'so'** or **'such a great'**: *Ho una tale paura!* ('I am so afraid'), *Non potevo immaginare un tale successo!* ('I could not imagine such a great success!');
- **replace all the demonstratives** *questo, questa, quello*, etc.: *Ho capito perfettamente, tali [= questi] concetti mi sono molto chiari* ('I understood perfectly; these concepts are very clear to me');
- form the construction **tale e quale** meaning 'identical' or 'the same': *Tu e io siamo tali e quali* ('You and I are identical');
- correspond to the English **'like ..., like ...'** when doubled: *tale padre, tale figlio* ('like father, like son').

11.7 Altro, altra, altri, *and* altre

Altro can be an adjective as well as a pronoun and indicates 'another' person, animal, or thing different from the one considered as a point of reference: *Vuoi questo libro, o ne vuoi un altro?* ('Do you want this book or do you want another one?'). When used as a pronoun, it can generically signify *un'altra cosa* ('another thing', 'something else'): *Facciamo altro* ('Let's do something else').

Altro is often used combined with other adjectives, pronouns, prepositions, and adverbs. Here are the most frequent expressions:

- ***altro ... altro*** ('... something ... something else'): *Altro è parlare, altro è agire* ('Speaking is something, acting someting else'). If the second *altro* is preceded by *tutto* (*tutt'altro*), the concept of difference is intensified and can be translated with the English 'something quite different': *Altro è lavorare, tutt'altro è sgobbare* ('Working is something, toiling something quite different');
- ***l'uno ... l'altro, l'una ... l'altra, gli uni ... gli altri, le une ... le altre*** are equivalent to the English 'one ... the other', 'these people ... the others': *L'uno è nuovo, l'altro vecchio* ('One is new, the other old'); or correspond to the structure 'the former ... the latter' if referring to someone or something previously mentioned: *I gatti e i cani sono diversi: gli uni sono indipendenti, gli altri molto legati al padrone* ('Cats and dogs are different: the former are independent, the latter very tied to their owner');
- ***l'uno e l'altro, l'una e l'altra, gli uni e gli altri, le une e le altre*** all mean 'both': *L'uno e l'altro dei miei figli portano gli occhiali* ('Both my sons wear glasses');
- ***l'un l'altro, l'una l'altra*** (without the conjunction *e*) express the reciprocal meaning 'each other': *Amate l'un l'altro* ('Love each other');
- ***senz'altro*** expresses strength, confidence, and conviction, and can be equated with the English 'for sure', 'certainly', 'without any doubt': *Senz'altro visiterò il Colosseo* ('I will certainly visit the Colosseum');
- ***altroché*** (also written *altro che*) is generally used in exclamations and means the same as *senz'altro*: *Guardi la partita di calcio? – Altroché!* ('Are you watching the soccer match? – Certaintly!');
- ***altro che* + noun** is used to state a refusal, denial and is equivalent to the English 'of course not': *Altro che vacanza! Questa estate rimani a casa* ('Vacation this summer? Of course not! You will stay home');
- ***tutt'altro*** means 'not nearly', 'not at all' and is generally used in short answers to assert the opposite of the question posed: *Sei stanco? – Tutt'altro, sono pieno di energia* ('Are you tired? – Not at all, I am full of energy');
- ***per altro*** and ***tra l'altro*** both mean 'in addition', 'moreover': *Per altro, non ha neppure chiamato* ('Moreover, he did not even call'), *Tra l'altro, sei proprio maleducato* ('In addition, you are really impolite');
- ***nient'altro*** means 'nothing else': *Vuoi qualcos'altro? – No, nient'altro, grazie!* ('Do you want something else? – No, nothing else, thank you!'); when followed by *che* + noun, it can be equated with the English 'nothing but': *Non voglio nient'altro che un gelato* ('I want nothing but an ice cream').

11.8 Chiunque, qualunque, *and* qualsiasi

The pronoun **chiunque** is a singular invariable word meaning 'anybody', 'anyone': *Consegna questa scatola a chiunque vuoi* ('Give this box to anyone you want'). When *chiunque* is used as a relative indefinite, it generally corresponds to 'whoever': *Chiunque tu sia, vieni avanti* ('Whoever you are; come forward').

Qualunque and its equivalent **qualsiasi** are the corresponding adjectives of the pronoun *chiunque.* They are invariable and used only in the singular. When they are placed in front of the noun they modify, they mean 'any', 'every': *qualunque persona* ('every person'), *qualsiasi uomo* ('every man'). If they follow the noun instead, they mean 'ordinary', in the sense of not having any particular quality: *un uomo qualunque* ('an ordinary man'), *una giornata qualsiasi* ('an ordinary day').

Qualunque cosa and **qualsiasi cosa** correspond to 'whatever': *Qualunque cosa tu voglia, dimmi* ('Whatever you want, tell me'), *Qualsiasi cosa tu faccia, è troppo tardi* ('Whatever you do, it is too late').

11.9 Ogni, ognuno, *and* ciascuno

Ogni ('every', 'each', 'any') is a singular invariable adjective. It never stands alone but must always be followed by the noun it modifies: *ogni uomo* ('each man'), *ogni anno* ('every year').

Ognuno and **ognuna** are the corresponding pronouns of the adjective *ogni*. They are both singular and mean 'everyone': *Ognuno ha i propri difetti* ('Everyone has his/her own faults'). When they are followed by the preposition *di* (*ognuno di, ognuna di*), they are equivalent to 'each of': *Ognuno di voi sa che cosa fare* ('Each of you knows what to do').

Ciascuno and **ciascuna** are singular adjectives or pronouns. When they function as adjectives, they are equivalent to *ogni*: *Ciascun* [= *ogni*] *uomo ha il proprio destino* ('Every man has his own destiny'). Instead, as pronouns, they correspond to *ognuno* and *ognuna*: *Ciascuno* [= *ognuno*] *di voi sa cosa fare* ('Each of you knows what to do').

11.10 The Negative nessuno, niente, *and* nulla

The negative pronouns **nessuno** ('nobody), **niente** ('nothing') and its identical **nulla** are equivalent not only to the English negative pronouns, but also to 'anybody', 'anything', 'any' when they are used with a negative verb: *Nessuno è perfetto* ('Nobody is perfect'), *Niente è impossibile* ('Nothing is impossible'), *Non vedo nessuno* ('I don't see anybody'), *Non ho nulla* ('I don't have anything').

In Italian *nessuno, niente* and *nulla* require the negative *non* when they follow a verb even if they are themselves negative. In contrast, if they come before the verb, they do not need another negative. Whatever position they occupy in the sentence, the meaning stays the same: *Non mi ha chiamato nessuno* is equivalent to *Nessuno mi ha chiamato* ('Nobody called me'), *Non mi piace niente* is equivalent to *Niente mi piace* ('I don't like anything'), *Non è sicuro nulla* is equivalent to *Nulla è sicuro* ('Nothing is sure').

In addition, the negative *non* is not necessary in some interrogative sentences when *nessuno* means *qualcuno* ('someone'), and *niente* and *nulla* mean *qualcosa* ('something'): *Hai visto nessuno* [= *qualcuno*]? ('Did you see somebody?'), *Vuoi niente* [= *qualcosa*]? ('Do you want something?').

Below are their specific uses in detail:

- **nessuno** and **nessuna**, which can be adjectives ('no ...', 'any') and pronouns ('nobody', 'anybody'), are only singular. In negative sentences *nessuno* and *nessuna* can be replaced

by *alcuno* and *alcuna*, especially in a formal context: *Non ho alcuna* [= *nessuna*] *informazione a proposito* ('I don't have any information about it');
- **niente** and **nulla** (both meaning 'nothing', 'anything') are only pronouns and are invariable: *Non ho detto niente/nulla* ('I did not say anything'). In Italian, when *niente* and *nulla* combine with an adjective (always singular and masculine), it is necessary to insert the preposition *di* in between: *niente di buono* ('nothing good'), *nulla di bello* ('nothing beautiful'); the phrases *nient'altro* and *null'altro* (both meaning 'nothing else'), written without *di*, are a noteworthy exception to this rule. *Niente* (but not *nulla*) can be used in colloquial Italian as an invariable adjective to replace the singular *nessuno* and *nessuna*: *Niente* [= *nessuna*] *paura!* ('No fear!').

11.11 Some Rare Forms: alcunché, taluni, certuni, *etc.*

Though rare in contemporary Italian, the following forms are worth including in this discussion since they still occur. Below is a simple explanation:

- **alcunché** is equivalent to *niente* and *nulla* ('nothing', 'anything'), but more uncommon. Like *niente* and *nulla*, it is usually found in negative sentences and followed by the preposition *di*: *Non ci trovo alcunché* [= *niente/nulla*] *di interessante* ('I find nothing interesting');
- **qualcheduno** and **qualcheduna** are literary forms equivalent to *qualcuno* and *qualcuna* ('somebody'): *Qualcheduno* [= *qualcuno*] *pagherà per questo* ('Somebody will pay for it');
- **certuni** and **certune** are used only in the plural and are equivalent to *alcuni* and *alcune* ('some', 'a few'), but used only in literary contexts: *Certuni* [= *alcuni*] *di voi sono giunti da lontano* ('Some of you arrived from far away');
- **taluni** and **talune**, like *certuni* and *certune*, are equivalent to *alcuni* and *alcune* but are used only in formal Italian: *Taluni* [= *alcuni*] *non hanno fede in Dio* ('Some don't have faith in God');
- **che**, as an indefinite pronoun, is equivalent to *qualcosa* ('something') and can be preceded by the article *un* alone (*un che*) or in combination with other words (*un certo che, un non so che*). It is typical of colloquial Italian: *C'è un che di strano nell'aria* ('There is something strange in the air'), *Sento un certo non so che allo stomaco* ('I feel something in my stomach');
- **qualsivoglia** is invariable and corresponds to *qualunque* and *qualsiasi* (both meaning 'any'). It is a literary form which is extremely rare in everyday Italian: *Qualsivoglia* [= *qualunque/qualsiasi*] *decisione è possibile* ('Any decision is possible');
- **chicchessia** is equivalent to *chiunque* ('anyone') but is nowadays rather unusual: *Non è timido, parla con chicchessia* [= *chiunque*] ('He's not shy; he talks to anyone');
- **ciascheduno** and **cadauno** are equivalent to *ciascuno* ('each', 'each one'). *Cadauno* is still used in the language of commerce: *Queste magliette vengono € 20 cadauna* [= *ciascuna*] ('These T-shirts are € 20 each').

11.12 Tutto, tutta, tutti, *and* tutte

When used as **adjectives,** the singular **tutto** and **tutta** mean 'all' in the sense of 'the whole', 'the entire amount': *con tutto il mio amore* ('with all my love'), *tutta la storia* ('the whole story'). Instead, the plural forms *tutti* and *tutte* mean 'all' in the sense of 'every', 'each': *tutti gli uomini* ('all men'), *tutte le volte* ('each time'). These adjectives, unlike most of the others, are not placed before or after the noun, but are followed, as is shown above, by an **article + noun** construction. Nonetheless, *tutto* does not require an article when meaning 'completely' (*tutto sporco* 'completely dirty'), when combined with numbers (*tutti e tre* 'all three') in which case it is followed by the conjunction *e*, and in special constructions such as *di tutto cuore* ('with all my heart'), *di tutto punto* ('fully'), *in tutta fretta* ('in a great hurry'). When a demonstrative (*questo*, *quello*, etc.) is combined with *tutto,* the demonstrative always comes after *tutto*: *tutto quello spazio* ('all that space'), *tutte quelle case* ('all those houses').

When used as **pronouns** the singular *tutto* and *tutta* always refer to things, never to people: *Ho mangiato tutto* ('I ate it all'), *Ecco la lettera, l'ho riguardata tutta* ('Here is the letter; I reviewed it all'). The masculine plural *tutti* ('everyone') denotes generic people, men, and women: *Tutti hanno bisogno di una casa* ('Everyone needs a house'). The feminine *tutte* is used specifically to refer to female persons: *Non tutte hanno un lavoro* ('Not all women have a job').

11.13 The Gradation of Degrees: poco, alquanto, parecchio, molto, tanto, *and* troppo

All these words can be used as indefinite adjectives, pronouns, and adverbs and indicate a graduation in quantity or number compared to a normal value. The scale can be represented by the table below:

A little less	A little more	A lot more	Much more
poco ('a little', 'a few')	**alquanto** ('some', 'several')	**molto, tanto, parecchio** ('much', 'many')	**troppo** ('too much', 'too many')

As adjectives, they always agree with the nouns they modify, while as adverbs, they are invariable: note the difference between *molti spaghetti* ('a lot of spaghetti') where *molti* ('a lot of') is an adjective and agrees with *spaghetti*, and *molto buoni* ('very good') where *molto* ('very') does not change its form because it is an adverb.

Plural forms are often followed by the preposition *di* or *fra* to indicate a part of a group: *molti di noi* ('many of us'), *parecchi fra gli insegnanti* ('many among the teachers').

The expression *un poco* ('some', 'a little') is generally shortened to *un po'* and combined with the preposition *di* (*un po' di*) to indicate a small quantity of something: *un po' di acqua* ('some water'), *un po' di caramelle* ('some candy'). However, *di* is always omitted when *un po'* refers to a verb (*Abbiamo studiato un po'* 'We studied a little'), an adverb (*Ho mangiato un po' troppo* 'I ate a little too much'), or an adjective (*Sei un po' noioso* 'You are a little boring').

12. Numerals and Numeral Constructions

> **Numerals**: Numerals are a part of speech that principally define the number of items like *uno* ('one'), *due* ('two'), *tre* ('three'), or the order of items such as *primo* ('first'), *secondo* ('second'), *terzo* ('third'). The first are called cardinals while the second ones are ordinals. Next to these two main types of numerals, like English, Italian has collective numbers (*un paio* 'a pair', *una dozzina* 'a dozen'), multiplicative (*doppio* 'double', *triplo* 'triple') numbers, and several numeral expressions to indicate percentages, fractions, and so on.

12.1 Cardinal Numbers from 0 to 99

Cardinal numbers are the most useful to know. The following tables display the numbers from 0 to 49 and from 50 to 99:

0-9	10-19	20-29	30-39	40-49
0 zero	10 dieci	20 venti	30 trenta	40 quaranta
1 uno	11 undici	21 ventuno	31 trentuno	41 quarantuno
2 due	12 dodici	22 ventidue	32 trentadue	42 quarantadue
3 tre	13 tredici	23 ventitré	33 trentatré	43 quarantatré
4 quattro	14 quattordici	24 ventiquattro	34 trentaquattro	44 quarantaquattro
5 cinque	15 quindici	25 venticinque	35 trentacinque	45 quarantacinque
6 sei	16 sedici	26 ventisei	36 trentasei	46 quarantasei
7 sette	17 diciassette	27 ventisette	37 trentasette	47 quarantasette
8 otto	18 diciotto	28 ventotto	38 trentotto	48 quarantotto
9 nove	19 diciannove	29 ventinove	39 trentanove	49 quarantanove

50-59	60-69	70-79	80-89	90-99
50 cinquanta	60 sessanta	70 settanta	80 ottanta	90 novanta
51 cinquantuno	61 sessantuno	71 settantuno	81 ottantuno	91 novantuno
52 cinquantadue	62 sessantadue	72 settantadue	82 ottantadue	92 novantadue
53 cinquantatré	63 sessantatré	73 settantatré	83 ottantatré	93 novantatré
54 cinquantaquattro	64 sessantaquattro	74 settantaquattro	84 ottantaquattro	94 novantaquattro
55 cinquantacinque	65 sessantacinque	75 settantacinque	85 ottantacinque	95 novantacinque

56 cinquantasei	66 sessantasei	76 settantasei	86 ottantasei	96 novantasei
57 cinquantasette	67 sessantasette	77 settantasette	87 ottantasette	97 novantasette
58 cinquantotto	68 sessantotto	78 settantotto	88 ottantotto	98 novantotto
59 cinquantanove	69 sessantanove	79 settantanove	89 ottantanove	99 novantanove

Just a few simple rules to remember:

- all numbers are **written as one word** and are never hyphenated as they are in English: *quarantaquattro* ('forty-four'), *cinquantaquattro* ('fifty-four');
- all the numbers are **invariable and plural with the exception of *uno***. *Uno* follows the same pattern as the indefinite article (see 2.2), so *uno* becomes *un* as in *un gatto* ('one/a cat'), *una* as in *una bambina* ('one/a girl'), or *un'* as in *un'amica* ('one/a girfriend') depending on the word that follows it;
- *venti*, *trenta*, *quaranta*, and so on drop the last vowel in front of *uno* and *otto*: *ventuno* ('twenty-one'), *trentotto* ('thirty-eight');
- when *tre* is the last digit of a bigger number, it takes an accent (*-tré*) : *ventitré* ('twenty-three'), *trentatré* ('thirty-three');
- the **final -*o* of numerals ending in -*uno*** can simply be omitted when the number is used directly in front of a noun: *ventun amici* ('twenty-one friends'), *quarantun biciclette* ('forty-one bicycles');
- the **final -*o* of numerals ending in -*quattro*, -*otto*** is sometimes replaced by an apostrophe when the number is followed by a word starting with a vowel, especially *ore* ('hours') and *anni* ('years'): *ventiquattr'ore* ('twenty-four hours'), *diciott'anni* ('eighteen years'). *Quattro* can also drop the final -*o* and replace it with an apostrophe in a few very common idiomatic expressions such as *a quattr'occhi* ('face to face'), and *in quattro e quattr'otto* ('in short order').

12.2 Cardinal Numbers above 100

The following table indicates the numbers from 100:

100-111	200-999	1000-999.999	From and above 1.000.000
100 cento	200 duecento	1.000 mille	1.000.000 un milione
101 centouno	201 duecentouno	1.001 milleuno	1.000.001 un milione e uno ...
102 centodue	203 duecentotré	1.002 milledue ...	1.000.100 un milione e cento
103 centotré	204 duecentoquattro ...	1.100 millecento ...	1.000.101 un milione e centouno ...
104 centoquattro	300 trecento ...	1.200 milleduecento ...	2.000.000 due milioni
105 centocinque	400 quattrocento ...	2.000 duemila	2.000.001 due milioni e uno ...
106 centosei	500 cinquecento ...	2.001 duemilauno ...	100.000.000 cento milioni ...
107 centosette	600 seicento ...	2.100 duemilacento ...	200.000.000 duecento milioni ...
108 centootto	700 settecento ...	3.000 tremila ...	1.000.000.000 un miliardo
109 centonove	800 ottocento ...	10.000 diecimila ...	1.000.000.001 un miliardo e uno ...

| 110 centodieci | 900 novecento ... | 100.000 centomila | 2.000.000.000 due miliardi |
| 111 centoundici ... | 999 novecentonovantanove | 999.999 novecentonovantanovemila | 2.000.000.001 due miliardi e uno... |

Just a few simple rules to remember:

- even if numbers usually form one word, in case of **multiples of cento and mille,** they can sometimes be divided into three elements, **number + e + number**: *cento e uno* ('a hundred and one'), *mille e due* ('a thousand and two'); from **un milione and above** numbers are always written as separate words: *un milione e uno* ('a million and one'), *due millardi e due* ('two billion and two');
- Italian, unlike English, does not use the indefinite article *un* ('a' or 'an') with *cento* and *mille* when directly followed by a noun: *cento uomini* ('a hundred men'), *mille studenti* ('a thousand students');
- **cento** is invariable (*cento* 'a hundred', *duecento* 'two hundred'), but it can lose its final *-o* when immediately preceding a word starting with a vowel, especially *ore* ('hours') and *anni* ('years'): *cent'ore* ('a hundred hours'), *duecent'anni* ('two hundred years');
- although the forms *centouno* ('a hundred and one'), *centootto* ('a hundred and eight'), *centoundici* ('a hundred and eleven'), *duecentouno* ('two hundred and one'), and so on are preferable, the same numbers can be written without the *-o* of *cento* or *-cento*: *centuno*, *centotto*, *centundici*, *duecentuno*;
- **mille** makes its plural in *-mila*: *duemila* ('two thousand'), *tremila* ('three thousand');
- **milione** ('million') and **miliardo** ('billion') **make their plural in milioni and miliardi**: *due milioni* ('two million'), *tre miliardi* ('three billion'); *milione* and *miliardo*, and their plural, unless combined with additional numbers (*due milioni/miliardi e trecento mila uomini* 'two million/billion and three thousand men'), **need the preposition di** before an immediately following noun: *due milioni/miliardi di uomini* ('two million/billion men');
- **Italian uses periods where English uses commas**: 1.000 ('a thousand'), 200.000 ('two hundred thousand'). On the contrary, commas are required to indicate decimal points: *1,3* ('one point three'), *2,4* ('two point four').

12.3 Uses of Cardinal Numbers

Cardinal numbers have extensive and different uses in Italian as they do in English although there does not exist one-to-one correspondences between the two languages.

Below are those cases where Italian differs from English:

- **years** (see also 12.5): cardinal numbers are preceded by the article *il* when denoting a calendar year: *Il 2001 è stato un anno tristissimo* ('Two thousand and one was a really sad year'). The article forms articulated prepositions when combined with *di* (*un giorno del 1972* 'a day in nineteen seventy-two'), *in* (*nato nel 1967* 'born in nineteen sixty-seven'), and *da* (*dal 2000 in poi* 'from two thousand on');

- **dates** (see also 12.5): unlike English, Italian uses cardinal numbers, except for the ordinal *primo* ('first'), to denote the days of the month. As in English they are preceded by the definite article: *il primo di giugno* ('the first of June'), *il due di marzo* ('the second of March'), *il quattro di aprile* ('the fourth of April');
- **time** (see also 12.6): cardinal numbers are preceded by the definite feminine articles *l'* or *le* when indicating time: *È l'una* ('It's one o'clock'), *Sono le cinque* ('It's five o'clock'), *Sono le sette* ('It's seven o'clock'). As shown in the examples above the feminine *l'una* is used instead of *uno* and, except for this case, all the other numbers denoting time require a plural verb, which is different from English usage. The articles *l'* and *le* form articulated prepositions when combined with *a* (*all'una* 'at one o'clock', *alle due* 'at two o'clock') and *da* (*dall'una* 'from one o'clock', *dalle due* 'from two o'clock');
- **percentages** (see also 12.8): cardinal numbers are preceded by the article *il* or *l'* and followed by the simple or articulated preposition *di* when denoting percentages: *il 25 per cento di noi* ('25 per cent of us'), *l'otto per cento delle donne* ('eight per cent of women').

12.4 Ordinal Numbers

Ordinal numbers indicate the order of people or items and always agree in gender and number with the nouns they modify. In Italian, as in English, they are usually preceded by a definite article: *il primo uomo* ('the first man'), *la seconda volta* ('the second time').

They generally come before nouns, unless used with names of kings, queens, and popes: *Carlo quinto* ('Charles V'), *Elisabetta prima* ('Elisabeth I'), *Giovanni Paolo secondo* ('John Paul II'). If combined with another numeral, the ordinal number can precede or follow the latter: *i tre primi piatti* is equivalent to *i primi tre piatti* ('the first three dishes').

The following table lists the ordinal numbers:

1-10	11-20	From and above 21
1st *primo*	11th *undicesimo*	21st *ventunesimo* ...
2nd *secondo*	12th *dodicesimo*	100th *centesimo*
3rd *terzo*	13th *tredicesimo*	101st *centunesimo* ...
4th *quarto*	14th *quattordicesimo*	1000th *millesimo*
5th *quinto*	15th *quindicesimo*	1001st *millunesimo* ...
6th *sesto*	16th *sedicesimo*	1000000th *milionesimo* ...
7th *settimo*	17th *diciassettesimo*	
8th *ottavo*	18th *diciottesimo*	
9th *nono*	19th *diciannovesimo*	
10th *decimo*	20th *ventesimo*	

Just a few simple rules to remember:

- **ordinal numbers above *decimo*** are formed by dropping the last vowel of the cardinal number and replacing it with *-esimo*: *undici > undic > undicesimo* ('eleventh'), *dodici >*

dodic > *dodicesimo* ('twelfth'). But numbers ending in *-tré* and *-sei* do not lose their final vowel: *ventitré* > *ventitreesimo* ('twenty-third'), *trentasei* > *trentaseiesimo* ('thirty-sixth');
- unlike **ordinal abbreviations** in English, Italian ones are written according to the gender of the noun they refer to (° for masculine and ª for feminine) regardless of the number itself: *il 1° piano* ('the 1st floor'), *la 1ª canzone nella lista* ('the 1st song in the list'), *la 15ª pagina* ('the 15th page'); ordinals, as in English, can also be expressed using Roman numerals, especially when referring to kings, queens, popes, and centuries: *Giovanni Paolo II* ('John Paul II'), *il XX secolo* ('the twentieth century').

12.5 Cardinals and Ordinals with Dates, Years, and Centuries

Italian uses cardinal numbers, preceded by the definite article, except for the ordinal *primo* 'first,' to denote the **dates of a month** (see also 12.3): *Oggi è il primo ottobre, domani sarà il due* ('Today is October the first; tomorrow will be the second').

Cardinal numbers are similarly used to indicate **years.** In such cases the number, preceded by the article *il*, is usually written in figures and always pronounced as one word: *il 1420, il 2000*. The last two figures introduced by an apostrophe can be used alone if the reader or the listener can easily infer the century in question from the context: *Andrea Bocelli è nato nel '58* ('Andrea Bocelli was born in 1958'), *La seconda guerra mondiale cominciò nel '39* ('World War II begun in 1939').

As in English, the **century** can be expressed by ***il* + ordinal number + *secolo*** ('century'): *il primo secolo* ('the first century'), *il quattordicesimo secolo* ('the fourteenth century'). From the 13th to the 20th century it is also possible to indicate centuries by a capitalized cardinal as indicated in the table below:

From 13th to the 20th century
il Duecento ('13th century')
il Trecento ('14th century')
il Quattrocento ('15th century')
il Cinquecento ('16th century')
il Seicento ('17th century')
il Settecento ('18th century')
l'Ottocento ('19th century')
il Novecento ('20th century')

This use of cardinals is especially prevalent in literature, art, and history: *un poeta del Duecento* ('a 13th century poet'), *un ritratto del Cinquecento* ('a 16th century portrait'). If digits are used, the first number is replaced by an apostrophe: *il '200* ('13th century'), *il '300* ('14th century').

In Italian **decades** are indicated by ***gli anni* + cardinal number:** *gli anni settanta* ('the Seventies'), *gli anni novanta* ('the Nineties').

12.6 Numbers Expressing Time

In Italian one can ask the time using either **Che ora è?** or **Che ore sono?** both equivalent to the English 'What time is it?'. One will answer using numbers, except for *mezzogiorno* ('noon') or *mezzanotte* ('midnight'): *È mezzanotte* ('It's midnight'), *È mezzogiorno* ('It's noon').

Since the word *ora* ('hour') is feminine, the feminine article precedes the number: *la* in case of *una* (*l'una* 'one o'clock') and *le* for all other hours (*le due* 'two o'clock', *le tre* 'three o'clock'). The singular verb *è* is used with *una* (*È l'una* 'It's one o'clock') and, as seen before, with *mezzogiorno* ('noon') and *mezzanotte* ('midnight'), while the plural *sono* for all other times (*Sono le due* 'It's two o'clock', *Sono le cinque* 'It is five o'clock').

Minutes are expressed by adding the conjunction *e* for those past the hour, and *meno* for those before the hour: *Sono le due e dieci* ('It's ten past two'), *Sono le due meno dieci* ('It's ten to two'). The fractions *un quarto* ('a quarter'), *mezzo* or *mezza* (both 'a half'), and *tre quarti* ('three quarters') often replace the equivalent *quindici* ('fifteen'), *trenta* ('thirty') and *quarantacinque* ('fourty-five'): *Sono le cinque e un quarto* ('It's five and a quarter'), *Sono le cinque e mezzo/mezza* ('It's five and a half'), *Sono le cinque e tre quarti* ('It's five and three quarters').

To indicate **AM** Italians usually add the time expression *di notte* ('at night') or *di mattina* ('in the morning') to the hour; to indicate **PM** they add *del pomeriggio* ('in the afternoon') and *di sera* ('in the evening'). But they can also use, especially in a formal context, the **24 hour clock** and indicate 1PM with *13*, 2PM with *14* and so on. The 24 hour clock is typical of official schedules: *Il treno parte alle 20* ('The train leaves at 8PM'), *L'appuntamento è fissato alle 16* ('The appointment has been scheduled for 4 PM').

12.7 Numbers Expressing Age

Unlike English, age is indicated in Italian by the phrase **avere + cardinal number + anni**: *Ho venti anni* ('I am twenty years old'), *Noi abbiamo quaranta anni* ('We are forty years old'). The equivalent to the English 'to turn + number' is the Italian construction **compiere + cardinal number + anni**: *Ieri Giovanni ha compiuto dieci anni* ('Yesterday Giovanni turned ten'). The word *anni*, unlike the English 'years', must always be expressed in all cases.

12.8 Numbers in Mathematics

To execute **the four basic operations,** cardinal numbers in digits are used with the signs *più* ('plus'), *meno* ('minus'), *per* ('multiplied by'), *diviso* ('divided by'), and *uguale* ('equal').

When preceded by *il* or *l'*, cardinal numbers are also used to denote a **percentage** (*il 25%, l'8%*). As for **fractions**, they are expressed by a combination of cardinal and ordinal numbers written as two separate words: *un terzo* ('a third'), *un decimo* ('a tenth'). Since ordinals always agree in gender and number with the nouns they modify (see 12.4), denominators are plural when the nominator is bigger than *uno*: *due quinti* ('two-fifths'), *tre quarti* ('three-quarters'). If the dominator is the number 'two', Italian always uses the adjective *mezzo* ('half'): *un mezzo* ('a half'), *tre mezzi* ('three-halves').

The expressions **al quadrato** and **al cubo** are equivalent to the English 'squared' and 'cubed': *due al quadrato* ('2^2'), *quattro al cubo* ('4^3').

12.9 How to Express 'half of ...': mezzo and la metà di ...

'Half of' something (for fractions see 12.8) is always indicated in Italian with the adjective **mezzo**, which agrees with the singular noun it modifies: *mezzo mondo* ('half of the world'), *mezza mela* ('half of an apple'). As can be seen from the examples above, unlike English, Italian never uses an article or a preposition with *mezzo*.

The construction **la metà di** + **noun or pronoun** is possible to indicate 'half of' something with plural words: *la metà degli uomini* ('half of the men'), *la metà di voi* ('half of you').

12.10 Numbers Expressing Measurements

Measurements are expressed in Italian by an **adjective** (*lungo* 'long', *alto* 'high', etc.) + **cardinal number** + **unit of measurement**: *un palazzo alto cinquanta metri* ('a building fifty meters high'), *una buca larga tre metri* ('a hole three meters wide'). The adjective, when it can be easily inferred, is often omitted and replaced by the preposition *di*. If we consider the two examples above, we see how the first one could be rewritten as *un palazzo di cinquanta metri*, while the second one could not, since some ambiguity between *larga* ('wide') and *profonda* ('deep') can result.

> **N.B.** It must be kept in mind that in Italy, unlike in the United States, the metric system is used: *metro* ('meter'), *chilo* ('kilo'), *litro* ('liter'), and their decimals.

12.11 Multiplicatives: doppio, triplo, etc.

The most common multiplicatives are **doppio** ('double'), **triplo** ('triple'), and **quadruplo** ('quadruple'). The rest of them, like *quadruplo*, end in *-uplo* (*quintuplo* 'quintuple', *sestuplo* 'sextuple', etc), but they are extremely rare. In these cases, it is always preferable to use the structure **cardinal number + volte**: *cinque volte* ('five times'), *venti volte* ('twenty times'). When the multiplicatives are used, they are preceded by the article *il* (or *l'*) and followed by the simple or articulated preposition *di*: *Io guadagno il doppio di te* ('I make twice what you make'), *Avrei voluto avere il triplo delle occasioni che ho avuto* ('I wish I had three times the chances I had').

Adjectives ending in *-plice* are multiplicative words equivalent to the English adjectives ending in '-fold': *duplice* ('twofold'), *triplice* ('threefold').

12.12 Collective Numbers and Approximate Values: un paio, una dozzina, etc.

Collectives are words that represent a certain number of people or objects. In Italian they are much more common than in English and, except for *paio* ('pair') and *dozzina* ('dozen'), they do not have single word equivalents in English.

In Italian, the collectives are always followed by the preposition *di* when the noun or the pronoun that follows is explicitly indicated: *una ventina di amici* ('about twenty friends'), *una trentina di noi* ('about thirty of us').

Apart from the singular masculine *un paio* ('a pair'), *un centinaio* ('about a hundred'), and *un migliaio* ('about a thousand'), all the others, singular and plural, are considered feminine, so they end in *-a* when preceded by *una* and in *-e*, when preceded by other numbers: *una quindicina di ragazzi* ('about fifteen boys'), *due dozzine di uova* ('two dozen eggs').

When a singular collective (*un paio* 'a pair', *una decina* 'about ten', etc.) is used, in Italian unlike English the verb agrees with the number and is therefore singular as well: *Un paio di studenti è in classe* ('A pair of students are in class'), *Una dozzina di uova è in frigo* ('A dozen eggs are in the fridge'). However, in contemporary Italian the plural form is accepted, at least in the spoken language. For example, 'A dozen students were at the party' can be translated as *Una decina di studenti era alla festa* or *Una decina di studenti erano alla festa*, depending on whether the verb agrees with *decina*, or *studenti*.

The following table indicates the collective numbers, their plural when not formed regularly, and their English equivalents:

Singular	Irregular plurals
paio ('pair' or 'couple')	*paia* (fem.)
decina ('about ten')	
dozzina ('dozen')	
quindicina ('about fifteen')	
ventina ('about twenty')	
trentina ('about thirty')	
quarantina ('about forty')	
cinquantina ('about fifty')	
sessantina ('about sixty')	
settantina ('about seventy')	
ottantina ('about eighty')	
novantina ('about ninety')	
centinaio ('about a hundred'), etc.	*centinaia* (fem.)
migliaio ('about a thousand'), etc.	*migliaia* (fem.)

12.13 Idiomatic Uses of Some Numbers: quattro gatti, due passi, *etc.*

The numbers **due** ('two') and **quattro** ('four') are often used with the idiomatic meaning of an 'unspecified small number': *Mi passi due pistacchi?* ('Could you pass me a few pistachios?'), *Facciamo due/quattro passi* ('Let's take a short walk'). Italian uses the number *quattro* followed by the word *gatti* (literally 'cats') to indicate 'a small number of people': *Al concerto c'erano quattro gatti* ('There were only a handful of people at the concert'). On the contrary, the numbers **cento** ('hundred'), **mille** ('thousand'), and the phrase **un milione di ...** ('a million ...') can have the idiomatic meaning of an 'unspecified large number': *Ho cento/mille/un milione di cose da fare* ('I have a lot of things to do').

Apart from these particular cases, other numbers are used in idiomatic phrases. Here are the most common of them and their English meaning: *Di prima mano* ('First hand'), *Di seconda mano* ('Used'), *Essere al settimo cielo* ('To be in seventh heaven'), *Essere il primo della lista* ('To be the first to go'), *Essere una prima donna* ('To be a diva'), *Fare a mezzo* ('To split'), *Fare il terzo grado* ('To give the third degree'), *Farsi in quattro* ('To leave no stone unturned'), *Grazie mille* ('Thank you so much'), *Non fermarsi un secondo* ('Do not stop for a second'), and *Passare un brutto quarto d'ora* ('To have the worst fifteen minutes of one's life').

13. Personal Pronouns

> **Personal Pronouns**: Personal pronouns are used as substitutes for proper or common nouns, so they replace the people or things that are being talked about. Like other pronouns, they can be masculine or feminine (*lui* 'he', *lei* 'she'), singular or plural (*io* 'I', *noi* 'we') and function as subjects (*Loro studiano* 'They study') or objects (*Le porto dei fiori* 'I bring her flowers').

13.1 Subject Pronouns: io, tu, lui, *etc.*

As subjects, pronouns replace nouns denoting people, animals, or things. For example in *Carlo suona la chitarra* ('Carlo plays the guitar'), *Carlo* can be replaced by *lui* ('he'): *Lui suona la chitarra* ('He is playing the guitar'). The word *lui* is a subject pronoun as are *io* ('I'), *tu* ('you'), *noi* ('we'), and so on. The following table indicates all the Italian subject pronouns and their English equivalents:

Persons	Italian	English	Rare Italian Forms
1st pers. sing.	*io*	('I')	
2nd pers. sing.	*tu* (informal)	('you' sing.)	
3rd pers. sing.	*lui, lei, Lei*	('he', 'she', 'you' sing. formal)	*egli, ella, esso, essa*
1st pers. pl.	*noi*	('we')	
2nd pers. pl.	*voi*	('you' plur.)	
3rd pers. pl.	*loro*	('they')	*Loro* ('you' pl. formal), *essi, esse*

As can be seen from the table above, not all the correspondences between Italian and English subject pronouns are one-to-one.

The 1st person singular:

- unlike its English equivalent 'I', the pronoun *io* is never capitalized (*Oggi, io non vado a scuola* 'Today, I'm not going to school') unless it occupies the initial position in a sentence: *Io voglio un gatto* ('I want a cat');
- in compound subject constructions, *io* generally comes last for courtesy: *Tu, Giacomo ed io partiremo insieme* ('You, Giacomo, and I will leave together'). This position, however, is not mandatory and *io* can be found in any other position as well: *Io, tu e Gianni siamo buoni amici da sempre* ('You, Gianni, and I have been good friends for ever');

- the pronoun *io* can sometimes be used as a noun. *Io* then refers to one's personality or conscience and can be considered equivalent to the English 'self': *Tu non conosci il mio vero io* ('You do not know my true self').

The 2nd person singular:

- *tu* is equivalent to 'you' singular. Like the English 'you', but less frequently, the pronoun *tu* can be used as an impersonal subject meaning 'one': *Che bel film. Tu lo guardi e non ti stanchi mai* ('What a nice movie. You watch it and you never get tired of it');
- in colloquial Italian, the pronoun *tu* is frequently replaced by *te*: *Te [= Tu] come stai?* ('How are you?'), *Te [= Tu] non puoi venire* ('You can't come'). Learners of Italian should be aware that in written Italian, however, *te* as subject is considered incorrect and should be avoided. The form *te* is, on the contrary, appropriate and mandatory when it follows *io* in the construction *io e te* ('you and I'): *Io e te siamo molto felici insieme* ('You and I are happy together').

The 3rd person singular:

- *lui* and *lei* are equivalent to 'he' and 'she' respectively and refer to people: *Lui arriva questa sera, lei sarà qui domani* ('He is arriving tonight; she will be here tomorrow'). However, in Italian as in English, both pronouns can be used to refer to pets: *Il mio gatto si chiama Micio; lui ha tre anni* ('My cat is called Micio; he is three years old');
- the pronoun *lei* has a double function: it can be equivalent to 'she' as seen above, or it can replace *tu* ('you') when one wants to be polite and respectful (see 13.3). In this case, a capitalized *Lei* is generally used in written Italian to emphasize the formal context: *Adesso, Lei può parlare* ('Now, you can talk');
- besides the common pronoun *lui*, the form *egli* is still possible in formal contexts, especially in written Italian: *Egli si è presentato gentilmente* ('He introduced himself courteously'). The forms *esso* (for *lui*), *ella* (for *lei*), and *essa* (for *lei*) have, nowadays, disappeared and can only be found in literature.

The 1st person plural:

- *noi* is the equivalent of 'we': *Noi studiamo Italiano* ('We study Italian'). It is often used in Italian as a collective subject ('we the people') to replace constructions with the impersonal *si* (23.13): *In Italia noi mangiamo [= si mangia] molta pasta* ('We eat a lot of pasta in Italy');
- moreover, *noi* is used more often than *io* in articles, essays, and other formal contexts: *Noi crediamo [= Io credo] che il presidente abbia commesso un errore* ('I believe that the president made a mistake').

The 2nd person plural:

- in addition to its common meaning of 'you' plural, the pronoun *voi* was also used until a few decades ago instead of *tu* as a formal pronoun: *Caro dottore, voi siete molto gentile* ('Dear doctor, you are very kind'). Although this pronoun is no longer used as a polite form in contemporary Italian, having been replaced by the formal *Lei* (*Caro dottore, Lei è molto gentile*), it is still possible to hear it in some parts of Southern Italy, especially in Sicily.

The 3rd person plural:

- the Italian *loro* ('they') refers only to people not to things, unlike its English equivalent (for Italian 'they' as subjects other than people see 13.2);
- the form *Loro* (capitalized) can sometimes be used instead of *voi* ('you' pl.) in really formal situations to address strangers or people in authority (see 13.3): *Loro non hanno niente da temere* ('You have nothing to fear');
- the forms *essi* (for *loro* m.) and *esse* (for *loro* f.) are seldom used today and can be found only in literature.

13.2 Italian Equivalents of Neuter English 'it' and 'they'

There is no equivalent form for **'it'** to refer to things. In this case Italian can use a demonstrative pronoun (*questo/questa* 'this', *quello/quella* 'that') as a substitute for 'it' in subject position, but generally, it just lets the verb stand alone: *Marco ha una moto veloce. Questa è una Ducati* or *Marco ha una moto veloce. È una Ducati* ('Marco has a motorbike. It is a Ducati').

Although **'they'** referring to people is equivalent to *loro*, it has no Italian equivalent when it refers to things and other non-human subjects. In such contexts, Italian can use a demonstrative pronoun (*questi/queste* 'these', *quelli/quelle* 'those') as a substitute for 'they', but generally it just omits 'they', letting the verb stand alone: *Anna ha molti libri. Questi sono tutti romanzi* or *Anna ha molti libri. Sono tutti romanzi* ('Anna has a lot of books. They are all novels').

13.3 Formal Lei *and* Loro

Unlike English, Italian has two forms for expressing the singular and plural 'you': one informal and one formal.

Singular 'you':

- ***tu*** is informal and used with family members, friends, and peers: *Tu sei un caro amico* ('You are a dear friend'), *Ascolta Marco, tu devi essere coraggioso* ('Listen Marco; you must be brave');
- ***Lei*** is formal and required when addressing strangers, adults, and people in authority, male or female. When written, the formal pronoun *Lei* is usually capitalized to distinguish it from

lei meaning 'she'. Note that the verb must be conjugated at the 3rd person singular, not at the 2nd: *Buongiorno, Lei è la professoressa di francese?* ('Good morning, are you the professor of French?'), *Lei dimostra sempre grandi capacità* ('You always display great skills').

Plural 'you':

- *voi* is the most common second person plural pronoun. It is, nowadays, used indistinctly in informal situations (*Voi dovete venire a cena* 'You must come to dinner') as well as in more formal contexts (*Senatori, voi potete votare adesso* 'Senators, you can vote now');
- *Loro* can replace *voi* in a few cases. Although this form is becoming increasingly rare in contemporary Italian, it is worth remembering that in very formal situations such as addressing strangers or people in authority, especially during official meetings, galas, conferences, the use of *Loro* is not uncommon: *Cortesemente, Loro vengano da questa parte* ('Kindly proceed this way'). Like *Lei,* the formal *Loro* is usually capitalized to distinguish it from *loro,* meaning 'they'. Note that the verb must be conjugated at the 3rd person plural, not at the 2nd: *Buongiorno, Loro sono gli ambasciatori europei?* ('Good morning, are you the European ambassadors?').

> **N.B.** In Italian *tu* is used with people with whom one is on a first name basis; therefore, it is frequent for people to ask acquaintances they have known for a little while (never people in authority) *Possiamo darci del "tu"?* ('May we switch to "tu"?'), and because such a request is hardly ever refused, they start using the informal pronoun *tu.*

13.4 Use and Omission of Subject Pronouns

Subject pronouns, when expressed, usually precede the verb (*Loro cantano una canzone* 'They sing a song', *Tu sei molto gentile* 'You are very kind'), but they can sometimes follow it, especially to emphasize the pronoun: *Oggi pulisci tu la stanza* ('Today, you clean the room'), *Hai rotto tu il computer?* ('Did you break the computer?').

Unlike English, Italian often omits subject pronouns because the verb forms themselves clearly indicate the subjects. For instance, in *Oggi ho molta fame* ('I am really hungry today'), the verb form *ho* itself restricts the choice of subjects to *io*. However, if the omission of the pronoun creates ambiguity in the sentence, the subject pronoun becomes mandatory. For example, in the sentence *Anna ha parlato con Marco e lui ha avuto piacere* ('Anna spoke with Marco and he was happy about it'), the pronoun *lui* ('he') is necessary to understand that it is Marco who was happy, not Anna. For this reason, it is helpful to keep in mind a few practical rules that highlight when subject pronouns are necessary and must, therefore, be expressed. This is the case when:

- the same verb form can be used for more than one person as, for instance, in the present subjunctive: *È importante che tu venga* ('It is important that you come'), *Credo che lui venga* ('I think he will come');
- emphasis or contrast is desired: *No, non sei tu la persona che cerco* ('No, you are not the person I am looking for'), *Io canto, tu suoni* ('I sing; you play music');
- the pronoun follows conjunctions such as *anche* ('also', 'too'), *neanche* ('not even'), *almeno* ('at least'): *Anche noi andremo in Italia quest'anno* ('We will go to Italy this year, too'), *Almeno tu hai una casa grande* ('At least you have a big house');
- the pronoun combines with other pronouns (*Lui e lei sono molto carini* 'He and she are really nice'), nouns (*Noi professori siamo in sciopero* 'We professors are on strike'), adjectives (*Lui schizzinoso non mangia* 'He, being squeamish, is not eating'), and numerals (*Voi due siete una bella coppia* 'You two are a nice couple');
- the subject pronoun is followed by a relative pronoun: *Tu, che ami tanto gli animali, non dovresti aver paura dei ragni* ('You, who love animals so much, should not be scared of spiders').

13.5 Stressed and Unstressed Object Pronouns: me/mi, te/ti, *etc.*
Unlike English, Italian has two forms of object pronouns:

- **stressed forms** (*me, te, lui,* etc.) are used to carry emphasis, hence their name; they come after a verb (*Chiamo lui* 'I call him') or after a preposition (*Parlo con/di/a voi* 'I am talking with/about/to you');
- **unstressed forms** (*mi, ti, lo,* etc.) do not carry emphasis and tend to blend with the words they occur with. They are never preceded by a preposition and come directly before a verb (*Lo chiamo* 'I call him', *Vi parlo* 'I am talking to you') or attach to an infinitive verb (*Vai a incontrarli* 'Go to meet them'), an imperative (*Parlale* 'Talk to her'), a gerund (*Guardandoti, mi sento felice* 'Looking at you makes me happy'), or a past participle (*Mangiatolo, mi sono sentito male* 'Having eaten it, I felt bad').

When both unstressed indirect and direct object pronouns occur in the same sentence, they combine (see 13.10) and change forms: *Glielo porterai* ('You will bring it to him'), *Chiamameli* ('Call them for me').

Below is a complete list of the stressed and unstressed pronouns for each person. Most function as both direct (13.6) and indirect objects (see 13.9); when such pronouns have only one function, it is indicated:

Persons	Stressed Pronouns	Unstressed Pronouns
1st pers. sing.	*me* ('me')	*mi* ('me')
2nd pers. sing.	*te* ('you')	*ti* ('you')
3rd pers. sing. m.	*lui* ('him')	*lo* ('him', 'it') only direct obj., *gli* ('him') only indirect obj.
3rd pers. sing. f.	*lei* ('her')	*la* ('her', 'it') only direct obj., *le* ('her') only indirect obj.

3rd pers. sing. m./f. (formal)	*Lei* ('you' sing. formal)	*La* ('you' sing. formal) only direct obj.
		Le ('you' sing. formal) only indirect obj.
3rd pers. sing. refl.	*sé* ('himself', 'herself', 'oneself')	*si* ('himself', 'herself', 'oneself')
1st pers. pl.	*noi* ('us')	*ci* ('us')
2nd pers. pl.	*voi* ('you' pl.)	*vi* ('you' pl.)
3rd pers. pl. m.	*loro* ('them')	*li* ('them') only direct obj., *gli/loro* ('them') only indirect obj.
3rd pers. pl. f.	*loro* ('them')	*le* ('them') only direct obj., *gli/loro* ('them') only indirect obj.
3rd pers. pl. m./f. (formal)	*Loro* ('you' pl. formal)	*Li* ('you' pl. m. formal) only direct obj.
		Le ('you' pl. f. formal) only direct obj.
3rd pers. pl. refl.	*sé* ('themselves')	*si* ('themselves')

Even though theoretically these two forms are interchangeable, Italians generally use unstressed pronouns much more frequently, especially in spoken language in order to make the sentence more fluid. In fact, for example, it is clearly much easier to pronounce *Mi parli* than *Parli a me* ('You talk to me'). On the contrary, English speakers tend to prefer stressed forms because they are comparable to English constructions. In this case, they should strive to use unstressed forms more often to sound like native Italians.

Stressed forms, however, are always required after a verb to distinguish between multiple objects, pronouns, and nouns: *Invita lui, ma non loro* ('Invite him, but not them'), *Ho spedito un regalo a te e a tuo fratello* ('I sent a gift to you and to your brother').

Stressed forms are also preferable when greater emphasis on the pronoun is desired. For instance, although the two sentences *Amo lei* and *La amo* have the same meaning ('I love her'), the first one focuses much more attention and stress on the pronoun, conveying the impression that the person who loves, loves *lei* ('her') exclusively.

13.6 Direct Object Pronouns: mi, me, lo, la, *etc.*

A direct object is a noun or pronoun that receives the action of a verb directly, without a preposition. A direct object pronoun is used to replace a direct object noun, especially in order to avoid repetition. For instance, in *Oggi vedo Marco, lo incontro in biblioteca* ('I will see Marco today; I will meet him in the library'), the pronoun *lo* ('him') replaces *Marco.*

There are two sets of direct object pronouns: stressed and unstressed (see 13.5). Even though these two forms are generally interchangeable, Italians use unstressed direct pronouns more readily, especially in spoken language for ease of pronunciation. Stressed forms are preferred instead when greater emphasis is desired (*Chiamano te* 'They are calling you') and are always required after a verb to distinguish between multiple objects (*Chiama loro, ma non tuo fratello* 'Call them, but not your brother').

The table below displays the two sets of direct object pronouns, their English equivalents, and a sample of their use:

Persons	Unstressed & stressed pronouns	Examples
1st pers. sing.	**mi** = **me** ('me')	*Mi vedi? = Vedi me?* ('Do you see me?')
2nd pers. sing.	**ti** = **te** ('you')	*Ti invito a cena = Invito te a cena* ('I invite you for dinner')
3rd pers. sing. m.	**lo** = **lui** ('him') (**lo** is also 'it')	*Non lo conosco = Non conosco lui* ('I don't know him')
3rd pers. sing. f.	**la** = **lei** ('her') (**la** is also 'it')	*La incontro oggi = Incontro lei oggi* ('I see her today')
3rd pers. sing. m./f. (formal)	**La** = **Lei** ('you' sing. formal)	*La chiamo domani = Domani chiamo Lei* ('I'll call you tomorrow')
1st pers. pl.	**ci** = **noi** ('us')	*Ci vieni a trovare? = Vieni a trovare noi?* ('Are you coming to visit us?')
2nd pers. pl.	**vi** = **voi** ('you' pl.)	*Vi trovo bene = Trovo voi bene* ('I find you well')
3rd pers. pl. m.	**li** = **loro** ('them') (**li** is also 'them' neuter)	*Marco li guarda = Marco guarda loro* ('Marco is watching them')
3rd pers. pl. f.	**le** = **loro** ('them') (**le** is also 'them' neuter)	*Anna le rimprovera = Anna rimprovera loro* ('Anna is scolding them')
3rd pers. pl. m. (formal)	**Li** = **Loro** ('you' pl. m. formal)	*Li invito ad entrare = Invito Loro ad entrare* ('I invite you all to come in')
3rd pers. pl. f. (formal)	**Le** = **Loro** ('you' pl. f. formal)	*Le invito ad entrare = Invito Loro ad entrare* ('I invite you ladies to come in')

Just a few rules to remember:

- unstressed pronouns are generally placed right before the verb, while the stressed ones follow it: *Io ti vedo / Io vedo te* ('I see you'). However, unstressed pronouns attach to the infinitive verb form after the latter has dropped its final -e: *Penso di conoscerti* ('I think I know you'). If the infinitive follows *potere* ('can'), *dovere* ('must'), or *volere* ('to want'), the pronoun may either attach to the infinitive (*Posso/Devo/Voglio conoscerti* 'I can/must/want to know you') or precede the entire verb phrase (*Ti posso/devo/voglio conoscere* 'I can/must/want to know you'). Unstressed forms also always attach to an imperative (*Chiamala* 'Call her'), a gerund (*Lasciandoti, sono triste* 'Leaving you, makes me sad'), or a past participle (*Conosciutolo, siamo subito diventati amici* 'Having met, we immediately became friends');
- the singular pronouns *lo*, *la*, but never *li* and *le*, can elide (*l'*) in front of compound verb forms using *avere* as auxiliary: *L'ho visto oggi* ('I saw him today'), *L'ho incontrata ieri* ('I met her yesterday');
- the unstressed pronouns *la* and *lo* (but not the stressed *lui* or *lei*), *li* and *le* (but not *loro*) can refer to people, animals, or objects, so they can also mean 'it' and 'them' neuter: *Ho visto un bel cappotto, lo devo comprare* ('I saw a beautiful coat; I have to buy it'), *Che belle mele! Le mangio volentieri* ('What beautiful apples! I will gladly eat them');

- the stressed pronoun *loro* and the unstressed *li* and *le* (usually capitalized *Loro*, *Li*, and *Le* when written) could also be used for the formal 'you' plural: *Chiamo Loro, entrino* ('I am calling you all; come in'), *Signore, Le invito a restare* ('Ladies, I invite you to stay'). However, these forms are extremely rare in contemporary Italian and only used in very formal situations such as addressing strangers or people in authority, especially during official meetings, galas, and conferences;
- sometimes in informal Italian the unstressed pronouns *lo, la, le,* and *li* can be found together with the direct object nouns they should replace: *Lo vedi Antonio?* ('Do you see Antonio?'), *La mangi la carne?* ('Do you eat meat?'). This redundant usage is typical of a colloquial register and should be avoided.

> **N.B.** Not all transitive Italian verbs are transitive in English, and vice versa (see 22.1, 22.2). This means that a verb that takes a direct object noun and accordingly a direct object pronoun in Italian may not do so in English: *Beatrice aspetta il treno, lo aspetta dalle 14.00* ('Beatrice is waiting for the train; she has been waiting for it since 2:00PM'). A good dictionary should indicate whether a verb takes a direct object or not.

13.7 Direct Object Pronouns and Past Participle Agreement: L'ho mangiato / L'ho mangiata

The past participle of a verb conjugated with *avere* ('to have') is invariable (see 20.13), unless a 3rd person direct object pronoun *lo, la, li,* or *le* precedes the verb. In this case the past participle must agree in gender and number with the direct object pronoun preceding the auxiliary *avere* (see 21.61). The table below explains the rules of agreement:

Rules of Agreement	Examples: Answers with direct object pronouns
with *lo* the past part. ends in *-o*	Hai visto il professore? – Sì, lo/l'ho vist**o** in classe ('Did you see the professor? – Yes, I saw him in class')
with *la* the past part. ends in *-a*	Hai mangiato la mela? – Sì, la/l'ho mangiat**a** ('Did you eat the apple? – Yes, I ate it')
with *li* the past part. ends in *-i*	Hai comprato i libri? – No, non li ho ancora comprat**i** ('Did you buy the books? – No, I haven't bought them yet')
with *le* the past part. ends in *-e*	Hai spedito le cartoline? – Sì, le ho spedit**e** ieri ('Did you send the postcards? – Yes, I sent them yesterday')

Although possible, agreement between the past participle and the other unstressed pronouns (*mi, ti, ci,* etc.) is nowadays rare, especially in colloquial Italian. Thus, a sentence like *Carla, ti ho chiamata cento volte* ('Carla, I have called you a hundred times'), where *chiamata* agrees with *ti* referring back to the feminine *Carla*, is grammatically correct but less common than the equivalent *Carla, ti ho chiamato cento volte*, where there is no agreement. Thus, with all the direct object pronouns other than *lo, la, li,* or *le*, the past participle tends to end invariably in *-o*.

> **N.B.** The singular forms *lo* and *la* (not the plurals *li* and *le*) can be elided and take the apostrophe (*l'*) in front of the forms of *avere*.

13.8 Ecco + Direct Object Pronouns: eccomi, eccoli, eccovi, *etc.*

The word *ecco* means 'here/there is': *Ecco Giovanna* ('Here is Giovanna'), *Ecco il libro* ('Here is the book'). When *ecco* is used with a direct object pronoun rather than a noun, the pronoun is always unstressed and must attach to *ecco*: *Eccomi* ('Here I am'), *Eccoti* ('There you are').

13.9 Indirect Object Pronouns: mi = a/per me, gli = a/per lui, *etc.*

When the action of a verb is done *a* ('to') or *per* ('for') a person, the recipient of that action constitutes an indirect object: *Sto parlando a Maria* ('I am talking to Maria'), *Maria fa tutto per i suoi figli* ('Maria does everything for her sons'). In order to avoid repetition, the noun of the person receiving the action is often replaced by a pronoun: for instance, in *Hai l'indirizzo di Ferruccio? Manda a lui questo pacco* ('Do you have Ferruccio's address? Send him this package'), the pronoun *lui* ('him') replaces *Ferruccio*.

Like the direct object pronouns, the indirect ones have two forms, unstressed (used alone) and stressed (used with the preposition *a* or *per*). Here, too, Italians have a marked preference for the unstressed pronouns, especially in spoken language. The stressed forms are required to distinguish between multiple indirect objects (*Parlo a te e a tuo fratello, non a tua sorella* 'I am talking to you and to your brother, not to your sister'), and preferred when placing greater emphasis on the pronoun.

The table below displays the two sets of pronouns, their English equivalents, and a sample of their use:

Persons	Unstressed & Stressed Pronouns	Examples
1st pers. sing.	*mi = a/per me* ('to/for me')	*Mi puoi parlare? = Puoi parlare a me?* ('Can you talk to me?')
2nd pers. sing.	*ti = a/per te* ('to/for you' sing.)	*Ti offro un caffè = Offro a te un caffè* ('I am offering you a coffee')
3rd pers. sing. m.	*gli = a/per lui* ('to/for him')	*Gli dico di venire = Dico a lui di venire* ('I am telling him to come')
3rd pers. sing. f.	*le = a/per lei* ('to/for her')	*Le faccio un piacere = Faccio a lei un piacere* ('I am doing her a favor')
3rd pers. sing. m./f. (formal)	*Le = a/per Lei* ('to/for you' sing. formal)	*Le chiediamo scusa = Chiediamo a Lei scusa* ('We beg your pardon')
1st pers. plur.	*ci = a/per noi* ('to/for us')	*Ci hai dato un libro = Hai dato a noi un libro* ('You gave us a book')
2nd pers. plur.	*vi = a/per voi* ('to/for you' pl.)	*Vi preparo un tè = Preparo per voi un tè* ('I am making you a tea')
3rd pers. plur. m./f.	*gli = a/per loro* ('to/for them')	*Gli dico la verità = Dico [a] loro la verità* ('I am telling them the truth')
3rd pers. plur. m./f. (formal)	[*a/per*] *Loro* (only stressed) ('to/for you' plur. formal)	*Parlo [a] Loro* ('I am talking to you all')

Just a few simple rules to remember:

- unstressed pronouns are generally placed right before the verb, while stressed forms follow it: *Io ti parlo / Io parlo a te* ('I am talking to you'). However, unstressed pronouns must attach to the infinitive verb form, which always drops its final -e: *Credevo di averti detto di venire* ('I thought I told you to come'). If the infinitive follows *potere* ('can'), *dovere* ('must'), or *volere* ('to want') the pronoun may either attach to the infinitive (*Posso/Devo/Voglio parlarvi* 'I can/must/want to talk to you') or precede the entire verb phrase (*Vi posso/devo/voglio parlare* 'I can/must/want to talk you'). Unstressed forms also attach to an imperative verb (*Offrile un tè*, 'Offer her a tea'), a gerund (*Convincerai tuo padre semplicemente parlandogli* 'You will convince your father by simply talking to him'), or a past participle (*Confessatole la verità, sono stato meglio* 'Having confessed the truth to her, I felt better');
- if in English the prepositions 'to' or 'for' can sometimes be omitted before an indirect object noun or pronoun ('Marco bought Marta/her a gift' or 'Marco bought a gift for Marta/her'), in Italian the preposition *a* or *per* must always precede the indirect object noun or the indirect stressed pronoun (*Marco ha comprato un regalo per Marta/lei*). The only exception to this rule (see below) is with the pronoun *loro*;
- the preposition *a* can be omitted when placed before the plural stressed pronoun *loro* (and the formal *Loro*): *Di' [a] loro di venire* ('Tell them to come'). This case of omission is not frequent in colloquial Italian but preferred in formal contexts (see below);
- the stressed pronoun *loro* (usually capitalized *Loro* when written) could also be used for the formal plural 'you': *Mi rivolgo [a] Loro* ('I am addressing you all'). However, this form is extremely rare in contemporary Italian;
- the singular *gli* form often replaces the feminine *la* in colloquial Italian: *Ho visto Giovanna e gli ho detto di venire* ('I saw Giovanna and I told her to come'). Though very common, this usage is considered ungrammatical and must be avoided;
- in colloquial Italian, unstressed and stressed pronouns can both occur at the same time: *A me non mi parli?* ('Aren't you talking to me?'). This redundant usage is typical of colloquial registers and should be avoided;
- sometimes in very informal Italian the unstressed pronouns *gli* and *le* can appear together with the nouns they should replace. For example, it is possible to hear *Gli hai portato a Giovanni il libro?* ('Did you bring Giovanni the book?'), where *Gli* and *a Giovanni* appear at the same time, instead of the more grammatical *Gli hai portato il libro?* or *Hai portato il libro a Giovanni?* This redundant usage is typical of colloquial register and it is best to avoid it.

> **N.B.** Not all Italian verbs that take an indirect object, and accordingly an indirect object pronoun, have an English equivalent with the same construction, and vice versa (see 22.3). This means that a verb may take an indirect object and thus an indirect object pronoun in Italian but not in English: *Telefono al professore, gli telefono questa sera.* ('I'll call the professor; I'll call him tonight'). A good dictionary should indicate if a verb takes a direct object or not.

13.10 Double Object Pronouns: melo, gliela, vele, *etc.*

There are times when the same verb takes both a 3rd person unstressed direct object pronoun (*lo, la, li,* and *le*; see 13.6) and an unstressed indirect object pronoun (*mi, ti, gli,* etc.; see 13.9). In *Ho comprato un libro per Marco* ('I bought a book for Marco') *un libro* can be replaced by *lo* ('it') and *per Marco* by *gli* ('for him'), forming the sentence *Glielo ho comprato* ('I bought it for him'). When both pronouns appear in Italian, they combine according to the following rules:

- the indirect object pronoun always comes before the direct one;
- the indirect object pronouns *mi, ti, ci,* and *vi* change respectively into *me, te, ce,* and *ve*;
- the indirect object pronouns *gli, le,* and the formal *Le* all become *glie-* when followed by direct object pronouns and the two are written as single new words: *glielo, gliela, glieli,* and *gliele*.

The following chart presents all the double object pronouns:

Indirect object pronouns	Direct object pronouns			
	lo	la	li	le
mi	me lo	me la	me li	me le
ti	te lo	te la	te li	te le
gli, le, Le	glielo	gliela	glieli	gliele
ci	ce lo	ce la	ce li	ce le
vi	ve lo	ve la	ve li	ve le
gli	glielo	gliela	glieli	gliele

Just a few simple rules to remember:

- the combined pronouns, like all unstressed pronouns, generally precede the conjugated verb: *Te lo darò domani* ('I will give it to you tomorrow');
- they always attach to an infinitive verb form, which in this case drops its final *-e*, and the construction verb + pronoun becomes a single word: *Credevo di avertelo portato* ('I thought I had brought it to you');
- an infinitive follows *potere* ('can'), *dovere* ('must'), or *volere* ('to want'), the pronouns may either attach to the infinitive and form one word with it (*Posso/Devo/Voglio spedirtela* 'I can/must/want to send it to you') or precede the entire verb phrase (*Te la posso/devo/voglio spedire* 'I can/must/want to send it to you');
- the combined forms also always attach to an imperative verb (*Portaglielo,* 'Bring it to him/her'), a gerund (*Donandomelo, fai la cosa giusta* 'Giving it to me is the right thing'), or a past participle (*Confessatoglielo mi sento meglio* 'Having confessed to him/her, I feel better').

Sometimes in informal Italian double direct objects can occur in a sentence where a direct object noun and the pronoun, which should replace it, are both present. For example, it is possible to hear *Me la dai una matita?* (where the words *matita* and *la* appear at the same time) instead of the more grammatical *Mi dai una matita?* ('Are you giving me a pencil?'), or *Me la dai?* ('Are you giving it to me?'). This redundant usage is typical of colloquial register and should be discouraged.

> **N.B.** It is also possible to combine the direct object pronouns *lo, la, li,* and *le* with reflexive pronouns. Since all the reflexive pronouns (see 13.13) are identical in form to the unstressed direct or indirect object pronouns, except the 3rd pers. sing. and pl. *si,* they combine with *lo, la, li,* and *le* following the rules explained above. Just remember that the reflexive *si* changes into *se* when combined with these indirect pronouns (*se lo, se la, se li,* and *se le*): *Lui, la cravatta? Macché, non se la sa legare* ('He, a tie? No way! He wouldn't know how to tie it').

13.11 Double Object Pronouns and Past Participle Agreement: Gliel'ho dato / Gliel'ho data

When a double object pronoun (see 13.10) precedes a verb in sentences with compound tenses using *avere* as auxiliary, the past participle of the main verb must agree in gender and number with the direct object pronoun *lo, la, li,* and *le,* according to the rules previously indicated (see 13.7): *Ho comprato una nuova auto. Me la hanno consegnata questa mattina* ('I bought a new car. They delivered it this morning'). Remember that the singular *lo* and *la* can be elided and take an apostrophe (*l'*) before the forms of *avere*: *Il quaderno? Te l'ho dato ieri* ('The notebook? I gave it to you yesterday'), *Che storia! Ve l'hanno raccontata?* ('What a story! Did they tell you about it?').

13.12 Object Prepositional Pronouns: di lui, con voi, fra noi, *etc.*

A prepositional pronoun is a special form of a pronoun used as the object of a preposition. Any preposition (for *a* and *per,* see indirect object pronouns 13.9) combined with a stressed pronoun forms an object prepositional pronoun (*di lui, con voi, fra noi,* etc.). Except for *me* ('me') and *te* ('you'), the prepositional pronouns have the same form as the subject pronouns.

The following chart indicates all the Italian prepositional pronouns and their English equivalents:

Persons	Prepositional pronouns
1st pers. sing.	**prep. +** ***me*** (prep. + 'me')
2nd pers. sing.	**prep. +** ***te*** (prep. + 'you' sing.)
3rd pers. sing. m.	**prep. +** ***lui*** (prep. + 'him')
3rd pers. sing. f.	**prep. +** ***lei*** (prep. + 'her')
3rd pers. sing. m. and f. (formal)	**prep. +** ***Lei*** (prep. + 'you' sing. formal)
1st pers. plur.	**prep. +** ***noi*** (prep. + 'us')
2nd pers.plur.	**prep. +** ***voi*** (prep. + 'you' pl.)
3rd pers. plur. m. and f.	**prep. +** ***loro*** (prep. + 'they')
3rd pers. plur. m. and f. (formal)	**prep. +** ***Loro*** (prep. + 'you' pl. formal)

Italian uses the prep + *Lei* construction instead of prep. + *te* in formal situations (see 13.3). The prep + *voi* construction can be also replaced by the structure prep. + *Loro* to address strangers or people in authority (*Tutto è pronto per Loro* 'Everything is ready for you all'), even if this form is nowadays extremely rare.

> **N.B.** English speakers must be aware that Italian and English verbs are not always followed by the same preposition (see chapter 22): *Non ridere di me* ('Don't laugh at me'), *Mi sto innamorando di te* ('I am falling in love with you'). A good Italian dictionary always indicates what preposition follows what verb.

13.13 Reflexive Pronouns: mi, si, ci, *etc.*

In Italian as in English, reflexive pronouns are used to indicate that the doer and the receiver of the action of a verb are one and the same: *Io mi lavo* ('I wash myself'), *Tu ti vesti* ('You dress yourself'). They are identical in form to the unstressed direct (see 13.6) or indirect (see 13.9) object pronouns, except the 3rd person singular and plural *si*.

These pronouns are used with reflexive verbs (see 23.4) and must always be expressed in Italian whereas in English they can be omitted: *Lei si pettina i capelli* ('She combs her hair [herself]'), *Lui si veste bene* ('He dresses [himself] well'). Reflexive pronouns can function as both direct object pronouns (*Tu ti diverti* 'You entertain yourself') and indirect object pronouns (*Lia si compra un nuovo computer* 'Lia is buying a new computer for herself').

The following chart indicates all the Italian reflexive pronouns, and their English equivalents:

Persons	Reflexive pronouns
1st pers. sing.	*mi* ('myself' or 'to/for myself')
2nd pers. sing.	*ti* ('yourself' or 'to/for yourself')
3rd pers. sing. m. and f.	*si* ('himself'/'herself' or 'to/for himself/herself')
3rd pers. sing. m. and f. (formal)	*Si* ('yourself' or 'to/for yourself' formal)
1st pers. pl.	*ci* ('ourselves' or 'to/for ourselves')
2nd pers. pl.	*vi* ('yourselves' or 'to/for yourselves')
3rd pers. pl. m. and f.	*si* ('themselves' or 'to/for themselves')
3rd pers. pl. m. and f. (formal)	*Si* ('yourselves' or 'to/for yourselves' formal)

Just a few simple rules to remember:

- just like unstressed pronouns, reflexive pronouns usually occur before a conjugated verb: *Si lavano ogni mattina* ('They wash [themselves] every morning');
- if they occur with an infinitive, the infinitive drops its final *-e* and the pronouns attach to it: *Hai bisogno di divertirti di più* ('You need to have more fun'). If the infinitive is preceded by a form of *potere* ('can'), *dovere* ('must'), or *volere* ('to want'), the pronouns may either

attach to the infinitive (*Posso/Devo/Voglio lavarmi* 'I can/must/want to wash myself') or precede the entire verb phrase (*Mi posso/devo/voglio lavare* 'I can/must/to wash myself');
- the reflexives also always attach to an imperative verb (*Lavatevi bene* 'Wash yourself well'), a gerund (*Conoscendomi, non credo di venire* 'Knowing myself, I don't think I'll come'), or a past participle (*Cambiatomi, sono pronto a uscire* 'Having changed [myself], I am ready to go out');
- the reflexive *mi*, *ti*, *si*, and *vi* may drop the *i* before vowels and take an apostrophe (*M'annoio* 'I get bored', *V'annoiate* 'You get bored'), but *ci* may drop the *i* only before another *i* or an *e* (*Non c'innervosiamo* 'Let's not become nervous');
- a formal *Si* can, on rare occasions, replace *vi* as the reflexive form for the formal *Loro* when addressing strangers or people in authority in very ceremonious situations: *Per favore, Loro Si presentino* ('Please, introduce yourselves').

13.14 The Reflexive Pronoun sé

The stressed reflexive pronoun *sé* ('himself', 'herself', and 'themselves') can replace, even if rarely, the reflexive pronoun *si*: *Lui immaginò sé davanti al giudice* is equivalent to *Lui si immaginò davanti al giudice* ('He imagined himself in front of the judge'). The pronoun *sé* is instead used extensively when preceded by prepositions (*a sé, con sé, di sé*, etc.): *Maria parla di sé tutto il tempo* ('Maria talks about herself all the time'), *Carla pensa più agli altri che a sé* ('Carla cares more about the others than about herself'). The pronun *sé* is preferably combined with the adjective *stesso* (see 13.15). In this case the pronoun is written *se*, without the accent: *Maria parla di se stessa tutto il tempo; Carla pensa più agli altri che a se stessa*.

13.15 The Reflexive Use of stesso: me stesso, loro stessi, *etc.*

The word *stesso* can be inflected to mean 'oneself' when it is used with stressed personal pronouns, forming reflexive phrases equivalent to the reflexive pronouns (see 13.13). The table below shows these constructions and their equivalent reflexive pronouns:

Forms with *stesso*
me stesso/me stessa ('myself') = *mi*
te stesso/te stessa ('yourself') = *ti*
se stesso/se stessa ('himself'/'herself') = *si* sing.
noi stessi/noi stesse ('ourselves') = *ci*
voi stessi/voi stesse ('yourselves') = *vi*
se stessi/se stesse ('themselves') = *si* pl.
loro stessi/loro stesse ('themselves') = *si* pl.

Since *stesso* must agree with the subject, two forms (as shown in the table above) are possible for each person, depending on the gender and number of the subject: *Marta loda troppo se stessa* ('Marta brags too much about herself'), *Le madri spesso rimproverano se stesse* ('Mothers often blame themselves').

Constructions with *stesso* are considered stressed pronouns, so unlike their reflexive equivalents, they always follow the verb: *Giovanni considera se stesso il migliore* ('Giovanni considers himself the best').

Such constructions can also combine with prepositions: *Elisa pensa sempre a se stessa* ('Elisa always thinks about herself'), *Non essere arrabbiato con te stesso* ('Do not be upset with yourself').

The phrases *loro stessi* and *loro stesse* are also possible next to *se stessi* and *se stesse*, even if less common: *Non pensano che a loro stessi* [= *se stessi*] ('They think just about themselves').

13.16 Reciprocal Pronouns: ci, vi, si, *etc.*

Reciprocal pronouns are used with reciprocal verbs (see 23.5) and are equivalent to the English 'each other': *abbracciarsi* ('to embrace each other'), *rispettarsi* ('to respect each other'), and so on. They are identical in form to the reflexive pronouns (see 13.13) and follow the same rules. By definition, a reciprocal action involves a plural subject: *Ci amiamo* ('We love each other'), *Vi incontrate questa sera* ('You will meet each other tonight').

Italian can also indicate reciprocity with the phrase *l'un l'altro, l'un l'altra* and the plural *gli uni e gli altri, le une e le altre* (all equivalent to 'each other' and 'one another'), which can replace or be added to the reciprocal pronouns for more emphasis: *Confortano l'un l'altro* is equivalent to *Si confortano l'un l'altro* ('They comfort each other').

The adverbs **reciprocamente** and **a vicenda** (both meaning 'reciprocally') can also be added for redundancy (*Aiutatevi reciprocamente* 'Help each other'), but they are especially used when a reciprocal or reflexive meaning is ambiguous. For example, a sentence such as *Si ammirano* could have a reflexive meaning ('They admire themselves') or a reciprocal one ('They admire each other'); to avoid confusion while stressing the reciprocal meaning, one of the adverbs mentioned above would be used in Italian: *Si ammirano l'un l'altro* or *Si ammirano a vicenda* ('They admire each other').

> **N.B.** The only case where a reciprocal act involves a singular subject is when this subject implies a plurality as it happens in Italian with the singular words *famiglia* ('family') and *gente* ('people'): *La famiglia si riunisce la prossima domenica* ('The family is getting together next Sunday'), *La gente si insulta per strada* ('People are insulting each other on the street').

14. THE PARTICLES *CI* AND *NE*

> **Particles**: Particles are uninflected function words that do not easily fit into the established system of parts of speech. The Italian particles *ci* ('there', 'about it', 'of it') and *ne* ('some', 'of it', 'of them') function as unstressed pronouns. However, *ci* and *ne* have other special uses that are specific to the Italian language, and therefore make literal translation impossible.

14.1 The Particle ci

Ci as an unstressed (direct, indirect, reflexive, or reciprocal) pronoun corresponding to the first person plural (*Marco ci chiama* 'Marco is calling us', *Anna ci parla* 'Anna is talking to us', *Noi ci salutiamo* 'We greet each other') was discussed in the chapter on personal pronouns (see chapter 13). However, other uses of *ci* merit discussion and will be detailed in this section. Such cases may lead to *ci* changing positions inside the sentence, but always according to the rules governing the position of unstressed pronouns within the sentence (see 13.6, 13.9). Therefore, *ci* can:

- be used as an **adverb of location, replacing a noun indicating position or direction to**. In this case *ci* is equivalent to the English 'here' or 'there'. The following examples can clarify this particular use of *ci*: *Vivo in Italia* > *Ci vivo* ('I live here/there'), where *ci* replaces *in Italia*; *Vado al cinema* > *Ci vado* ('I am going there'), where *ci* substitutes for *al cinema*; *Lui non è in casa* > *Lui non c'è* ('He is not here/there'), where *ci* replaces *in casa*;
- have a locative meaning when **it replaces the preposition *da* followed by names** (*da Mario, da Giovanni*)**, or professional nouns** (*dal dottore* 'to the doctor's', *dall'avvocato* 'to the lawyer's'). With names *ci* means 'at/to somebody's place' (generally 'home' or 'restaurant', if the name is a restaurant's name), while with professional nouns it means 'at/to the office of'. The following examples can clarify this particular use of *ci*: *Andiamo da Giovanni* > *Ci andiamo* ('Let's go to Giovanni's place'), where *ci* replaces *da Giovanni*; *Sono andato dal dottore* > *Ci sono andato* ('I went there'), where *ci* stands for *dal dottore*;
- **replace a word or phrase introduced by the prepositions *a*, *con*, *in*, *su***. The following examples can clarify this particular use of *ci*: *Penso a Marco* > *Ci penso* ('I am thinking about him'), where *ci* replaces *a Marco*; *Sto bene con voi* > *Ci sto bene* ('I feel good with you'), where *ci* replaces *con voi*; *Credo in Dio* > *Ci credo* ('I believe in God'), where *ci* replaces *in Dio*; *Conto sull'amicizia* > *Ci conto* ('I rely on friendship'), where *ci* replace *sull'amicizia*;

- **replace infinitive phrases that start with the preposition *a***: *Vado a studiare > Ci vado* ('I am going to study') where *ci* replaces *a studiare*; *Pensi sempre a mangiare > Ci pensi sempre* ('You're always thinking about eating'), where *ci* replaces *a mangiare*;
- be used in everyday speech, often **with the verb *avere***, to add emphasis to sentences: *Ci ho fame* ('I am hungry'), *Ci abbiamo fatto le cinque del pomeriggio* ('We waited till 5 o'clock in the afternoon'). Even if in these cases *ci* is usually pronounced as *c'*, especially in front of *h*, it is important to keep in mind that this particular elision must be avoided in written Italian (see 1.12);
- be used **with reflexive or reciprocal verbs to make impersonal constructions** with the third person singular form of the verb: *Quando piove ci si bagna* ('When it rains one gets wet'), *Lavorando troppo, ci si stanca* ('Working too much, makes one tired').

14.2 The Locative ci in Combination with Direct Object Pronouns: mi ci, ce lo, *etc.*

The locative *ci* can combine with all unstressed direct object pronouns (see 13.6) except the first person plural *ci* (to avoid the repetitive combination *ci ci*). Note that *ci* always follows *mi, ti, vi* but precedes the pronouns *lo, la, li,* and *le*, changing into *ce*. The table below lists all the possible combinations with a sample of their use:

Ci + direct obj. pron.	Examples
mi ci	*So che vai a scuola; mi ci accompagni?* ('I know you're going to school; can you take me there?')
ti ci	*È tardi, non ti ci posso portare* ('It's late; I can't take you there')
ce lo/ce l'	*Tuo figlio vuole andare al cinema; portacelo* ('Your son wants to go to the movies; take him there')
ce la/ce l'	*Carla va a scuola in auto ogni mattina; ce l'accompagna suo padre* ('Carla goes to school by car every morning; her father takes her there')
vi ci	*Se volete andare al parco vi ci accompagno io* ('If you want to go to the park, I will take you there')
ce li	*Gli studenti non sanno dove è la biblioteca; portaceli tu* ('The students don't know where the library is; take them there')
ce le	*Alle nostre figlie piace Disneyland; quest'anno ce le portiamo* ('Our daughters like Disneyland; this year we are taking them there')

- The **combined forms generally precede the conjugated verb** (*Ti ci accompagno domani* 'I will take you there tomorrow') but always attach to the infinitive verb. In this case the verb always drops its final *-e*, and the construction is written as a single word: *Portarmici è stato un errore* ('It was a mistake to take me there'). If the infinitive follows the verbs *potere* ('can'), *dovere* ('must'), or *volere* ('to want'), the combined form may either attach to the infinitive (*È una buona scuola. Posso/Devo/Voglio mandarcelo* 'It is a good school. I can/must/want to send him there') or precede the entire verb phrase (*È una buona scuola. Ce* *lo posso/devo/voglio mandare* 'It is a good school. I can/must/want to send him there'). Similarly, the combined forms always attach to the verb even if the verb is an imperative (*Portamici*, 'Take me there'), a gerund (*Conducendoceli, fai la cosa giusta* 'Your accompanying them there is the right thing to do'), or a past participle (*Portativici, sarete contenti* 'Once taken there, you will be happy').

- When the forms *ce lo, ce la, ce li* or *ce le* are used **with a compound tense using the auxiliary *avere***, the past participle must agree in gender and number with the unstressed pronoun preceding the verb *avere* (see 13.17): *Ce li ho portati io* ('I took them there'), *Lui ce le ha accompagnate con l'auto* ('He took them there by car').
- The rare combination **ce La**, and the equivalent plurals **ce Li** and **ce Le** can be used to express respectively the formal singular and plural 'you' (*Vada senza paura; ce La conduce il mio assistente* 'Go without fear; my assistant will escort you there').

> **N.B.** In the verb *farcela* (deriving from *fare* + *ce la*), the combination of *ce* and *la* does not have a locative value but the idiomatic meanings 'to succeed', 'to overcome', or 'to manage' (see 23.9): *Ce l'abbiamo fatta, l'esame è passato* ('We succeeded; the exam is over'), *Non ce la faccio più* ('I can't manage it anymore').

14.3 Ci *and the Verb* essere: c'è, ci sono, *etc.*

The particle of place *ci* frequently combines with the verb *essere* ('to be') to form the verb **esserci** from which come the expressions *c'è* ('there is'), *ci sono* ('there are'), *c'era* ('there was'), and so on, meaning 'to be in a place' or 'to be there'. Additionally, *esserci* expresses a variety of nuances and can be used for the following purposes:

- to say that someone understood something: *Ci sono, finalmente!* ('I got it, finally!');
- to indicate the arrival of someone: *Ci siamo, siamo appena arrivati* ('Here we are; we have just arrived');
- to let someone know one is ready: *Ci sono, andiamo* ('I am ready; let's go');
- to begin a story: *C'era una volta ...* ('Once upon a time ...');
- to excuse or justify oneself when combining *esserci* with the expressions *niente di male* ('nothing bad') and *niente di sbagliato* ('nothing wrong'): *Non c'è niente di male a parlare tanto* ('There's nothing wrong with talking a lot');
- to indicate that nothing has changed: *Ci siamo di nuovo* ('Here we go again').

14.4 Ci *in Idiomatic Expressions:* non ci casco, non c'entro, *etc.*

The particle *ci* often combines with verbs to give them an idiomatic connotation (see also 23.7). Such idiomatic constructions are extremely common in Italian, but they can be really hard for English speakers to understand because they may completely differ in meaning from the source verbs. For this reason, the following table indicating the most significant verbs of this kind with a sample of their use should be useful for the English speaking learners:

Verbs	Examples
arrivarci ('to understand')	*Non ci arrivo* ('I do not understand')
cascarci ('to fall for a joke')	*Ci sono cascati* ('They fell for it')
entrarci ('to have something to do with')	*Io non c'entro* ('I don't have anything to do with it')
metterci ('to take a certain amount of time')	*Ci metto un giorno a finire questo lavoro* ('It takes me one day to finish this job')
scommetterci ('to bet')	*Ci scommettiamo?* ('Do you want to bet?')
sentirci ('to be able to hear')	*Non ci sentirò bene* ('I will not be able to hear well')
starci ('to agree')	*Ci stai?* ('Do you agree?')
vederci ('to be able to see')	*Ci vediamo bene* ('We are able to see well')
volerci ('to be necessary', 'to take a certain amount of time')	*Ci vuole una penna per scrivere una lettera* ('A pen is necessary to write a letter'); *Ci vuole un'ora ad arrivare a Milano* ('It takes one hour to get to Milan')

14.5 Vi *Equivalent to* ci

As already discussed (see chapter 13), **vi** can function as an unstressed direct, indirect, reflexive, or reciprocal pronoun for the second person plural *voi* ('you'), but it can also substitute for the particle *ci* to indicate a place: *V'è molta gente qui intorno* ('There are many people around here'), *Vorrei andarvi* ('I'd like to go there'). The difference between the locative *ci* and *vi* is not in their meaning but in their use. *Ci* is much more frequent than *vi*, which occurs only in very formal and sophisticated contexts: *Quando siamo arrivati all'hotel, non v'era nessuno ad attenderci* ('When we arrived at the hotel, no one was there to wait for us').

14.6 The Particle ne

Ne is an invariable particle, which like *ci*, can be used in different ways. In terms of position, *ne*, like any unstressed pronouns (see 13.5), occurs directly before a conjugated verb, or attaches to the end of infinitive, imperative, past participle, and gerund forms.

In term of agreement, when *ne* is used with a compound tense using the auxiliary *avere*, the past participle agrees in gender and number with the noun *ne* is replacing. For example, in *Ho comprato dieci mele e ne ho mangiate tre* ('I bought ten apples and I ate three of them'), the past participle *mangiate* is feminine plural to agree with *ne*, which in this context replaces the feminine plural *mele*.

The pronoun *ne* can mean 'about', 'any', 'some', 'of it', 'of them' and it can have a partitive function as well as replace a locative construction. These particular uses of *ne* are explained in detail below:

- *ne* can stand for a prepositional phrase beginning with *di*. In this case *ne* works as a pronoun and is approximately equivalent to the English **'of it'**. The following examples can clarify this particular use of *ne*: *Prendo una fetta di torta* > *Ne prendo una fetta* ('I'll have a slice of it'), where *ne* replaces *di torta* ('of the cake'); *Non ho voglia di studiare* > *Non ne ho voglia* ('I don't feel like it'), where *ne* replaces *di studiare* ('to study');

- *ne* meaning 'of it' and 'of them' (omitted at times in English) is also used in Italian to replace nouns in **expressions of quantity** indicated by numbers or adjectives such as *molto, troppo, poco*. An example is the use of *ne* in answers to questions asking about a number ('How many?') or a quantity ('How much?'): *Quanti fratelli hai? – Ne ho quattro* ('How many brothers do you have? – I have four of them'), where *ne*, equivalent to 'of them', replaces *di fratelli* ('of brothers'); *Quanto gelato mangi? – Ne mangio molto* ('How much ice cream do you eat? – I eat a lot of it'), where *ne*, equivalent to 'of it', replaces *di gelato* ('of ice cream');
- *ne* is used with verbs like *parlare* ('to talk'), *chiedere* ('to ask'), *discutere* ('to discuss') to mean **'about it'**: *Parlerò del mio viaggio > Ne parlerò* ('I will talk about it'), where *ne* replaces *del mio viaggio* ('about my trip');
- *ne* simply **adds emphasis** when used in addition to the phrase that it should replace. In a sentence like the above, if the particle *ne* does not replace but occurs with *del mio viaggio* (*Del mio viaggio ne parlerò*), it conveys the speaker's desire to put a special stress on what he or she is saying. This particular use is typical of colloquial language;
- *ne* can also replace a **partitive construction** (see chapter 15). In this case its English equivalent is 'some' or 'any' when placed in a negative sentence: *Vuoi del caffè? – Sì, ne voglio* ('Do you want some coffee? – Yes, I want some'), *Vuoi della frutta? No, non ne voglio* ('Do you want some fruit? – No, I don't want any');
- *ne* has a **locative** function when it refers to a real or figurative location from where someone comes or leaves. In this case *ne* stands for the prepositional phrase *da* + noun and is equivalent to the English 'from here', 'from there'. In *Appena arrivato a scuola, ne sono subito uscito* ('As soon as I arrived in school, I turned right back from there'), the particle *ne* substitutes for *da scuola* ('out of school');
- when *ne* **combines with *ecco*** it must attach to the end of it: *Ho comprato le mele, eccone due* ('I bought some apples; here are two of them').

14.7 Idiomatic Uses of ne

Like the particle *ci*, *ne* often combines with verbs to give them an idiomatic connotation (see also 23.8, 23.11). Even though such idiomatic constructions are quite common in Italian they can be very hard for English speakers to comprehend because they may differ in meaning from the source verbs. In view of this fact, the next paragraphs indicate the most significant verbs of this kind with a sample of their use.

The particle *ne* combines with reflexive pronouns and the verbs *andare* ('to go'), *tornare* ('to come back'), and *stare* ('to stay') to form **andarsene, tornarsene**, and **starsene**, which simply add more emphasis to the context: *Me ne vado subito da qui* ('I am leaving from here right away'), *Dovresti startene tranquillo* ('You should stay calm').

The same construction can be found in the colloquial verbs **uscirsene** ('to come out'), **importarsene** or **fregarsene** ('to care'), and **infischiarsene** ('not to give a damn'): *Se ne è uscito dicendo che lui è il più intelligente* ('He came out saying that he is the most intelligent'), *Me ne importa molto di questo* ('I really care about it'), *Me ne infischio di te* ('I don't give a damn about you').

Ne is also used in the construction ***valerne la pena*** ('to be worth it') and the negative ***non poterne più*** ('to have had enough'): *Lo compro, ne vale la pena* ('I'll buy it; it's worth it'), *Non ne posso più di te* ('I had enough of you'). Another common verb combined with *ne* is ***volerne*** ('to hold it against'): *Non me ne volere* ('Don't hold it against me').

15. Partitives

> **Partitives**: A partitive is a determiner used to indicate an indefinite quantity that is part of a whole (*un po' di acqua* 'some water') or a part of a group of people (*alcuni ragazzi* 'some boys'), animals (*qualche cane* 'some dogs'), or things (*delle mele* 'some apples').

15.1 Partitives in Italian: Like and Unlike English

In Italian, partitives function in almost the same way as in English, with only a few differences. Unlike English, which normally expresses the idea of a partitive with 'some' and 'any', Italian conveys the same idea with various forms. These forms are presented in detail in the next paragraphs.

15.2 The Partitive Article: del, dello, della, *etc.*

The partitive article is formed by the preposition **di + definite article** (see 16.10) and is equivalent to the English 'some' or 'any', and 'a few'.

While in English 'some' is used in affirmative sentences, 'any' in negative ones, and 'some' or 'any' in interrogative sentences, Italian has just one form regardless of the structure of the sentence: *Voglio dell'acqua* ('I want some water'), *Non voglio dell'acqua* ('I don't want any water'), *Vuoi dell'acqua?* ('Do you want some/any water?').

In its **singular forms,** the partitive article occurs with uncountable nouns (nouns denoting substances or abstract concepts that not are discrete or separable into individual countable units) to indicate an unspecified quantity: *Bevo dell'acqua minerale* ('I am drinking some mineral water'), *Dimostri davvero del coraggio* ('You're really showing some courage'); or to indicate a part of the whole, a piece of something: *Mangio del pane* ('I am eating some bread'), *Ho comprato dell'ottimo formaggio* ('I bought some very good cheese').

In its **plural forms**, the partitive article is used with plural countable nouns (nouns that can be pluralized and counted) to indicate an unspecified number or amount: *Ti ho portato delle fragole* ('I brought you some strawberries'), *Gradiresti dei biscotti?* ('Would you like some cookies?'). However, it is also possible to encounter the plural partitives with uncountable nouns such as *acqua* ('water'), *vino* ('wine'), *birra* ('beer'), and so on, where they indicate an unspecified number of 'containers of': *delle acque, dei vini, delle birre*, all implying *delle bottiglie/lattine/caraffe di acqua/vino/birra* ('some bottles/cans/carafes of water/wine/beer').

It is important to keep in mind the **difference in meaning between the use of the singular and plural partitive articles with countable nouns**. Compare these two sentences: *Vuoi della banana?* ('Do you want some of the banana?') and *Vuoi delle banane?* ('Do you want some bananas?'). As in English, *della banana* ('some of the banana') in the first sentence indicates an unspecified quantity of the whole 'banana', while the plural *delle banane* ('some bananas') in the second one indicates an unspecified number of 'bananas'.

A partitive article generally precedes uncountable nouns although they may occur without one. The **non-occurrence of the partitive** creates a subtle difference in meaning. In fact, in such constructions, the emphasis is more on the concept expressed by the noun than on an unspecified quantity of it. For example, in *Mangio pane ogni giorno* ('I eat bread every day') the absence of a partitive stresses the habit of eating bread everyday with no consideration for the quantity; while in *Passami del pane* ('Give me some bread'), the occurrence of the partitive *del* emphasizes that a certain quantity of bread is requested.

15.3 Other Partitive Expressions: un po', qualche, *and* alcuni/alcune

The partitive articles *del, dello, della*, etc. (see 15.2) can always be replaced by the following words or phrases:

- **un po' di** ('a little bit of', 'some', 'a few') can be used in front of singular nouns to indicate an unspecified quantity: *un po' di acqua* ('some water'), *un po' di pane* ('some bread'). It can also be placed in front of the plural to indicate an unspecified number: *un po' di fragole* ('a few strawberries'), *un po' di persone* ('a few persons');
- **qualche** ('some', 'a few') is invariable and is always followed by a singular noun even though its meaning is plural (see also 11.2): *qualche ragazzo* ('some boys'), *qualche ciliegia* ('some cherries'). *Qualche* can only indicate an unspecified number, never an unspecified quantity of something. Consequently, it is generally not used with uncountable nouns such as *acqua* ('water'), *coraggio* ('courage'), and so on because they denote entities such as substances, and abstract concepts, which by definition cannot be counted. When it does occur with such uncountable nouns, it can only imply an unspecified number of 'containers of': *qualche acqua, qualche vino, qualche birra* all implicitly mean *qualche bottiglia/lattina/caraffa di acqua/vino/birra* ('some bottles/cans/carafes of water/wine/beer');
- **alcuni** and **alcune** ('some', 'a few') are equivalent to *qualche* but always followed by a plural noun (see also 11.4). Both can only indicate an unspecified number of something: *alcuni ragazzi* ('some boys'), *alcune ciliege* ('some cherries'). As the examples above show, *alcuni* is used for masculine nouns while *alcune* is used for feminine ones.

16. PREPOSITIONS

> **Prepositions:** Prepositions are words that precede nouns, pronouns, or verbs to specify direction (*vado a scuola* 'I go to school'), time (*studio da 2 ore* 'I have been studying for 2 hours'), possession (*il libro di Carlo* 'Carlo's book'), cause (*Non studiano per molte ragioni* 'They don't study for many reasons'), purpose (*Ho fatto domanda per ottenere questo posto* 'I applied for this position'), means (*Mi piace viaggiare in treno* 'I like to travel by train'), and so on. The most common prepositions in Italian are *a, con, da, di, fra* (or *tra*), *in, per,* and *su*. They do not change their form, regardless of the number and gender of the word they are referring to, except when combined with an article (*della, nel, sui,* etc.).

16.1 The Preposition a

The Italian preposition *a* can mean 'in', 'at', or 'to', depending on the context in which it is used. When *a* is followed by a definite article, the two combine to form one word (see 16.10). The preposition *a* can indicate:

- **the idea of staying or going** somewhere with names of towns, cities, and small islands: *Abito a Roma* ('I live in Rome'), *Questa estate vado a Capri* ('This summer I am going to Capri'). The preposition *a* is always used with words like *scuola* (*a scuola* 'at/in/to school'), *letto* (*a letto* 'in/to bed'), and so on (see 16.3);
- **to whom or what** the action expressed by a verb refers: *Porto un fiore a mia mamma* ('I am bringing a flower to my mother'), *A che cosa attribuisci il tuo successo?* ('To what do you attribute your success?');
- **age** at which one does something: *Ho letto il primo romanzo a dieci anni* ('I read my first novel at the age of ten'), *A diciotto anni si diventa maggiorenni* ('One reaches majority at the age of eighteen');
- **time and months** in which one does something: *Arriverò a mezzogiorno* ('I will arrive at noon'), *Andiamo in vacanza a luglio* ('We will go on vacation in July'). In this last case the preposition *in* (see 16.2) can also be used. The preposition *a* also occurs in time expressions like *a colazione* ('at breakfast time'), *a pranzo* ('at lunch time'), *a cena* ('at dinner time');
- **price** at which one thing is bought or sold: *Ho comprato un cappotto a 100 euro* ('I paid 100 Euros for a coat'), *Le ciliegie vanno a 10 euro al chilo* ('Cherries are 10 euros a kilo'). In these cases the preposition *per* could also be used instead of *a* (see 16.8)
- **games** one plays: *Giocare a tennis, a scacchi, a carte* ('To play tennis, chess, cards');

- **speed**: *La mia moto va a 100 km all'ora* ('My motorcycle goes 100 km/h'), *Per un po' di tempo lui può correre a più di 20 miglia all'ora* ('For a brief amount of time he can run over 20 mph');
- **distance from** someone or something: *Abito a 100 metri da Marco* ('I live 100 meters from Marco'), *Roma è a 28 chilometri dal mare* ('Rome is 28 km from the sea');
- **feature** of something: *una camicia a maniche lunghe* ('a long-sleeved shirt'), *un trapano a batteria* ('a battery-powered drill');
- **manner**: *parlare a alta voce* ('to talk aloud'), *pasta fatta a mano* ('handmade pasta');
- **means** with the two expressions *a piedi* ('on foot'), *a cavallo* ('on horseback');
- **purpose** when it follows expressions of exhortation, invitation, or obligation: *Ti invito a essere puntuale* ('I suggest you be on time').

The preposition *a* is also used **after many verbs** (see 22.3) followed by an infinite form (*Io vado a vedere un film* 'I am going to see a movie', *Cominciamo a studiare* 'Let's start studying') and with some **idiomatic expressions** like *a mano a mano, a poco a poco, a piccoli passi* (all meaning 'little by little'), *a lungo andare* ('in the long run'), *a tempo debito* ('in due course').

> **N.B.** The preposition *a* becomes *ad* before words starting with vowels (*ad Enrico, ad ordinare*, etc.), in particular before an *a* (*ad Angela, ad agosto,* etc.). It is always used with the word *esempio* (*ad esempio* 'for example').

16.2 The Preposition in

The Italian preposition *in* is usually equivalent to the English 'in', but it can also mean 'at', 'to', and 'by', depending on the context in which it is used. When *in* is followed by a definite article, they combine to form one word (see 16.10). The preposition *in* can indicate:

- **the idea of staying or going** somewhere with names of locations bigger than cities: *Abito in Italia* ('I live in Italy'), *Questa estate vado in America* ('This summer I am going to America'). *In* is also used with other locations like *in biblioteca* ('at/in/to the library'), *in banca* ('at/in/to the bank'), and so on (see 16.3);
- **years, months, and seasons** in which one does something or something is done: *Roma è stata fondata nel 753 A.C.* ('Rome was founded in 753 BC'), *Veniamo in settembre* ('We will come in September'), *In inverno fa freddo* ('It is cold in the winter'). The preposition *a* (see 16.1) can also be used with months;
- **amount of time** in which one does something or something is done: *Ho fatto i compiti in 10 minuti* ('I did my homework in 10 minutes'), *Luigi si veste sempre in 5 minuti* ('Luigi always gets dressed in 5 minutes'). *In* is also used with time expressions like *in tempo* or *in orario* ('on time') and *in ritardo* ('late');

- **material** of something: *un tavolo in legno* ('a wooden table'), *un vaso in plastica* ('a plastic vase'). In this case the preposition *di* (see 16.5) is more common;
- **means** like *in treno* ('by train'), *in auto* ('by car'), *in autobus* ('by bus'), *in aereo* ('by airplane'), and so on. The preposition *con*, followed by an article, can be used in these cases instead of *in* (see 16.7):
- **quantity or number of persons**: *Oggi siamo in tre* ('Today, we are three'), *In famiglia siamo in sei* ('We are six in the family');
- **field in which one is specialized, or is good, bad at**: *Sono un esperto in informatica* ('I am an expert in computer science'), *Sei bravo in matematica* ('You are good at math').

The preposition *in* is also used in **particular expressions** such as *in verità* ('as a matter of fact'), *in coscienza* ('in all conscience'), *in fede* ('faithfully').

16.3 A Difficult Choice: in *or* a*?*
As explained above, the prepositions *in* and *a*, and their combined forms with definite articles (*nel, alla, negli*, etc.) are both used as **locators of place**. If at times the context clearly indicates which of the two is the more appropriate, at other times the choice is not as definite, which makes selecting the right preposition troublesome for non-native speakers. It is, therefore, useful to repeat some general rules and list some particularities or exceptions:

- *a* is used before names of towns, cities, small islands, but also against the rule with some states (*a Cuba, a San Marino*) and it is preferably used with *casa* ('home'), *scuola* ('school'), *letto* ('bed'), *tavola* ('table'), *teatro* ('theater');
- *a* + **article** (*allo, alla, all'*, etc.) is always used before *cinema, mercato* ('market'), *museo* ('museum'), *ristorante* ('restaurant'), *stadio* ('stadium'), *supermercato* ('supermarket'); it can also be used instead of *in* with *aeroporto* ('airport'), *bagno* ('bathroom'), *stazione* ('station');
- *in* is used with names of location bigger than cities and big islands, with *piazza* ('square'), *via* ('street'), *chiesa* ('church'), *aeroporto* ('airport'), *banca* ('bank'), *ufficio* ('office'), *piscina* ('swimming pool'), *cucina* ('kitchen'), *camera* ('bedroom'), *bagno* ('bathroom'), *salotto* ('living room'), *centro* ('downtown'), *periferia* ('suburbs'), *montagna* ('mountain'); it is also used with all words ending in *-teca*, like *biblioteca* ('library'), and all words ending in *-ria*, like *pizzeria*.

> **N.B.** When a location is modified by an adjective (*biblioteca pubblica* 'public library') or by a prepositional phrase (*biblioteca della scuola* 'school library'), the articulated prepositions *al, allo, nel, nello, nell'*, etc. must always be used instead of the simple *a* or *in*. Note the difference between *Studio in biblioteca* ('I study at the library') and *Studio nella biblioteca pubblica* ('I study at the public library') or the difference between *Vado a teatro* ('I am going to the theatre') and *Vado al teatro della scuola* ('I am going to the school theatre').

16.4 The Preposition da

The Italian preposition **da** can be equivalent to the English 'from', 'to', 'at', or 'by' and can have a special meaning depending on the context in which it is used. When *da* is followed by a definite article, it combines with it to form one word (see 16.10). The preposition *da* can express:

- **motion from** with names of towns, cities, small islands (*Partiamo da Firenze* 'We are departing from Florence') and names of squares, streets, avenues (*Vengo da Piazza Tasso*, 'I am coming from Piazza Tasso'). With the words *scuola* ('school') and *casa* ('home'), the simple preposition *da* is used as in the cases above; with all other locations, *da* combines with the appropriate article to form an articulated preposition: *Vengo dall'aeroporto* ('I am coming from the airport'), *Loro arrivano dagli Stati Uniti* ('They are arriving from the USA');
- **distance from**: *La mia scuola è a 5 km da casa* ('My school is 5 km from home'), *Marco abita lontano da qui* ('Marco lives far from here');
- **idea of staying or going** somewhere when used with proper names (*Sono da Franco* 'I am at Franco's', *Vado da Maria* 'I am going to Maria's'), names denoting family members (*Mangio dai nonni* 'I am eating at my grandparents', *Faccio un salto da mamma* 'I am stopping at Mom's'), and names of professions (*Sono dal dottore* 'I am at the doctor's', *Vado dal panettiere* 'I am going to the baker's');
- **past time** when used before nouns or adjectives describing stages of life with the verb usually in the imperfect tense: *Da bambino ero molto buono* ('I was really good when I was a kid'), *Da piccoli si giocava sempre* ('When we were young kids, we used to play a lot');
- **duration in time of something started in the past**. In this case the English equivalent of *da* can be 'since' (*Suono il piano da quando avevo cinque anni* 'I have been playing the piano since I was five') or 'for' (*Studio da due ore* 'I have been studying for two hours');
- **specific purpose** of something: *abito da sera* ('black tie'), *camera da letto* ('bedroom'), *scarpe da corsa* ('running shoes');
- **obligation or necessity** to do something. This is expressed by the use of *da* before the infinitive form of a verb: *La bolletta è da pagare* ('The bill must be paid'), *Ho molto da leggere* ('I have a lot to read');
- **consequence** of something. This is the case when *da* is used in combination with *così*, *talmente*, *troppo*, or *tanto*, all equivalent to the English 'so' and 'too': *È così caro da venire a trovarci!* ('He is so nice as to come to visit us!'), *È talmente intelligente da avere tutti voti alti* ('She is so intelligent as to get only good grades'), *È troppo difficile da fare* ('It is too difficult to do');
- **physical or moral characteristics**: *una bambina dagli occhi verdi* ('a green-eyed girl'), *un ragazzo dal buon carattere* ('a boy of good character'), *una voce da bambino* ('a child's voice'). The use of *da* translated in English by 'as' or 'like' can be considered part of this category: *comportarsi da maleducato* ('to behave like a rude person'), *vestirsi da Pinocchio* ('to dress up as a Pinocchio');
- **value** of something: *un vestito da 1000 euro* ('a 1000 euro dress'), *una cosa da poco* ('a thing of little value or meaning');

- **agent** of an action: *una composizione scritta da uno studente* ('a composition written by a student'), *un dolce fatto dalla mamma* ('a cake made by Mom').

The preposition *da* is also used **after many verbs** (see 22.5) followed by a noun (*Ha divorziato dal marito,* 'She is divorced from her husband'), a pronoun (*Dipende da te,* 'It depends on you'), and with expressions such as *d'altra parte* ('on the other hand'), *d'altro canto* ('but then'), *da vicino* ('closely'), *da lontano* ('from a distance'), *fin da ora* ('from now on').

16.5 The Preposition di

The Italian preposition **di** is the most versatile one and has several different meanings depending on the context in which it is used. However, it is not difficult for English speakers to use correctly. In fact, *di* expresses most often the **genitive case**, formed in English by adding the clitic 's ('John's') to the word or inserting 'of' before it ('of mine'). When *di* is followed by a noun starting with a vowel, it usually drops the vowel *i* and takes an apostrophe (*d'argento*); when followed by a definite article, it combines with it to form one word (see 16.10). The preposition *di* can express:

- **possession**: *il libro di Mario* ('Mario's book'), *la casa di mia zia* ('my aunt's house'), *le ruote della bicicletta* ('the bicycle wheels');
- **relationships**: *la sorella di Carlo* ('Carlo's sister'), *gli amici di Maria* ('Maria's friends');
- **material**: *un anello d'oro* ('a gold ring'), *un tavolo di legno* ('a wood table');
- **author** of something: *"La Vita è bella" è un film di Benigni* ('*Life Is Beautiful* is a film by Benigni'), *"Io non ho paura" è un libro di Niccolò Ammaniti* ('*I'm Not Scared* is a book by Niccolò Ammaniti');
- **characteristics**: *un uomo di alta statura* ('a tall man'), *un quadro di valore* ('a valuable painting');
- **elements of something**: *un chilo di patate* ('a kilo of potatoes'), *un gruppo di amici* ('a group of friends');
- **times of the day**: *Esco di casa di pomeriggio* ('I leave home in the afternoon'), *Di notte non studio mai!* ('I never study at night'). In these cases *di* can be easily replaced by the definite article: *Esco di casa il* [= *di*] *pomeriggio*; *La* [= *Di*] *notte non studio mai!* The preposition *di* is also used in expressions like *le due di notte* ('two o'clock at night'), *alle tre di domani* ('at three o'clock tomorrow'), and so on;
- **second element of a comparison** (see also 6.4 and 6.6): *Maria è più buona di te* ('Maria is nicer than you'), *Matteo è il migliore di voi tutti* ('Matteo is the best of all of you');
- **means involving substances**: *Riempi la pentola d'acqua* ('Fill the pot with water'), *Dipingiamo la stanza di colore rosso* ('Let's paint the room red'); though means is more commonly expressed in Italian with the preposition *con* (see 16.7), it is possible to use *di* when using nouns denoting substance or material as in the two examples above;

- **cause:** *Luigi è morto d'infarto* ('Luigi died of an heart attack'), *Tu impazzisci di gioia* ('You leap with joy'); though means is more commonly expressed in Italian with the preposition *per* (see 16.8), it is possible to use *di* in the same context;
- **age** (see also 12.7): *Ho un figlio di due anni* ('I have a two-year old son'), *È un'auto di un anno!* ('It is a one-year old car');
- **topic:** *Parliamo di calcio* ('Let's talk about soccer'), *È un libro di matematica!* ('It is a math book');
- **origin** when part of the Italian construction **essere + di + the name of a city or a town:** *Maria è di Palermo* ('Maria is from Palermo'), *Noi siamo di Sangimignano* ('We are from Sangimignano').

The preposition *di* can come **after many verbs** (see 22.4) followed by an infinitive form (*Mi sono dimenticato di andare* 'I forgot to go', *Prometto di studiare* 'I promise to study'), a noun (*Sono innamorato di Maria* 'I am in love with Maria'), or a pronoun (*Mi fido di te* 'I trust you'). Furthermore, *di* can be found in **some special expressions** such as *per merito di* ('thanks to'), *per colpa di* ('because of'), *a causa di* ('due to').

16.6 The Prepositions fra *and* tra

Fra and ***tra*** are two interchangeable Italian prepositions, the use of which depends mostly on one's preference. As with most Italian prepositions, their meaning varies with the context in which they are used. For this reason it is worthwhile to take a closer look at them. *Fra* and *tra* can express:

- **future time:** *Parto fra una settimana* ('I am leaving in a week'), *Tra cinque minuti finisco* ('I will be done in five minutes'). As can be seen from the above examples *fra* and *tra* are equivalent in this case to the English 'in';
- **location:** *Roma è fra Firenze e Napoli* ('Rome lies between Florence and Naples'), *Mi siedo tra voi due* ('I will sit between you two'). In this case *fra* and *tra* are equivalent of the English 'between';
- **relationships:** *Qui siamo fra amici* ('We are among friends here'), *Tra zio Giorgio e zia Anna c'è grande stima* ('There is great esteem between uncle Giorgio and aunt Anna'). As can be concluded from the above examples, Italian uses *fra* or *tra* indistinctly, regardless of the number of people or things involved whereas English prefers using 'between' for two things or people and 'among' when more than two things or people are involved. *Tra* and *fra* can combine with personal pronouns (*me, te, lui*, etc.) with or without the preposition *di* occurring between them: *Fra [di] noi c'è grande amicizia* ('There is great friendship between us');
- **comparison** (see also 6.6) with a group of people or objects: *Mario è il migliore fra tutti voi* ('Mario is the best among all of you'), *Questo film è fra i peggiori che abbia mai visto* ('This film is one of the worst I have ever seen').

16.7 The Preposition con

The Italian preposition **con** is equivalent to the English 'with', but it can also have special meanings depending on the context. *Con* can express:

- **accompaniment or union** between people or objects: *Vieni con me* ('Come with me'), *Il gelato è buono con le fragole* ('Ice cream is good with strawberries');
- **means**: *Scrivo con una penna* ('I am writing with a pen'). This case also includes means of transportation; in fact, *con*, followed by an article, can be used in Italian instead of *in* (see 16.2): *Vado a Napoli con il* [= *in*] *treno* ('I am going to Naples by train'), *Lui è partito con l'* [= *in*] *autobus* ('He left by bus');
- **manner**: *Faccio questo con tutto il mio amore* ('I am doing this with all my heart'), *Ti vedrò con molto piacere* ('It will be a great pleasure to see you');
- **characteristics**: *È quello con la barba* ('He is the one with the beard'), *Lei indossa scarpe con tacchi alti* ('She is wearing shoes with high heels');
- **seasons and months**: *Con la primavera fioriscono i fiori* ('Flowers bloom in the spring'), *Con novembre arriva il freddo* ('With November comes the cold');
- **cause**: *Con il tuo brutto carattere non otterrai niente* ('You'll never get anywhere with that bad character'), *Con questo traffico arriveremo in ritardo* ('We will get there late with such traffic'). In this case *con* is equivalent to the English 'with' meaning 'because of' or 'due to'.
- **manner**: *Non si chiede attenzione con l'urlare* ('One does not draw attention by yelling'). The construction *con* + article + infinitive is equivalent to the English 'by + -ing' (see also 22.5).

16.8 The Preposition per

The Italian preposition **per** is generally equivalent to the English 'for', but it can also be translated as 'to', 'in order to', 'by', or 'as' depending on the context. *Per* can express:

- **motion through**: *Cammina per il bosco* ('He is walking through the woods'), *Le volpi corrono per i campi* ('Foxes are running across the fields'). In this case the preposition *per* is used with verbs of motion and is equivalent to the English 'through' or 'across';
- **location in or at** to express the idea of being in or staying on the street or on the ground: *Sono per strada* ('I am in the street'), *Il bambino è per terra* ('The child is on the floor');
- **direction to**: *Oggi parto per Firenze* ('I am leaving for Florence today'), *Il treno per Milano è in partenza* ('The train for Milan is departing');
- **duration in time:** *Bocelli ha cantato per tre ore* ('Bocelli sang for three hours'), *Oggi sarò disponibile per quattro ore* ('Today I will be available for four hours'). As in English the preposition *per* can easily be omitted in these cases: *Ho aspettato [per] tre giorni* ('I waited three days');
- **recipient of an action** indicating for 'whom' or 'what' the action is done: *Faccio questo per mia mamma* ('I am doing this for my mother'), *Lo compro per il nostro appartamento* ('I am buying it for our apartment');

- **purpose**: *Sono qui per il lavoro* ('I am here for the job'), *Sono venuto per l'esame* ('I came for the exam'). Purpose can be indicated in Italian by the structure *per* + noun (as the above examples show), or *per* + infinitive, in which case *per* is equivalent to the English preposition 'to' or the expression 'in order to': *Studio per avere buoni voti* ('I study to get good grades'), *Ascoltiamo la musica per rilassarci* ('We listen to music in order to relax');
- **cause**: *Non ho studiato per la stanchezza* ('I have not studied due to tiredness'), *Per la neve le strade sono chiuse* ('The streets are closed due to the snow'). In this case *per* corresponds to 'for' meaning 'because of' or 'due to';
- **means**: *Spedisco il pacco per posta* ('I am sending the package by mail'), *Rimaniamo in contatto per telefono* ('Let's keep in touch by phone');
- **price** when indicating the price of something bought or sold: *Ho comprato un cappotto per 100 euro* ('I paid 100 euros for a coat'), *Questa auto è in vendita per 3000 dollari* ('This car is on sale for 3,000 dollars'). In these cases *a* could be used instead of *per* (see 16.1);
- **exchange**: *L'ho scambiato per Marco* ('I mistook him for Marco'). In this case *per* corresponds to the English 'for', meaning 'instead of';
- **opinion**: *Per me va bene* ('For me it is fine'), *Se per lui è giusto, io sono d'accordo* ('If it is all right with him, I agree');
- **exclamations**: *Per l'amor di Dio!* ('For the love of God!'), *Per la miseria!* ('Holy smoke!').

16.9 The Preposition su

The Italian preposition ***su*** is generally equivalent to the English 'on', 'over', but it can be translated as 'in', 'about', or 'around' depending on the context. When *su* is followed by a definite article, it combines with it to form one word (see 6.10). The preposition *su* can express:

- **place on or over**: *I libri sono sul banco* ('The books are on the desk'), *L'aereo vola su Roma* ('The plane is flying over Rome');
- **topic**: *È un programma sulla musica rock* ('It is a program about rock music'), *Su che cosa vuoi discutere?* ('What topic do you want to talk about?'). In this case *su* can replace the more common *di* (see 16.5);
- **approximate age**: *Marco è sui venti anni* ('Marco is about twenty years old'), *Sui cinquanta si comincia ad avere qualche acciacco* ('Around fifty we start having aches and pains');
- **approximate price**: *Il prezzo è sui venti euro* ('The price is around twenty euros'), *Ho pagato sui mille euro* ('I paid around a thousand euros');
- **approximate measure**: *Lui è alto sul metro e mezzo* ('He is about one and a half meters tall'), *Questa bistecca è sul chilo* ('This steak weighs about a kilo').

16.10 Articulated Prepositions and Their Uses: del, alla, negli, *etc.*

In Italian, when an article is required after the prepositions *a, da, di, in,* and *su*, it combines with the prepositions to form one word. For example, instead of saying *a il ristorante*, or *da la strada* one says *al ristorante* ('to the restaurant') or *dalla strada* ('from the street').

Nouns that take simple prepositions when standing alone usually take an articulated preposition when modified. Note the difference between *Vengo da scuola* ('I come from school') and *Vengo dalla scuola media* ('I come from middle school'), or *Sono in biblioteca* ('I am in the library') and *Sono nella biblioteca del College* ('I am in the College library').

These prepositions take the forms listed below. Note that when combined with an article, *di* becomes **de-** and *in* becomes **ne-**:

Prepositions	Articles						
	il	lo	l'	la	i	gli	le
a	al	allo	all'	alla	ai	agli	alle
da	dal	dallo	dall'	dalla	dai	dagli	dalle
di	del	dello	dell'	della	dei	degli	delle
in	nel	nello	nell'	nella	nei	negli	nelle
su	sul	sullo	sull'	sulla	sui	sugli	sulle

The preposition **con** may sometimes form one word with the article (*col, collo, coll', colla, coi, cogli, colle*), but this usage is becoming rare in contemporary Italian. All the other prepositions (*fra/tra, per*) remain detached (*per il, fra i, tra le,* etc.).

The preposition **in**, when indicating 'movement to/at' and preceding a modified noun, is **replaced by the articulated preposition formed with *a***. Note the difference between *Vado in ufficio* ('I am going to the office') and *Vado all'ufficio postale* ('I am going to the Post Office'), or between *Siamo andati in banca* ('We went to the bank') and *Siamo andati alla Banca dei Paschi* ('We went to the Paschi Bank').

Articulated prepositions formed by **di + article** also express a **partitive meaning** (see 15.2) indicated in English by 'some': *Ho comprato del latte* ('I bought some milk'), *Mi passi del pane?* ('Can you pass me some bread?').

16.11 Other Prepositions: dopo, eccetto, fuori, *etc.*

In Italian some adverbs, adjectives, past participles, and special phrases can function as prepositions. Below is a list of the most common with examples of their use:

Prepositional phrases	Examples
a causa di ('because of')	*Siamo in ritardo a causa del traffico* ('We are late because of traffic')
a differenza di ('unlike')	*A differenza di voi non sono stanco* ('Unlike you I am not tired')
a nome di ('on behalf of')	*A nome di tutti faccio un annuncio* ('I am making an announcement on behalf of everybody')
accanto a ('next to')	*Vieni accanto a me* ('Come next to me')
eccetto (or *ad eccezione di*) ('except', 'with the exception of')	*Eccetto Marco tutti erano là* ('Except for Marco, everybody was there')
al di là di ('beyond')	*Al di là del muro c'è il giardino* ('Beyond the wall there is the garden')
al di sotto di ('beneath')	*Al di sotto della strada corre la metropolitana* ('The subway runs beneath the street')
all'interno di ('within')	*Venga all'interno del negozio* ('Come within the store')

attraverso ('across')	*Viaggio attraverso l'Europa* ('I am traveling across Europe')
contro ('against')	*Non essere sempre contro tutti!* ('Don't always go against everybody!')
davanti a ('in front of')	*Non stare davanti a me, non vedo niente* ('Do not stay in front of me, I can't see anything')
dentro ('inside')	*Vieni dentro* ('Come inside')
di fronte a ('in front of')	*La scuola si trova di fronte al teatro* ('The school is in front of the theater')
dietro a ('behind')	*Il ragazzo corre dietro al suo cane* ('The boy is running behind his dog')
dopo ('after')	*Ho finito i compiti dopo cena* ('I finished my homework after dinner')
durante ('during')	*Non ho dormito durante tutto il viaggio* ('I did not sleep during the whole trip')
entro ('within')	*Sarò là entro due ore* ('I will be there within two hours')
fino a ('up to', 'until')	*Dormirò fino a mezzogiorno* ('I will sleep until noon')
fuori ('outside')	*Venite fuori* ('Come outside')
giù ('down')	*Marco è giù in cantina* ('Marco is down in the basement')
intorno a ('around')	*Lui ha viaggiato intorno al mondo* ('He traveled around the world')
invece di ('instead of')	*Invece di questo libro, prendi quel CD* ('Instead of this book, take that CD')
lontano da ('far from')	*Vivono lontano dal parco* ('They live far from the park')
nei pressi di (or *presso*) ('close to', 'near', 'nearby')	*C'è un buon ristorante nei pressi della stazione* ('There is a good restaurant near the station')
nonostante ('despite', 'in spite of')	*Nonostante il freddo, siamo uscite* ('We went out in spite of the cold')
prima di ('before')	*Prima di cena, ho fatto una passeggiata* ('I took a walk before dinner')
riguardo a ('concerning')	*Riguardo al viaggio, ti invierò le informazioni* ('I will send you information concerning the trip')
secondo ('in someone's opinion')	*Secondo me siete fortunati* ('In my opinion, you are lucky')
senza [di] ('without')	*Non voglio andare senza [= di] te* ('I don't want to go without you')
sotto a ('under')	*Il gatto è sotto al tavolo* ('The cat is under the table')
tramite ('through')	*Ho preso i biglietti tramite un'agenzia* ('I got the tickets through an agency')
verso ('toward')	*Vieni verso me* ('Come toward me')
vicino a ('near', 'close to')	*Vivono vicino al cinema* ('They live near the movie theater')

17. CONNECTIVES: CONJUNCTIONS AND CONJUNCTIVE PHRASES

> **Connectives**: A connective is a word or a phrase that connects words, phrases, or clauses together. Coordinating connectives such as *e* ('and') and *ma* ('but') are used to join two grammatically similar constructions, words, phrases, or clauses: *Marco e Giovanni* ('Marco and Giovanni'), *Verrò con voi, ma non mangerò* ('I will come with you, but I won't eat'). Subordinating connectives such as *quando* ('when') and *perché* ('because') instead connect dependent clauses to main clauses, providing information about time, place, cause, and so on: *Non ero in casa quando sei arrivato* ('I was not home when you arrived'), *Mangio perché ho fame* ('I am eating because I am hungry').

17.1 Copulative Connectives: e, anche, inoltre, *etc.*

The copulative connectives are coordinating conjunctions or phrases used to denote addition:

- ***e*** ('and') is the most common conjunction and, as in English, can join elements of any kind: *tu e lei* ('you and her'), *È arrivato e ha mangiato* ('He arrived and he ate'). The variant form ***ed*** may sometimes be used before a word starting with a vowel, especially in front of forms of *essere* ('to be'): *tu ed io* ('you and I'), *Non lavora ed è sempre stanco* ('He does not work and he is always tired'). Like the English 'and', the conjunction *e* can combine with other prepositions such as *anche* (*e anche* 'and also'), *allora* (*e allora* 'and so'), and so on;
- ***anche*** and ***pure*** are equivalent and mean 'too', 'also': *Vengo anche/pure io* ('I am coming too'), *Voglio anche/pure qualcosa da bere* ('I want something to drink also'). Although the two conjunctions are interchangeable, *anche* is more frequent in contemporary Italian;
- ***inoltre*, *in più*, *fra l'altro*, *per di più***, all meaning 'moreover', can be used at the beginning of a clause. In this case, as in English, they should be separated from the rest of the sentence by a comma: *Inoltre/In più/Fra l'altro/Per di più, non so che cosa dire* ('Moreover, I do not know what to say');
- ***né*** ('nor') is the equivalent of ***e non*** ('and not') and can only be used in negative sentences: *Marco non studia, né lavora* ('Marco does not work, nor does he study'). Italian can use *né* where English would usually use the conjunction 'or', especially if *né* introduces the second of two conjoined elements, the first of which begins with *senza* ('without'): *Sono infelice, senza parenti, né amici* ('I am sad, without relatives or friends');

- **neppure**, **neanche**, and **nemmeno** are all interchangeable and equivalent to the English 'not even'; they can only be used in negative contexts: *È arrivato e neppure/neanche/nemmeno ha salutato* ('He arrived and he did not even say hello').

17.2 Disjunctive Connectives: o *and* oppure

Disjunctive connectives join two parts of speech that exclude one another. The conjunctions **o** and **oppure** are perfectly interchangeable and can simply be considered equivalent to the English 'or': *Vuoi un gelato o/oppure una pizza?* ('Do you want ice cream or pizza?').

17.3 Adversative Connectives: ma, però, invece, *etc.*

These are coordinating conjunctions used to express contrast:

- **ma** ('but') is by far the most common adversative conjunction in Italian: *Non voglio questo, ma quello* ('I do not want this one, but that one'), *Io non parto oggi, ma parto domani* ('I am not leaving today but tomorrow'). As in English, *ma* can be used to intensify an element: *Non ho mangiato niente, ma proprio niente* ('I had nothing to eat, but really nothing'); or, contrary to English, to express surprise or annoyance when used at the beginning of a sentence: *Ma che dici?* ('What are you saying?'), *Ma smettila, per favore!* ('Do stop it, please!'). *Ma* can be intensified by some prepositions forming expressions such as *ma tuttavia* ('but yet'), *ma invece* ('but instead'), and *ma però* ('but'), which should be avoided in written Italian despite being quite common in colloquial registers;
- **però** can sometimes simply mean 'but' and replace *ma*: *Ascolta, però [= ma] non parlare* ('Listen, but do not talk'); also, it can be used as the equivalent of the English 'however': *Non ci sono riuscito, però questa esperienza è stata importante* ('I did not make it; however, it was an important experience'). When *però* is placed at the beginning of a sentence, it expresses surprise or annoyance: *Però, che forza!* ('What strength!'), *Però, ora basta!* ('Now, that's enough!');
- **invece** ('instead') is a really common conjunction, which is used extensively in Italian when a clear and strong contrast is desired: *Noi lavoriamo, voi invece vi riposate tutto il giorno* ('We work; you rest all day instead'). When *invece* combines with the infinitive form of a verb, it must be followed by *di* or *che* and be translated in English with 'instead of + -ing'. The forms *invece di* and *invece che* are perfectly interchangeable: *Mangia, invece di/che parlare* ('Eat instead of talking');
- **mentre** ('while') and **quando** ('when'), like *invece*, can be used interchangeably to contrast two actions: *Hai voluto agire subito, mentre/quando dovevi pensarci di più* ('You wanted to act immediately, while/when you should have thought a little more about it'). Often, as happens in English, they are used to reinforce *invece*: *mentre invece* ('while instead'), *quando invece* ('when instead');
- **eppure** and **tuttavia** (both meaning 'yet' or 'however'): *Sono stanco, eppure/tuttavia continuo a lavorare* ('I am tired; however, I will keep working');

- **anzi** and **al contrario** (both meaning 'on the contrary'): *Non è simpatico, anzi/al contrario è antipaticissimo* ('He is not pleasant; on the contrary, he is really unpleasant');
- **viceversa** ('vice versa') is considered quite informal and is not used much: *Tu mi aiuti e viceversa io aiuto te* ('You help me, and vice versa'). Unlike its English equivalent, it can easily substitute for *invece* in contexts where English would require the use of 'instead' or 'on the contrary', never 'vice versa': *Ti avevo detto di stare zitto, viceversa [= invece] tu hai parlato* ('I have told you to be quiet; on the contrary, you spoke');
- **piuttosto** ('rather'): *Non una birra, bevo piuttosto un bicchiere d'acqua* ('Not a beer, I'd rather have a glass of water');
- **altrimenti** ('otherwise'): *Certo che vado al concerto; altrimenti non avrei comprato un biglietto* ('Of course I am going to the concert; otherwise, I wouldn't have bought a ticket').

17.4 Declarative Connectives: cioè, infatti, ovvero, *etc.*

Declarative connectives are meant to introduce elements that support, explain, or confirm what has already been said or written:

- **cioè** is undoubtedly the most used declarative conjunction. It is equivalent to the English 'that is': *Vengo il 10, cioè fra una settimana* ('I am coming on the 10th, that is, in a week'). Often in informal contexts *cioè* is used just as a verbal tic, and is approximately equivalent to 'I mean' in English: *Lui, cioè Marco, è bravo, cioè è un bravo ragazzo* ('He, I mean Marco, is good, I mean a good boy');
- **ovvero** and **ossia** can be considered equivalent to *cioè* in meaning ('that is') but are quite rare in spoken Italian. They can still occur in formal contexts and in written language: *Le dico che non ho fatto niente, ovvero non sono colpevole* ('I'm telling you that I did not do anything; that is, I am not guilty');
- **vale a dire** ('that is to say'): *Questo è necessario; vale a dire lo dovete fare* ('This is necessary; that is to say, you must do it'). Expressions like **o meglio**, **in altre parole**, and **in altri termini** (meaning 'in other words') are similar to *vale a dire* and can easily replace it;
- **infatti** and its less used equivalent **difatti** and **in effetti** all mean 'indeed': *Ho detto che sarei partito ed infatti/difatti/in effetti l'ho fatto* ('I said that I would leave, and indeed I did').

17.5 Conclusive Connectives: dunque, pertanto, tanto che, *etc.*

Conclusive connectives introduce a clause caused by or resulting from what was said or written before:

- **dunque, quindi, pertanto,** and **perciò** (and the regional *sicché*) are all interchangeable and all mean 'so': *Studio, dunque/quindi/pertanto/perciò prenderò un buon voto* ('I study, so I'll get a good grade');

- **per cui** and **di conseguenza** can replace all the above in a more colloquial and informal context: *Ti avevo avvertito, per cui/di conseguenza non mi infastidire* ('I warned you, so do not bother me');
- **tanto che** ('so', 'so that'): *Non mi piace per niente Marco, tanto che non lo saluto mai* ('I do not like Marco at all, so I never say hello to him');
- **allora** translates into the English 'then' and 'so' in the sense of 'in that case': *Se non hanno telefonato, allora va tutto bene* ('If they haven't called, then everything is fine'), *Non ho detto niente; allora perché mi guardi in quel modo?* ('I haven't said a word; so why do you look at me that way?');
- **ebbene** ('well'): *Ebbene, ci vediamo domani* ('Well, I'll see you tomorrow');
- **ora** ('now') introduces a sequence in time: *Io ho parlato, ora è il tuo turno* ('I have spoken; now it's your turn'). When *ora* is followed by *che* (**ora che**), it always corresponds to the English 'since': *Ora che sei venuto, devi rimanere* ('Since you came, you must stay').

17.6 Correlative Connectives: e ... e, o ... o, ma ... anche, etc.

Correlative connectives are pairs of conjunctions or conjunctive phrases that work in pairs, joining various sentence elements that should be treated as grammatically equal:

- **sia ... che** is the most frequent way to express the English 'both ... and': *Sia mia madre, che mio padre sono insegnanti* ('Both my mother and my father are teachers'). The word *che* can always be replaced by another *sia*, creating the phrase **sia ... sia**: *Sia mio fratello, sia [= che] mia sorella sono studenti* ('Both my sister and my brother are students');
- **e ... e** means 'both ... and' like *sia ... che* and *sia ... sia*, but it is less used in contemporary Italian and usually limited to formal written language: *Sono invitati e professori e studenti* ('Both professors and students are invited');
- **tanto ... che** or **tanto ... quanto** are two other conjunctions that mean 'both ... and': *Tanto Marco che Maria sono italiani* ('Both Marco and Maria are Italian'), *Tanto tu quanto Anna siete miei amici* ('Both you and Anna are my friends');
- **o ... o** ('either ... or'): *O vai o rimani* ('Either you go or you stay');
- **né ... né** can only be used in a negative sentence and means 'neither ... nor': *Non voglio né la torta né il gelato* ('I want neither cake nor ice cream');
- **non solo ... ma anche** ('not only ... but also'): *Non solo non ti scusi, ma anche ti lamenti!* ('Not only you do not apologize, but you also complain!'); *addirittura* and *perfino* (both meaning 'even') can be used instead of *anche* to reinforce a contrast: *Non solo sei colpevole, ma addirittura accusi me!* ('You're not only guilty, but you even accuse me!');
- **se ... o** ('whether ... or'): *Mario non è sicuro se diventare dottore o avvocato* ('Mario is not sure whether to become a doctor or a lawyer');
- **così ... come** ('as ... as'): *La tua macchina non va così bene come va la mia* ('Your car doesn't run as well as mine does').

17.7 Uses of the Conjunction che

Che is one of the most frequently used words in Italian. It can be a relative (see 8.3), an interrogative pronoun (see 9.2), or a conjunction. As a conjunction, *che* introduces a clause with the **indicative** or **subjunctive** moods according to their respective rules (see chapter 21).

In Italian the conjunction *che* is generally expressed in contexts in which its English equivalent 'that' can be easily omitted (see 17.8): *So che sei intelligente* ('I know you are smart'). The conjunction *che* frequently combines with other words to form conjunctive phrases such as *dal momento che* ('since'), *in modo che* ('so that'), and so on. *Che* can play several functions corresponding to different English meanings.

Below is a list of the uses of the conjunction *che*:

- **che declarative,** equivalent to the English 'that', introduces an explanation: *Dicono che tu sei simpatico* ('They say that you are nice'), *Vorrei che tu fossi qui* ('I wish you were here'). The construction *che* + indicative or *che* + subjunctive must be replaced by the structure **di + infinitive** when the subject of both clauses is the same. Compare the two sentences: *Sono contento che studi italiano* ('I am happy you study Italian'), *Sono contento di studiare italiano* ('I am happy to study Italian'). In the second sentence *di* + infinitive is used because the implicit subject of both clauses is *io*;
- **che introducing a result**: *Parla in modo che io capisca* ('Speak so that I can understand'), *Ero talmente stanco che mi sono addormentato subito* ('I was so tired that I fell asleep immediately'). In this particular case, as can be seen from the examples above, the conjunction *che* is generally introduced in the main clause by words or expressions such as *così, tanto, talmente, in modo, in maniera*, all approximately equivalent to the English 'so';
- **che introducing a purpose**: *Prega che mi diano il lavoro* ('Pray that they give me the job'), *Chiedi che escano da qui* ('Tell them to get out of here');
- **che expressing time**: *Sono due anni che ci conosciamo* ('We have known each other for two years'), *È il momento che partiate* ('It's time you leave');
- **che introducing an indirect command**: *Che entri il primo, per favore* ('Can the first one come in, please'), *Che non si parli più di loro* ('Let's not talk about them anymore'). In this case *che* must be combined with the present subjunctive;
- **che introducing a limitation** is equivalent to the English 'as far as': *Franco non è ancora arrivato, che io sappia* ('As far as I know, Franco has not arrived yet');
- **che introducing an exception** corresponds to the English 'but': *Non fa altro che giocare* ('He does nothing but play');
- **che as a concessive conjunction** creates a specific relationship contrasting two or more pieces of information: *Che ne dicano i tuoi amici, non mi interessa* ('What your friends have to say about it is of no interest to me'), *Non che lei non fosse felice, ma non lo dimostrava* ('She was not unhappy, but she was not showing it');
- **che as a disjunctive conjunction combined with *o*** is equivalent to the English 'whether ... or': *Che tu venga o no, non mi interessa* ('Whether you come or not is of no interest to me');

- **_che_ expressing comparison** is equivalent to the English 'than': *Leggere è più importante che scrivere* ('Reading is more important than writing'). *Che* used in comparative phrases is always preceded by *più* 'more' or *meno* 'less' (see 6.4).

17.8 Omission of the Conjunction *che*

In subordinate clauses with indicative verbs, the omission of *che* is not allowed whereas its English equivalent 'that' can easily be omitted: *Dicono che sei un bravo studente* ('They say you are a good student'). However, **with subjunctive verbs the omission is common** enough in contemporary Italian (see 21.20). In this case constructions with or without *che* are perfectly interchangeable: *Credo che abbiano studiato abbastanza* and *Credo abbiano studiato abbastanza* ('I think they have studied enough') or *Voglio che tu venga con me* and *Voglio tu venga con me* ('I want you to come with me') are perfectly equivalent.

17.9 The Causal Conjunction *ché*

The form **_ché_** with an accent mark is not to be confused with the other forms of *che* without the accent. *Ché* must be considered an abbreviated form of a conjunction like *perché* ('because', 'since'), *affinché* ('so') that have a causal meaning (*Non chiamo Marco, ché non mi piace* 'I am not calling Marco because I don't like him') or result meaning (*Svegliami alle 7.00, ché non sia in ritardo* 'Wake me up at 7.00AM so that I won't be late'). Today the form *ché* is really rare in the colloquial register and can be found only in written and formal Italian.

17.10 Causal Connectives: *perché, poiché, siccome, etc.*

Causal connectives introduce a clause that explains the cause or the reason for what is expressed in the main clause. All such conjunctions introduce dependent clauses that require the **indicative** forms of the verb:

- **_perché_** ('because' or 'since') is the most common causal conjunction: *Ho fame perché non ho mangiato* ('I am hungry because I haven't eaten'), *Non parlo perfettamente italiano, perché sono tedesco* ('Since I am German, I do not speak Italian perfectly'). *Perché*, unlike its equivalents listed below, can never be placed at the beginning of a sentence in Italian;
- **_poiché, giacché, siccome_** ('because' or 'since') are all equivalent to *perché* but less common in everyday Italian. Unlike *perché*, they can be placed at the beginning of the sentence: *Poiché/Giacché/Siccome non ho mangiato, ho fame* ('Since I haven't eaten, I am hungry');
- **_in quanto_, _dal momento che_, _per il fatto che_, _considerato che_, _visto che_** are all conjunctive phrases meaning 'because' or 'since': *Non sono venuto in quanto/dal momento che/per il fatto che/considerato che/visto che tu non mi hai invitato* ('I did not come since you did not invite me').

17.11 Purpose Connectives: perché, affinché, acciocché, *etc.*

Purpose connectives introduce a clause that explains why or for what purpose what is expressed in the main clause occurs. All such conjunctions introduce dependent clauses that require the **subjunctive** or in some cases the **infinitive** forms of the verb:

- ***perché*** ('so that') is the most common purpose conjunction: *Ti chiamo perché tu venga* ('I am calling you so that you come');
- ***affinché*** and ***acciocché*** mean 'so that' and are perfectly interchangeable with *perché* although *affinché* is restricted to written Italian and *acciocché* is nowadays rare: *Ti parlo affinché/acciocché* [= *perché*] *tu mi ascolti* ('I am talking to you so that you listen to me'). *Perché, affinché, acciocché* must all be replaced by ***per* + infinitive** when the subject of both clauses is the same. Compare these two sentences: *Lavoro perché tu possa frequentare il college* ('I work so that you can attend college') and *Lavoro per poter frequentare il college* ('I work to attend college'). In the second sentence *per* + infinitive is used because the implicit subject of the two clauses is *io* ('I');
- ***in modo che*** and ***di modo che*** ('so that'): *Dico questo in modo che/di modo che tu possa credermi* ('I am telling you this so that you can believe me');
- ***in modo da*** ('in order to') is used instead of *in modo che* or *di modo che* when the subject of both sentences is the same and an infinitive form of the verb is used: *Organizzati in modo da venire domani* ('Get organized in order to come tomorrow');
- ***al fine di***, followed by an infinitive, is another way to mean 'in order to'. It is typical of the formal register: *Al fine di ottenere la verità sono disposto a tutto* ('I will do anything in order to get the truth');
- ***pur di*** ('just to') is always followed by an infinitive: *Farò di tutto pur di andare* ('I will do anything just to go').

17.12 Time Connectives: quando, mentre, dopo che, *etc.*

Time connectives are used to introduce a clause that indicates the time when an action occurs in relation to something else. They all require the **indicative** forms of the verb except *prima che* ('before'), followed by the subjunctive instead:

- ***quando*** ('when'): *Quando sei arrivato, io ero già uscito* ('When you arrived, I had already left'), *Chiamami quando sei pronto* ('Call me when you are ready'). In a colloquial context, the final *o* of *quando* can be deleted and replaced by the apostrophe (***quand'***) before a word beginning with a vowel (or *h*), especially with the forms of *essere* ('to be'): *Quand'è partito non ero in casa* ('I wasn't home when he left'). When *quando* is preceded by the preposition *da* (***da quando***), it is equivalent to the English 'since' (see also 16.4): *Suona la chitarra da quando aveva dieci anni* ('He's been playing the guitar since he was ten');

- ***fino a quando*** ('until'): *Lapo non è uscito fino a quando non ha finito i compiti* ('Lapo did not go out until he finished his homework');
- ***ogni [qual] volta*** means 'whenever' in the sense of 'every time': *Ogni [qual] volta che ti vedo sei sempre più grande* ('Whenever I see you, you are bigger'), *Vieni ogni [qual] volta ti fa piacere* ('Come whenever you like');
- ***mentre*** ('while'): *Io studio mentre tu guardi la televisione* ('I am studying while you are watching TV'). In colloquial Italian the phrase *mentre che* can substitute for the simple *mentre*: *Mentre che facevi i compiti, io sono uscito* ('While you were doing your homework, I went out'). However, it is recommended not to use this form;
- ***prima*** ('first', 'before') is usually used with *poi, dopo,* or *in seguito* (all meaning 'then') to simply indicate a sequence of actions: *Prima studio, poi gioco* ('First I study, then I play'). In Italian as opposed to English, when *prima* introduces a subordinate clause, it is always followed by *che* and requires the subjunctive (***prima che* + subjunctive**): *Passo prima che tu parta* ('I will stop by before you leave'). If the subject of both clauses is the same, the construction with the subjunctive must be replaced by ***prima di* + infinitive**: *Passo prima di partire* ('I will stop by before I leave');
- ***dopo, poi, in seguito*** (all meaning 'then') can be directly followed by the verb when correlated to another connective (usually *prima* 'first', 'before') simply to indicate a sequence of actions in compound sentences: *Prima mangi, dopo/poi/in seguito guardi la TV* ('First you eat, then you watch TV'). In Italian, as opposed to English, when *dopo* introduces a subordinate clause, it must be combined with *che* followed by the indicative form of the verb (***dopo che* + indicative**): *Lia sarà triste, dopo che tu sarai partito* ('Lia will be sad after you leave'). If the subject of both clauses is the same, the construction with the indicative is replaced by ***dopo* + past infinitive**: *Sarò triste dopo essere partito* ('I will be sad after I leave'). In Italian, as in English, *dopo* can be combined with a noun instead of a past infinitive (***dopo* + noun**) without changing the meaning: *Lia sarà triste, dopo la tua partenza* ('Lia will be sad after your departure'). In this case, as can be seen from the example, a possessive adjective must be added to specify who is leaving;
- ***all'inizio*** ('at first') and ***alla fine*** ('at last', 'in the end') are usually used in compound sentences to indicate a sequence of actions: *All'inizio mi piaceva molto, alla fine non lo sopportavo più* ('At first I liked it a lot, but in the end I could not stand it anymore'). The conjunctions *poi, dopo,* or *in seguito* (all meaning 'then') can also be combined with *all'inizio*: *All'inizio giocavo a calcio, in seguito ho giocato a tennis* ('At first I used to play soccer, then I played tennis');
- ***appena*** ('as soon as'): *Appena arrivi chiamami* ('As soon as you arrive, call me'). It is frequent in contemporary Italian to find the exact equivalent structure ***non appena*** where the use of *non* is stylistic rather than negative: *Non appena arrivi chiamami* ('As soon as you arrive, call me');
- ***come*** can work as a time conjunction. In this case it is equivalent to *appena* and so means 'as soon as': *Come [= appena] è arrivato, lo ho abbracciato* ('As soon as he arrived, I gave him a hug');
- ***finché, fino a che***, and ***fino a quando*** are all equivalent to the English 'until' or 'as long as': *Non ceneremo finché/fino a che/fino a quando tu sarai qui* ('We won't have dinner until

you get here'), *Rimango con te finché/fino a che/fino a quando vuoi* ('I will stay with you as long as you want');
- **da quando**, **dal momento che**, **da che** (also written **dacché**) all mean 'since': *Sono felice da quando/dal momento che/da che tu sei con me* ('I am happy since you are with me').

17.13 Conditional Connectives: se, semmai, qualora, *etc.*

Conditional connectives indicate hypotheses or conditions showing that the completion of a clause in a sentence rests upon the fulfillment of another. All such conjunctions take the **subjunctive** except *se* when used to introduce a hypothetical situation presented as real (see 23.29):

- **se** is the conjunction most used to express a hypothesis and can be easily translated with the English 'if': *Se io avessi tempo, studierei musica* ('If I had time, I would study music'). When combined with *anche* (**anche se**), it means 'even if': *Anche se tu non fossi mio figlio, ti vorrei bene lo stesso* ('Even if you were not my son, I would love you just the same');
- **semmai**, **caso mai**, and **qualora** are equivalent and close in meaning to *se* in the sense of 'in case': *Fammi sapere, semmai/caso mai/qualora incontrassi Marco* ('Let me know in case you meet Marco');
- **purché**, **a patto che**, **a condizione che**, and **sempre che** express a necessary condition for something else to happen and can be considered equivalent to the English 'on the condition that' or 'as long as': *Purché/a patto che/a condizione che/sempre che tu voglia, questa sera usciamo* ('As long as you want, we will go out tonight');
- **a meno che** ('unless'): *Pago io, a meno che tu non ti offenda* ('I will pay unless you get offended'). Note that in Italian, contrary to English, this connective introduces a negative clause.

17.14 Concessive Connectives: benché, sebbene, quantunque, *etc.*

Concessive connectives imply concession. The following concessive connectives always require the **subjunctive**:

- **benché** and **sebbene** are perfectly equivalent and mean 'although': *Benché/Sebbene non mi piaccia, lo mangerò* ('Although I don't like it, I will eat it');
- **nonostante** and **malgrado** are both equivalent to 'although' or 'despite the fact that', but *malgrado* is less used: *Sono venuto nonostante/malgrado avessi un altro impegno* ('I came although I had another committment'). In colloquial Italian, it is not uncommon to find these two conjunctions followed by *che*: *Abbiamo fatto una passeggiata nonostante che/malgrado che piovesse* ('We took a walk despite the fact that it was raining'). Often, as in English, they can be used before a noun conveying the same meaning as an entire clause. For example, the sentence before can be changed into *Abbiamo fatto una passeggiata nonostante/malgrado la pioggia* ('We took a walk despite the rain') where *pioggia* replaces *che piovesse*;
- **ammesso che** ('assuming that') and **quand'anche** ('even if') introduce a sentence with a hypothetical concession and often express skepticism: *Ammesso che tu ce l'abbia, dammi*

il tuo compito ('Assuming that you have your homework, hand it to me'), *Quand'anche fosse così, io sarei soddisfatto* ('Even if it were so, I would be satisfied').

The following concessive connectives can use **verbal modes other than the subjunctive**:

- **anche se** can easily be translated with the English 'even though'. It generally requires the **indicative**: *Anche se sei qui, non conta* ('Even though you are here, it doesn't count'); However, it must be used with the subjunctive if it works as a conditional conjunction expressing probability or impossibility (see 23.29): *Anche se potessi, non andrei in vacanza* ('Even if I could, I wouldn't go on vacation');
- **pur** ('although') is generally followed by a **gerund**: *Pur non essendo in grande forma, ha vinto la gara* ('Although he wasn't in great shape, he won the race'). The gerund can sometimes be omitted without modifying the meaning of the sentence: *Pur non in grande forma, ha vinto la gara* ('Though not in great shape, he won the race').

Expressions like **tuttavia** ('however'), **ugualmente** ('all the same'), **allo stesso modo** ('in the same way') are often used in the main clause to intensify the contrast with the concessive clause: *Benché non abbia ancora cenato, tuttavia non ho assolutamente fame* ('Although I haven't had dinner yet, I am not hungry at all').

17.15 Modal Connectives: come, comunque, quasi, *etc.*

Modal connectives describe the manner in which the action of the main clause is carried out. They are followed by the **indicative** when they present something as real (*Lui agisce sempre come vuole* 'He always does as he pleases'), but they are **mainly used with the subjunctive** to indicate a doubt or a possibility (*Fai come tu fossi a casa tua* 'Make yourself at home'):

- **come** ('as'): *Mi vesto sempre come mi suggerisce mia moglie* ('I always dress as my wife suggests'). When *come* is followed by *se* (**come se**), it means 'as if' and always requires the subjunctive: *Mi dici tutto questo come se io non lo sapessi già* ('You are telling me all about it as if I didn't know already');
- **quasi** ('as if') can be considered equivalent to *come se*, but is certainly less common: *Mi rimproveri, quasi [= come se] avessi combinato un disastro* ('You scold me as if I made a mess'). *Quasi* is often followed by *che* (**quasi che**) without a change in meaning: *Ti comporti quasi che tu fossi un bambino* ('You behave as if you were a child');
- **comunque** ('however'): *Comunque le cose vadano, io non cambio idea* ('However things go, I won't change my mind');
- **senza che** ('without'): *Ti ho riconosciuto, senza che tu dicessi una parola* ('I recognized you without you saying a word'). Note that *che* is dropped and only *senza* is used when the subject of both verbs is the same. In this case *senza* always requires the infinitive: *Ho studiato tutta la notte, senza dormire* ('I have studied all night long without sleeping').

17.16 Connectives of Exception: salvo che, fuorché, tranne che, *etc.*

Connectives of exception are a class of connectives that introduce an exception to something in the sentences in which they are used:

- **a parte**, **salvo**, and **tranne** all mean 'apart from' when introducing a noun or pronoun: *a parte/salvo/tranne Marco e te* ('apart from Marco and you'). However, they mean 'on the condition that' when followed by *che* and introducing a dependent clause with the subjunctive: *Non vado a parte che/salvo che/tranne che tu non venga con me* ('I am only going on the condition that you come with me'). If the subject of both verbs is the same, the structure **per + infinitive** (equivalent to the English 'except') follows directly *che*: *Non esco a parte che/salvo che/tranne che per andare in biblioteca* ('I am not going out except to the library');
- **a meno che** is equivalent to the English 'unless' and introduces a dependent clause with the subjunctive: *Non ti aiuterò a meno che tu non lo chieda* ('I won't help you unless you ask me to');
- **se non** is 'apart from' or 'except' and can be used only in a negative context: *Nessuno può rimanere se non il professore e voi* ('No one, apart from the professor and you, can stay'), *Non mi diverte niente se non giocare a calcio* ('I don't like doing anything except playing soccer'). The phrase **se non per** ('but for') is always followed by the infinitive and indicates the exclusive reason why something is done: *Non ti ho chiamato, se non per salutarti* ('I called you just to say hello');
- **fuorché** ('apart from') and **eccetto** ('except') can be used before nouns or pronouns: *Fuorché/Eccetto lui, sono tutti partiti* ('Apart from/Except for him, all have left'); more frequently they occur before the infinitive form of a verb: *Posso sopportare tutto fuorché/eccetto dormire in tenda* ('I can tolerate anything apart from/except sleeping in a tent');
- **ad eccezione di** and **all'infuori di** ('apart from', 'except) are two expressions perfectly equivalent to *fuorché* and *eccetto* but more formal: *Ad eccezione di/All'infuori di Maria eravamo tutti stanchi* ('Apart from/Except for Maria, we were all tired'). In the presence of an infinitive, *che* replaces *di* (**ad eccezione che**, **all'infuori che**): *Non mi piace niente ad eccezione che/all'infuori che leggere* ('I don't like doing anything except reading').

17.17 Restrictive Connectives: per quanto, da quello che, a quel che, *etc.*

These connective phrases express restrictions and are most often used with the **subjunctive** to emphasize a speaker's doubt. Note the difference between *Per quanto ne so io, Marco è qui* and *Per quanto ne sappia io, Marco è qui*. Although, both constructions can be rendered in English with 'For all I know, Marco is here', the use of the subjunctive in the second sentence casts doubt on the presence of Marco.

The most common restrictive connectives are **per quanto**, **a quanto**, **per quel che**, **a quel che** all meaning 'as far as': *Per quanto capisca la matematica, questo esercizio è sbagliato* ('As far as I understand math, this exercise is wrong'), *A quel che so io, Carlo si trova in biblioteca in questo momento* ('As far as I know, Carlo is at the library at the moment').

17.18 Comparative Connectives: così ... come, più ... che, meglio ... che, *etc.*

The structure of comparative constructions between nouns or pronouns was previously studied (see 6.4). The following discussion concerns only the use of the comparative subordinating conjunctions **più** ('more'), **meno** ('less'), **meglio** ('better'), **peggio** ('worse') followed by **che** or **di quanto** (both meaning 'than'). One of their distinguishing characteristics is that they all require the **subjunctive**: *Il film mi è piaciuto più di quanto immaginassi* ('I liked the movie more than I imagined I would'), *Abbiamo pagato meno di quanto ci aspettassimo* ('We paid less than we expected'). The indicative can sometimes be found as well, but it is typical of the colloquial register (*È meglio di quanto pensavo* 'It is better than I thought') and, as such, should be avoided in more formal Italian.

18. NEGATIVE STRUCTURES

> **Negatives:** A negative states that something is not true, correct, or negates something. The occurrence of negative words such as *non* ('not'), *niente* ('nothing'), *mai* ('never') is a feature that makes negative constructions easily recognizable.

18.1 Structure of Negative Sentences with the Simple non

In Italian, the most common way of negating something is to use the adverb **non.** *Non* is generally placed directly in front of the verb: *Non studio* ('I don't study'), *Tu non sei gentile* ('You are not nice'). When a direct or an indirect objet pronoun occurs before the verb, it keeps its position and the adverb *non* is placed before it: *Non ti conosco* ('I don't know you'), *Non gli parlo* ('I don't talk to him').

As in English, *non* negates the verb immediately following it and not another that could appear in the same sentence: *Non dico di essere il più bravo della classe* ('I am not saying that I am the best in the class'), *Dico di non essere il più bravo della classe* ('I am saying that I am not the best in the class'). However, with verbs expressing opinion, doubt, desire, or fear like *pensare* ('to think'), *sembrare* ('to seem'), *volere* ('to want'), *non* can be placed indistinctly in front of these verbs or the following verbs without changing the meaning of the sentence: *Non penso di andare* ('I don't think I will go') is equivalent to *Penso di non andare* ('I think I won't go').

Albeit not common in Italian, *non* can occur in front of nouns, adjectives, or pronouns to lend more emphasis to a statement. For example, comparing the sentences *Hai un aspetto non sereno oggi* and *Non hai un aspetto sereno oggi* (both meaning 'You do not look serene today'), the first one, in which *non* negates the adjective *sereno*, has more impact because it focuses on the look of the person.

Moreover, *non*, meaning 'not' or 'non-' can also appear in front of nouns, adjectives, pronouns, or adverbs to negate the second element of an identical couple: *Voglio un gelato, non una pizza* ('I want an ice cream, not a pizza'), *Pronti o non pronti, partiamo* ('Ready or not ready, we're leaving'), *Lavoratori e non lavoratori hanno manifestato contro le scelte del governo* ('Workers and non-workers alike demonstrated against the government's decisions').

18.2 Common Negative Phrases with non: non ... ancora, non ... più, *etc.*

In addition to the structures already discussed, *non* can combine with adverbs, pronouns, and conjunctions to form negative phrases. Below is a list of these and a sample of their use:

Negative constructions	Examples
non ... affatto ('not ... at all')	*Non ho affatto fame* ('I am not hungry at all')
non ... ancora ('not ... yet')	*Non è ancora arrivato* ('He has not arrived yet')
non ... che ('no ... but')	*Non ho che questa casa* ('I have no home but this one')
non ... mai ('never')	*Tu non parli mai* ('You never talk')
non ... né ... né ('neither ... nor')	*Non sono né felice, né triste* ('I'm neither happy nor sad')
non ... neanché/neppure/nemmeno ('not ... even')	*Non ho neanche/neppure/nemmeno un euro* ('I don't even have a euro')
non ... nessuno ('nobody', 'not ... anybody')	*Non parte nessuno* ('Nobody leaves')
non ... niente/nulla ('nothing', 'anything')	*Non ho niente/nulla da dire* ('I don't have anything to say')
non ... più ('no more', 'no longer')	*Non lavoro più là* ('I no longer work there')
non ... mica ('not ... at all')	*Non sono mica matto* ('I am not crazy at all')

As demonstrated in the examples above, *non* precedes the verb while the companion negative word follows it. However, the use of *non* is not obligatory in all the negative structures above. In fact, some of these admit the **omission of *non*** and just place the companion negative before the verb. They are *mai* (*Mai parli* 'You never talk'), *né ... né* (*Né sono felice, né triste* 'I am neither happy nor sad'), *neanche, neppure, nemmeno* (*Neanche/Neppure/Nemmeno ho un euro* 'I don't even have a euro'), *nessuno* (*Nessuno parte* 'Nobody leaves'), *niente, nulla* (*Niente/Nulla ho da dire* 'I don't have anything to say'), *mica* (*Mica sono matto* 'I am not crazy at all').

Though typical of the informal register, **mica** is really common in Italian. It is used to highlight the negative meaning of a sentence and can be considered an emphatic variant of *non*, either when combined with it (*Non sono mica scemo* 'I am not stupid at all') or on its own (*Mica sono scemo* 'I am not stupid at all').

> **N.B.** A colloquial alternative to *mica* is the negative **punto**, a typical expression in Tuscany. However, *punto*, unlike *mica*, must always be used with *non* and before nouns with which it agrees in gender and number. It can be translated into English with 'any', or with the phrase 'at all': *Non ho punti soldi* ('I don't have any money'), *Non ho punta fame* ('I am not hungry at all').

18.3 Negatives with Compound Tenses: non ho mai mangiato del pesce

As seen before *non* is placed directly in front of the auxiliary or, if a direct or indirect object pronoun precedes the verb, it is placed directly in front of the pronoun (see 18.1). When *non* combines with other negative expressions, it precedes the auxiliary while the words *che* (*Non ho avuto che questa casa* 'I've had no other home than this one'), *nessuno* (*Non è partito nessuno* 'Nobody left'), and *niente* or *nulla* (*Non ho avuto niente/nulla da dire* 'I had nothing to say') always follow the past participle (see 18.2).

All the other negative words used with *non* may appear either between the auxiliary verb and the past participle or after the past participle: *Tu non hai mai parlato* is equivalent to *Tu non hai parlato mai* ('You never talked'), *Non ho neanche avuto un euro* is equivalent to *Non ho avuto neanche un euro* ('I didn't even have a euro').

When *non* is omitted (see 18.2), the negative companions must always precede the auxiliary verb: *Mai hai parlato* ('You never talked'), *Neanche ho avuto un euro* ('I didn't even have a euro').

18.4 Negative Answers

Italian is similar to English in that it answers a question negatively using a simple, isolated *no* ('no') or a *no* accompanied by more information: *No, non sono io la persona che stai cercando* ('No, I'm not the person you are looking for'). This explanation barely skims over this structure, the finer points of which are covered in chapter 9 (see 9.5)

19. WORD DERIVATION: PREFIXES AND SUFFIXES

> **PREFIXES AND SUFFIXES**: Prefixes and suffixes are grammatical elements that attach to words to make derived or inflected forms. A prefix, as its name indicates, occurs at the beginning of a base word to alter its meaning and form a new word: *bisnonno* ('great-grandfather'), *ex moglie* ('ex-wife'). In contrast, a suffix occurs at the end of a base word: *piccoletto* ('quite short'), *giornataccia* ('a really bad day').

19.1 Word Derivation

One of the most important features of a language is its vocabulary, which, if rich, gives the language the flexibility to express shades of meaning or otherwise serve as an effective means of communication. To such ends word derivation, changing words through the use of affixes, serves as an effective method of ensuring that this vocabulary is rich enough, varied enough by enhancing the stock of words a language makes available to its users. Italian is a language that makes particularly good use of word derivation.

Italian words fall into three groups: 1) simple words, 2) derived words, and 3) combined words:

- **simple words** constitute the majority of the Italian vocabulary. They are original and do not derive from other words: *cane* ('dog'), *piazza* ('square'), *mangiare* ('to eat'), and so on;
- **compound words** (see 3.19, 3.20) are formed by the combination of two or more existing words like *capo* + *squadra* > *caposquadra* ('team captain') or *sempre* + *verde* > *sempreverde* ('evergreen'), just to give a couple of examples;
- **derived words**, on the other hand, are formed by the combination of existing base words with a prefix, a suffix, or both. Prefixes are added to the beginning of the base word (*ambi-* + *destro* > *ambidestro* 'both-hands') whereas suffixes are added to the end of the base word (*vento* + *-icello* > *venticello* 'a light wind').

Prefixes occur with a relatively equal frequency in Italian and English, but suffixes are more common in Italian where they can be used to express particular nuances or convey personal emotions and points of view. To illustrate this point, just consider that from a base word like *casa* ('house'), it is possible to derive the following eight words, most of which can only be rendered in English by using entire phrases (see 19.3–19.7): *casato, casina, casetta, casuccia, casona, casaccia, casettina, casettuccia*.

19.2 The Most Common Prefixes: a-, dis-, inter-, *etc.*

It is almost impossible to draw up a list of Italian prefixes because of their sheer number, and because it is a task better suited for a dictionary than a reference grammar. Nevertheless, knowledge of the most common Italian prefixes can help English speakers to recognize many Italian words. In addition, since most have a Latin origin, the same prefix can be found in both Italian and English.

Below is a list of the most useful prefixes with their English meaning and examples:

Prefixes	Meaning	Examples
a-	('not')	*acefalo* ('acephalous')
ambi-	('both')	*ambivalente* ('ambivalent')
ante-	('before')	*anteguerra* ('prewar')
anti-	('against')	*anticiclone* ('anticyclone')
arci-	('chief' with nouns, 'very' with adjectives)	*arcivescovo* ('archbishop'), *arcicontento* ('very happy')
auto-	('self')	*autobiografia* ('autobiography')
avan-	('before')	*avanguardia* ('avant-guarde')
bis-/bi-	('two')	*bisnonno* ('great-grandfather'), *bilingue* ('bilingual')
circum-	('around')	*circumnavigare* ('circumnavigate')
co-	('together')	*coabitare* ('to live together')
contro-	('opposite')	*controsenso* ('contradiction')
dis-	('opposite')	*disdire* ('to cancel')
ex-	('former')	*ex moglie* ('ex-wife')
in-	('not')	*insensatezza* ('senselessness')
infra-/intra-	('inside')	*intramuscolare* ('intramuscolar')
inter-	('between')	*internazionale* ('international')
iper-	('over, big')	*iperattivo* ('hyperactive')
ipo-	('below')	*ipocalorico* ('low-calorie')
macro-	('very big')	*macrocosmo* ('macrocosm')
maxi-	('big')	*maxischermo* ('big screen')
mega-	('big')	*megafono* ('megaphone')
megalo-	('big')	*megalomane* ('megalomaniac')
meta-	('beyond')	*metafisica* ('metaphysics')
micro-	('very small')	*microscopio* ('microscope')
mini-	('small')	*minigonna* ('mini-skirt')
mono-	('one')	*monolingue* ('monolingual')
multi-	('many')	*multiuso* ('multipurpose')
neo-	('new')	*neonato* ('newborn')
oltre-	('over')	*oltremare* ('overseas')
omo-	('same')	*omonimo* ('homonymous')
onni-	('all')	*onnivoro* ('omnivore')
para-	('similar')	*paralegale* ('paralegal')
pluri-	('several')	*pluripartitico* ('multi-party')

poli-	('many')	*polivalente* ('multipurpose')
post-	('after')	*postmoderno* ('postmodern')
pre-	('before')	*preveggente* ('foresighted')
re-/ri-	('back', 'again')	*reazione* ('reaction'), *ritorno* ('return')
retro-	('backward')	*retrospettiva* ('retrospective')
s-	('opposite')	*sfortuna* ('bad luck')
semi-	('half', 'almost')	*semicerchio* ('semicircle'), *seminuovo* ('almost new')
sopra-/sovra-	('above')	*sovrannaturale* ('supernatural')
sotto-	('below')	*sottomarino* ('submarine')
stra-	('immensely')	*straricco* ('immensely rich')
sub-	('below')	*subacqueo* ('underwater')
super-	('more than')	*supervisore* ('superintendent')
sur-	('beyond')	*surreale* ('surreal')
trans-	('across')	*transatlantico* ('transatlantic')
ultra-	('extremely')	*ultramoderno* ('ultramodern')
vice-	('in place of')	*vicepresidente* ('vice-president)'

19.3 The Most Common Suffixes: -aggio, -eria, -ista, etc.

When a suffix is added to nouns or adjectives, these drop their last vowel: *dente* + *-ista* > *dentista* ('dentist'), *bello* + *-ezza* > *bellezza* ('beauty'). To accept suffixes, verbs drop the infinitive endings *-are*, *-ere*, or *-ire*: *udire* + *-ibile* > *udibile* ('audible'), *ammirare* + *-evole* > *ammirevole* ('admirable').

Suffixes are a very versatile and practical method to alter words to fit some desired purpose. Some suffixes create new words from existing ones: *gelato* ('ice cream') + *-eria* > *gelateria* ('ice-cream parlor'), *pane* ('bread') + *-ificio* > *panificio* ('bakery'). Others instead simply modify the meanings of the base words (see 19.4): *gatto* ('cat') + *-ino* > *gattino* ('kitten'), *piccolo* ('short') + *-etto* > *piccoletto* ('quite short').

Listed below are the most common suffixes and the meanings associated with them, with the letter 'x' always referring to the noun, adjective, or verb that serves as the base word. Because feminine forms and plurals can be derived regularly, only the masculine forms are indicated:

- **-aggio** is added to verbs to indicate 'an action derived from x': *atterrare* > *atterraggio* ('landing'), *lavare* > *lavaggio* ('washing');
- **-aio** is added to nouns to indicate 'someone doing an activity linked to x': *biglietto* > *bigliettaio* ('ticket clerk'), *libro* > *libraio* ('bookseller'); it can also indicate 'something that contains x': *grano* > *granaio* ('granary'), *pollo* > *pollaio* ('henhouse');
- **-aiolo** is added to nouns to indicate 'someone who has something to do with x': *festa* > *festaiolo* ('party goer'), *pizza* > *pizzaiolo* ('pizza maker');
- **-ano** is added to proper nouns or names designating geographical places to indicate 'typical of x', 'follower of x', or 'coming from x': *Francesco* > *francescano* ('Fransciscan'), *Italia* > *italiano* ('Italian'), *monte* > *montano* ('mountainous');

- **-ario** is added to nouns to indicate 'a container of x': *ricetta* > *ricettario* ('recipe book'), *vocabolo* > *vocabolario* ('vocabulary');
- **-ato** is added to nouns to indicate 'the base of x': *console* > *consolato* ('consulate'), *vescovo* > *vescovato* ('bishopric');
- **-abile** is added to verbs in *-are*, **-ibile** to verbs in *-ere*, and *-ire* to indicate 'something that can be x' ('x' representing in this case the past participle of the verb): *amare* > *amabile* ('lovable'), *vendere* > *vendibile* ('saleable'), *compatire* > *compatibile* ('compatible');
- **-eria** is added to nouns or verbs to indicate 'the place where x is produced or sold': *gioiello* > *gioielleria* ('jewelry store'), *stirare* > *stireria* ('dry-cleaning store');
- **-esco** is added to nouns to form adjectives denoting a quality 'typical of x': *romanzo* > *romanzesco* ('of a novel'), *Settecento* > *settecentesco* ('eighteenth-century');
- **-esimo** is added to adjectives to form nouns indicating 'movements or ideologies linked to x': *pagano* > *paganesimo* ('paganism'), *umano* > *umanesimo* ('humanism');
- **-evole**, added to nouns, forms adjectives indicating 'a characteristic of x': *amore* > *amorevole* ('loveable'); or, added to verbs, it indicates 'someone/something doing x' or 'deserving to be x' ('x' representing in this case the past participle of the verb): *girare* > *girevole* ('revolving'), *ammirare* > *ammirevole* ('admirable');
- **-ezza** is added to adjectives to form nouns denoting 'a characteristic of someone/something x is': *bello* > *bellezza* ('beauty'), *stanco* > *stanchezza* ('tiredness');
- **-iere** is added to nouns to indicate 'someone doing an activity related to x': *giardino* > *giardiniere* ('gardener'), *spedizione* > *spedizioniere* ('forwarding agent'); *-iere* is also added to nouns to indicate 'an object linked to x': *candela* > *candeliere* ('candlestick'), *pane* > *paniere* ('basket');
- **-ificio** is added to nouns to indicate 'the place where x is produced or sold': *cemento* > *cementificio* ('cement factory'), *pane* > *panificio* ('bakery');
- **-ino** (for the diminutive value of *-ino* see 19.5) added to nouns indicates 'something pertaining to x': *mare* > *marino* ('marine'), *mira* > *mirino* ('sights'); *-ino* added to verbs indicates 'someone doing an activity related to x': *imbiancare* > *imbianchino* ('painter'), *ballare* > *ballerino* ('dancer');
- **-ismo** is added to nouns, adjectives, verbs, and adverbs to form nouns indicating 'movements, ideologies, attitudes linked to x': *razza* > *razzismo* ('racism'), *terrore* > *terrorismo* ('terrorism');
- **-ista**, is added to nouns to indicate 'someone doing an activity related to x': *auto* > *autista* ('driver'), *terrore* > *terrorista* ('terrorist');
- **-ità** is added to adjectives to form nouns indicating 'characteristics of someone/something x is': *felice* > *felicità* ('happiness'), *oscuro* > *oscurità* ('darkness');
- **-itudine** is added to adjectives to form nouns indicating 'a condition of someone/something x is': *beato* > *beatitudine* ('beatitude'), *grato* > *gratitudine* ('gratitude');
- **-oso** is added to nouns to form adjectives indicating 'someone/something having x as a characteristic': *ansia* > *ansioso* ('anxious'), *noia* > *noioso* ('boring');
- **-uto** is added to nouns to form adjectives indicating 'someone/something having x': *barba* > *barbuto* ('bearded'), *pancia* > *panciuto* ('pot-bellied').

19.4 Evaluative Suffixes

Unlike most suffixes, evaluative ones do not create new words but change the meaning of the base word, expressing a speaker or writer's emotions or points of view. Nouns, adjectives, verbs, and adverbs of this kind are unique to the Italian language and are extensively used, especially in the informal register. Italian, in fact, has suffixes to give a particular nuance to a word where other languages can only express the same meaning by resorting to a combination of words. For example, a word like *passeggiatina* (*passeggiata* + *-ina*) refers to a 'walk' that is not only short but also nice and enjoyable. The same shade of meaning in English (but also in Spanish or in French) can only be expressed by means of a phrase.

It must be kept in mind that the same evaluative suffix can carry more than one meaning and sometimes even opposite meanings, depending on the context or on the speaker's/writer's point of view. For example, *-uccio* can add a nuance of endearment (*Che calduccio!* 'What a nice warm temperature!') as well as a negative connotation (*Ho fatto un affaruccio* 'I did not have a really good deal').

The next few paragraphs enumerate the evaluative suffixes grouped by their main meaning and with examples of their use.

19.5 Diminutive and Affective Suffixes: -ino, -etto, -ello, etc.

Listed below are the diminutive and affective suffixes and the meanings associated with them. Because feminine forms and plurals can be derived regularly, only the masculine forms are indicated:

- **-ino** is probably the most common evaluative suffix. It is generally used to denote smallness: *tavolo > tavolino* ('small table'), *ragazzo > ragazzino* ('small boy'). At the same time it can convey the idea of something lovely and enjoyable: *casa > casina* ('cute, nice, little house'), *cosa > cosina* ('cute, nice, little thing'). When attached to a word expressing a negative connotation, *-ino* softens the negative nuance: *sporco > sporchino* ('not really clean'), *male > malino* ('not very well'). In some cases *-ino* is not attached directly to the base word but **-ic-** or **-ol-** can be placed in between: *bastone > bastoncino* ('small stick'), *mazzo > mazzolino* ('small bunch');
- **-etto** like *-ino*, indicates smallness (*bar > baretto* 'small bar') and can convey the idea of something lovely and enjoyable (*casa > casetta* 'a nice, little house'). It can also be used to soften an original meaning that could sound insulting by adding a clear nuance of affection: *piccolo > piccoletto* ('nice, short guy'), *vecchio > vecchietto* ('nice, old man');
- **-ettino** results from the combination of *-etto + -ino*; in fact, a word can combine two suffixes to accentuate its evaluative meaning: *casa > casettina* ('a nice, cozy, little house'), *zaino > zainettino* ('a nice, cool, small backpack');
- **-ello** and **-otto**, and their combination **-ottello,** indicate smallness or even a negative connotation tinged with affection, appreciation, or liking: *povero > poverello* ('poor, nice, little guy'), *ignorante > ignorantotto* ('ignorant but nice guy'), *grasso > grassottello* ('chubby, little guy');

- **-uccio,** which may also be used as a pejorative suffix (see 19.7), is especially used in reference to kids and in this context the suffix adds a nuance of affection: *bocca* > *boccuccia* ('nice, little mouth'), *occhi* > *occhiucci* ('nice, little eyes');
- **-igno, -occio, -ognolo** are generally used with adjectives to soften their meaning: *aspro* > *asprigno* ('a little sour'), *brutto* > *bruttoccio* ('not really beautiful'), *giallo* > *giallognolo* ('a little yellow').

19.6 Augmentative Suffixes: -one, -ona, -acchione, *and* -acchiona

Listed below are the augmentative suffixes and the meanings associated with them. In this section, only the singular masculine and feminine forms are indicated since the plural can be derived regularly:

- **-one (-ona f.)** is the most common suffix to indicate largeness: *libro* > *librone* ('big book'), *tavola* > *tavolona* ('big table'). This suffix does not simply express the measure of something, but it usually conveys at the same time a nuance of appreciation or, on the contrary, a derogatory tinge: *affare* > *affarone* ('great deal'), *naso* > *nasone* ('huge nose'). It is pervasively used in Italian and can be combined with nouns (as in the examples above), adjectives (*bello* > *bellone* 'really good looking', *pigro* > *pigrone* 'really lazy') and adverbs (*bene* > *benone* 'really well'). Sometimes *-one* is used instead of its equivalent feminine *-ona* with some feminine nouns to give them a masculine overtone. This is especially true of *un donnone* ('a huge woman'), *un macchinone* ('a showy and powerful car'), *un fontanone* ('a huge fountain');
- **-acchione (-acchiona f.)** is sometimes used with adjectives to intensify their meaning with a touch of humor: *furbo* > *furbacchione* ('smart aleck'), *matto* > *mattacchione* ('joker').

19.7 Pejorative Suffixes: -accio, -astro, -uccio, *etc.*

Listed below are the pejorative suffixes and the meanings associated with them. Because feminine and plural forms can be derived regularly, only the masculine ones are indicated:

- **-accio** is the most common pejorative suffix, clearly denoting the unpleasant and unlikable character of something: *giornata* > *giornataccia* ('a really bad day'), *ragazzo* > *ragazzaccio* ('rude boy'). It is extensively used in colloquial Italian and can be combined with nouns (as in the two examples above), adjectives (*amaro* > *amaraccio* 'unpleasantly bitter'), and adverbs (*male* > *malaccio* 'really badly') as well;
- **-astro** if combined with nouns imparts a pejorative connotation to them: *poeta* > *poetastro* ('a bad poet'), *professore* > *professorastro* > ('bad professor'). If instead it is combined with adjectives, the suffix softens the intensity or pureness of them: *dolce* > *dolciastro* ('sweetish'), *verde* > *verdastro* ('greenish');
- **-iccio** adds a relatively light pejorative connotation to adjectives: *bagnato* > *bagnaticcio* ('a little unpleasantly wet'), *bianco* > *bianchiccio* ('kind of dingy white');

- **-uccio**, which can also be used to convey a nuance of affection (see 19.5), generally adds a nuance of mediocrity to a word: *macchina* > *macchinuccia* ('not a really good car'), *romanzo* > *romanzuccio* ('not a really good novel').

19.8 The Special Cases of patrigno, matrigna, fratellastro, *and* sorellastra

The suffixes **-igno**, **-igna**, **-astro** and **-astra** added to *padre*, *madre*, *fratello*, and *sorella* form respectively the words *patrigno* ('stepfather'), *matrigna* ('stepmother'), *fratellastro* ('stepbrother'), and *sorellastra* ('stepsister'). Because of their original negative connotation, stemming from the old Italian culture of traditional families, these words are not used anymore in contemporary Italian, except when referring to fairy-tale characters. Anyone addressing living people with the above epithets in today's Italy is doing so intentionally, meaning to inflict emotional injury. For this reason, they are usually replaced by phrases like *la moglie di mio padre* ('my father's wife'), *il marito di mia madre* ('my mother's husband'), *il figlio di mio padre* ('my father's son'), and so on.

19.9 Typical Verb Suffixes: -acchiare, -erellare, -ettare, *etc.*

Not only nouns and adjectives but also verbs can combine with suffixes. If a good number of the suffixes seen above (see 19.3) can bind to verbs to form nouns (*ballare* + *ino* > *ballerino* 'dancer') or adjectives (*amare* + *ibile* > *amabile* 'lovable'), other suffixes are added to verb forms having dropped *-are*, *-ere*, and *-ire*, to soften the action expressed by the base verb or convey a sense of its repetition or imperfection. Listed below are the suffixes of this kind with the meanings associated with them:

- **-acchiare, -icchiare, -ucchiare**: *vivere* > *vivacchiare* ('to scrape out a living'), *cantare* > *canticchiare* ('to croon'), *leggere* > *leggiucchiare* ('to skim reading material');
- **-erellare** (or the equivalent **-ellare**): *giocare* > *giocherellare* ('to fiddle around'), *saltare* > *saltellare* ('to jump around');
- **-ettare, -ottare**: *picchiare* > *picchiettare* ('to tap repetitively'), *parlare* > *parlottare* ('to mumble').

20. VERB FORMS: REGULAR AND IRREGULAR CONJUGATIONS

> **Verbs and verb conjugations:** The verb is the most important part of the sentence. It communicates something about the subject and expresses actions or states of being. One of the most significant things about the verb is its relationship to time. A verb, in fact, tells when something takes place: if it has already happened, if it is occurring later, or if it is going on now. Verb conjugation is the process by which the root of the verbs is modified according to the subjects of the verbs (*io* 'I', *tu* 'you', etc.), tenses (present, imperfect, etc.), and moods (indicative, subjunctive, etc.).

20.1 Italian Verbs Unlike English Verbs

Verb conjugation in English is relatively simple whereas in Italian it is quite complex. Indeed, Italian verbs undergo changes involving six different forms for every tense, one form for each subject pronoun. Thus, studying Italian verbs is unquestionably a harder task than studying English verbs due to the great number of verbal forms. English speakers, however, should not be discouraged because many verbs are regular, so it is easy enough to memorize model forms and apply them to other verbs of the same group.

20.2 The Three Conjugations: *-are, -ere, and -ire*

Regular verbs are divided into three classes, called conjugations, according to whether their infinitive forms end in *-are* (*parlare* 'to talk'), *-ere* (*temere* 'to fear'), or *-ire* (*dormire* 'to sleep'). Each conjugation has its specific endings related to the mood, tense, and subject of the verb. Endings are attached directly to the root of the verb, which is obtained by dropping *-are*, *-ere*, and *-ire* from the infinitive form:

- the **first conjugation** includes all verbs ending in *-are* (*amare* 'to love', *cantare* 'to sing', *giocare* 'to play', etc.) and is the most extensive of all the three conjugations;
- the **second conjugation** involves all verbs ending in *-ere* (*leggere* 'to read', *scrivere* 'to write', *vedere* 'to see', etc.); it covers a lot of irregular verbs and is the least extensive of the three conjugations;

- the **third conjugation** encompasses all verbs ending in -*ire* (*annuire* 'to nod', *fuggire* 'to run away', *gradire* 'to appreciate', etc.); it is more extensive than the second conjugation but considerably less extensive than the first one.

20.3 Person, Gender, Number

There are **six personal forms** in Italian (see also 13.1), three singular and three plural:

Personal forms	
1st sing. pers.	*io* ('I')
2nd sing. pers.	*tu* ('you' sing.)
3rd sing. pers.	*lui* ('he'), lei ('she'); *Lei* ('you' sing. formal)
1st pl. pers.	*noi* ('we')
2nd pl. pers.	*voi* ('you' pl.)
3rd pl. pers.	*loro* ('they'); *Loro* ('you' pl. formal)

Since Italian verb endings almost always (see chapter 20 for verb conjugations) indicate the subject (*amo* 'I love', for example, can only have *io* as its subject because it ends in -*o*), the **subject pronouns** *io* ('I'), *tu* ('you'), and so on, unlike their English counterparts, **are generally omitted** (see 21.21 for exceptions): *Studiano molto* ('They study a lot'), *Parlerò al professore* ('I'll talk to the professor'). Otherwise, they are used for emphasis: *Io sono italiano, tu invece americano* ('I am Italian; you are American'), *Voi ripetete sempre le stesse cose* ('You always repeat the same things').

Although there is no gender distinction in Italian verbs, some rules of agreement must be applied where auxiliaries are concerned. Thus, compound forms that take the auxiliary *essere* ('to be') must agree in gender and number with the subject (see 20.9): *Lei è uscita* ('She went out'), *Loro sono partiti* ('They have left'). Compound forms taking the auxiliary *avere* ('to have') must instead agree with direct object or compound pronouns when they occur (see 20.9): *Li ho salutati* ('I said hello to them'), *Gliela ho data* ('I gave it to her').

> **N.B.** Unlike English, Italian has two formal pronouns *Lei* ('you' sing.) and *Loro* ('you' pl.) used when addressing strangers, adults, and people in authority (see 13.3).

20.4 Moods and Tenses

Verbs can be conjugated in different **moods** that indicate the manner in which the action or condition is conceived or intended. The Italian language identifies four finite moods: the **indicative** (used to state facts), the **subjunctive** (used to convey possibility, opinions, feelings, judgments, necessity), the **conditional** (used to express wishes and conditions, real or hypothetical), and the **imperative** (used to express commands). In addition to these four moods, there are three indefinite forms, which unlike the finite ones, do not indicate an explicit subject. They are the **infinitive**, the **participle**, and the **gerund** forms.

Each mood is further subdivided in two or more tenses. Tenses can be classified as **simple** (present, imperfect, preterite, and future) or **compound** (present perfect, pluperfect, preterite perfect, past, and future perfect).

> **N.B.** Since there does not exist a perfect correspondence between Italian and English tenses, there is a multiplicity of English terms applied to Italian tenses. For example, what is referred to here as the Preterite can be called Absolute Past or Simple Past, and what is called here the Preterite Perfect can be called Past Anterior, and so on. For this reason, it is not a bad idea to memorize the original Italian names: *Presente* ('Present'), *Imperfetto* ('Imperfect'), *Passato Remoto* ('Preterite'), *Futuro* ('Future'), *Passato Prossimo* ('Present Perfect'), *Trapassato Prossimo* ('Pluperfect'), *Trapassato Remoto* ('Preterite Perfect'), *Futuro Anteriore* ('Future Perfect'), *Passato* ('Past').

20.5 Transitive and Intransitive: Italian vs English

Italian verbs are divided into two categories: transitive and intransitive. A **transitive** verb expresses an action that transits directly (without any preposition) from the subject to an object. A transitive verb is usually followed by a direct object, a noun, or pronoun that directly receives the action of the verb: *Lo studente scrive il tema* ('The student is writing the essay'), *Conosco bene tuo fratello* ('I know your brother well'). In the examples above, the words *tema* and *tuo fratello* are the direct objects of the transitive verbs *scrivere* and *conoscere*. It is easy to recognize a direct object since it answers the question *Che cosa?* ('What?') or *Chi?* ('Whom?'). Everytime these two questions can be formulated, the verb can be considered transitive, even if the object is not expressed. In fact, a transitive verb does not always require a direct object to complete its meaning, but always answers the questions *Chi?* or *Che cosa?*. For example, in *Il professore scrive* ('The professor is writing'), the direct object is not explicit, but the action of 'writing' itself implies an object of writing, whether it is a letter, a postcard, or an essay. A transitive verb, and only a transitive verb, can take the passive form (see 23.1): *Il tema è scritto dallo studente* ('The essay is written by the student').

An **intransitive** verb is never followed by a direct object but may have an object preceded by a preposition: *Gli studenti vanno a scuola* ('The students are going to school'), *Parlo a te* ('I am speaking to you'). An intransitive verb answers the questions *Dove?* ('Where?'), *A chi?* ('To whom?'), *Con che cosa?* ('With what?'), and so on but never *Chi?* or *Che cosa?*. Intransitive verbs do not take the passive form.

If most transitive verbs in English are also transitive in Italian and vice-versa, sometimes they contrast. In fact, there are several very common verbs that take a direct object in Italian whereas their English equivalents are followed by a preposition + object construction (see 22.2): *Lia ascolta una canzone* ('Lia is listening to a song'). Likewise, several Italian verbs taking an object preceded by a preposition have English equivalents that take a direct object (see 22.3): *Paolo assomiglia a suo zio* ('Paolo looks like his uncle').

20.6 The Verb essere

The verb ***essere*** ('to be') is an irregular verb that must be memorized because it does not completely follow any of the three conjugation patterns. *Essere* can function as an auxilary verb to "help" other verbs to form compound tenses (see 20.8), or it can be used independently. In the latter case, *essere*:

- translates in most cases into the English **'to be'**: *Io sono Marco* ('I am Marco'), *Noi siamo felici* ('We are happy'), *Erano a casa* ('They were at home');
- is the equivalent of the English structure **'there + to be'** (see 14.3) when preceded by the particle *ci* (see 14.3): *Ci sono due cani* ('There are two dogs'), *C'è ancora tempo* ('There is still time'), *Marco ci sarà* ('Marco will be there');
- can mean **'to exist'**, when used alone without any specification: *Dio è e sarà sempre* ('God exists and always will exist').

Below are indicated the forms of ***essere*** ('to be').

INDICATIVE		SUBJUNCTIVE	
Present	**Present Perfect**	**Present**	**Past**
io sono	*io sono stato/a*	*io sia*	*io sia stato/a*
tu sei	*tu sei stato/a*	*tu sia*	*tu sia stato/a*
lui/lei/(Lei) è	*lui/lei/(Lei) è stato/a*	*lui/lei/(Lei) sia*	*lui/lei/(Lei) sia stato/a*
noi siamo	*noi siamo stati/e*	*noi siamo*	*noi siamo stati/e*
voi siete	*voi siete stati/e*	*voi siate*	*voi siate stati/e*
loro/(Loro) sono	*loro/(Loro) sono stati/e*	*loro/(Loro) siano*	*loro/(Loro) siano stati/e*
Imperfect	**Pluperfect**	**Imperfect**	**Pluperfect**
io ero	*io ero stato/a*	*io fossi*	*io fossi stato/a*
tu eri	*tu eri stato/a*	*tu fossi*	*tu fossi stato/a*
lui/lei/(Lei) era	*lui/lei/(Lei) era stato/a*	*lui/lei/(Lei) fosse*	*lui/lei/(Lei) fosse stato/a*
noi eravamo	*noi eravamo stati/e*	*noi fossimo*	*noi fossimo stati/e*
voi eravate	*voi eravate stati/e*	*voi foste*	*voi foste stati/e*
loro/(Loro) erano	*loro/(Loro) erano stati/e*	*loro/(Loro) fossero*	*loro/(Loro) fossero stati/e*
		CONDITIONAL	
Preterite	**Preterite Perfect**	**Present**	**Past**
io fui	*io fui stato/a*	*io sarei*	*io sarei stato/a*
tu fosti	*tu fosti stato/a*	*tu saresti*	*tu saresti stato/a*
lui/lei/(Lei) fu	*lui/lei/(Lei) fu stato/a*	*lui/lei/(Lei) sarebbe*	*lui/lei/(Lei) sarebe stato/a*
noi fummo	*noi fummo stati/e*	*noi saremmo*	*noi saremmo stati/e*
voi foste	*voi foste stati/e*	*voi sareste*	*voi sareste stati/e*
loro/(Loro) furono	*loro/(Loro) furono stati/e*	*loro/(Loro) sarebbero*	*loro/(Loro) sarebbero stati/e*

		IMPERATIVE	
Future	Future Perfect	Present	
io sarò	io sarò stato/a	sii (tu)	
tu sarai	tu sarai stato/a	siamo (noi)	
lui/lei/(Lei) sarà	lui/lei/(Lei) sarà stato/a	siate (voi)	
noi saremo	noi saremo stati/e		
voi sarete	voi sarete stati/e	**N.B.** The 3rd sing. and pl. persons of the present subj. *sia*	
loro/(Loro) saranno	loro/(Loro) saranno stati/e	(*Lei*) and *siano* (*Loro*) are used to express formal commands.	

INFINITIVE		PARTICIPLE		GERUND	
Present	Past	Present	Past	Present	Past
essere	essere stato/a/i/e	ente/i	stato/a/i/e	essendo	essendo stato/a/i/e

> **N.B.** a. The past participle of *essere*, which is used to form the compound tenses, always agrees in number and gender with the subject: *La bambina è stata buona* ('The little girl has been good'), *Gli studenti sono stati in Italia quest'anno* ('The students have been to Italy this year'). b. The present participle *ente/i* and the preterite perfect of *essere* are in complete disuse in contemporary Italian.

20.7 The Verb avere

The verb ***avere*** ('to have'), like *essere* ('to be'), is an irregular verb that must be memorized because it does not completely follow any of the three conjugation patterns.

Avere can function as an auxiliary verb to "help" other verbs to form compound tenses (see 20.8) or can be used independently. In the latter case *avere* can indicate:

- **possession**: *Ho una bella casa* ('I have a beautiful house'), *Lei ha grande fascino* ('She has great charm');
- **relationship**: *Ho due fratelli* ('I have two brothers'), *Abbiamo molti amici* ('We have many friends');
- **duty** when followed by the construction ***da* + infinitive** (see also 16.4): *Ho da spedire una lettera* ('I have to send a letter'), *Abbiamo da fare la spesa* ('We have to go grocery shopping');
- **age** (see also 12.7): *Marco ha venti anni* ('Marco is twenty years old'), *La mia moto è nuova, ha appena qualche giorno* ('My motorcycle is new; it is just a few days old');
- **feelings and physical sensations**: *Hai paura?* ('Are you afraid?'), *Hanno molta fame* ('They are really hungry').

Below are indicated the forms of ***avere*** ('to have')

INDICATIVE		SUBJUNCTIVE	
Present	**Present Perfect**	**Present**	**Past**
io ho	io ho avuto	io abbia	io abbia avuto
tu hai	tu hai avuto	tu abbia	tu abbia avuto
lui/lei/(Lei) ha	lui/lei/(Lei) ha avuto	lui/lei/(Lei) abbia	lui/lei/(Lei) abbia avuto
noi abbiamo	noi abbiamo avuto	noi abbiamo	noi abbiamo avuto
voi avete	voi avete avuto	voi abbiate	voi abbiate avuto
loro/(Loro) hanno	loro/(Loro) hanno avuto	loro/(Loro) abbiano	loro/(Loro) abbiano avuto
Imperfect	**Pluperfect**	**Imperfect**	**Pluperfect**
io avevo	io avevo avuto	lo avessi	io avessi avuto
tu avevi	tu avevi avuto	tu avessi	tu avessi avuto
lui/lei/(Lei) aveva	lui/lei/(Lei) aveva avuto	lui/lei/(Lei) avesse	lui/lei/(Lei) avesse avuto
noi avevamo	noi avevamo avuto	noi avessimo	noi avessimo avuto
voi avevate	voi avevate avuto	voi aveste	voi aveste avuto
loro/(Loro) avevano	loro/(Loro) avevano avuto	loro/(Loro) avessero	loro/(Loro) avessero avuto
		CONDITIONAL	
Preterite	**Preterite Perfect**	**Present**	**Past**
io ebbi	io ebbi avuto	io avrei	io avrei avuto
tu avesti	tu avesti avuto	tu avresti	tu avresti avuto
lui/lei/(Lei) ebbe	lui/lei/(Lei) ebbe avuto	lui/lei/(Lei) avrebbe	lui/lei/(Lei) avrebbe avuto
noi avemmo	noi avemmo avuto	noi avremmo	noi avremmo avuto
voi aveste	voi aveste avuto	voi avreste	voi avreste avuto
loro/(Loro) ebbero	loro/(Loro) ebbero avuto	loro/(Loro) avrebbero	loro/(Loro) avrebbero avuto
		IMPERATIVE	
Future	**Future Perfect**	**Present**	
io avrò	io avrò avuto	abbi (tu)	
tu avrai	tu avrai avuto	abbiamo (noi)	
lui/lei/(Lei) avrà	lui/lei/(Lei) avrà avuto	abbiate (voi)	
noi avremo	noi avremo avuto		
voi avrete	voi avrete avuto	**N.B.** The 3rd sing. and pl. persons of the present subj. *abbia* (*Lei*)	
loro/(Loro) avranno	loro/(Loro) avranno avuto	and *abbiano* (*Loro*) are used to express formal commands.	

INFINITIVE		PARTICIPLE		GERUND	
Present	**Past**	**Present**	**Past**	**Present**	**Past**
avere	avere avuto	avente	avuto	avendo	avendo avuto

20.8 Compound Tenses: essere or avere?

Compound tenses are formed by using the auxiliary verbs *essere* ('to be') or *avere* ('to have') with the verb we want to conjugate. Grammatically speaking, there are no general and unequivocal rules for choosing either *essere* or *avere* as auxiliaries, but rather some practical clues. Having said that, verbs taking *avere* are more numerous than those taking *essere*. The following guidelines can help in making the right choice.

The verb **essere** is used:

- as **auxiliary for itself** when it is the main verb: *Sono stato bravo* ('I was being good'), *Saresti stata felice* ('You would have been happy');
- with **most of the intransitive verbs** (see 20.5), especially those involving movement (*andare* 'to go', *partire* 'to leave'), inactivity (*stare* 'to stay', *rimanere* 'to remain'), transformation in the state of being (*crescere* 'to grow', *morire* 'to die'), appearance (*sembrare* 'to seem', 'to look like') and events (*avvenire* 'to happen');
- with **reflexive verbs** (see 23.4): *Si sono alzati presto* ('They got up early'), *Si è lavata* ('She washed herself');
- to make **the passive form** (see 23.1): *Gli studenti sono rimproverati dal professore* ('The students are scolded by the professor'), *Sono stato invitato da Giovanni* ('I was invited by Giovanni').

The auxiliary **avere** is used:

- as **auxiliary for itself** when it is the main verb: *Ho avuto due biciclette* ('I had two bicycles'), *Ho avuto molta paura* ('I was really afraid');
- with **all transitive verbs** (see 20.5): *Ho letto un libro* ('I read a book'), *Ho deciso di venire a trovarti* ('I decided to come to visit you');
- with **some intransitive verbs** (see 20.10 for a list of them): *Ho dormito benissimo* ('I slept very well'), *Hanno parlato per due ore* ('They spoke for two hours');
- with the verbs ***incominciare*** and ***cominciare*** (both meaning 'to start'), ***finire*** ('to finish'), ***smettere*** ('to quit'), ***continuare*** ('to continue'), when followed by *a* or *di* + infinitive: *Ho cominciato a suonare la chitarra* ('I started playing the guitar'), *Ho smesso di fumare* ('I quit smoking');
- with all verbs expressing **animal sounds**: *Il cane ha abbaiato* ('The dog barked'), *I gatti hanno miagolato tutta la notte* ('Cats caterwauled all night long').

20.9 Past Participle Agreement with essere *and* avere

The past participle of the verb conjugated **with *essere* always agrees in number and gender with the subject**: *Maria è arrivata* ('Maria arrived'), *I miei genitori sono partiti* ('My parents left').

In contrast, in compound tenses **with the auxiliary *avere*, the past participle does not agree with the subject,** but always ends in *-o* regardless of the gender and number of the subject: *Maria ha cantato* ('Maria sang'), *Loro hanno mangiato* ('They ate'). However, the past participle does agree with the object, if it is a third person direct object pronoun (see 13.7) *lo, la, li,* or *le* as can be seen in the sentence *I musicisti erano sul palco, li abbiamo salutati* ('The musicians were on the stage; we said hello to them') where *salutati* ends in *-i* because it agrees with the pronoun *li* that stands for the masculine and plural *musicisti*.

Agreement also occurs when the direct object pronouns combine with indirect ones (see 13.10) to form *glielo, gliela, gliele,* or *glieli*: *Abbiamo comprato fiori per nostra mamma e glieli abbiamo dati* ('We bought flowers for our mother, and we gave them to her'). In this case *dati* ends in *-i* because it agrees with the pronoun *-li* of *glieli*, which stands for the masculine and plural *fiori*.

20.10 Intransitive Verbs Taking the Auxiliary avere

The majority of intransitive verbs use *essere* ('to be') though some form their compound tenses with *avere* ('to have'). The most common ones are:

Intransitive verbs with *avere*	Examples
camminare ('to walk')	*Ho camminato per due ore* ('I walked for two hours')
cenare ('to have dinner')	*Abbiamo cenato con Carlo* ('We had dinner with Carlo')
dormire ('to sleep')	*Avete dormito bene?* ('Did you sleep well?')
gridare ('to shout out')	*Lei ha gridato per la gioia* ('She shouted for joy')
nuotare ('to swim')	*Ho nuotato molto oggi* ('I swam a lot today')
parlare ('to speak')	*Hai parlato con mamma?* ('Did you speak with Mom?')
passeggiare ('to take a walk')	*Abbiamo fatto una bella passeggiata* ('We took a nice walk')
pranzare ('to have lunch')	*Hanno pranzato insieme* ('They had lunch together')
sciare ('to ski')	*Lei ha sciato benissimo* ('She skied very well')
urlare ('to scream')	*Lui ha gridato fortissimo* ('He screamed really loud')
viaggiare ('to travel')	*Lei ha viaggiato molto* ('She traveled a lot')

20.11 Verbs with Double Auxiliaries: essere *and* avere

Usually one auxiliary verb excludes the other, but some verbs can indistinctly take either *essere* ('to be') or *avere* ('to have'), depending on whether they are used transitively (with *avere*) or intransitively (with *essere*). The chart below provides a list of the most common of these verbs:

verbs	with *avere*	with *essere*
aumentare ('to increase', 'to raise')	*Tu hai aumentato il prezzo* ('You raised the price')	*La benzina è aumentata* ('The price of gasoline has increased')
cambiare ('to change')	*Abbiamo cambiato scuola* ('We changed schools')	*Il tempo è cambiato* ('The weather has changed')
cominciare ('to start', 'to begin')	*Ho cominciato il tema* ('I started my essay')	*Il film è cominciato* ('The movie has started')
continuare ('to continue', 'to go on')	*Lui hai continuato a parlare* ('He went on talking')	*La lezione è continuata* ('Class went on')
correre ('to run')	*Avete corso un miglio* ('You ran a mile')	*Siamo corsi a casa* ('We ran back home')
diminuire ('to reduce')	*Abbiamo diminuito il prezzo* ('We reduced the price')	*Il prezzo è diminuito* ('The price is reduced')
finire ('to finish', 'to end')	*Ho finito i compiti* ('I finished my homework')	*Il concerto è finito alle 23* ('The concert ended at 11 PM')
iniziare ('to start', 'to begin')	*Ho iniziato il lavoro per te* ('I started the work for you')	*La conferenza è iniziata alle 9* ('The conference started at 9 AM')
migliorare ('to improve', 'to get better')	*Ho migliorato i miei voti* ('I improved my grades')	*Sono molto migliorato* ('I really got better')
passare ('to pass')	*Ho passato l'esame* ('I passed the exam')	*È passato molto tempo* ('A lot of time passed')
vivere ('to live')	*Ho vissuto a Roma* ('I lived in Rome')	*È vissuta ottanta anni* ('She lived for eighty years')

In the case of **impersonal verbs indicating weather conditions** like *piovere* ('to rain'), *nevicare* ('to snow'), and so on, the use of *essere* or *avere* is perfectly equivalent: *Ha piovuto/È piovuto* ('It rained'), *Ha nevicato/È nevicato* ('It snowed').

20.12 The Verbs essere and avere with Modal Verbs

Common modal verbs (see also 23.14) like *potere* ('can', 'to be able to'), *dovere* ('must', 'to have to'), and *volere* ('to want to') are usually followed by an infinitive verb: *Posso cantare* ('I can sing'), *Dobbiamo partire* ('We must leave'), *Vogliono uscire* ('They want to go out'). They can use either *essere* or *avere* depending on the auxiliary required by the infinitive verb. For example, in *Non ho potuto lavorare* ('I couldn't work'), the compound tense of *potere* is formed with *avere* (*ho*) because the verb *lavorare* requires *avere*; in a sentence like *Marco non è voluto uscire* ('Marco did not want to go out'), the compound tense of *volere* is formed with *essere* (*è*) because *uscire* requires the auxilary *essere*.

If the infinitive is one of the verbs for which *essere* or *avere* are perfectly equivalent (see 20.11), one or the other will work: *Secondo le previsioni sarebbe/avrebbe dovuto piovere tutto il giorno* ('According to the weather forecast it should have rained all day long').

When used alone, without an infinitive following them, modal verbs always form their compound tenses with *avere*: *Non ho potuto* ('I couldn't'), *Hai voluto* ('You wanted').

20.13 Compound Tense Formation

To form compound tenses, it can be helpful to keep in mind the correspondences between simple and compound forms as indicated in the following chart:

Simple tenses	Compound tenses
INDICATIVE	
Present	Present Perfect
Imperfect	Pluperfect
Preterite	Preterite Perfect
Future	Future Perfect
SUBJUNCTIVE	
Present	Past
Imperfect	Pluperfect
CONDITIONAL	
Present	Past
GERUND	
Present	Past
INFINITIVE	
Present	Past

There are three simple steps to forming compound tenses:

- choosing the right auxiliary verb between *essere* or *avere* (see 20.8);
- choosing the simple tense of *essere* or *avere* corresponding to the compound we want to form;
- adding the past participle of the verb being conjugated.

To form the indicative present perfect of *cantare* ('to sing'), for example, we must first choose *avere* as auxiliary, then we take the present tense of *avere* (*io ho, tu hai*, etc.), and at last we add the past participle *cantato*: *io ho cantato* ('I sang'), *tu hai cantato* ('you sang'), and so on. If the verb we want to make compound requires the auxiliary *essere*, we follow exactly the same steps, but we must remember that the past participle combined with *essere* always agrees in gender and number with the subject (see 20.9): *Marta è andata in vacanza in Italia* ('Marta went on vacation in Italy'), *Loro sono arrivati puntuali* ('They arrived on time').

As can be seen from the examples above, the auxiliary always precedes the past participle. The only words that can come between the auxiliary and the past participle are adverbs like *sempre* ('always'), *mai* ('never'), *ancora* ('yet'), *già* ('already'): *Non ho mai incontrato i tuoi amici italiani* ('I have never met your Italian friends'), *Abbiamo già mangiato* ('We have already eaten').

20.14 The First Conjugation: Verbs in -are

All the regular verbs in *-are* are conjugated by dropping the infinitive ending *-are* and adding the appropriate endings to the resulting stem. The compound forms use *avere* or *essere* (see 20.8) depending on the specific verb being conjugated.

The regular forms of verbs in ***-are*** (***parlare*** 'to talk')

INDICATIVE		SUBJUNCTIVE	
Present	**Present Perfect**	**Present**	**Past**
*io parl**o***	*io ho parlato*	*io parl**i***	*io abbia parlato*
*tu parl**i***	*tu hai parlato*	*tu parl**i***	*tu abbia parlato*
*lui/lei/(Lei) parl**a***	*lui/lei/(Lei) ha parlato*	*lui/lei/(Lei) parl**i***	*lui/lei/(Lei) abbia parlato*
*noi parl**iamo***	*noi abbiamo parlato*	*noi parl**iamo***	*noi abbiamo parlato*
*voi parl**ate***	*voi avete parlato*	*voi parl**iate***	*voi abbiate parlato*
*loro/(Loro) parl**ano***	*loro/(Loro) hanno parlato*	*loro/(Loro) parl**ino***	*loro/(Loro) abbiano parlato*
Imperfect	**Pluperfect**	**Imperfect**	**Pluperfect**
*io parl**avo***	*io avevo parlato*	*io parl**assi***	*io avessi parlato*
*tu parl**avi***	*tu avevi parlato*	*tu parl**assi***	*tu avessi parlato*
*lui/lei/(Lei) parl**ava***	*lui/lei/(Lei) aveva parlato*	*lui/lei/(Lei) parl**asse***	*lui/lei/(Lei) avesse parlato*
*noi parl**avamo***	*noi avevamo parlato*	*noi parl**assimo***	*noi avessimo parlato*
*voi parl**avate***	*voi avevate parlato*	*voi parl**aste***	*voi aveste parlato*
*loro/(Loro) parl**avano***	*loro/(Loro) avevano parlato*	*loro/(Loro) parl**assero***	*loro/(Loro) avessero parlato*

		CONDITIONAL	
Preterite	**Preterite Perfect**	**Present**	**Past**
io parl**ai**	io ebbi parlato	io parl**erei**	io avrei parlato
tu parl**asti**	tu avesti parlato	tu parl**eresti**	tu avresti parlato
lui/lei/(Lei) parl**ò**	lui/lei/(Lei) ebbe parlato	lui/lei/(Lei) parl**erebbe**	lui/lei/(Lei) avrebbe parlato
noi parl**ammo**	noi avemmo parlato	noi parl**eremmo**	noi avremmo parlato
voi parl**aste**	voi aveste parlato	voi parl**ereste**	voi avreste parlato
loro/(Loro) parl**arono**	loro/(Loro) ebbero parlato	loro/(Loro) parl**erebbero**	loro/(Loro) avrebbero parlato
		IMPERATIVE	
Future	**Future Perfect**	**Present**	
io parl**erò**	io avrò parlato	parla (tu)	
tu parl**erai**	tu avrai parlato	parliamo (noi)	
lui/lei/(Lei) parl**erà**	lui/lei/(Lei) avrà parlato	parlate (voi)	
noi parl**eremo**	noi avremo parlato		
voi parl**erete**	voi avrete parlato	**N.B.** The 3rd sing. and pl. persons of the present subj. *parli*	
loro/(Loro) parl**eranno**	loro/(Loro) avranno parlato	(Lei) and *parlino* (Loro) are used to express formal commands.	

INFINITIVE		PARTICIPLE		GERUND	
Present	**Past**	**Present**	**Past**	**Present**	**Past**
parl**are**	avere parlato	parl**ante**	parl**ato**	parl**ando**	avendo parlato

Verbs in -*are* conjugated with *essere* (*tornare* 'to come back', *cambiare* 'to change', and so on) have past participle forms and compound tenses that agree (see 20.9) in gender and number with the subject (*io sono tornato/a, loro sono cambiati/e,* and so on).

20.15 *Particularities of Verbs in* -care, -gare, -iare, *and* -eare

Several first conjugation verbs present some particularities, depending on the vowels or consonants preceding -*are*. Below are all the possible cases:

- verbs ending in **-care** and **-gare** acquire an **h** in front of all endings starting with *e* and *i* in order to preserve the hard sound of *c* and *g*: *giocare* ('to play') > *tu giochi, noi giochiamo, loro giocheranno*, and so on; *navigare* ('to sail') > *tu navighi, noi navighiamo, loro navigheranno*, and so on;
- verbs ending in **-iare** presenting a stress (indicated in the following Italian verbs by the underlined vowel) on the *i* in the 1st pers. sing. of the present tense (*io avvio, io scio*) maintain that *i* even in front of another *i* (*tu avvii, noi sciiamo*); on the contrary, verbs ending in -*iare* but presenting an unstressed *i* in the 1st pers. sing. of the present tense (*io studio, io viaggio*) drop that *i* in front of another *i* (*tu studi, noi viaggiamo*);

- verbs ending in *-eare* maintain the *e* even in front of another *e*: *sottolineare* ('to underline') > *io sottolineerò, noi sottolineeremo, loro sottolineeranno*.

20.16 Irregular Verbs in -are

The verbs in this section are the most common irregular verbs in *-are*. Only the irregular patterns are listed, the others are regular:

Andare ('to go')

Present Indic.	Future	Present Subj.	Present Cond.
io vado	io andrò	io vada	io andrei
tu vai	tu andrai	tu vada	tu andresti
lui/lei/(Lei) va	lui/lei/(Lei) andrà	lui/lei/(Lei) vada	lui/lei/(Lei) andrebbe
noi andiamo	noi andremo	noi andiamo	noi andremmo
voi andate	voi andrete	voi andiate	voi andreste
loro/(Loro) vanno	loro/(Loro) andranno	loro/(Loro) vadano	loro/(Loro) andrebbero

Imperative	
vai/va' (tu)	**N.B.** a) The form *va'* (*tu*) with the apostrophe is also very common, especially in spoken Italian.
andiamo (noi)	b) The 3rd sing. and pl. persons of the present subj. *vada* (*Lei*) and *vadano* (*Loro*) are used to express formal commands.
andate (voi)	

Dare ('to give')

Present Indic.	Preterite	Future	Present Subj.
io do	io detti (diedi)	io darò	io dia
tu dai	tu desti	tu darai	tu dia
lui/lei/(Lei) dà	lui/lei/(Lei) dette (diede)	lui/lei/(Lei) darà	lui/lei/(Lei) dia
noi diamo	noi demmo	noi daremo	noi diamo
voi date	voi deste	voi darete	voi diate
loro/(Loro) danno	loro/(Loro) dettero (diedero)	loro/(Loro) daranno	loro/(Loro) diano

Imperfect Subj.	Present Cond.	Imperative	
io dessi	io darei	dai/da' (tu)	
tu dessi	tu daresti	diamo (noi)	
lui/lei/(Lei) desse	lui/lei/(Lei) darebbe	date (voi)	
noi dessimo	noi daremmo		
voi deste	voi dareste	**N.B.** a) The form *da'* (*tu*) with the apostrophe is also very common, especially in spoken Italian. b) The 3rd sing. and pl. persons of the present subj. *dia* (*Lei*) and *diano* (*Loro*) are used to express formal commands.	
loro/(Loro) dessero	loro/(Loro) darebbero		

As can be seen in the table above, *dare* can take the forms *io diedi, lui/lei/(Lei) diede, loro (Loro) diedero* in addition to the preterite forms *io detti, lui/lei/(Lei) dette, loro (Loro) dettero*.

Fare ('to make', 'to do')

Present Indic.	Imperfect Indic.	Preterite	Future
io faccio	io facevo	io feci	io farò
tu fai	tu facevi	tu facesti	tu farai
lui/lei/(Lei) fa	lui/lei/(Lei) faceva	lui/lei/(Lei) fece	lui/lei/(Lei) farà
noi facciamo	noi facevamo	noi facemmo	noi faremo
voi fate	voi facevate	voi faceste	voi farete
loro/(Loro) fanno	loro/(Loro) facevano	loro/(Loro) fecero	loro/(Loro) faranno
Present Subj.	**Imperfect Subj.**	**Present Cond.**	**Imperative**
io faccia	io facessi	io farei	fai/fa' (tu)
tu faccia	tu facessi	tu faresti	facciamo (noi)
lui/lei/(Lei) faccia	lui/lei/(Lei) facesse	lui/lei/(Lei) farebbe	fate (voi)
noi facciamo	noi facessimo	noi faremmo	
voi facciate	voi faceste	voi fareste	**N.B.** a) The form *fa'* (*tu*) with the apostrophe is also very common, especially in spoken Italian. b) The 3rd sing. and pl. persons of the present subj. *faccia* (*Lei*) and *facciano* (*Loro*) are used to express formal commands.
loro/(Loro) facciano	loro/(Loro) facessero	loro/(Loro) farebbero	
Past Participle	**Present Gerund**		
fatto	facendo		

All verbs formed with *-fare* are conjugated like *fare*: *contraffare* ('to forge'), *disfare* ('unmake', 'undo'), and so on.

Stare ('to stay')

Present Indic.	Preterite	Future	Present Subj.
io sto	io stetti	io starò	io stia
tu stai	tu stesti	tu starai	tu stia
lui/lei/(Lei) sta	lui/lei/(Lei) stette	lui/lei/(Lei) starà	lui/lei/(Lei) stia
noi stiamo	noi stemmo	noi staremo	noi stiamo
voi state	voi steste	voi starete	voi stiate
loro/(Loro) stanno	loro/(Loro) stettero	loro/(Loro) staranno	loro/(Loro) stiano
Imperfect Subj.	**Present Cond.**	**Imperative**	
io stessi	io starei	stai/sta' (tu)	
tu stessi	tu staresti	stiamo (noi)	
lui/lei/(Lei) stesse	lui/lei/(Lei) starebbe	state (voi)	
noi stessimo	noi staremmo		
voi steste	voi stareste	**N.B.** a) The form *sta'* (*tu*) with the apostrophe is also very common, especially in spoken Italian. b) The 3rd sing. and pl. persons of the present subj. *stia* (*Lei*) and *stiano* (*Loro*) are used to express formal commands.	
loro/(Loro) stessero	loro/(Loro) starebbero		

All verbs formed with *-stare* are conjugated like *stare*: *contrastare* ('to contrast'), *restare* ('to remain'), and so on.

20.17 The Second Conjugation: Verbs in -ere

All the regular verbs in *-ere* are conjugated by dropping the infinitive ending *-ere* and adding the appropriate endings to the resulting stem. The compound forms use *avere* or *essere* (see 20.8), depending on the specific verb being conjugated.

The regular forms of verbs in ***-ere*** (***temere*** 'to fear') follow:

INDICATIVE		SUBJUNCTIVE	
Present	**Present Perfect**	**Present**	**Past**
io temo	*io ho temuto*	*io tema*	*io abbia temuto*
tu temi	*tu hai temuto*	*tu tema*	*tu abbia temuto*
lui/lei/(Lei) teme	*lui/lei/(Lei) ha temuto*	*lui/lei/(Lei) tema*	*lui/lei/(Lei) abbia temuto*
no temiamo	*noi abbiamo temuto*	*noi temiamo*	*noi abbiamo temuto*
voi temete	*voi avete temuto*	*voi temiate*	*voi abbiate temuto*
loro/(Loro) temono	*loro/(Loro) hanno temuto*	*loro/(Loro) temano*	*loro/(Loro) abbiano temuto*
Imperfect	**Pluperfect**	**Imperfect**	**Pluperfect**
io temevo	*io avevo temuto*	*io temessi*	*io avessi temuto*
tu temevi	*tu avevi temuto*	*tu temessi*	*tu avessi temuto*
lui/lei/(Lei) temeva	*lui/lei/(Lei) aveva temuto*	*lui/lei/(Lei) temesse*	*lui/lei/(Lei) avesse temuto*
noi temevamo	*noi avevamo temuto*	*noi temessimo*	*noi avessimo temuto*
voi temevate	*voi avevate temuto*	*voi temeste*	*voi aveste temuto*
loro/(Loro) temevano	*loro/(Loro) avevano temuto*	*loro/(Loro) temessero*	*loro/(Loro) avessero temuto*
		CONDITIONAL	
Preterite	**Preterite Perfect**	**Present**	**Past**
io temetti (temei)	*io ebbi temuto*	*io temerei*	*io avrei temuto*
tu temesti	*tu avesti temuto*	*tu temeresti*	*tu avresti temuto*
lui/lei/(Lei) temette (temé)	*lui/lei/(Lei) ebbe temuto*	*lui/lei/(Lei) temerebbe*	*lui/lei/(Lei) avrebbe temuto*
noi tememmo	*noi avemmo temuto*	*noi temeremmo*	*noi avremmo temuto*
voi temeste	*voi aveste temuto*	*voi temereste*	*voi avreste temuto*
loro/(Loro) temettero (temerono)	*loro/(Loro) ebbero temuto*	*loro/(Loro) temerebbero*	*loro/(Loro) avrebbero temuto*
		IMPERATIVE	
Future	**Future Perfect**	**Present**	
io temerò	*io avrò temuto*	*temi (tu)*	
tu temerai	*tu avrai temuto*	*temiamo (noi)*	
lui/lei/(Lei) temerà	*lui/lei/(Lei) avrà temuto*	*temete (voi)*	
noi temeremo	*noi avremo temuto*		
voi temerete	*voi avrete temuto*	**N.B.** The 3rd sing. and pl. persons of the present subj. *tema* (*Lei*) and *temano* (*Loro*) are used to express formal commands.	
loro/(Loro) temeranno	*loro/(Loro) avranno temuto*		

INFINITIVE		PARTICIPLE		GERUND	
Present	Past	Present	Past	Present	Past
tem*ere*	*avere* tem*uto*	tem*ente*	tem*uto*	tem*endo*	*avendo* tem*uto*

Verbs in *-ere* conjugated with *essere* (*crescere* 'to grow up', *cadere* 'to fall', and so on) have past participle forms and compound tenses that agree (see 20.9) in gender and number with the subject (*io sono cresciuto/a, loro sono caduti/e,* and so on).

> **NB:** As can be seen in the table above, *temere* and other similar verbs in *-ere* (see 20.18) take the forms *io temei, lui/lei/(Lei) temé, loro (Loro) temerono* in addition to the preterite forms *io temetti, lui/lei/(Lei) temette, loro (Loro) temettero.*

20.18 Particularities of Second Conjugation Regular Verbs

The second conjugation presents a lot of irregularity. It is not enough to know that numerous verbs belonging to this category are irregular, it must be kept in mind that even the verbs that are regular have some particularities:

- unlike the verbs of the first conjugation, verbs ending in *-cere* and *-gere*, do not aquire an *h* in front of all endings starting with *e* and *i*: *vincere* ('to win') > *tu vinci, lui vince, io vincevo,* etc.; *reggere* ('to hold') > *tu reggi, lui regge, io reggevo,* etc.;
- the preterite can present two forms for the first and third person singular and the third person plural: **-ei/-etti, -é/-ette, -erono/-ettero.** If some verbs, like *temere* (see 20.17), can admit both forms, other verbs, according to the contemporary usage of Italian, take preferably the forms *-etti, -ette,* and *-ettero.* Most verbs whose root ends in *t* (*potere* 'can', *riflettere* 'to reflect', etc.) take instead the endings *-ei, -é,* and *-erono*. When in doubt, it is always a good idea to consult a dictionary to see what form is admitted or preferred.

20.19 Irregular Verbs in -ere

Most verbs ending in *-ere* are irregular verbs, the most common of which are presented in this section. Only the major patterns of irregularity are listed; the rest follow the regular patterns:

Bere ('to drink')

Preterite	Future	Present Cond.
io bevvi	io berrò	io berrei
tu bevesti	tu berrai	tu berresti
lui/lei/(Lei) bevve	lui/lei/(Lei) berrà	lui/lei/(Lei) berrebbe
noi bevemmo	noi berremo	noi berremmo
voi beveste	voi berrete	voi berreste
loro/(Loro) bevvero	loro/(Loro) berranno	loro/(Loro) berrebbero

All other forms are made by adding the regular endings to the stem **bev-**: *bevo, bevevi,* and so on.

Cadere ('to fall')

Preterite	Future	Prensent Cond.
io caddi	*io cadrò*	*io cadrei*
tu cadesti	*tu cadrai*	*tu cadresti*
lui/lei/(Lei) cadde	*lui/lei/(Lei) cadrà*	*lui/lei/(Lei) cadrebbe*
noi cademmo	*noi cadremo*	*noi cadremmo*
voi cadeste	*voi cadrete*	*voi cadreste*
loro/(Loro) caddero	*loro/(Loro) cadranno*	*loro/(Loro) cadrebbero*

All verbs formed with *-cadere* are conjugated like *cadere*: *accadere* ('to happen'), *scadere* ('to expire'), and so on.

Cogliere ('to pick')

Present Indic.	Preterite	Present Subj.	Past Participle
io colgo	*io colsi*	*io colga*	*colto*
tu cogli	*tu cogliesti*	*tu colga*	
lui/lei/(Lei) coglie	*lui/lei/(Lei) colse*	*lui/lei/(Lei) colga*	
noi cogliamo	*noi cogliemmo*	*noi cogliamo*	
voi cogliete	*voi coglieste*	*voi cogliate*	
loro/(Loro) colgono	*loro/(Loro) colsero*	*loro/(Loro) colgano*	

All verbs formed with *-gliere* are conjugated like *cogliere*: *accogliere* ('to receive'), *raccogliere* ('to collect'), and so on.

Dovere ('to have to' 'must')

Present Indic.	Future	Present Subj.	Present Cond.
io devo	*io dovrò*	*io debba*	*io dovrei*
tu devi	*tu dovrai*	*tu debba*	*tu dovresti*
lui/lei/(Lei) deve	*lui/lei/(Lei) dovrà*	*lui/lei/(Lei) debba*	*lui/lei/(Lei) dovrebbe*
noi dobbiamo	*noi dovremo*	*noi dobbiamo*	*noi dovremmo*
voi dovete	*voi dovrete*	*voi dobbiate*	*voi dovreste*
loro/(Loro) devono	*loro/(Loro) dovranno*	*loro/(Loro) debbano*	*loro/(Loro) dovrebbero*
Imperative			
devi (*tu*)			
dobbiamo (*noi*)			
dovete (*voi*)			
N.B. The 3rd sing. and pl. persons of the present subj. *debba* (*Lei*) and *debbano* (*Loro*) are used to express formal commands.			

In addition to the most common forms in *-v-* , the 1st per. sing. and the 3rd pers. pl. of the present indicative take forms in *-bb-*: *io debbo, loro debbono*.

Piacere ('to please')

Present Indic.	Preterite	Present Subj.	Past Participle
io piaccio	io piacqui	io piaccia	piaciuto
tu piaci	tu piacesti	tu piaccia	
lui/lei/(Lei) piace	lui/lei/(Lei) piacque	lui/lei/(Lei) piaccia	
noi piacciamo	noi piacemmo	noi piacciamo	
voi piacete	voi piaceste	voi piacciate	
loro/(Loro) piacciono	loro/(Loro) piacquero	loro/(Loro) piacciano	
Imperative			
piaci (tu)			
piacciamo (noi)			
piacete (voi)			

N.B. The 3rd sing. and pl. persons of the present subj. *piaccia* (*Lei*) and *piacciano* (*Loro*) are used to express formal commands.

All verbs formed with *-acere* are conjugated like *piacere*: *dispiacere* ('to be sorry'), *tacere* ('to be silent'), and so on.

Potere ('to be able', 'can')

Present Indic.	Future	Present Subj.
io posso	io potrò	io possa
tu puoi	tu potrai	tu possa
lui/lei/(Lei) può	lui/lei/(Lei) potrà	lui/lei/(Lei) possa
noi possiamo	noi potremo	noi possiamo
voi potete	voi potrete	voi possiate
loro/(Loro) possono	loro/(Loro) potranno	loro/(Loro) possano

Rimanere ('to stay')

Present Indic.	Preterite	Future	Present Subj.
io rimango	io rimasi	io rimarrò	io rimanga
tu rimani	tu rimanesti	tu rimarrai	tu rimanga
lui/lei/(Lei) rimane	lui/lei/(Lei) rimase	lui/lei/(Lei) rimarrà	lui/lei/(Lei) rimanga
noi rimaniamo	noi rimanemmo	noi rimarremo	noi rimaniamo
voi rimanete	voi rimaneste	voi rimarrete	voi rimaniate
loro/(Loro) rimangono	loro/(Loro) rimasero	loro/(Loro) rimarranno	loro/(Loro) rimangano
Present Cond.		**Past Participle**	
io rimarrei		rimasto	
tu rimarresti			
lui/lei/(Lei) rimarrebbe			
noi rimarremmo			
voi rimarreste			
loro/(Loro) rimarrebbero			

The verb *permanere* ('to linger') is conjugated like *rimanere*.

Sapere ('to know', 'to be able to')

Present Indic.	Preterite	Future	Present Subj.
io so	io seppi	io saprò	io sappia
tu sai	tu sapesti	tu saprai	tu sappia
lui/lei/(Lei) sa	lui/lei/(Lei) seppe	lui/lei/(Lei) saprà	lui/lei/(Lei) sappia
noi sappiamo	noi sapemmo	noi sapremo	noi sappiamo
voi sapete	voi sapeste	voi saprete	voi sappiate
loro/(Loro) sanno	loro/(Loro) seppero	loro/(Loro) sapranno	loro/(Loro) sappiano
Present Cond.		**Imperative**	
io saprei		sappi (tu)	
tu sapresti		sappiamo (noi)	
lui/lei/(Lei) saprebbe		sappiate (voi)	
noi sapremmo			
voi sapreste		**N.B.** The 3rd sing. and pl. persons of the present subj. *sappia*	
loro/(Loro) saprebbero		(*Lei*) and *sappiano* (*Loro*) are used to express formal commands.	

Sedere ('to sit')

Present Indic.	Present Subj.
io siedo	io sieda
tu siedi	tu sieda
lui/lei/(Lei) siede	lui/lei/(Lei) sieda
noi sediamo	noi sediamo
voi sedete	voi sediate
loro/(Loro) siedono	loro/(Loro) siedano

The verb *possedere* ('to own') is conjugated like *sedere*.

Tenere ('to hold')

Present Indic.	Preterite	Future	Present Subj.
io tengo	io tenni	io terrò	io tenga
tu tieni	tu tenesti	tu terrai	tu tenga
lui/lei/(Lei) tiene	lui/lei/(Lei) tenne	lui/lei/(Lei) terrà	lui/lei/(Lei) tenga
noi teniamo	noi tenemmo	noi terremo	noi teniamo
voi tenete	voi teneste	voi terrete	voi teniate
loro/(Loro) tengono	loro/(Loro) tennero	loro/(Loro) terranno	loro/(Loro) tengano
Present Cond.		**Imperative**	
io terrei		tieni (tu)	
tu terresti		teniamo (noi)	
lui/lei/(Lei) terrebbe		tenete (voi)	
noi terremmo			
voi terreste		**N.B.** The 3rd sing. and pl. persons of the present subj. *tenga*	
loro/(Loro) terrebbero		(*Lei*) and *tengano* (*Loro*) are used to express formal commands.	

All verbs formed with *-tenere* are conjugated like *tenere*: *appartenere* ('to belong to'), *contenere* ('to contain'), and so on.

Vedere ('to see')

Preterite	Future	Present Cond.	Past Participle
io vidi	io vedrò	io vedrei	visto (or the regular veduto)
tu vedesti	tu vedrai	tu vedresti	
lui/lei/(Lei) vide	lui/lei/(Lei) vedrà	lui/lei/(Lei) vedrebbe	
noi vedemmo	noi vedremo	noi vedremmo	
voi vedeste	voi vedrete	voi vedreste	
loro/(Loro) videro	loro/(Loro) vedranno	loro/(Loro) vedrebbero	

Vivere ('to live')

Preterite	Future	Present Cond.	Past Participle
io vissi	io vivrò	io vivrei	vissuto
tu vivesti	tu vivrai	tu vivresti	
lui/lei/(Lei) visse	lui/lei/(Lei) vivrà	lui/lei/(Lei) vivrebbe	
noi vivemmo	noi vivremo	noi vivremmo	
voi viveste	voi vivrete	voi vivreste	
loro/(Loro) vissero	loro/(Loro) vivranno	loro/(Loro) vivrebbero	

Verbs like *convivere* ('to live together') and *sopravvivere* ('to survive') are conjugated like *vivere*.

Volere ('to want')

Present Indic.	Preterite	Future	Present Subj.
io voglio	io volli	io vorrò	io voglia
tu vuoi	tu volesti	tu vorrai	tu voglia
lui/lei/(Lei) vuole	lui/lei/(Lei) volle	lui/lei/(Lei) vorrà	lui/lei/(Lei) voglia
noi vogliamo	noi volemmo	noi vorremo	noi vogliamo
voi volete	voi voleste	voi vorrete	voi vogliate
loro/(Loro) vogliono	loro/(Loro) vollero	loro/(Loro) vorranno	loro/(Loro) vogliano

Present Cond.		Imperative	
io vorrei		vuoi (tu)	
tu vorresti		vogliamo (noi)	
lui/lei/(Lei) vorrebbe		volete (voi)	
noi vorremmo			
voi vorreste		N.B. The 3rd sing. and pl. persons of the present subj. *voglia*	
loro/(Loro) vorrebbero		(*Lei*) and *vogliano* (*Loro*) are used to express formal commands.	

20.20 Irregularities of the Preterite and/or Past Participle of verbs in -ere

The verbs in *-ere* listed below display some irregularity only in their preterite tense and/or past participle forms.

Verbs	Preterite		Past Participle
accendere ('to turn on')	*io accesi* *tu accendesti* *lui/lei/(Lei) accese*	*noi accendemmo* *voi accendeste* *loro/(Loro) accesero*	*acceso*
appendere ('to hang')	*io appesi* *tu appendesti* *lui/lei/(Lei) appese*	*noi appendemmo* *voi appendeste* *loro/(Loro) appesero*	*appeso*
chiedere ('to ask')	*io chiesi* *tu chiedesti* *lui/lei/(Lei) chiese*	*noi chiedemmo* *voi chiedeste* *loro/(Loro) chiesero*	*chiesto*
chiudere ('to close')	*io chiusi* *tu chiudesti* *lui/lei/(Lei) chiuse*	*noi chiudemmo* *voi chiudeste* *loro/(Loro) chiusero*	*chiuso*
conoscere ('to know')	*io conobbi* *tu conoscesti* *lui/lei/(Lei) conobbe*	*noi conoscemmo* *voi conosceste* *loro/(Loro) conobbero*	*conosciuto*
correre ('to run')	*io corsi* *tu corresti* *lui/lei/(Lei) corse*	*noi corremmo* *voi correste* *loro/(Loro) corsero*	*corso*
crescere ('to grow')	*io crebbi* *tu crescesti* *lui/lei/(Lei) crebbe*	*noi crescemmo* *voi cresceste* *loro/(Loro) crebbero*	*cresciuto*
cuocere ('to cook')	*io cossi* *tu cuocesti* *lui/lei/(Lei) cosse*	*noi cuocemmo* *voi cuoceste* *loro/(Loro) cossero*	*cotto*
decidere ('to decide')	*io decisi* *tu decidesti* *lui/lei/(Lei) decise*	*noi decidemmo* *voi decideste* *loro/(Loro) decisero*	*deciso*
difendere ('to defend')	*io difesi* *tu difendesti* *lui/lei/(Lei) difese*	*noi difendemmo* *voi difendeste* *loro/(Loro) difesero*	*difeso*
dipingere ('to paint')	*io dipinsi* *tu dipingesti* *lui/lei/(Lei) dipinse*	*noi dipingemmo* *voi dipingeste* *loro/(Loro) dipinsero*	*dipinto*
discutere ('to discuss')	*io discussi* *tu discutesti* *lui/lei/(Lei) discusse*	*noi discutemmo* *voi discuteste* *loro/(Loro) discussero*	*discusso*
dividere ('to divide')	*io divisi* *tu dividesti* *lui/lei/(Lei) divise*	*noi dividemmo* *voi divideste* *loro/(Loro) divisero*	*diviso*
esprimere ('to express')	*io espressi* *tu esprimesti* *lui/lei/(Lei) espresse*	*noi esprimemmo* *voi esprimeste* *loro/(Loro) espressero*	*espresso*
leggere ('to read')	*io lessi* *tu leggesti* *lui/lei/(Lei) lesse*	*noi leggemmo* *voi leggeste* *loro/(Loro) lessero*	*letto*
mettere ('to put')	*io misi* *tu mettesti* *lui/lei/(Lei) mise*	*noi mettemmo* *voi metteste* *loro/(Loro) misero*	*messo*
muovere ('to move')	*io mossi* *tu muovesti* *lui/lei/(Lei) mosse*	*noi muovemmo* *voi muoveste* *loro/(Loro) mossero*	*mosso*
nascere ('to be born')	*io nacqui* *tu nascesti* *lui/lei/(Lei) nacque*	*noi nascemmo* *voi nasceste* *loro/(Loro) nacquero*	*nato*

nascondere ('to hide')	io nascosi tu nascondesti lui/lei/(Lei) nascose	noi nascondemmo voi nascondeste loro/(Loro) nascosero	nascosto
perdere ('to lose')	io persi tu perdesti lui/lei/(Lei) perse	noi perdemmo voi perdeste loro/(Loro) persero	perso (or the regular perduto)
piangere ('to cry')	io piansi tu piangesti lui/lei/(Lei) pianse	noi piangemmo voi piangeste loro/(Loro) piansero	pianto
prendere ('to take')	io presi tu prendesti lui/lei/(Lei) prese	noi prendemmo voi prendeste loro/(Loro) presero	preso
rendere ('to give back')	io resi tu rendesti lui/lei/(Lei) rese	noi rendemmo voi rendeste loro/(Loro) resero	reso
rispondere ('to answer')	io risposi tu rispondesti lui/lei/(Lei) rispose	noi rispondemmo voi rispondeste loro/(Loro) risposero	risposto
rompere ('to brake')	io ruppi tu rompesti lui/lei/(Lei) ruppe	noi rompemmo voi rompeste loro/(Loro) ruppero	rotto
scoprire ('to discover')	io scoprii tu scopristi lui/lei/(Lei) scoprì	noi scoprimmo voi scopriste loro/(Loro) scoprirono	scoperto
scrivere ('to write')	io scrissi tu scrivesti lui/lei/(Lei) scrisse	noi scrivemmo voi scriveste loro/(Loro) scrissero	scritto
spegnere ('to turn off')	io spensi tu spegnesti lui/lei/(Lei) spense	noi spegnemmo voi spegneste loro/(Loro) spensero	spento
trascorrere ('to pass')	io trascorsi tu trascorresti lui/lei/(Lei) trascorse	noi trascorremmo voi trascorreste loro/(Loro) trascorsero	trascorso
vincere ('to win')	io vinsi tu vincesti lui/lei/(Lei) vinse	noi vincemmo voi vinceste loro/(Loro) vinsero	vinto

20.21 Verbs Without Preterite and Past Participle Forms

A few second conjugation verbs lack a preterite and past participle. In such cases, other verbs or alternative expressions are used to replace them. Following are the most common ones: *competere* ('to compete'), *distare* ('to be distant'), *divergere* ('to diverge'), *incombere* ('to be incumbent upon someone'), *prudere* ('to itch').

20.22 Verbs in -arre, -orre, -urre

Several Italian second conjugation verbs ending in **-arre, -orre, -urre** are contracted forms of the original Latin verbs. To be able to conjugate these verbs correctly, it is necessary to take their extended original infinitives and drop *-ere* in order to obtain the stem. For example, the verb *trarre* ('to draw') comes from 'tra[h]ere', so its stem is *tra-*; the verb *porre* ('to place') comes from 'ponere', so its stem is *pon-*; and *condurre* ('to lead') comes from 'conducere', so its stem is *conduc-*. These verbs are conjugated as shown below:

Forms of Verbs in *-arre* (*trarre* 'to draw')

INDICATIVE		SUBJUNCTIVE	
Present	**Present Perfect**	**Present**	**Past**
io traggo	io ho tratto	io tragga	io abbia tratto
tu trai	tu hai tratto	tu tragga	tu abbia tratto
lui/lei/(Lei) trae	lui/lei/(Lei) ha tratto	lui/lei/(Lei) tragga	lui/lei/(Lei) abbia tratto
noi traiamo	noi abbiamo tratto	noi traiamo	noi abbiamo tratto
voi traete	voi avete tratto	voi traiate	voi abbiate tratto
loro/(Loro) traggano	loro/(Loro) hanno tratto	loro/(Loro) traggano	loro/(Loro) abbiano tratto
Imperfect	**Pluperfect**	**Imperfect**	**Pluperfect**
io traevo	io avevo tratto	io traessi	io avessi tratto
tu traevi	tu avevi tratto	tu traessi	tu avessi tratto
lui/lei/(Lei) traeva	lui/lei/(Lei) aveva tratto	lui/lei/(Lei) traesse	lui/lei/(Lei) avesse tratto
noi traevamo	noi avevamo tratto	noi traessimo	noi avessimo tratto
voi traevate	voi avevate tratto	voi traeste	voi aveste tratto
loro/(Loro) traevano	loro/(Loro) avevano tratto	loro/(Loro) traessero	loro/(Loro) avessero tratto
		CONDITIONAL	
Preterite	**Preterite Perfect**	**Present**	**Past**
io trassi	io ebbi tratto	io trarrei	io avrei tratto
tu traesti	tu avesti tratto	tu trarresti	tu avresti tratto
lui/lei/(Lei) trasse	lui/lei/(Lei) ebbe tratto	lui/lei/(Lei) trarrebbe	lui/lei/(Lei) avrebbe tratto
noi traemmo	noi avemmo tratto	noi trarremmo	noi avremmo tratto
voi traeste	voi aveste tratto	voi trarreste	voi avreste tratto
loro/(Loro) trassero	loro/(Loro) ebbero tratto	loro/(Loro) trarrebbero	loro/(Loro) avrebbero tratto
		IMPERATIVE	
Future	**Future Perfect**	**Present**	
io trarrò	io avrò tratto	trai (tu)	
tu trarrai	tu avrai tratto	traiamo (noi)	
lui/lei/(Lei) trarrà	lui/lei/(Lei) avrà tratto	traete (voi)	
noi trarremo	noi avremo tratto		
voi trarrete	voi avrete tratto	**N.B.** The 3rd sing. and pl. persons of the present subj. *tragga*	
loro/(Loro) trarranno	loro/(Loro) avranno tratto	(*Lei*) and *traggano* (*Loro*) are used to express formal commands.	

INFINITIVE		PARTICIPLE		GERUND	
Present	**Past**	**Present**	**Past**	**Present**	**Past**
trarre	avere tratto	traente	tratto	traendo	avendo tratto

All verbs ending in *-arre* (all derived from *trarre*) are conjugated like *trarre*. They are just a few and here are the most common ones: *astrarre* ('to abstract'), *attrarre* ('to attract'), *con-*

trarre ('to contract'), *distrarre* ('to distract'), *estrarre* ('to extract'), *protrarre* ('to protract'), *ritrarre* ('to retract'), *sottrarre* ('to subtract').

Forms of Verbs in **-orre** (***porre*** 'to place')

INDICATIVE		SUBJUNCTIVE	
Present	**Present Perfect**	**Present**	**Past**
io pongo	*io ho posto*	*io ponga*	*io abbia posto*
tu poni	*tu hai posto*	*tu ponga*	*tu abbia posto*
lui/lei/(Lei) pone	*lui/lei/(Lei) ha posto*	*lui/lei/(Lei) ponga*	*lui/lei/(Lei) abbia posto*
noi poniamo	*noi abbiamo posto*	*noi poniamo*	*noi abbiamo posto*
voi ponete	*voi avete posto*	*voi ponete*	*voi abbiate posto*
loro/(Loro) pongono	*loro/(Loro) hanno posto*	*loro/(Loro) pongano*	*loro/(Loro) abbiano posto*
Imperfect	**Pluperfect**	**Imperfect**	**Pluperfect**
io ponevo	*io avevo posto*	*io ponessi*	*io avessi posto*
tu ponevi	*tu avevi posto*	*tu ponessi*	*tu avessi posto*
lui/lei/(Lei) poneva	*lui/lei/(Lei) aveva posto*	*lui/lei/(Lei) ponesse*	*lui/lei/(Lei) avesse posto*
noi ponevamo	*noi avevamo posto*	*noi ponessimo*	*noi avessimo posto*
voi ponevate	*voi avevate posto*	*voi poneste*	*voi aveste posto*
loro/(Loro) ponevano	*loro/(Loro) avevano posto*	*loro/(Loro) ponessero*	*loro/(Loro) avessero posto*
		CONDITIONAL	
Preterite	**Preterite Perfect**	**Present**	**Past**
io posi	*io ebbi posto*	*io porrei*	*io avrei posto*
tu ponesti	*tu avesti posto*	*tu porresti*	*tu avresti posto*
lui/lei/(Lei) pose	*lui/lei/(Lei) ebbe posto*	*lui/lei/(Lei) porrebbe*	*lui/lei/(Lei) avrebbe posto*
noi ponemmo	*noi avemmo posto*	*noi porremmo*	*noi avremmo posto*
voi poneste	*voi aveste posto*	*voi porreste*	*voi aveste posto*
loro/(Loro) posero	*loro/(Loro) ebbero posto*	*loro/(Loro) porrebbero*	*loro/(Loro) avrebbero posto*
		IMPERATIVE	
Future	**Future Perfect**	**Present**	
io porrò	*io avrò posto*	*poni (tu)*	
tu porrai	*tu avrai posto*	*poniamo (noi)*	
lui/lei/(Lei) porrà	*lui/lei/(Lei) avrà posto*	*ponete (voi)*	
noi porremo	*noi avremo posto*		
voi porrete	*voi avrete posto*	**N.B.** The 3rd sing. and pl. persons of the present subj. *ponga* (*Lei*)	
loro/(Loro) porranno	*loro/(Loro) avranno posto*	and *pongano* (*Loro*) are used to express formal commands.	

INFINITIVE		PARTICIPLE		GERUND	
Present	**Past**	**Present**	**Past**	**Present**	**Past**
porre	*avere posto*	*ponente*	*posto*	*ponendo*	*avendo posto*

All verbs ending in *-orre* (just a few and all derived from *porre*) are conjugated like *porre*. Here are the most common ones: *anteporre* ('to attract'), *comporre* ('to compose'), *deporre* ('to put down'), *imporre* ('to impose'), *opporre* ('to oppose'), *posporre* ('to postpone'), *proporre* ('to propose'), *supporre* ('to suppose'), *trasporre* ('to transpose').

Forms of Verbs in **-urre** (***condurre*** 'to lead')

INDICATIVE		SUBJUNCTIVE	
Present	**Present Perfect**	**Present**	**Past**
io conduco	*io ho condotto*	*io conduca*	*io abbia condotto*
tu conduci	*tu hai condotto*	*tu conduca*	*tu abbia condotto*
lui/lei/(Lei) conduce	*lui/lei/(Lei) ha condotto*	*lui/lei/(Lei) conduca*	*lui/lei/(Lei) abbia condotto*
noi conduciamo	*noi abbiamo condotto*	*noi conduciamo*	*noi abbiamo condotto*
voi conducete	*voi avete condotto*	*voi conduciate*	*voi abbiate condotto*
loro/(Loro) conducono	*loro/(Loro) hanno condotto*	*loro/(Loro) conducano*	*loro/(Loro) abbiano condotto*
Imperfect	**Pluperfect**	**Imperfect**	**Pluperfect**
io conducevo	*io ebbi condotto*	*io conducessi*	*io avessi condotto*
tu conducevi	*tu avesti condotto*	*tu conducessi*	*tu avessi condotto*
lui/lei/(Lei) conduceva	*lui/lei/(Lei) ebbe condotto*	*lui/lei/(Lei) conducesse*	*lui/lei/(Lei) avesse condotto*
noi conducevamo	*noi avemmo condotto*	*noi conducessimo*	*noi avessimo condotto*
voi conducevate	*voi aveste condotto*	*voi conduceste*	*voi aveste condotto*
loro/(Loro) conducevano	*loro/(Loro) ebbero condotto*	*loro/(Loro) conducessero*	*loro/(Loro) avessero condotto*
		CONDITIONAL	
Preterite	**Preterite Perfect**	**Present**	**Past**
io condussi	*io ebbi condotto*	*io condurrei*	*io avrei condotto*
tu conducesti	*tu avesti condotto*	*tu condurresti*	*tu avresti condotto*
lui/lei/(Lei) condusse	*lui/lei/(Lei) ebbe condotto*	*lui/lei/(Lei) condurrebbe*	*lui/lei/(Lei) avrebbe condotto*
noi conducemmo	*noi avemmo condotto*	*noi condurremmo*	*noi avremmo condotto*
voi conduceste	*voi aveste condotto*	*voi condurreste*	*voi avreste condotto*
loro/(Loro) condussero	*loro/(Loro) ebbero condotto*	*loro/(Loro) condurrebbero*	*loro/(Loro) avrebbero condotto*
		IMPERATIVE	
Future	**Future Perfect**	**Present**	
io condurrò	*io avrò condotto*	*conduci (tu)*	
tu condurrai	*tu avrai condotto*	*conduciamo (noi)*	
lui/lei/(Lei) condurrà	*lui/lei/(Lei) avrà condotto*	*conducete (voi)*	
noi condurremo	*noi avremo condotto*		
voi condurrete	*voi avrete condotto*	**N.B.** The 3rd sing. and pl. persons of the present subj. *conduca* (*Lei*)	
loro/(Loro) condurranno	*loro/(Loro) avranno condotto*	and *conducano* (*Loro*) are used to express formal commands.	

INFINITIVE		PARTICIPLE		GERUND	
Present	**Past**	**Present**	**Past**	**Present**	**Past**
condurre	*avere condotto*	*conducente*	*condotto*	*conducendo*	*avendo condotto*

All verbs ending in *-urre* are conjugated like *condurre*. They are few and following are the most common ones: *dedurre* ('to deduce'), *indurre* ('to induce'), *introdurre* ('to introduce'), *produrre* ('to produce'), *ridurre* ('to reduce'), *sedurre* ('to seduce').

> **N.B.** The infinitive *redarre*, often used in contemporary Italian, is not part of this group because it is a simplified version of the correct infinitive *redigere* ('to draw up'), which follows the patterns of the regular second conjugation (*Redigiamo questo contratto* 'Let's draw up this contract').

20.23 The Third Conjugation: Verbs in -ire

All regular verbs in *-ire* are conjugated by dropping the infinitive ending *-ire* and adding the appropriate endings to the resulting stem. The compound forms use *avere* or *essere* (see 20.8), depending on the specific verb being conjugated.

The Regular Forms of Verbs in ***-ire*** (***dormire*** 'to sleep')

INDICATIVE		SUBJUNCTIVE	
Present	**Present Perfect**	**Present**	**Past**
io dorm**o**	io ho dormito	io dorm**a**	io abbia dormito
tu dorm**i**	tu hai dormito	tu dorm**a**	tu abbia dormito
lui/lei/(Lei) dorm**e**	lui/lei/(Lei) ha dormito	lui/lei/(Lei) dorm**a**	lui/lei/(Lei) abbia dormito
noi dorm**iamo**	noi abbiamo dormito	noi dorm**iamo**	noi abbiamo dormito
voi dorm**ite**	voi avete dormito	voi dorm**iate**	voi abbiate dormito
loro/(Loro) dorm**ono**	loro/(Loro) hanno dormito	loro/(Loro) dorm**ano**	loro/(Loro) abbiano dormito
Imperfect	**Pluperfect**	**Imperfect**	**Pluperfect**
io dorm**ivo**	io avevo dormito	io dorm**issi**	io avessi dormito
tu dorm**ivi**	tu avevi dormito	tu dorm**issi**	tu avessi dormito
lui/lei/(Lei) dorm**iva**	lui/lei/(Lei) aveva dormito	lui/lei/(Lei) dorm**isse**	lui/lei/(Lei) avesse dormito
noi dorm**ivamo**	noi avevamo dormito	noi dorm**issimo**	noi avessimo dormito
voi dorm**ivate**	voi avevate dormito	voi dorm**iste**	voi aveste dormito
loro/(Loro) dorm**ivano**	loro/(Loro) avevano dormito	loro/(Loro) dorm**issero**	loro/(Loro) avessero dormito
		CONDITIONAL	
Preterite	**Preterite Perfect**	**Present**	**Past**
io dorm**ii**	io ebbi dormito	io dorm**irei**	io avrei dormito
tu dorm**isti**	tu avesti dormito	tu dorm**iresti**	tu avresti dormito
lui/lei/(Lei) dorm**ì**	lui/lei/(Lei) ebbe dormito	lui/lei/(Lei) dorm**irebbe**	lui/lei/(Lei) avrebbe dormito
noi dorm**immo**	noi avemmo dormito	noi dorm**iremmo**	noi avremmo dormito
voi dorm**iste**	voi aveste dormito	voi dorm**ireste**	voi avreste dormito
loro/(Loro) dorm**irono**	loro/(Loro) ebbero dormito	loro/(Loro) dorm**irebbero**	loro/(Loro) avrebbero dormito
		IMPERATIVE	
Future	**Future Perfect**	**Present**	
io dorm**irò**	io avrò dormito	dorm**i** (tu)	
tu dorm**irai**	tu avrai dormito	dorm**iamo** (noi)	
lui/lei/(Lei) dorm**irà**	lui/lei/(Lei) avrà dormito	dorm**ite** (voi)	
noi dorm**iremo**	noi avremo dormito		
voi dorm**irete**	voi avrete dormito	**N.B.** The 3rd sing. and pl. persons of the present subj. *dorma* (*Lei*)	
loro/(Loro) dorm**iranno**	loro/(Loro) avranno dormito	and *dormano* (*Loro*) are used to express formal commands.	

	INFINITIVE		PARTICIPLE		GERUND	
	Present	**Past**	**Present**	**Past**	**Present**	**Past**
	dormire	*avere dormito*	*dormente (-iente)*	*dormito*	*dormendo*	*avendo dormito*

Verbs in *-ire* conjugated with *essere* (*partire* 'to leave', *fuggire* 'to run away', and so on) have past participle forms and compound tenses that agree (see 20.9) in gender and number with the subject (*io sono partito/a, loro sono fuggiti/e,* and so on).

> **N.B.** A few verbs in *-ire* can take in addition to the regular present participle in *-ente* an old Latinized form in *-iente*. Like *dormire* (see table above), the verbs *finire* ('to finish'), *impedire* ('to restrain'), *nutrire* ('to feed'), *partorire* ('to give birth'), *percepire* ('to perceive'), *progredire* ('to progress'), *venire* ('to come') can get both forms.

20.24 Verbs with -isc-: *finire, capire, pulire, etc.*

A great number of regular verbs of the third conjugation make their present indicative and subjunctive forms (except the 1st and 2nd pl. persons), and their 2nd person sing. of the imperative by inserting *-isc-* between the stem of the verb and the ending forms. The table below displays the patterns for these verbs, using *finire* ('to finish') as a model:

Special Forms of Verbs in *-ire-* (*finire* 'to finish')

Present Indic.	**Present Subj.**	**Imperative**
io finisco	*io finisca*	*finisci (tu)*
tu finisci	*tu finisca*	*finiamo (noi)*
lui/lei/(Lei) finisce	*lui/lei/(Lei) finisca*	*finite (voi)*
noi finiamo	*noi finiamo*	
voi finite	*voi finiate*	**N.B.** The 3rd sing. and pl. persons of the present subj.
loro/(Loro) finiscono	*loro/(Loro) finiscano*	*finisca* (*Lei*) and *finiscano* (*Loro*) are used to express formal commands.

Finire serves as a model of conjugation for more than 400 Italian verbs. Here are the most common ones: *capire* ('to understand'), *costruire* ('to build'), *esaurire* ('to exhaust'), *fallire* ('to fail'), *impazzire* ('to go mad'), *obbedire* ('to obey'), *preferire* ('to prefer'), *pulire* ('to clean'), *restituire* ('to give back'), *spedire* ('to send'), *tradire* ('betray'), *unire* ('to join').

> **N.B.** If a few verbs can still accept a double form, with and without -*isc*- (*applaudire* 'to applaud', *assorbire* 'to absorb', *mentire* 'to lie'), the forms with -*isc*- are always preferable.

20.25 Irregular Verbs in -ire

Several verbs ending in -*ire* are irregular verbs, the most common of which are presented in this section. Only the major patterns of irregularity are listed, the rest following regular patterns (see 20.23):

Apparire ('to appear')

Present Indic.	Preterite	Present Subj.	Past Participle
io appaio	io apparvi	io appaia	apparso
tu appari	tu apparisti	tu appaia	
lui/lei/(Lei) appare	lui/lei/(Lei) apparve	lui/lei/(Lei) appaia	
noi appariamo	noi apparimmo	noi appaiamo	
voi apparite	voi appariste	voi appariate	
loro/(Loro) appaiono	loro/(Loro) apparvero	loro/(Loro) appaiano	

Dire ('to say')

Present Indic.	Preterite	Future	Imperfect Subj.
io dico	io dissi	io dirò	io dicessi
tu dici	tu dicesti	tu dirai	tu dicessi
lui/lei/(Lei) dice	lui/lei/(Lei) disse	lui/lei/(Lei) dirà	lui/lei/(Lei) dicesse
noi diciamo	noi dicemmo	noi diremo	noi dicessimo
voi dite	voi diceste	voi direte	voi diceste
loro/(Loro) dicono	loro/(Loro) dissero	loro/(Loro) diranno	loro/(Loro) dicessero
Imperative			**Past Participle**
di' (tu)			detto
diciamo (noi)			
dite (voi)			
N.B. The 3rd sing. and pl. persons of the present subj. *dica* (*Lei*) and *dicano* (*Loro*) are used to express formal commands.			

All other forms are obtained by adding the regular endings to **dic-** (*dicevo*, *dica*, etc.). *Dire* serves as a model for the conjugation of a few verbs formed with -*dire*, except for the 2nd sing. person of the imperative (-*dici*, and not -*di'*, in the compound verbs): *contraddire* ('to contradict'), *disdire* ('to cancel'). However, the majority of verbs in this category (*spedire* 'to send', *ubbidire* 'to obey', and so on) follow instead the patterns of *finire* (see 20.24).

Morire ('to die')

Present Indic.	Future	Present Subj.
io muoio	io morrò (morirò)	io muoia
tu muori	tu morrai (morirai)	tu muoia
lui/lei/(Lei) muore	lui/lei/(Lei) morrà (morirà)	lui/lei/(Lei) muoia
noi moriamo	noi morremo (moriremo)	noi moriamo
voi morite	voi morrete (morirete)	voi moriate
loro/(Loro) muoiono	loro/(Loro) morranno (moriranno)	loro/(Loro) muoiano
Present Cond.		**Past Participle**
io morrei (morirei)	noi morremmo (moriremmo)	morto
tu morresti (moriresti)	voi morreste (morireste)	
lui/lei/(Lei) morrebbe (morirebbe)	loro/(Loro) morrebbero (morirebbero)	

The verb *morire*, as can be seen from the above table, accepts double forms (both regular and irregular) in the future and in the present conditional.

Udire ('to hear')

Present Indic.	Future	Present Subj.
io odo	io udrò (udirò)	io oda
tu odi	tu udrai (udirai)	tu oda
lui/lei/(Lei) ode	lui/lei/(Lei) udrà (udirà)	lui/lei/(Lei) oda
noi udiamo	noi udremo (udiremo)	noi udiamo
voi udite	voi udrete (udirete)	voi udiate
loro/(Loro) odono	loro/(Loro) udranno (udiranno)	loro/(Loro) odano
Present Cond.		
io udrei (udirei)	noi udremmo (udiremmo)	
tu udresti (udiresti)	voi udreste (udireste)	
lui/lei/(Lei) udrebbe (udirebbe)	loro/(Loro) udrebbero (udirebbero)	

The verb *udire*, as can be seen from the above table, accepts double forms (both regular and irregular) in the future and in the present conditional.

Uscire ('to exit', 'to go out')

Present Indic.	Present Subj.
io esco	io esca
tu esci	tu esca
lui/lei/(Lei) esce	lui/lei/(Lei) esca
noi usciamo	noi usciamo
voi uscite	voi usciate
loro/(Loro) escono	loro/(Loro) escano

The verb *riuscire* ('to succeed') is conjugated like *uscire*.

Venire ('to come')

Present Indic.	Preterite	Future	Present Subj.
io vengo	*io venni*	*io verrò*	*io venga*
tu vieni	*tu venisti*	*tu verrai*	*tu venga*
lui/lei/(Lei) viene	*lui/lei/(Lei) venne*	*lui/lei/(Lei) verrà*	*lui/lei/(Lei) venga*
noi veniamo	*noi venimmo*	*noi verremo*	*noi veniamo*
voi venite	*voi veniste*	*voi verrete*	*voi veniate*
loro/(Loro) vengono	*loro/(Loro) vennero*	*loro/(Loro) verranno*	*loro/(Loro) vengano*
Present Cond.		**Past Participle**	
io verrei	*noi verremmo*	*venuto*	
tu verresti	*voi verreste*		
lui/lei/(Lei) verrebbe	*loro/(Loro) verrebbero*		

21. VERBS: USES OF MOODS AND TENSES

> **Moods and tenses**: The mood of a verb (indicative, subjunctive, etc.) is the manner in which the action or condition is conceived or intended while the tense of a verb (present, future, etc.) is a grammatical category that locates an action in time to indicate when the action takes place.

21.1 The Indicative Mood

The indicative is the most used verbal mood in Italian. Its function is to represent something as a fact and to convey both certainty and objectivity. The indicative has **four simple tenses** (present, imperfect, preterite, and future) and **four compound tenses** (present perfect, pluperfect, preterite perfect, and future perfect). Their use will be detailed in the next few paragraphs.

21.2 Uses of the Present Indicative

The main use of the present tense (for verb conjugations see chapter 20) is to indicate that **something is happening at the time of speaking or writing** (*Leggo un libro* 'I am reading a book'), to represent **habitual actions** (*Vado in palestra ogni giorno* 'I go to the gym every day'), or to state **general truths** (*Firenze è in Toscana* 'Florence is in Tuscany').

The Italian present tense corresponds essentially to the English simple present (*parlo* 'I talk') as well as to the emphatic present (*parlo* 'I do talk') and the present progressive (*parlo* 'I am talking'). In fact, the present progressive has a more restricted use in Italian than it does in English (see 21.3, 21.15) and can almost always be replaced by the simple present: *Aspetta un momento, mangio* [= *sto mangiando*] ('Wait a moment; I am eating').

In addition to these main uses, the present tense has other applications. It is also frequently employed to express **future actions** that tend to indicate plans or intentions: *Ho deciso; studio filosofia* ('I have decided; I am going to study philosophy'). It is used as well to indicate events taking place in the near future, especially when another expression of future time appears in the sentence: *Domani vado al supermercato* ('Tomorrow, I'll go to the supermarket'), *Esco di casa fra un paio di ore* ('I'll leave home in a couple of hours').

The present can also refer to the past; in this case it is called **historic present**. This use, typical of historic narrative, makes the account more dramatic by presenting something distant in time as happening right now: *Nelle Idi di marzo Giulio Cesare muore per mano di Bruto* ('On the Ides of March Julius Caesar dies at the hand of Brutus'), *Dante Alighieri nasce a Firenze nel 1265* ('Dante Alighieri was born in Florence in 1265'). The historic present is really frequent in contemporary Italian and typical of newspaper, radio, TV headings, and sportscasting: *Come previsto, il parlamento approva la legge* ('As expected, the Parliament passes the law'), *Totti segna e la Roma vince la partita* ('Totti scores and Roma wins the match').

The present tense can often replace, in spoken language, the imperative to **convey commands**: *Ora ti alzi [= alzati] e mangi [= mangia]* ('Now get up and eat').

When preceded by the preposition *da* (**da + present**), the present tense indicates something that started in the past and continues uninterrupted in the present. This use is equivalent to the English construction 'perfect tense + for/since': *Studio chitarra da cinque anni* ('I have been studying the guitar for five years'), *Non vado in vacanza da quando è nato mio figlio* ('I haven't gone on vacation since my son was born'). This construction can be replaced in colloquial Italian by the phrase *è [da]/sono + time espression + che*: *È [da] tanto tempo che non vieni a trovarmi* ('It has been a long time since you last visited me'), *Sono tre ore che aspetto* ('I have been waiting for three hours'). Note that *da* is never used with the plural *sono*.

21.3 Italian vs English Present Progressive

The present progressive (or continuous), as all the progressive tenses (see 21.15), is formed in Italian with *stare* + gerund. Compared to the English '-ing' construction, the Italian tense has a more restricted usage. In fact, it can only be employed to indicate an action that is going on at the moment (*In questo momento sto studiando* 'Right now I am studying') and never to express habitual actions (*Uso il computer ogni giorno* 'I am using my computer every day'), states of affairs (*Oggi, Marco indossa una bella cravatta* 'Today, Marco is wearing a beautiful tie'), and future actions (*Presto usciremo* 'We are leaving soon'), respectively expressed in Italian with the present and future tenses. That said, in Italian as opposed to English, the present progressive can nearly always be replaced by the simple present: *Sto mangiando [= Mangio] una mela* ('I am eating an apple'), *Stanno studiando [= Studiano] i verbi Italiani* ('They are studying Italian verbs').

21.4 Uses of the Future Tense

In English the future is expressed with 'will' or the phrase 'to be going to' whereas in Italian the future, like all the other Italian tenses, is simply formed by adding specific endings to the root of the verb (for verb conjugations see chapter 20). The simple future tense indicates **actions that have not yet occurred**: *I miei genitori arriveranno domani* ('My parents will arrive tomorrow'), *Noi andremo presto in vacanza* ('We will go on vacation soon'). Unlike English, Italian requires the use of the future tense after connectives of time such as *quando* ('when') and *appena* ('as soon as'): *Sarai felice, quando sarai con me* ('You will be happy when you are with me'). It also requires it after *se* ('if') in hypothetical clauses (see 23.29) expressing a future action, a case in which English uses the simple present: *Se studierai, avrai buoni voti* ('If you study, you will have good grades').

Besides this main use, the future tense has other applications. It can carry a conjectural value communicating **speculation and probability** not referring to the future, but to the present: *Mia mamma sarà a casa a quest'ora* ('My mother must be home at this time'), *Quel ragazzo sembra molto giovane, non avrà più di quindici anni* ('That boy looks really young; he must be no more than fifteen').

The future is also frequently employed to express **doubt and skepticism**: *Sarà anche vero, ma io non ci credo* ('It may even be true, but I don't believe it'), *Tuo zio avrà anche molti soldi, ma vive come un povero* ('Your uncle may have a lot of money, but he lives like a poor man').

As in English, the future in Italian can replace the imperative form to **convey a command**, especially in more formal contexts: *Le parlerai* [= *Parlale*] ('You will talk to her'), *Non ruberai* [= *Non rubare*] ('You will not steal'); and it can be used as well to **ask to be excused or forgiven**: *Mi perdonerai, ma non posso venire* ('You will forgive me, but I can't come').

In some *che* clauses the future is also often used instead of the more appropriate present subjunctive (see 21.19): *Credo che mia sorella arriverà* [= *arrivi*] *domani* ('I think my sister will arrive tomorrow').

> **N.B.** In spoken Italian the present is often used instead of the future. In fact, it is preferred when expressing plans and intentions or events scheduled in the near future (see 21.2): *Domani finalmente vado* [= *andrò*] *in vacanza* ('I'm finally going on vacation tomorrow').

21.5 Uses of the Future Progressive

The future progressive (or continuous) is formed with the **future of *stare* + gerund**. It can only be used to indicate an **action that will be going on when another action happens** (*Quando arriverete, noi staremo dormendo* 'When you arrive, we will be sleeping') or to express **speculation or probability** not referring to the future, but to the present (*Staranno mangiando a quest'ora* 'They must be eating at this time').

21.6 Uses of the Future Perfect

The future perfect is formed (for verb conjugations see chapter 20) with **the future of the auxiliary *essere* or *avere* plus the past participle** of the verb (*avrò parlato, sarai andato*). As in English, the future perfect is used to indicate **what will have taken place by a certain time in the future**: *Alle sette saremo arrivati a Milano* ('By seven o'clock, we will have arrived in Milan'); or it is used to express **an action in the future that will have already occurred before another future action takes place**: *Avrò finito i miei compiti, prima che tu arrivi* ('I will have finished my homework before you arrive').

Unlike English, Italian requires the use of the future perfect tense after connectives of time such as *quando* ('when'), *appena* ('as soon as'), *dopo che* ('after'): *Quando avrai mangiato, starai meglio* ('When you have eaten, you will feel better'). Also, the future perfect tense is obligatory after *se* ('if') in hypothetical clauses (see 23.29) referring to a future condition whose consequence is conveyed by the simple future: *Se avrai studiato bene, passerai l'esame* ('If you have studied well, you will pass the exam').

Like the simple future (see 21.4), the future perfect can be used to express **speculation and probability** related to the present: *Mio padre sarà arrivato a lavoro a quest'ora* ('My father must have arrived at work by this time'); or to indicate **doubt and skepticism** about something that has already occurred: *Sarà stato un brav'uomo, ma io non ci credo* ('He may have been a good man, but I don't believe it').

> **N.B.** Nowadays, **the future perfect is rare in spoken language**. In fact, Italians prefer instead to use the simple future instead, without any indication of the sequence in time of the actions: *Quando finirò la cena, andrò a letto* ('When I finish my dinner, I'll go to bed'). Sentences like this one are really common in contemporary Italian, replacing the more grammatical ones formed with the future perfect: *Quando avrò finito la cena, andrò a letto* ('When I have finished my dinner, I'll go to bed').

21.7 Uses of the Imperfect

The imperfect is mainly used to express **ongoing past actions** (*Io studiavo, mentre tu guardavi la televisione* 'I was studying while you were watching TV') and **habitual actions in the past** (*Come tutti i bambini giocavo a calcio* 'Like all boys I used to play soccer'). In these cases the Italian imperfect corresponds respectively to the English phrases 'was/were + -ing' and 'used to + base form of verb'.

The imperfect (for verb conjugations see chapter 20) is also used as in English to indicate **physical, physiological, and mental states** (*Faceva freddo* 'It was cold', *Carlo stava male* 'Carlo was not feeling well', *Ero felice* 'I was happy'), as well as **time and age** in the past (*Erano le cinque* 'It was five o'clock', *Aveva venti anni quando si è trasferito a Roma* 'He was twenty when he moved to Rome').

Besides these main uses, the imperfect tense has other applications. It is employed in spoken language instead of the present indicative to make a more **polite request**: when, for example, one asks for an ice cream, one never says *Voglio un gelato* ('I want an ice cream'), which would sound rude, but *Volevo un gelato* ('I would like an ice cream'). In this case the imperfect can be considered the colloquial equivalent of the present conditional form generally used in polite requests (see 21.29): *Volevo* [= *Vorrei*] *un panino* ('I would like a sandwich'). Common expressions such as *telefonavo per ...* ('I am calling for ...'/'I called for ...') or *venivo perché ...* ('I am coming because ...'/'I came because ...'), which are part of the polite use of the imperfect, soften the tone of statements and can replace both the present indicative and the present perfect.

The imperfect is often used as a **narrative** verb where a preterite or present perfect would be expected since the action is not going on but is completed. This occurs especially in dream narrations and in newspaper reports: *Ieri, il Senato approvava* [= *ha approvato*] *la legge sul conflitto di interessi* ('Yesterday, the Senate passed the law on the conflict of interest'). The effect is to make the narration more vivid and project the reader or listener inside the story.

In spoken Italian, the imperfect is frequently used to form a **hypothetical construction** (see 23.29) expressing something that did not happen and its consequence (*Se tu venivi, ero* *felice* 'If you had come, I would have been happy') where the subjunctive *fossi venuto* and conditional *sarei stato* would be expected instead (*Se tu fossi venuto sarei stato felice* 'If you had come, I would have been happy').

21.8 The Imperfect Progressive

The imperfect progressive (or continuous) is formed with the **imperfect of *stare* + gerund**. It can only be used to describe an ongoing action in the past. In this case, and only in this case, it can replace the imperfect: *Noi stavamo dormendo* [= *noi dormivamo*]*, quando siete arrivati* ('We were sleeping, when you arrived').

21.9 Uses of the Preterite

The preterite (for verb conjugations see chapter 20), or historic past, is a simple tense used to refer to **completed actions or events that have happened in the distant past** relative to the speaker or writer: *L'anno scorso andammo in treno* ('Last year we went by train'), *Lo incontrammo la prima volta a Roma* ('We met him for the first time in Rome'). Although in some parts of Italy the preterite is still used in spoken Italian, this tense is nowadays **mostly restricted to the written language**, especially in literary and academic contexts.

Students of Italian should learn the preterite in order to recognize and understand the forms that they could hear or read, but they can always use the present perfect (see 21.10) to replace the preterite in speaking and in daily writing as well: *L'anno scorso siamo andati* [= *andammo*] *a Venezia in treno* ('Last year we went to Venice by train'), *Lo abbiamo incontrato* [= *incontrammo*] *la prima volta a Roma* ('We met him for the first time in Rome').

21.10 Uses of the Present Perfect

The present perfect (for verb conjugations see chapter 20) is a compound tense formed by **the present of the auxiliary *essere* or *avere* and the past participle** of the main verb (*ho mangiato, sei venuto*, etc.). It expresses **actions completed in the past whose effects continue in some way in the present.** The Italian present perfect mainly corresponds to the English simple past (*Ho parlato* 'I talked'), but sometimes the English present perfect (*Ho parlato* 'I have talked') or the emphatic past (*Ho parlato* 'I did talk') can be better equivalents.

Despite its name (*passato prossimo*, literally 'near past'), the present perfect refers both to recent events and actions that happened in the distant past but which are still present in the speaker's or writer's mind. In fact, more than proximity in time, the present perfect expresses psychological nearness. For example, in a sentence like *Dieci anni fa abbiamo visitato l'Italia. Che bel viaggio!* ('Ten years ago we visited Italy. What a nice trip!'), the present perfect is appropriately used to indicate that whoever is speaking or writing vividly remembers the trip, even though it goes back ten years. On the contrary, if the action completed in the past is no longer felt to have any relation to the present, it would be better to use the preterite (*passato remoto* in Italian, literally 'distant past'), at least in formal written Italian (see 21.9).

Just as the present can replace the future (see 21.2), so can the present perfect replace the future perfect (see 21.6), especially in spoken Italian: *Quando ho finito* [= *avrò finito*] *il liceo, andrò all'università* ('When I finish high school, I will go to college').

21.11 Preterite vs Present Perfect
As already explained (see 21.9, 21.10), the preterite expresses completed actions in the distant past, while the present perfect expresses actions that occurred not too long ago or actions that, having occurred in the distant past, are still felt to be related to the present by the speaker or writer. Note the difference between the two tenses in the following sentences: *Andai al mare a dieci anni* and *Sono andato al mare a dieci anni*. In the first sentence the event is represented by the preterite (*Andai*) as completed in time and it is mentally felt as unrelated to the present; in the second one instead, even though the experience was completed ten years before, the experience is not felt to be over or completely done because it is expressed in the present perfect (*Sono andato*). If the first sentence can be translated as 'I went to the beach when I was ten', the second one is better rendered by the English construction 'have + past participle', which would result in the sentence 'I have gone to the beach when I was ten'.

Despite what was said above, the present perfect tends to replace extensively the preterite, which has become essentially restricted to formal writing in contemporary Italian. In fact, if in Tuscany and in the deep south of Italy the preterite still somehow occurs in daily conversation (especially in Sicily where the speakers have a great tendency to use it), in the rest of the country even educated people tend to employ exclusively the present perfect. The only case where the preterite is still generally used without distinction is in relation to dead persons in order to avoid any ambiguity. In fact, the present perfect may imply that they are still alive. Note the difference between *Mio padre visse a Roma dieci anni* and *Mio padre ha vissuto a Roma dieci anni*. Although both sentences can be translated as 'My father lived in Rome ten years', the first one, using the preterite, makes it clear in Italian that the 'father' is dead.

21.12 Uses of the Pluperfect
The pluperfect (for verb conjugations see chapter 20) is a compound tense formed by **the imperfect of the auxiliary *essere* or *avere* and the past participle** of the main verb (*avevo mangiato, eri andato*, etc.). It expresses an **action that occurred before another one in the past**, so it is not used alone but generally in combination with other past tenses. The English equivalent construction is always 'had + past participle': *Quando sono arrivato, tu eri già uscito* ('When I arrived, you had already left'), *Avevamo mangiato prima che tu chiamassi* ('We had eaten before you called').

Like the imperfect (see 21.7), the pluperfect can be used **to soften or make more polite a request** in spoken Italian. In this case it replaces the present perfect: *Ero venuto* [= *Sono venuto*] *per chiederti se vuoi uscire con me* ('I came to ask you if you want to go out with me').

The phrase **dopo che + pluperfect** can be replaced by *dopo* + past infinitive when the subject is the same in both clauses: *Dopo essere arrivato* [= *Dopo che ero arrivato*] *ho guardato* *un film* ('After having arrived, I watched a movie'). Even the past participle alone (or preceded by *dopo*, *una volta*, or *appena*) can be used instead of the phrase *dopo che* + pluperfect, when the subject is the same in both clauses: *Mangiato* [= *Dopo che avevo mangiato*], *mi sono sentito male* 'Having eaten, I felt bad'.

21.13 Uses of the Preterite Perfect

The preterite perfect (for verb conjugations see chapter 20) is a compound tense formed by **the preterite of the auxiliary *essere* or *avere* and the past participle** of the main verb (*ebbe mangiato*, *furono partiti*, etc.). This tense is extremely uncommon in contemporary spoken Italian and is rarely employed even in formal and written language. That said, it can be considered an alternative to the pluperfect since it is used to express past actions that occurred before others expressed by the preterite: *Dopo che ebbe mangiato, Mario andò a letto* ('After he had eaten, Mario went to bed'), *Appena furono partiti, io cominciai a studiare* ('As soon as they had left, I started to study'). Similarly to the pluperfect (see 21.12), the preterite perfect can also be replaced by the past infinitive or the past participle alone when the subject is the same in both clauses: *Dopo aver studiato/Studiato* [= *Dopo che ebbe studiato*], *Franco andò in palestra* ('After he had studied, Franco went to the gym').

21.14 Combining the Imperfect and the Present Perfect

It is not always easy for an English speaker to decide whether to use the Italian imperfect or the present perfect, since in English the same verb form can sometimes translate both, depending on the context. As mentioned before (see 21.7), in Italian, the imperfect tense mainly describes ongoing actions or states of affairs in the past, while the present perfect (see 21.10) expresses events that have already occured and are completed. This contrast could be synthesized with the opposition **continuing action or state of affairs in the past** versus **completed action**. When both tenses occur together in the same sentence each of them carries out its usual function:

- **the imperfect describes an ongoing action when something else expressed by the present perfect occurs:** *Studiavo quando l'allarme è suonato* ('I was studying when the alarm rang'), *Mangiavamo quando siete arrivati* ('We were eating when you arrived');
- **the imperfect gives the background state of affairs when the action expressed by the present perfect occurs:** *Era già buio quando sono arrivato a Milano* ('It was already dark when I arrived in Milan'), *Faceva molto caldo quando mi sono sentito male* ('It was really hot when I felt bad').

> **N.B.** When the imperfect describes an ongoing action in the past, it can always be replaced, as in English, with the imperfect progressive (21.8). Thus, the two examples above can be also written as *Stavo studiando* [= *studiavo*], *quando l'allarme è suonato* and *Stavamo mangiando* [= *mangiavamo*], *quando siete arrivati*.

21.15 The Progressive Tenses: Italian Unlike English

Italian has progressive forms similar to English ones. Instead of the auxiliary *essere* ('to be'), Italian uses the verb **stare** ('to stay') **followed by a gerund**: *Io sto magiando* ('I am eating'), *Stava nevicando* ('It was snowing'), *Domani, a quest'ora, starò viaggiando in treno* ('Tomorrow, at this time, I will be traveling by train').

Compared to the English 'to be + -ing' construction, the Italian progressive tense has more restricted applications. Unlike the English construction, it can only be used in the present, imperfect, and the future, and it is not used at all in the passive voice. This means that an English passive sentence like, for example, 'I'm being advised to change my job' cannot be translated literally keeping 'I' (*io*) as the subject by using the progressive Italian form, but it must be transformed into an impersonal construction (see 23.12, 23.13) either by using the impersonal *si* (*Mi si consiglia di cambiare lavoro*) or the 3rd person plural of the verb *stare* followed by the gerund (*Mi stanno consigliando di cambiare lavoro*).

The typical future meaning of the progressive tense in English has no equivalent in Italian (*Vado al cinema questa sera* 'I am going to the movies tonight'), and the Italian progressive tense can never express a state of affairs (*Oggi, Maria porta un bel cappello* 'Today, Maria is wearing a beautiful hat').

Unlike their English counterparts, the Italian present and imperfect progressive tenses can always be replaced by the non-progressive equivalents without causing a change in meaning: *Che cosa fai/facevi* [= *Che cosa stai facendo/stavi facendo*]? ('What are/were you doing?'). In case of a future action, on the contrary, the progressive meaning can't be conveyed by the simple future tense, so the progressive tense is necessary to express an ongoing action in the future. For instance, note the difference in meaning between the sentence *Domani a quest'ora staremo mangiando spaghetti* ('Tomorrow, at this time, we will be eating spaghetti') and the sentence *Domani a quest'ora mangeremo spaghetti* ('Tomorrow, at this time, we will eat spaghetti'), where the action itself is pointed out, not its progression.

> **N.B.** The form *stare a* + infinitive can be found sometimes, especially in a slangy context, instead of **stare + gerund**: *Sto a guardare* [= *Sto guardando*] *la televisione* ('I am watching TV'). This construction is typical of Rome and its vicinity. However, this form must be avoided.

21.16 The Subjunctive

The subjunctive (for verb conjugations see chapter 20) has only four tenses: **two simple** (present and imperfect) and **two compound tenses** (past and pluperfect). It is a mood capable of expressing what the indicative does not. It is used to indicate possibility, uncertainty, opinions, wishes, commands, and so on. Since it emphasizes a speaker's or writer's feelings about facts, the subjunctive gives voice to a "subjective" point of view, whereas the indicative presents facts as certain and objective. Note, for example, the difference between *Sono certo che tu sei felice* ('I am sure you are happy') and *Spero che tu sia felice* ('I hope you are happy'). In the first sentence *sei* (indicative) is used in a context of certainty; on the contrary, in the second sentence *sia* (subjunctive) expresses hope and wish.

21.17 Uses of the Subjunctive in Independent Clauses

The subjunctive occurs mostly in subordinate clauses (see 21.18–21.27), but it can be used in independent sentences as well. In these cases the subjunctive, usually preceded by *che*, has the following applications.

- **Giving commands, advice, and exhortations**. The subjunctive provides forms of command for the missing third persons of the imperative (see 21.35): *Che lui/lei lavori fino a sera!* ('He/She shall work till night!'), *Che loro parlino più forte* ('They shall speak up'). The subjunctive can also replace the imperative with *tu*, *noi*, and *voi* in order to soften a request or demand: *Che entri, per favore!* ('Come in, please'), *Che facciate prima possibile* ('Do it as soon as possible'). To issue a formal command, one should use *Lei* and *Loro* (though the latter is rarely used) followed respectively by the third singular and the plural forms of the verb (see also 21.37): *Lei esca, per favore* ('You, get out please'), *Loro non vadano via* ('You, do not leave').
- **Expressing doubt and conjecture**. When the present or the present perfect subjunctive tenses are used in a direct interrogative sentence, they express doubt or conjecture in the present or in the past. In a sentence like *Marco non risponde. Che sia fuori?* ('Marco isn't answering. Could he be out?'), the interrogative does not really ask a question but makes a supposition. The interrogative *Che sia fuori?* is in this case equivalent to *Forse è fuori* ('Maybe he is out'). The same doubt or conjecture meaning is typical of questions introduced by *se*, often preceded by the conjunction *e*: *E se fossimo fatti l'uno per l'altro?* ('What if we were made for each other?').
- **Making an exclamation**. An exclamation mark or the tone of the voice makes this meaning of the subjunctive clear, distinguishing it from the interrogative subjunctive expressing doubt or conjecture. A sentence like *Che Gianna esca tutti i giorni!*, for example, is perfectly equivalent in meaning to *È incredibile che Gianna esca tutti i giorni!* ('It is incredible that Gianna goes out everyday!'). The subjunctive exclamatory is also frequent with the second person singular and plural of verbs such as *sapere* ('to know'), *vedere* ('to see'), and *sentire* ('to hear') usually preceded by *se* ('if'): *Se tu sapessi quanto ti amo!* ('If you could know how much I love you!'), *Se voi aveste visto come si è comportato Mario!* ('If you all could have seen how Mario behaved!').

- **Expressing desire**. The imperfect or pluperfect subjunctive, usually preceded by *magari* or *almeno* (both meaning 'if only' in this case), express desire. The desire is related to the present or the future when the imperfect subjunctive is implied, or is related to the past if expressed by the pluperfect: *Magari piovesse!* ('If only it could rain!'), *Almeno avesse piovuto!* ('If only it had rained!'). If in the former case the desire is real because it can still be satisfied, the latter sentence instead expresses an unfulfilled wish. The same meanings can be conveyed in English with the phrase 'I wish …' or with 'I wish it would have …', depending on the tense of the Italian subjunctive. Similarly, the subjunctive of the verb *potere* is used to express a desire: *Potesse piovere!* ('I wish it would rain!'), *Tu potessi vincere!* ('I wish you could win!').

21.18 The Subjunctive in Dependent "che Clauses"

In most cases the **subjunctive occurs in subordinate clauses introduced by the conjunction *che***, when the subjects of the two clauses are different (otherwise the infinitive must be used, see. 21.23) and the context is presented by the main clause as opinion (*Penso che John vada in Italia* 'I think John is going to Italy'), doubt (*Dubito che John vada in Italia* 'I doubt that John will go to Italy'), hope (*Spero che John vada in Italia* 'I hope John goes to Italy'), wish and volition ('*Voglio che John vada in Italia* 'I want John to go to Italy'), fear (*Temo che John vada in Italia* 'I am afraid that John will go to Italy').

The most significant verbs and verbal constructions that require the subjunctive, grouped by category, are indicated below, with examples of their use.

- Verbs and verbal constructions expressing **personal opinion or conviction** such as *avere la convinzione/il dubbio/l'idea* ('to be certain/to doubt/to have the idea'), *considerare* ('to consider'), *credere* ('to believe'), *dubitare* ('to doubt'), *immaginare* ('to imagine'), *ipotizzare* ('to suspect'), *negare* ('to deny'), *pensare* ('to think'), *presumere* ('to presume'), *sospettare* ('to suspect'), *supporre* ('to suppose'): *Penso che tu abbia reagito male* ('I think you have reacted badly'), *Perché presumi che sia colpa mia?* ('Why do you presume it is my fault?').
- Verbs and verbal constructions expressing **impersonal and general opinions**. All the above verbs require the subjunctive also when they are used impersonally to express a general opinion: *Si pensa che …* ('People think that …'), *Qualcuno pensa che …* ('Someone thinks that …'). The verb *dire* ('to say'), and the equivalent *affermare* ('to affirm'), which regularly require the indicative (*Io dico che sei un bravo ragazzo* 'I say that you are a good boy'), must be followed by the subjunctive when they express a generic or undetermined subject: *Si dice/Dicono che tu sia un bravo ragazzo* ('People say that you are a good boy'). The third person of the verb *essere* ('to be'), combined with nouns such as *opinione* ('opinion'), *idea* ('idea'), *giudizio* ('judgment'), expresses the same generic thought and requires the subjunctive: *È opinione comune che tu sia un bravo ragazzo* ('It's everybody's opinion that you are a good boy'), *Era idea di tutti che Marco fosse partito* ('It was everybody's idea that Marco had left').

- Impersonal constructions expressing **look and appearance**. This is the case of the third person singular of the verbs *sembrare, apparire, parere*, meaning 'to look like', 'to sound', 'to appear': *Sembra che tu non voglia venire* ('It sounds as if you do not want to come'), *Pare che stiano tutti bene* ('It appears they are all well').
- Verbs expressing **volition** (including command, permission, or request) such as *chiedere* ('to ask'), *decidere* ('to decide'), *esigere* ('to require'), *ordinare* ('to order'), *permettere* ('to allow'), *pretendere* ('to expect'), *pregare* ('to pray'), *volere* ('to want'): *Voglio che tu stia con me* ('I want you to stay with me'), *Mio padre pretende che io diventi dottore* ('My father expects me to became a doctor'). The third person of the verb *essere* ('to be') combined with nouns such as *ordine* ('command'), *regola* ('rule'), *abitudine* ('habit') requires the subjunctive: *L'ordine è che tu rimanga qui con noi* ('The order is that you remain here with us'), *La regola è che tutti alzino la mano prima di parlare* ('The rule is that everybody raise his/her hand before speaking').
- Verbs and verbal constructions expressing **personal feelings** (including desire, fear, happiness or saddness, pleasure or dislike) such as *augurarsi* ('to wish'), *avere l'impressione* ('to be under the impression'), *avere la sensazione* ('to have the feeling'), *avere paura* ('to be afraid'), *essere contento* ('to be glad'), *essere felice* ('to be happy'): *Ho la sensazione che a loro non sia piaciuta la cena* ('I have the feeling they did not enjoy dinner'), *Hai paura che non arrivino in tempo?* ('Are you afraid they will be late?'). Other expressions of this category are *non vedere l'ora* ('to look forward to') and *non aspettare altro* ('just to wait for'): *Non vediamo l'ora che veniate a farci visita* ('We look forward to your visit'), *Non aspetto altro che cominci la scuola* ('I am just waiting for school to start').
- The third person singular of verbs such as *bisognare* ('to be necessary'), *convenire* ('to be convenient'), *occorrere* ('to be necessary'), *servire* ('to be useful') expressing **necessity or convenience**: *Bisogna che finiate il lavoro prima possibile* ('It is necessary that you finish your work as soon as possible'), *Conviene che rimaniate dove siete* ('It is convenient that you stay where you are').
- **Impersonal constructions** formed by the third person singular of the verb *essere* ('to be') followed by adjectives such as *è giusto* ('it is right'), *è bene* ('it is good'), *è naturale* ('it is normal'), *è meglio* ('it is better'), *è ovvio* ('it is obvious'), *è importante* ('it is important'), *è utile* ('it is useful'), *è strano* ('it is strange'): *È importante che ci pensiate a lungo prima di scegliere* ('It is important that you think it over before choosing'), *È naturale che tu sia felice* ('It is normal that you be happy').

> **N.B.** Despite the verb in the main clause, the subjunctive is mandatory when the *che* clause precedes the main one: *Che tu fossi stato a Roma lo sapevo* ('I knew that you had been to Rome'). Note that the indicative (*eri* and not the subjunctive *fossi*) would be used should the main clause (*lo sapevo già*) precede the *che* clause since the verb *sapere* does not require the subjunctive: *Lo sapevo già che eri stato a Roma*.

21.19 How to Use the Subjunctive Tenses in the Dependent "che Clauses"

The **present** of the subjunctive is used when the main clause is in the present or the future of the indicative and the action in the dependent clause occurs at the same time or in the future: *Dubito che Carlo compri un po' di pane* ('I doubt that Carlo will buy some bread'), *Crederanno che tu non venga* ('They will think you will not come').

The **past** of the subjunctive is used the main clause is in the present or the future of the indicative and the action in the dependent clause occurs before: *Dubito che Carlo abbia comprato un po' di pane* ('I doubt that Carlo bought some bread'), *Crederanno che tu non sia venuto* ('They will think you did not come').

On the other hand, the **imperfect** of the subjunctive is used when the main clause is in any past tense of the indicative or in the present conditional and the action in the dependent clause occurs at the same time or later than the action of the main one: *Dubitavo che Carlo comprasse un po' di pane* ('I doubted that Carlo bought some bread'), *Vorrei che tu venissi* ('I wish you would come').

As for the **pluperfec**t, it is used when the main clause is in any past tense of the indicative or in the past conditional and the action in the dependent clause occurs before the action in the main one: *Dubitavo che Carlo avesse comprato un po' di pane* ('I doubted that Carlo had bought some bread'), *Avrei voluto che tu fossi venuto* ('I would have liked it if you had come').

> **N.B.** In spoken Italian the future indicative is often used instead of the present subjunctive to refer to the future. For example, in the following sentence the future *verrà* can replace the subjunctive *venga*: *Credo che Matteo verrà* [= *venga*] *con me domani* ('I believe Matteo will come with me tomorrow').

21.20 Omission of che in Dependent Subjunctive Clauses

As said before (see 21.18), in most cases the subjunctive occurs in subordinate clauses introduced by the conjunction *che*. **When the subject of the subjunctive is a personal pronoun or it is implied, the conjunction *che* can be omitted.** The following two examples make this point clear: *Immagino* [*che*] *loro non possano venire* ('I imagine they can't come'), *Marco non ha chiamato, quindi credo* [*che*] *non venga* ('Marco hasn't called, so I think he is not coming'). In the first sentence *che* can be removed because of the personal pronoun *loro*, and in the second because the subject of *venga* (*Marco*) is implied rather than expressed. It must be kept in mind that **in all other cases the conjunction *che* is mandatory.**

21.21 Necessity of the Subject with the Subjunctive

While the subject pronoun is in some way optional with the indicative mood, with the subjunctive **it is mandatory because there is a possibility of ambiguity.** In a sentence like *Sperano che dorma* it would be impossible to understand who is the subject of *dorma*, since it could be *io* ('I'), *tu* ('you'), *lui* ('he'), *lei* ('she'), or *Lei* ('you' sing. form.). A sentence like this one would be the equivalent of the English 'They hope I/you sleep' and 'They hope he/she sleeps', so it is understandable why the subject must be expressed.

The subject can be omitted if it is easily inferred from the context. In *Non ho visto Maria, credo che [lei] sia in vacanza* ('I haven't seen Maria; I believe she is on vacation'), for example, the pronoun *lei* can be omitted since it is clear that *Maria* is the subject of *sia*.

21.22 Negative Constructions with the Subjunctive

When a verb or a verbal construction that expresses certainty is made negative, **the subjunctive must be used instead of the regular indicative in the *che* clause.** In fact, the negative (*non so* 'I do not know', *non sono certo* 'I am not sure') creates doubt and uncertainty. Note, for example, the difference between: *Sono sicuro che tu capisci* ('I am sure that you understand') and *Non sono sicuro che tu capisca* ('I am not sure that you understand'). The certainty expressed by *sono sicuro* is negated in the second sentence by *non*, so it becomes necessary to use the subjunctive *capisca* instead of the indicative *capisci*.

21.23 Di + Infinitive vs che + Subjunctive

The construction ***di* + infinitive must always replace *che* + subjunctive when the subject in both the main clause and the *che* clause is the same:** *Tu credi che tu sia il più bravo > Tu credi di essere il più bravo* ('You think you are the best'), *Io temo che io arrivi in ritardo > Io temo di arrivare in ritardo* ('I am afraid of being late').

In a few cases the infinitive is **without the preposition *di*** and follows directly the main clause. This is common with the third person of verbs expressing **necessity or convenience** such as *bisogna* ('it is necessary'), *conviene* ('it is convenient'), *necessita* ('it is necessary'): *Bisogna finire il lavoro* ('It is necessary to finish the work'), *Conviene partire presto* ('It is convenient to leave early'). This also happens with **impersonal constructions** formed by the third person of the verb *essere* ('to be') and some adjectives such as *è giusto* ('it is right'), *è bene* ('it is good'), *è naturale* ('it is normal'): *È naturale sperare in un buon risultato* ('It is normal to hope for a good result'), *È bene mostrare gentilezza* ('It is good to show kindness').

21.24 Indicative and Conditional Moods Instead of Subjunctive

It is really frequent in contemporary everyday spoken Italian to find **the indicative mood where the subjunctive ought to be.** This is especially common with verbs and constructions expressing personal opinions or convinctions: *Penso che tu sei intelligente* ('I think you are intelligent'), *Crediamo che avete mangiato bene* ('We imagine you ate well'). In the two sentences above the indicatives *sei* and *avete mangiato* replace respectively the more appropriate *sia* and *abbiate mangiato*. Even if this use is becoming increasingly common and can be accepted in colloquial contexts, it must be avoided in written and formal Italian where the non-mastery of the subjunctive is still considered a sign of a less than adequate formal education.

The future indicative and the past conditional are, on the contrary, accepted with verbs and constructions expressing personal opinions or convictions when the *che* clause indicates an action that happens after the time of the main clause (see 21.19). The future is used to replace the present subjunctive (*Penso che Mario verrà* 'I think Mario will come') and the past conditional to replace the imperfect subjunctive (*Pensavo che Mario sarebbe venuto* 'I thought Mario would have come'). In the two examples above *verrà* and *sarebbe venuto* replace respectively *venga* and *venisse* because the two actions they represent are located after *penso* and *pensavo* in time.

21.25 Mandatory Subjunctive After Some Conjunctions or Special Expressions: purché, se, *etc.*
The Italian subjunctive is required after a number of common conjugations and certain expressions (see also 17.7–17.18). The subjunctive is mandatory after the following words and phrases:

- *a condizione che, ammesso che, a patto che, purché, sempre che* (all meaning 'provided that') that express a **condition**: *Andrò a condizione che anche tu vada* ('I will go provided that you go, too'), *Sempre che tu mi inviti, verrò alla tua festa* ('I will come to your party, provided that you invite me');
- *se* ('if') introducing a **possible or unreal hypothetical situation** (see 23.29): *Se fossi ricco, comprerei una villa in Toscana* ('If I were rich, I would buy a villa in Tuscany'), *Se avessi saputo che saresti arrivato, ti avrei incontrato in aeroporto* ('If I had known that you were coming, I would have met you at the airport");
- *casomai, laddove, nel caso che, nell'eventualità che, qualora, ove* (all meaning 'in case') that express an **eventuality**: *Casomai Lia non potesse chiamarti, chiamala tu* ('In case Lia can't call you, you call her.'), *Qualora non fossi in casa, mi puoi trovare in biblioteca* ('In case I am not home, you can find me at the library');
- *affinché, acciocché, in modo che, perché* (all meaning 'so that', 'in order to') that express **purpose**: *Parla più forte in modo che ti senta* ('Speak up, so I can hear you'), *Faccio tutto questo perché tu possa essere felice* ('I am doing all this so that you can be happy'). Note that *perché* requires the subjunctive when it means 'in order to' but not when it means 'because'. In this latter case *perché* indicates a result (not an intention) and always requires the indicative: *Sono felice perché tu sei felice* ('I am happy because you are happy');
- *benché, malgrado [che], nonostante [che], per quanto, quantunque, sebbene, seppure* (all meaning 'although') that express a **contrast** with what is said or written in the main clause: *Benché Luigi abbia studiato molto, non ha passato l'esame* ('Although Luigi studied a lot, he did not pass the exam'), *Nonostante [che] faccia tutto per te, tu non sei mai contento* ('Although I do everything for you, you are never happy'). All the concessive conjunctions listed above could be replaced by *anche se* ('even though'), which, instead, takes the in-

dicative mood: *Anche se lo prometti* [= *Benché tu lo prometta*]*, io non mi fido di te* ('Even though you promise it, I do not trust you');
- *a meno che non, eccetto che, fuorché, salvo che non, tranne che* (all meaning 'unless') that express an **exception** to what is said or written in the main clause: *A meno che tu non mi inviti, io non verrò* ('Unless you invite me, I will not come'), *Non vado al cinema, salvo che non venga anche tu* ('I am not going to the movies unless you come, too');
- *prima che* ('before'), *fino a che, finché, fino a quando* (all meaning 'for as long as') that express **time**. If *prima che* always requires the subjunctive (*Parti, prima che sia tardi* 'Leave before it is too late'), the others take the subjunctive, usually preceded by *non*, when the duration of the time is given as unknown or indefinitive (*Staremo fino a quando la pioggia non cessi* 'We will stay until the rain stops') and the indicative when, on the contrary, the time is presented as known and definite (*Staremo fino a quando tu parti* 'We will stay until you leave').

The subjunctive is also required after *come se, quasi che* (both meaning 'as if'): *Parli come se mi conoscessi* ('You talk as if you know me'); after *senza che* ('without'): *Hai speso tanti soldi senza che me ne accorgessi* ('You spent a lot of money without me noticing it').

21.26 The Subjunctive in Relative Clauses: Marco cercava chi lo aiutasse

A relative clause usually takes the indicative (*Ho parlato con quello studente che conosci* 'I have spoken with that student you know'), but **when what is expressed in the main clause corresponds more to a desire or intention than to a fact, the subjunctive is required.** In a sentence like *Marco cercava chi lo aiutasse* ('Marco was looking for who would help him') the subjunctive *aiutasse* introduced by the relative pronoun *chi* indicates the purpose of the action not the action itself, which could simply be expressed by the indicative: *Marco cercava chi lo aiutava* ('Marco was looking for whoever was helping him').

The subjunctive is also used in relative sentences after a relative superlative (*il più ... che* 'the most ...', *il meno ... che* 'the least ...') and similar constructions (*il solo ... che* 'the only ...', *il primo che* 'the first ...'): *Tu sei il più bravo studente che io abbia* ('You are the best student that I have'), *Gianni è l'unico che io conosca* ('Gianni is the only one that I know').

21.27 The Subjunctive After Indefinite Adjectives and Pronouns: Chiunque tu sia ...

The subjunctive is required after common indefinite adjectives and pronouns (see also 11.8) such as *qualunque* ('whatever'), *chiunque* ('whoever'), and so on: *Qualunque cosa tu dica, ti credo* ('Whatever you say, I believe you'), *Chiunque venga non mi interessa* ('Whoever comes is of no interest to me'). This in particular occurs with indefinite antecedents to a relative clause meaning 'anyone who', 'anything that', and similar constructions: *Non c'è nessuno che mi aiuti* ('There is no one to help me'), *Non c'è niente che Anna possa fare* ('There is nothing Anna can do').

21.28 The Conditional

There are two conditional tenses in Italian (for verb conjugatiions see chapter 20): present and past. The **present conditional** is the equivalent of the English construction 'would' (conditional of all verbs), 'could' and 'might' (conditional of *potere*), 'should' and 'ought to' (conditional of *dovere*) followed by the base form of the verb: *Vorrei un gelato* ('I would like an ice cream'), *Non sono certo ti piacerebbe vivere in Italia* ('I am not sure you would like living in Italy'), *Se fossi te, non mi preoccuperei troppo* ('If I were you, I wouldn't be so worried').

The **past conditional** is the equivalent of the English construction 'would have' (conditional of all verbs), 'could have' and 'might have' (conditional of *potere*), 'should have' and 'ought to have' (conditional of *dovere*), plus the past participle of the main verb ('I would have done', 'You could have thought', etc.). It usually expresses the same situations as the present conditional but is set in the past: *Avrei voluto un gelato* ('I would have liked an ice cream'), *Non sono certo ti sarebbe piaciuto vivere in Italia* ('I am not sure you would have liked living in Italy'), *Se fossi stato te, non mi sarei preoccupato troppo* ('Had I been you, I wouldn't have been so worried'). For more details on these and other uses of the conditional, see the next paragraphs (21.29–21.32).

21.29 Uses of the Conditional in Independent Clauses

Even if in most cases the conditional is used in dependent clauses (see 21.30) to refer to a state of being or an action depending upon a condition (*Vivremmo meglio se avessimo più tempo libero* 'We would live better if we had more free time'), it is also possible to find the conditional in independent statements. This use is generally the result of a missing or unspoken condition in which a subjunctive would be used. For instance, in an independent sentence like *Prenderei un caffè* ('I would have a coffee') we can imagine clauses such as … *se tu me lo offrissi* ('… if you offered me one'), … *se non mi facesse male* ('… if it weren't bad for me').

In independent statements the conditional can be employed in one of the following circumstances.

- To express **politeness**. The use of the conditional rather than the present indicative is typical of requests when one wants to be courteous. In fact, the conditional makes the request less plain-spoken and adds a nuance of kindness: *Avrei bisogno di un chilo di pane* ('I need a kilo of bread, please'), *Vorrei un cappuccino* ('I would like a cappuccino'). Note that the English equivalent is not always 'would' so, to express the same politeness in English, it is necessary to use 'please', while in Italian the phrase *per favore* ('please') would just add more emphasis to what is already expressed in a kind way by the conditional. The conditional expresses a form of politeness also when an intention is declared: *Sono le due, io andrei adesso* ('It is two o'clock; I should go now'). This example omits the unspoken condition *se non ti dispiace* ('if you don't mind').

- To express **mitigation**. The use of the conditional softens the opinion expressed by someone: *Direi che possiamo andare* ('I would say we can leave'), *Sarebbe meglio non pensare a questo* ('It would be better not to think about it'). The use of the conditional in this context mitigates different opinions or possibilities, which can sound authoritative if expressed in the indicative mood.
- To express **probability**. The conditional, rather than the indicative, can also be used to introduce a present or past fact as probable, not certain. This use is typical of the journalistic style: *Il presidente avrebbe già lasciato Roma in aereo* ('The President would have already left Rome by plane'). In this example the journalist is essentially expressing his/her understanding of the facts.
- The conditional of *potere* and *dovere* ('could' and 'should') is used to present a **possibility in the future:** *Domani potrebbe piovere* ('It could rain tomorrow'), *Marco dovrebbe arrivare fra poco* ('Marco should be here soon').
- To issue **invitations**. In this case the conditional does not really make any difference and can be considered equivalent to the indicative. For example, the sentence *Verresti a cena?* is perfectly equivalent to *Vieni a cena?* ('Are you coming for dinner?').
- To express **desire**. In many cases desire is expressed by the conditional of the verb *volere* ('to want') or *piacere* ('to like'): *Vorrei avere un fratello* ('I wish to have a brother'), *Mi piacerebbe vivere in Sicilia* ('I would like to live in Sicily').

21.30 The Conditional in Dependent Clauses

The conditional can express politeness, mitigation, probability, invitation, and desire in a dependent clause also. If we take, for example, *Il presidente avrebbe già lasciato Roma in aereo* ('The President would have already left Rome by plane'), given as a sample of the conditional of probability (see 21.29), we can transform it from an independent clause to a dependent one by simply adding *Qualcuno riferisce che ...* ('Someone is saying ...'): *Qualcuno riferisce che il presidente avrebbe già lasciato Roma in aereo* ('Someone is saying the President has already left Rome by plane').

The conditional can also be used in a variety of dependent clauses such as indirect interrogatives (*Dimmi che cosa cosa avresti fatto tu* 'Tell me what you would have done'), relatives (*Ciò che vorrei chiederti è importante* 'What I would like to ask you is really important'), comparatives (*Ho dovuto lavorare più di quanto avrei potuto immaginare* 'I had to work more than I imagined I would have to'), and so on.

21.31 Past Conditional Expressing Future

Unlike English, which uses the present conditional to express the future aspect of an action viewed from a past perspective, Italian uses the past conditional for the same purpose: *Ero certo che Marco sarebbe arrivato in ritardo* ('I was sure Marco would be late'). In this sentence

Marco's lateness is viewed from a past perspective (*Ero certo*), making it a **future-in-the-past** action. This use of the past conditional is unique to Italian and has no equivalent in English.

This construction is also typical of indirect speech introduced by a verb in the past. When a direct statement is changed into an indirect one, the past conditional must always replace the future indicative: *Ho detto: "Ci vedremo presto"* > *Ho detto che ci saremmo visti presto* ('I said: "We will see each other soon"' > 'I said that we would see each other soon').

21.32 The Conditional in Hypothetical Sentences

The conditional can indicate the consequence of a condition expressed by *se* + subjunctive (see also 23.29). In particular the **present conditional** is used to talk about something that might happen or to talk about very improbable (though possible) conditions. In these cases the imperfect subjunctive occurs in the conditional clause and the present conditional in the consequent clause: *Se tu fossi con me, sarei felice* ('If you were with me, I would be happy'), *Comprerei una casa a Roma, se avessi i soldi* ('I would buy a house in Rome, if I had the money'). The present conditional is used as well when the condition, expressed by the pluperfect subjunctive, refers to the past but the consequence is in the present or future: *Se tu avessi vissuto più a lungo in Italia, oggi parleresti meglio l'italiano* ('If you had lived in Italy longer, you would speak better Italian today').

The **past conditional** indicates a consequence that is seen as impossible since it depends on a condition contrary-to-fact, expressed by the pluperfect subjunctive: *Se tu fossi stato con me sarei stato felice* ('If you had been with me, I would have been happy'), *Avrei comprato una casa a Roma, se avessi avuto i soldi* ('I would have bought a house in Roma, if I had had the money'). The past conditional is used as well when the condition, expressed by the imperfect subjunctive, refers to the present but the consequence is in the past: *Se tu mi volessi davvero bene, ieri non mi avresti offeso così tanto* ('If you really cared about me, you would not have hurt me so much yesterday').

> **N.B.** The conjunction *se* can be easily omitted without compromising the comprehension of the sentence. In fact, the combination of subjunctive and conditional is in itself sufficient to make the meaning clear: all the examples above could be presented without *se* and be absolutely understandable for an Italian listener or reader.

21.33 Indicative, Subjunctive, and Conditional with Pronouns

When unstressed direct or indirect object pronouns and their combined forms are used with the indicative, subjunctive, or the conditional moods of the verb, **they always precede the verbs:** *Lo bevo ogni giorno* ('I drink it every day'), *Gli potessi parlare!* ('I wish I could speak to him'), *Vorrei un cappuccino; lo vorrei con poco zucchero* ('I would like a cappuccino; I would like it with a little sugar').

21.34 The Imperative

The imperative mood is used for giving **commands** (*Parla* 'Talk'), **interdictions** (*Non fumare* 'Do not smoke'), or **advice** (*Evitate di stare troppo al sole!* 'Avoid staying too long under the sun!'). It is a simple form and has only one tense, the present.

21.35 The Subjects of the Imperative

Unlike its English counterpart, the Italian imperative has **three different forms** (for verb conjugations see chapter 20) depending on whom the command, the prohibition or the suggestion targets. The *tu* and *voi* imperatives are informal and used only to address family members and friends: *tu* refers to one person (*Vieni qua* 'Come here'), *voi* more than one (*Venite qua* 'Come here'). The *noi* form corresponds to the English 'let's' plus main verb and is not used to issue commands but to exhort (*Andiamo* 'Let's go'). It is easy to remember the imperative forms since they are identical to their correspondent indicative present forms, except *tu* in verbs in -*are*, which is equivalent to the 3rd form of the present (*Parla con me* 'Talk to me').

Since the 1st person singular imperative form does not exist, anyone who wants to direct an emphatic suggestion to himself/herself in Italian can use the imperative form for *tu* (*Rimani calmo, non ti preoccupare* 'Stay calm; do not worry') or the *noi* form (*Rimaniamo calmi, non ci preoccupiamo* 'Let's stay calm; let's not worry').

Remember that the subjet pronouns are not usually expressed with the imperative. They are used occasionally to add emphasis or to convey contrast: *Cantate voi adesso!* ('You sing now, please!'), *Esci tu, io rimango qua!* ('You leave! I stay here!'). In these cases, as the above examples show, the pronouns follow the verb, not precede it.

21.36 Negative Imperative: non urlate, non urlare

To express the negative imperative, **non is placed in front of the affirmative forms** for all verb forms (*Non parlate ad alta voce*, 'Do not talk loudly', *Non rimaniamo a casa questa sera* 'Let's not stay home tonight'), except for *tu*. In this case the negative imperative is formed with **non + infinitive**: *Non urlare* ('Do not yell'), *Non dire sciocchezze* ('Do not talk nonsense').

21.37 Formal Commands and Ways to Soften the Imperative

Since the imperative sounds sharp and abrupt, it is only used among friends, co-workers, relatives, or when addressing a child. For this reason, it must be avoided in other circumstances and replaced by other forms that make the command less outspoken and gentler.

In formal language the *tu* imperative form (affirmative as well as negative) is always replaced by the **3rd pers. sing. of the present subjunctive**: *Entri!* ('Come in'), *Non arrivi in ritardo!*

('Do not arrive late!'). When referring to more than one person, the formal use of the **3rd pers. pl. of the subjunctive** is also possible even though it is restricted in contemporary Italian to a very conventional context: *Entrino!* ('Come in'), *Non arrivino in ritardo!* ('Do not arrive late!').

Another way to make a command less direct and blunt is to add a **polite phrase** such as *per favore, per piacere, per cortesia, ti prego* (all equivalent to the English 'please'), or *pure* (equivalent to the exhortative 'do') to the sentence containing the imperative: *Esci, per favore!* ('Please, leave!'), *Entra pure!* ('Do come in!').

Often the command is formulated with a **turn of phrase** and presented as a question instead of an imperative. In this case, one can use expressions such as *Puoi/Potete ...?* ('Can you ...?') and *Ti dispiace/Vi dispiace ...?* ('Do you mind ...?'): *Puoi passarmi il pane?* ('Can you pass me the bread?'), *Vi dispiace portarmi a casa?* ('Do you mind giving me a ride home?').

The phrase **essere pregato di + infinitive** is typical of public service announcements (train stations, airport, aircraft). It replaces the imperative, making the call more polite: *Siete pregati di formare una sola fila* ('You are asked to form only one line'), *Signora, è pregata di mantenere le cinture allacciate* ('Madam, you are asked to keep your seatbelt fastened'). Note that *pregato* must always agree in gender and number with its subject.

21.38 The Imperative and Pronouns: svegliati; portamelo, *etc.*

When unstressed direct or indirect object pronouns and their combined forms are used with the imperative, **they follow the verbs and are attached to them:** *Passami la bottiglia d'acqua!* ('Pass me the bottle of water!'), *Vedete quell'uomo? Guardatelo attentamente!* ('Can you see that man? Look at him attentively!'). The same thing happens with reflexive pronouns: *Svegliati* ('Wake up'), *Alzatevi* ('Get up'). It is important to distinguish between an exhortation (imperative) and a simple statement (present indicative). In fact, in the former, the pronoun must be attached to the verb (*Ora alziamoci!* 'Let's get up, now!'), but in the latter, the pronoun precedes it (*Ora ci alziamo* 'We are getting up now').

As with affirmative commands, the pronouns always attach themselves to the verb forms in negative commands as well, except for the 2nd pers. sing. verb form. In this circumstance, the direct or indirect object pronouns, or their combined forms, can either attach themselves to the infinitive or precede it without changing the meaning: *Non incolparmi* is equivalent to *Non mi incolpare* ('Do not blame me'); *Non darglielo* is equivalent to *Non glielo dare* ('Do not give it to him').

With the 3rd persons subjunctive, used to express a command in a more formal way (see 21.37), the pronouns are always placed before the verb: *Mi dia una buona notizia* ('Give me some good news'), *Si siedano adesso* ('Sit now').

21.39 Other Common Uses of the Imperative: Instructions and Conversational Expressions

In addition to expressing commands, interdictions, or advice, the imperative *voi* form is generally used, besides the infinitive (see 21.43), for **giving instructions.** This is typical of recipes (*Tagliate il formaggio in cubetti e friggetelo* 'Cut the cheese into small cubes, and fry them') and operating manuals (*Avvitate la lampadina in senso orario* 'Screw in the bulb clockwise').

The imperative *tu* verb forms of *dare* (*dai*) and *sentire* (*senti*) are often used as conversational expressions in a familiar context. In this case they lose the imperative meaning of 'give' and 'listen' to function simply as **emphatic verbal inserts.** *Dai* corresponds to the English 'go on' or 'come on' (*Dai, non ti credo!* 'Go/Come on, I don't believe you!'), while *senti* is equivalent to 'look' or 'hey' (*Senti, io vado a casa* 'Look/Hey, I am going home').

21.40 The Infinitive

The infinitive form of the verb (see chapter 20), like the gerund, and the participle can't be conjugated since it does not have a specific subject: in fact, there is no *io, tu, lui* or *lei, noi, voi, loro* with the infinitive. This verb form includes only two tenses: **present** (simple) and **past** (compound). While the present consists of only one word (*scrivere* 'to write', *andare* 'to come'), the past is a compound tense formed by two parts, the simple infinitive of the auxiliary *avere* or *essere* plus the past participle of the main verb (*avere scritto* 'having written', *essere andato* 'having gone').

The infinitive, especially the present infinitive, is used extensively in Italian and is a really versatile verb form. Its English equivalent is either the infinitive 'to + verb' or the gerund '-ing' forms (*parlare* 'to talk', 'talking'). The infinitive is used after most prepositions (*Vado a mangiare* 'I am going to eat', *Prima di partire, chiama* 'Before you leave, call') and so can function as a noun (*Viaggiare è bello* 'Traveling is nice'), in which case it can even be preceded by an article (*Il mangiare troppo fa male* 'Too much eating is not good').

21.41 Agreement with the Past Infinitive: essere partiti, averla comprata

The present or simple infinitive is invariable whereas the past or compound infinitive displays some degree of change. In compound forms using the auxiliary *essere*, the past participle varies according to the subject (*Lui dice di essere arrivato in tempo, mentre lei ammette di essere arrivata in ritardo* 'He says he arrived on time whereas she admits that she arrived late') and, in those using the auxiliary *avere,* the past participle changes with the pronouns according with the rules of agreement (see 13.7, 13.11): *Che bella automobile! Sono contento di averla comprata* ('What a nice car! I am happy I bought it').

21.42 Use of the Infinitive in Independent Clauses

The use of the infinitive is not really frequent in independent clauses but it has several applications that must be remembered. Depending on the meaning of the clause, only the present or at times both the present and past infinitives can be used. Below are indicated all the possible applications of the infinitive. If just one example is given, only the present tense can be employed for that specific meaning, but if two examples are supplied, both tenses can be used (note that the English equivalent is not always an infinitive). The infinitive in independent clauses can:

- **express doubt** through an interrogative sentence: *Che pensare?* ('What should I think?');
- **make exclamations**: *Perdonare mio marito!* ('Forgive my husband!'), *Averlo saputo prima!* ('Having known it before!');
- **give commands or instructions** (see 21.43): *Avvitare la lampadina in senso orario* ('Screw in the bulb clockwise').

21.43 The Infinitive as Imperative and Instructional Form

As seen before (21.36) the present negative infinitive serves as the negative imperative form for *tu*: *Non parlare* ('Do not talk'), *Non partire, ti prego* ('Do not leave, I beg you').

Also, the infinitive, besides the imperative form (see 21.39), is often used for giving instructions. This is typical of recipes (*Aggiungere due cucchiaini di olio di oliva* 'Add two spoons of olive oil'), operating manuals (*Rimuovere il coperchio di plastica* 'Remove the plastic cover'), public notices *Spingere* 'Push', *Tirare* 'Pull') and announcements (*Allacciare le cinture* 'Fasten your seatbelts').

21.44 Uses of the Infinitive in Dependent Clauses: ... di fare ..., ... per essere stato ..., etc.

In general the infinitive is not used independently but introduced by prepositions or conjunctions in complex sentences in which both clauses, the main and the dependent one with the infinitive, have the same subject: *Risparmio dei soldi per andare in vacanza* ('I am saving money to go on vacation'), *Non credi di essere pronto* ('You do not think you are ready'). Note that in the two examples above, the implicit subject of the main clause and the dependent clause is the same person: *io* ('I') in the first case, *tu* ('you') in the second one. Had the subject been different, the subjunctive would have generally been used instead (see also 21.18, 21.23): *Risparmio dei soldi perché tu vada in vacanza* ('I am saving money so you can go on vacation'), *Non credo tu sia pronto* ('I do not think you are ready').

While the **present infinitive** indicates an action that occurs at the same time or in the future compared to the verb of the main clause (*Sono sicuro di vincere* 'I am sure to win', *Penso di fare meglio domani* 'I think I will do better tomorrow'), the **past infinitive** refers to an action that precedes that in the main clause, whether this is a past (*Sono andato in Italia dopo aver studiato l'italiano* 'I went to Italy, after having studied Italian'), a present (*Vado in Italia dopo aver studiato l'italiano* 'I am going to Italy, having studied Italian'), or a future tense (*Andrò in Italia dopo aver studiato l'italiano* 'I will go to Italy after having studied Italian').

Both present and past infinitives can be used in dependent clauses to indicate several meanings. Note that the English equivalent of the present and past infinitives is not always the same and can easily vary. The infinitive in a dependent clause can be used to:

- **formulate a completive clause**: *Mio figlio crede di avere talento* ('My son believes that he is talented'), *Bisogna alzarsi presto domani mattina* ('It is necessary that we get up early tomorrow morning'). Remember that a completive clause (also called noun clause or nominal clause) is the direct object of verbs such as *credere* ('to think'), *dubitare* ('to

doubt'), *temere* ('to fear') or impersonal expressions such as *è importante* ('it is important'), *bisogna* ('it is necessary'), *è meglio* ('it is better');
- **formulate a relative clause**: *Sono stato io a mangiare tutta la torta* ('I was the one who ate the entire cake'), *Sei sempre tu ad arrivare in ritardo* ('It is always you who arrives late'). In both cases the Italian infinitive replaces the relative pronoun *che* or the relative phrases *quello che ..., colui che ..., la persona che ...* all equivalent to the English 'who ...' (*Sei sempre tu ad arrivare* [= *che arrivi/colui che arriva*] *in ritardo*);
- **formulate a comparative clause or an opposition**: *Piuttosto che parlare ascolta* ('Rather than talking, listen'), *Invece di parlare di questo, fallo* ('Instead of talking about it; do it');
- **indicate a time**: *Studio prima di uscire* ('I study before I go out'), *Ti chiamo prima di partire* ('I'll call you before I leave'). The preposition *prima di* is typical of this construction;
- **indicate a lack, an exclusion, or an addition**: *Ho frequentato il corso di inglese senza fare l'esame* ('I attended the English course without taking the exam'), *Sono disposto a tutto fuorché a lasciare l'Italia* ('I am willing to do everything except leave Italy'), *Oltre ad essere molto intelligente, Chaira è anche una bella ragazza* ('Besides being really intelligent, Chiara is also a beautiful girl');
- **indicate a matter**: *Quanto a studiare non ho problemi* ('As for studying, I do not have any problems'), *Per quel che riguarda andare in vacanza, sono d'accordo con te* ('In the matter of going on vacation, I agree with you'). The phrases *a proposito di, riguardo a, per quanto riguarda, per quanto concerne* are all typical of this construction and can be translated with 'in the matter of + -ing';
- **express a purpose**: *Studio per imparare* ('I study to learn'), *Marco va in palestra per essere in forma* ('Marco is going to the gym to get fit'). The preposition *per* (more frequent than the equivalent phrases *allo scopo di* and *al fine di*) is typical of this construction;
- **express a cause**: *Ho sonno per non aver dormito abbastanza* ('I am sleepy because I haven't slept enough'), *Tu piangi per esserti fatto male* ('You are crying because of having hurt yourself'). In this case, only the past infinitive is possible;
- **express a consequence**: *Hai parlato così bene da lasciare tutti a bocca aperta* ('You spoke so well that everybody stood open-mouthed'), *Quell'uomo è brutto da far paura* ('That man is as ugly as sin'). The preposition *da* is typical of this construction (see also 16.4) and often creates an idiomatic meaning as in the second example;
- **express a contrast**: *Per avere dieci anni, sei molto alto* ('For a ten-year-old boy, you are really tall'), *Per aver pagato quella cifra, hai fatto un affare* ('Having paid so little for that, you got a bargain').

21.45 The Infinitive as a Noun: Riposare è importante

Besides being a verb, the present infinitive can function as a masculine and singular noun when it is used as the subject or object of another verb: *Nuotare fa bene alla salute* ('Swimming is good for your health'), *Ringraziare è segno di buona educazione* ('Saying thank you is a sign of good manners'). Where Italian uses the present infinitive, English can use the infinitive or the '-ing' form of the verb. Like all nouns, the infinitive can be preceded by an article

(*Il parlare una lingua straniera è molto utile* 'Speaking a foreign language is really useful'), a simple or articulated preposition (*Il desiderio di/del fuggire è comune fra i giovani* 'The desire to run away is common among young people'), and it can go together with an adjective (*È un bel respirare qui in campagna* 'It is good breathing fresh air here in the country') or an adverb (*Lavorare troppo mi stanca* 'Working too much makes me tired').

Most present infinitives remain basically verbs even when used as nouns, but a few of them have become independent forms that can be used as both singular and plural. These are *l'avere* and *gli averi* (*Questi sono tutti i miei averi* 'These are all my belongings'), *il piacere* and *i piaceri* (*Il piacere della tua compagnia è impareggiabile* 'The pleasure of your company is unparalleled'), *il dispiacere* and *i dispiaceri* (*Quanti dispiaceri nella vita!* 'How many regrets in life!'), *il dovere* and *i doveri* (*Il dovere prima di tutto!* 'Duty first!'), *il potere* and *i poteri* (*Il presidente ha tutti i poteri* 'The president has all the powers'), *il volere* and *i voleri* (*Mi piego al tuo volere!* 'I bend to your will').

21.46 Italian Infinitive vs. English Gerund in Simultaneous Actions: stare a ..., essere a ..., ect.

When simultaneous actions are expressed by verbs such as *stare*, *essere*, *trovarsi* (all meaning 'to be' in this case), *passare* ('to spend time'), or verbal phrases such as *essere impegnato* ('to be busy'), *essere seduto* ('to be sitting'), Italian uses the **infinitive form of the verb preceded by the preposition *a*** whereas English requires the '-ing' form: *Sono in biblioteca a studiare* ('I am in the library studying'), *Ho passato tutto il giorno a fare i compiti* ('I spent all day doing my homework'), *Sono impegnato a parlare al telefono* ('I am busy talking on the phone').

21.47 The Infinitive with Modal Verbs

When the common modal verbs *potere* ('can', 'to be able to'), *dovere* ('must', 'to have to'), *volere* ('to want to'), and the verb *sapere* ('to be able to') are themselves in the infinitive and are followed by another infinitive, they always drop their final *-e*: *È bello poter uscire con te* ('It is nice to be able to go out with you'), *Ho una macchina senza saper guidare* ('I have a car, but I can't drive').

21.48 The Infinitive with Pronouns

When the infinitive is combined with a direct, indirect, or double object pronoun, **the pronoun is affixed to the end of the present infinitive** (*mangiarlo, parlargli, comprartela*) **or to the end of the auxiliary of the past infinitive** (*averlo mangiato, avergli parlato, avertela comprata*); in both cases the infinitives drop the final *-e* in front of the pronoun: *Vederti è un piacere* ('Meeting you is a pleasure'), *Dopo averlo salutato, sono andato a casa* ('After having greeted him, I went home').

When an unstressed direct, indirect, or double object **pronoun is combined with *dovere*, *potere*, and *volere* + infinitive** (see 13.6, 13.9, 13.10), the pronoun can be attached to the end of the infinitive (*Posso vederti* 'I can see you', *Devo parlargli* 'I must talk to him'), or it can be placed before the modal verbs (*Ti posso vedere* 'I can see you', *Gli devo parlare* 'I must talk to him').

21.49 The Gerund

The gerund is a form of the verb (see chapter 20) that usually corresponds to the English '-ing' form and is used to provide background information. It has only two tenses: **present** (simple) and **past** (compound). While the present consists of only one word (*andando* 'going', *dormendo* 'sleeping'), the past is a compound tense formed by two elements, the simple gerund of the auxiliary *essere* or *avere* plus the past participle of the main verb (*essendo andato* 'having gone', *avendo dormito* 'having slept').

21.50 Uses of the Gerund

The gerund can never be used independently but must always be combined with another clause. The **present gerund** indicates an action that occurs at the same time, whether past, present, or future, as the main clause: *Giocando mi sono divertito/mi diverto/mi divertirò* ('Playing, I had/have/will have fun'). The **past gerund** refers to an action that precedes the time of the main clause, whether this is a past, present, or future action: *Avendo lavorato molto mi sono riposato/mi riposo/mi riposerò* ('Having worked a lot, I rested/I am resting/I will rest').

In contemporary spoken Italian the present gerund tends to replace the past, nowadays reserved for the formal and written language. For example, in a sentence like *Mangiando troppo mi sono sentito male* ('Having eaten too much, I felt ill'), it is clear that *Mangiando* is used instead of the more appropriate *Avendo mangiato* since the action of eating precedes the feeling of sickness.

21.51 The Agreement of the Past Gerund: essendo arrivata, avendoli comprati

The present gerund is invariable while in past gerund constructions with the auxiliary *essere*, the past participle varies according to the subject: *Maria ha perso il treno, essendo arrivata in ritardo* ('Maria missed the train, having arrived late'). Likewise, the past gerund formed with the auxiliary *avere*, which itself has pronouns attached to it, changes according to the rules of agreement (see 13.7, 13.11): *Non ho comprato quei libri, avendoli già letti* ('I did not buy those books, having already read them').

21.52 Subject of the Gerund

It is extremely important to remember that in Italian **the implicit subject of the gerund corresponds to the subject of the main clause verb.** In a sentence like *Carlo ha visto Marta tornando a casa*, the subject of *tornando* is *Carlo*, not *Marta* since *Carlo* is the subject of the main verb *ha visto*. The English equivalent of the above sentence is 'Carlo saw Marta on his way back home' and not 'Carlo saw Marta going back home'.

If the subject is different, in Italian, it is necessary to replace the gerund with a clause introduced by a relative pronoun (*che, il quale, la quale*, etc.) or by *mentre* ('while') plus an explicit subject. In this case we will have *Carlo ha visto Marta che tornava a casa* or *Carlo ha visto Marta mentre lei tornava a casa*, both equivalent to 'Carlo saw Marta going back home'.

The rule indicated above does not apply when the gerund forms a separate clause with its own explicit subject. In this case the subject always follows the simple gerund or is placed between the auxiliary and the past particle in the coumpound form: *Arrivando amici, preparo la camera degli ospiti* ('With friends arriving, I am preparing the guest room').

Another case where the subject of the gerund can be different from the subject of the main verb clause is when the subject can be interpreted as a generic one equivalent to 'one' or 'people' (*L'appetito vien mangiando* 'Appetite comes with eating'), or with impersonal expressions (*Essendo tardi, sono rimasto a casa* 'Since it was late, I stayed home').

21.53 Meanings of the Gerund and Its Equivalent Constructions

The gerund can express:

- **condition**: *Lavorando troppo, mi stanco* ('Working too much, I get tired'). In this case the gerund is equivalent to a hypothetical construction (see 23.29) and so could be replaced by *se* + conjugated verb: *Se lavoro* [= *Lavorando*] *troppo, mi stanco* ('If I work too much, I get tired');
- **cause**: *Avendo perso il treno, ho preso l'autobus* ('Having missed the train, I took the bus'). In this case the gerund is equivalent to a causal clause introduced by *perché* or similar expressions such as *in quanto, visto che, dato che* all meaning 'since' or 'because': *Perché ho perso* [= *Avendo perso*] *il treno, ho preso l'autobus* ('Since I had missed the train, I took the bus');
- **time**: *Passeggiando nel parco, ho incontrato Marco* ('Walking in the park, I met Marco'). In this case the gerund indicates what is going on while another action takes place. Equivalent to this construction is *mentre* ('while') + conjugated verb: *Mentre passeggiavo* [= *Passeggiando*] *nel parco, ho incontrato Marco* ('While I was walking in the park, I met Marco');
- **contrast**: *Pur essendo stanco, non riesco a dormire* ('Even though I am tired, I can't fall asleep'). In this case, the use of the gerund is concessive and corresponds to the construction *sebbene, benché, quantunque, nonostante* (all meaning 'although', 'even though') followed by the subjunctive (*Sebbene* [= *Pur essendo*] *sia stanco, non riesco a dormire*), or *anche se* ('even if') with the indicative (*Anche se sono stanco, non riesco a dormire*);
- **manner**: *Non si chiede attenzione urlando* ('One does not draw attention by yelling'). This construction is the equivalent of the articulated preposition *con* + article + infinitive and is always expressed in English with 'by + -ing': *Non si chiede attenzione con l'urlare* [= *urlando*].

> **N.B.** No preposition or conjunction is ever used in front of the gerund, except for *pure* or the equivalent *pur* ('even though'), as seen in the example above.

21.54 Gerund with stare, andare, *and* venire

Besides the above applications, the gerund can follow the verbs *stare* ('to stay'), *andare* ('to go') and rarely *venire* ('to come') to form a single expression. **Stare + gerund** is the equivalent of the English 'to be + -ing', and indicates a progressive action (see 21.15): *Sto studiando* ('I am studying'), *Stavo mangiando quando mi hai telefonato* ('I was eating when you called me').

Also **andare** + **gerund** and, less frequently, **venire** + **gerund** can indicate progressive actions, especially when the speaker or the reader wants to emphasize their repetition: *Vai/Vieni facendo sempre gli stessi errori* ('You are always going to make the same mistakes'). These two constructions are quite rare in contemporary Italian.

21.55 Participle
The participle has two forms (see chapter 20): **present** and **past**. It can function as a verb (*dormito* 'slept', *pagante* 'one paying'), a noun (*l'impiegato* 'the employee', *il cantante* 'the singer'), as well as an adjective (*una persona amata* 'a loved person', *una stella splendente* 'a bright star').

21.56 Uses of the Present Participle
The **present participle** works as an adjective with two endings (masculine and feminine singular -*e*, masculine and feminine plural -*i*), and it agrees with the noun it modifies (see 4.2 for agreement rules): *viaggio emozionante* ('exciting trip'), *gambe tremanti* ('trembling legs'). In contemporary Italian, the present participle is mainly used **as an adjective** (*una stella splendente* 'a bright star', *un colore predominante* 'a predominant color') or **as a noun** (*un cantante* 'a singer', *un insegnante* 'a teacher').

The present participle **as a verb** is rarely employed nowadays, except in bureaucratic language where it is still the norm: *Il certificato recante le informazioni richieste è giunto* ('The certificate indicating the required information has arrived'). In all other cases it tends to be **replaced by a relative clause**: *Un cesto che contiene* [= *contenente*] *alcune mele* ('A basket that contains a few apples').

21.57 The Past Participle
The **past participle** works as an adjective with four endingins (-*o, -a, -i, -e*). Although it can be used **as an adjective** that agrees (see 4.2 for agreement rules) with the noun it modifies (*una donna amata* 'a beloved woman', *alberi fioriti* 'trees in bloom'), the past participle is used mainly **as a verb** in compound tense constructions with *avere* or *essere*. In this case the past participle agrees with the subject when the auxiliary is *essere* (*Noi siamo andati a casa* 'We went home') and, when they occur, with the unstressed direct and compound pronouns when the auxiliary is *avere* (*Ho visto gli studenti e li ho salutati* 'I saw the students and I greeted them', *Ho preso una rosa per Maria e gliela ho data* 'I bought a rose for Maria, and I gave it to her') according to the rules of agreement (see 20.9).

Many past participles have in time acquired an independent meaning and become **nouns** such *impiegato* 'employee' (< *impiegare* 'to employ'), *certificato* 'certificate' (< *certificare* 'to certificate'), *abbonato* 'subscriber' (< *abbonare* 'to subscribe').

21.58 The Past Participle Used Alone and Its Equivalent Constructions

Apart from being used in compound tenses, the past participle can also be used alone in agreement with the subject of the main clause, if it is the same (*Partiti alle 6.00, gli studenti sono arrivati alle 10.00* 'Having left at 6:00AM, the students arrived at 10:00AM'), or its own subject, if different (*Mangiata la pizza, noi non volemmo altro* 'Having eaten pizza, we did not want anything else'). When a pronoun is present, it is attached to the participle: *Riconosciutomi, Marco mi salutò* ('Having recognized me, Marco said hello').

On its own the participle can express:

- **time**: *Arrivato a casa, sono corso a letto* ('As soon as I arrived at home, I hurried to bed'). In this case the past participle is usually preceded by *appena* ('as soon as') or *una volta* ('once') and can be replaced by a whole clause with a conjugated verb without a change in meaning: *Appena sono arrivato* [= *Arrivato*] *a casa, sono corso a letto*. The past participle expressing time can also be replaced by the construction *quando* ('when') or *dopo che* ('after') + conjugated verb (*Quando/dopo che avrò finito* [= *Finito*] *il mio tema, uscirò con gli amici* 'When I finish my composition, I'll go out with my friends'), or by *dopo* + past infinitive (*Dopo aver finito* [= *Finito*] *il mio tema, uscirò con gli amici* 'After I finish my composition, I'll go out with my friends');
- **condition**: *La televisione, guardata con intelligenza, può essere educativa* ('Television, if judiciously watched, can be educational'). In this case the past participle is equivalent in Italian, as in English, to a hypothetical construction (see 23.30) and can, therefore, be replaced by *se* + conjugated verb: *La televisione, se è guardata* [= *guardata*] *con intelligenza, può essere educativa*;
- **cause**: *Perso il cellulare, ne ho comprato un altro* ('Having lost my cellular phone, I bought another one'). Here the past participle is equivalent, as in English, to a causal clause introduced by *perché* or similar expressions such as *in quanto, visto che, dato che* all meaning 'since' or 'because' followed by a conjugated verb: *Perché ho perso* [= *Perso*] *il cellulare, ne ho comprato un altro*.

22. VERBS AND PREPOSITIONS:

22.1 Verbs and Prepositions: Italian vs English

Most Italian verbs are followed by prepositions that link them to nouns, pronouns, or infinitive forms. The most used prepositions are *a* and *di* but others (*con, da, in, per, su*) are also frequent. Some verbs can take more than one preposition depending on the meaning conveyed. It is important to remember that there are some differences between Italian and English concerning a few points:

- some Italian verbs require a preposition where their English equivalents do not and vice versa: *assomigliare a qualcuno* ('to resemble someone'), *aspettare qualcuno* ('to wait for someone');
- some Italian verbs can take one or more prepositions to express the same meaning, where their English equivalents do not and vice versa: *soffrire di/per solitudine* ('to suffer from loneliness'), *ridere di tutto* ('to laugh about/at everything');
- many Italian verbs take a preposition that does not always correspond to its English equivalent: *rimanere a letto* ('to stay in bed'), *dimenticarsi di tutto* ('to forget about everything');
- in Italian, prepositions can only precede the infinitive form of the verb while in English they can be placed in front of the gerund ('-ing' form) as well: *Grazie per essere così gentile con me* ('Thank you for being so kind to me').

22.2 Italian Verbs + Noun or Pronoun Without Prepositions

If most verbs not followed by a preposition are equivalent in Italian and English (*amare* 'to love', *cantare* 'to sing', etc.), some of them differ. The table below provides the most common Italian verbs used, unlike their English counterparts, without a preposition:

Verbs	Examples
ascoltare ('to listen to')	*Lia ascolta una canzone* ('Lia is listening to a song')
aspettare ('to wait for')	*Aspetto l'autobus* ('I am waiting for the bus')
cercare ('to look for')	*Cerco le chiavi* ('I am looking for my key')
chiedere ('to ask for')	*Chiedi un appuntamento* ('Ask for an appointment')
fissare ('to stare at')	*Non fissare quel ragazzo* ('Do not stare at that boy')
sognare ('to dream about')	*Ho sognato un appartamento nuovo* ('I dreamed about a new apartment')

22.3 Italian Verbs Followed by a + Noun or Pronoun

Not all the Italian verbs or verbal phrases followed by the preposition *a* (or its articulated forms) have their English equivalents followed by *to*. The table below provides the most common Italian verbs and verbal phrases of this kind that differ from English:

Verbs	Examples
assistere a ('to attend')	*Ho assistito al concerto* ('I attended the concert')
assomigliare a ('to look like')	*Paolo assomiglia a suo zio* ('Paolo looks like his uncle')
disubbidire a ('to disobey')	*Non disubbidire al capo* ('Do not disobey your boss')
credere a ('to believe in')	*Non credo a niente* ('I don't believe in anything')
dare fastidio a ('to bother')	*Leo dà fastidio a Franco* ('Leo is bothering Franco')
fare bene a ('to be good for')	*Lo sport fa bene a tutti* ('Sport is good for everyone')
fare male a ('to be bad for')	*Troppo vino fa male alla salute* ('Too much wine is bad for one's health')
fare piacere a ('to please')	*Non posso sempre fare piacere a mio fratello* ('I can't always please my brother')
fare vedere a ('to show')	*Fai vedere a Marco la moto* ('Show Marco your motorcycle')
fare visita a ('to visit')	*Facciamo visita alla nonna* ('Let's go visit grandmother')
giocare a ('to play')	*In Italia tutti giocano a calcio* ('In Italy everyone plays soccer')
interessarsi a ('to be interested in')	*Mi interesso all'arte* ('I am interested in art')
partecipare a ('to participate in')	*Partecipo a un gioco televisivo* ('I am participating in a game show')
pensare a ('to think about')	*Pensi sempre al lavoro* ('You always think about work')
raccomandarsi a ('to ask a favor of')	*Mi raccomando a te* ('I am asking a favor of you')
rinunciare a ('to give up')	*Ho dovuto rinunciare al viaggio* ('I had to give up my trip')
servire a ('to be good for')	*Una seconda lingua servirebbe al tuo CV* ('A second language would be good for your CV')
stringere la mano a ('to shake hands with')	*Stringo la mano alla gente* ('I shake hands with people')
tenere a ('to care about')	*Teniamo molto a te* ('We really care about you')
ubbidire a ('to obey')	*Ubbidisco ai miei genitori* ('I obey my parents')

22.4 Italian Verbs Followed by di + Noun or Pronoun

A great number of Italian verbs and verbal phrases are followed by the preposition *di* ('of'), or its articulated forms, while their English equivalents require different prepositions or none. The table below provides the most common Italian verbs and verbal phrases of this kind:

Verbs	Examples
accorgersi di ('to notice')	*Non mi ero accorto di voi* ('I did not notice you')
avere bisogno di '(to need')	*Hai bisogno di un nuovo zaino* ('You need a new backpack')
avere voglia di ('to have a desire for')	*Ho voglia di un gelato!* ('I have a desire for an ice-cream')
chiedere di ('to ask about')	*Perché non chiedi di tuo figlio?* ('Why don't you ask about your son?')
dimenticarsi di ('to forget about')	*Mi sono dimenticato della riunione* ('I forgot about the meeting')
fidarsi di ('to trust')	*Mi fido ciecamente di te* ('I trust you blindly')
informarsi di ('to find out about')	*Informati dell'orario* ('Find out about the schedule')

innamorarsi di ('to fall in love with')	*Mi sto innamorando di Laura* ('I am falling in love with Laura')
interessarsi di ('to be interested in')	*Ti interessi di cinema?* ('Are you interested in cinema?')
lamentarsi di ('to complain about')	*Non ti lamentare di tutto!* ('Do not complain about everything!')
meravigliarsi di ('to be surprised at')	*Mi meraviglio di me stesso* ('I am surprised at myself')
preoccuparsi di ('to worry about')	*Non ti preoccupare di questo* ('Do not worry about it')
ricordarsi di ('to remember')	*Ricordati di me* ('Remember me')
ridere di ('to laugh at')	*Non è bello ridere di qualcuno* ('It isn't nice to laugh at someone')
riempire di ('to fill with')	*Riempi d'acqua il bicchiere* ('Fill the glass with water')
soffrire di ('to suffer from')	*Carlo soffre d'ansia* ('Carl suffers from anxiety')
vivere di ('to live on')	*Mio cugino vive di un vitalizio* ('My cousin lives on a life annuity')

22.5 Italian Verbs Followed by con, da, in, per, and su + Noun or Pronoun

Numerous Italian verbs and verbal phrases followed by *con* ('with'), *da* ('from', 'by'), *in* ('in'), *per* ('for'), *su* ('on') or their articulated forms, have their English equivalents formed with other prepositions. The table below provides the most common Italian verbs and verbal phrases of this kind:

Verbs	Examples
confidare in ('rely on')	*Confidiamo tutti nel buon tempo* ('We all rely on good weather')
denunciare per ('to accuse of')	*Lo hanno denunciato per plagio* ('He was accused of plagiarism')
dipendere da ('to depend on')	*Dipende dal tempo* ('It depends on the weather')
dividere in ('to divide into')	*Dividiamolo in tre* ('Let's divide it into three')
imparare su ('to learn about')	*Voglio imparare di più sulla Grecia* ('I want to learn more about Greece')
perdere tempo in ('waste on')	*Non perdere il tempo in chiacchiere* ('Don't waste your time on chatting')
preoccuparsi per ('to worry about')	*Non preoccuparti per me* ('Don't worry about me')
protestare con ('to complain to')	*Non protesto con te* ('I'm not complaining to you')
scambiare qualcosa con ('to swap something for')	*Scambierò questo libro per quello* ('I will swap this book for that one')
scherzare su ('to joke about')	*Mi piace scherzare sulle tue imprese* ('I like to joke about your deeds')
scontrarsi con ('to crash into')	*Un capriolo si è scontrato con un'auto* ('A deer crashed into a car')
scusarsi con ('to apologize to')	*Mi scuso con te* ('I apologize to you')
soffrire per ('to suffer from')	*Soffro per amore* ('I suffer from love')
tradurre da ... in ('to translate from ... into')	*Traduco dal cinese in italiano* ('I translate from Chinese into Italian')
trasformarsi in ('to turn into')	*Tutto si è trasformato in uno scherzo* ('Everything turned into a joke')
travestirsi da ('to dress as')	*Si è travestito da re* ('He dressed as a king')

22.6 Verbs Requiring a and di + Infinitive

One of the most common occurrences of the infinitive is after prepositions. The use of a specific preposition can sometimes be required by the meaning the speaker or the writer wants to convey (for example *per* to express a purpose or *senza* to indicate a lack) but, in the case of *a* and *di*, the preposition is simply related to the verb or to the verbal phrase that introduces the infinitive. For this reason, it is useful to keep in mind a list of the most common verbs and verbal expressions followed by *a* or *di* + infinitive construction:

- ***a* + infinitive** is required after the verbs *abituarsi* ('to get used to'), *aiutare* ('to help'), *andare* ('to go'), *aspettare* ('to wait') *cominciare* ('to begin'), *continuare* ('to continue'), *costringere* ('to force'), *correre* ('to run') *decidersi* ('to make up one's mind'), *divertirsi* ('to have a good time'), *fare bene* ('to do right'), *fare meglio* ('to do better'), *fare presto* ('to be quick'), *fermarsi* ('to stop'), *imparare* ('to learn'), *mettersi* ('to put oneself'), *incoraggiare* ('to encourage'), *insegnare* ('to teach'), *invitare* ('to invite to'), *mandare* ('to send'), *obbligare* ('to oblige'), *passare* ('to stop by'), *pensare* ('to think about'), *persuadere* ('to convince'), *preparare* ('to prepare'), *provare* ('to try'), *rinunciare* ('to give up'), *riuscire* ('to succeed'), *sbrigarsi* ('to hurry up') *stare* ('to stay'), *tornare* ('to return'), *venire* ('to come');
- ***di* + infinitive** is required after the verbs *accettare* ('to accept'), *ammettere* ('to admit'), *aspettare* ('to wait for'), *augurare* ('to wish'), *avere bisogno* ('to need'), *cercare* ('to try to'), *chiedere* ('to ask'), *confessare* ('to confess'), *consigliare* ('to advise'), *credere* ('to believe'), *decidere* ('to decide'), *dimenticare* ('to forget'), *dubitare* ('to doubt'), *fingere* ('to pretend'), *finire* ('to finish'), *ordinare* ('to order'), *pensare* ('to plan'), *permettere* ('to permit'), *pregare* ('to beg'), *proibire* ('to prohibit'), *promettere* ('to promise'), *proporre* ('to propose'), *sapere* ('to know'), *smettere* ('to stop'), *sperare* ('to hope'), *suggerire* ('to suggest'), *tentare* ('to attempt'), *vietare* ('to avoid').

22.7 Nouns and Adjectives Followed by *a* or *di* + Infinite

In addition to verbs there are also adjectives and nouns that generally introduce the constructions *a* + infinite or *di* + infinite. Listed below are the most common of these words:

- ***a* + infinite** is generally found after nouns such as *attitudine* ('attitude'), *autorizzazione* ('authorization'), *impegno* ('commitment'), *interesse* ('interest'), *stimolo* ('stimulus') and adjectives such as *abituato* ('being used to'), *costretto* ('compelled'), *disponibile* ('available'), *interessato* ('interested'), *pronto* ('ready');
- ***di* + infinite** is generally found after nouns such as *desiderio* ('desire'), *intenzione* ('intention'), *paura* ('fear'), *obiettivo* ('goal'), *speranza* ('hope'), *volontà* ('will') and adjectives such as *curioso* ('curious'), *desideroso* ('eager'), *felice* ('happy'), *fiducioso* ('confident'), *triste* ('sad').

22.8 Verbs Requiring *da* + Infinitive

The construction **da + infinitive** is the equivalent of the phrase **qualcosa da + infinitive** ('something to + infinitive') and is introduced by the verbs *avere* ('to have'), *dare* ('to give'), *fare* ('to do'), *offrire* ('to offer'), *portare* ('to bring'), *preparare* ('to prepare'): *Ho preparato da* *mangiare* is equivalent to *Ho preparato qualcosa da mangiare* ('I made something to eat'); *Ho da fare* is equivalent to *Ho qualcosa da fare* ('I have something to do').

> **N.B.** *Qualcosa* can never be placed before *da + infinitive* when an adverb such as *molto* ('a lot'), *poco* ('a little'), *troppo* ('too much') occurs in the sentence: *Ho preparato molto da mangiare* ('I made a lot to eat'), *Ho poco da fare* ('I have a little to do').

22.9 Verbs Followed Directly by the Infinitive Without Prepositions

Several verbs do not require a preposition before an infinitive, which, in this case, follows them directly. The most common of these are *amare* ('to love'), *desiderare* ('to wish'), *dovere* ('to have to', 'must'), *fare* ('to make', 'to do'), *gradire* ('to appreciate'), *lasciare* ('to let'), *piacere* ('to like'), *potere* ('to be able to'), *preferire* ('to prefer'), *sapere* ('to know how'), *volere* ('to want'). Also the impersonal form *basta* ('it is enough'), *bisogna* ('it is necessary'), *pare* ('it seems') are directly followed by an infinitive without an intervening preposition.

23. SPECIAL VERBS AND VERB CONSTRUCTIONS

23.1 The Passive Form

Italian verbs, like English ones, can be used in the active or passive voice. When the verb is passive, the action is done to the subject and not performed by the subject as in the active voice. However, the meaning of both sentences is the same: *Marco chiama Maria* ('Marco calls Maria') is active, while *Maria è chiamata da Marco* ('Maria is called by Marco') is passive. The passive structure is much more common in English than in Italian, where its use is limited more to formal contexts and writing than to everyday speech.

While all verbs take the active form, the passive form is only possible with transitive verbs (see 20.5), which take a direct object. This means that verbs such as *andare* ('to go'), *parlare* ('to talk'), and so on do not take the passive form.

In terms of construction, **the passive form consists of the verb *essere* ('to be') followed by the past participle of the main verb.** It is easy to apply this formula, provided one pays attention to the verb tenses as is explained here. The verb *essere* should be in the same tense as the main verb in its corresponding active sentence: *io chiamo* (present active) > *io sono chiamato* (present passive). **The past participle always agrees in gender and number with the subject:** *lui è chiamato, lei è chiamata, noi siamo chiamati,* and so on. The agent, who or which performs the action, when expressed, is preceded by the preposition ***da*** ('by'), combined with an article if necessary: *La lettera è stata spedita da Marco* ('The letter was sent by Marco'), *Lo studente è stato rimproverato dal professore* ('The student was reprimanded by the professor').

Below are the passive forms of the verb *amare* ('to love') used as a model. Verbs in *-ere* and in *-ire* make their passive in the same way.

Passive Forms (*amare* 'to love')

INDICATIVE		SUBJUNCTIVE	
Present	Present Perfect	Present	Past
io sono amato/a	io sono stato/a amato/a	io sia amato/a	io sia stato/a amato/a
tu sei amato/a	tu sei stato/a amato/a	tu sia amato/a	tu sia stato/a amato/a
lui/lei/(Lei) è amato/a	lui/lei/(Lei) è stato/a amato/a	lui/lei/(Lei) sia amato/a	lui/lei(Lei) stato/a amato/a
noi siamo amati/e	noi siamo stati/e amati/e	noi siamo amati/e	noi siamo stati/e amati/e
voi siete amati/e	voi siete stati/e amati/e	voi siate amati/e	voi siate stati/e amati/e
loro/(Loro) sono amati/e	loro/(Loro) sono stati/e amati/e	loro/(Loro) siano amati/e	loro/(Loro) siano stati/e amati/e

Imperfect	Pluperfect	Imperfect	Pluperfect
io ero amato/a	io ero stato/a amato/a	io fossi amato/a	io fossi stato/a amato/a
tu eri amato/a	tu eri stato/a amato/a	tu fossi amato/a	tu fossi stato/a amato/a
lui/lei/(Lei) era amato/a	lui/lei/(Lei) era stato/a amato/a	lui/lei/(Lei) fosse amato/a	lui/lei/(Lei) fosse stato/a amato/a
noi eravamo amati/e	noi eravamo stati/e amati/e	noi fossimo amati/e	noi fossimo stati/e amati/e
voi eravate amati/e	voi eravate stati/e amati/e	voi foste amati/e	voi foste stati/e amati/e
loro/(Loro) erano amati/e	loro/(Loro) erano stati/e amati/e	loro/(Loro) fossero amati/e	loro/(Loro) fossero stati/e amati/e

		CONDITIONAL	
Preterite	**Preterite Perfect**	**Present**	**Past**
io fui amato/a	io fui stato/a amato/a	io sarei amato/a	io sarei stato/a amato/a
tu fosti amato/a	tu fosti stato/a amato/a	tu saresti amato/a	tu saresti stato/a amato/a
lui/lei/(Lei) fu amato/a	lui/lei/(Lei) fu stato/a amato/a	lui/lei/(Lei) sarebbe amato/a	lui/lei/(Lei) sarebbe stato/a amato/a
noi fummo amati/e	noi fummo stati/e amati/e	noi saremmo amati/e	noi saremmo stati/e amati/e
voi foste amati/e	voi foste stati/e amati/e	voi sareste amati/e	voi soreste stati/e amati/e
loro/(Loro) furono amati/e	loro/(Loro) furono stati/e amati/e	loro/(Loro) sarebbero amati/e	loro/(Loro) sarebbero stati/e amati/e

		IMPERATIVE	
Future	**Future Perfect**	**Present**	
io sarò amato/a	io sarò stato/a amato/a	sii amato/a (tu)	
tu sarai amato/a	tu sarai stato/a amato/a	siamo amati/e (noi)	
lui/lei/(Lei) sarà amato/a	lui/lei/(Lei) sarà stato/a amato/a	siate amati/e (voi)	
noi saremo amati/e	noi saremo stati/e amati/e		
voi sarete amati/e	voi sarete stati/e amati/e	**N.B.** The 3rd sing. and pl. persons of the present subj. *sia amato* (*Lei*)	
loro/(Loro) saranno amati/e	loro/(Loro) saranno stati/e amati/e	and *siano amati/e* (*Loro*) are used to express formal commands.	

INFINITIVE		GERUND	
Present	**Past**	**Present**	**Past**
essere amato/a/i/e	essere stato/a/i/e amato/a/i/e	essendo amato/a/i/e	essendo stato/a/i/e amato/a/i/e/

> **N.B. a.** Since the preterite perfect of *essere* is in almost complete disuse in contemporary Italian, the preterite perfect passive form can be considered nowadays obsolete. **b.** The present participle is not a passive form, while the past participle is the same form as the active one.

23.2 Alternative Auxiliaries for the Passive Form: venire *and* andare

Other than *essere*, the verbs *venire* ('to come') and *andare* ('to go') may sometimes be used as auxiliaries in the passive form:

- ***venire*** can always replace *essere* but only in simple tenses (present, imperfect, preterite, and future) and never in the forms of the imperative. Even if there is no difference in meaning and both verbs can be used indistinctly to make the passive form, *venire* is definitely less frequent than *essere*, and quite rare in everyday language. Nevertheless, *venire* is usually preferred when emphasizing a habit (*Notizie sul traffico vengono date* [= *sono date*] *ogni ora* 'The traffic report is given every hour') or putting more stress on the action (*Se continui*

così, verrai punito [= *sarai punito*] ('If you keep on behaving like this, you will be punished'). In this second case *venire* is often equivalent to the English 'to get': *Il mio libro verrà pubblicato* [= *sarà pubblicato*] *il prossimo anno* ('My book will get published next year');
- **andare** can replace the verb *essere* but carries two different connotations, depending on the past participle with which it occurs:
  - with a few past participles indicating **destruction** (*distrutto* 'destroyed', *rovinato* 'ruined'), **loss** (*disperso* 'dispersed', *smarrito* 'lost'), and **waste** (*perso* 'wasted', *speso* 'spent'), the verb *andare* admits the use of all moods and tenses. This application of *andare* with the past participle is the equivalent of the English 'to get' + past participle: *L'intera biblioteca è andata* [= *è stata*] *distrutta dalle fiamme* ('The entire library got burned down');
  - with all other past participles, *andare* can be used only in simple tenses (present, imperfect, preterite, and future) never in the forms of the imperative. This use of *andare* with the past expresses **obligation or necessity**: *Il professore va* [= *deve essere*] *ascoltato quando parla* ('The professor must be listened to when he is speaking'). The structure *andare* + past participle is, in this case, equivalent to *dover essere* + past participle and to *essere da* + infinitive (see also 16.4): *va ascoltato, deve essere ascoltato,* and *è da ascoltare* all translating into 'must be heard'. This use of *andare* is quite rare in contemporary Italian and is preferably used in formal contexts.

23.3 Si passivante: si + 3rd Person Forms of an Active Verb

The passive form can be expressed in Italian by the construction **si passivante.** It consists of the personal pronoun *si* + 3rd pers. sing. or plur. of an active verb followed by a direct object that can be considered the subject of a passive sentence with the same meaning: *Si mangiano le mele* is equivalent to *Le mele sono mangiate* ('Apples are eaten'). If the verb is followed by a singular direct object, the verb is singular: *Il caffè si beve al bar* ('Coffee is drunk at the bar'); if the direct object is plural, the verb is plural: *All'università si studiano le lingue straniere* ('Foreign languages are studied in college'). In compound verbs, the *si passivante* always uses *essere* as auxiliary, compelling the past participle to agree with the subject: *Si sono spesi molti soldi* ('A lot of money has been spent'), *Si è mangiata la torta di compleanno oggi* ('The birthday cake was eaten today').

The *si passivante* is frequently used in contemporary Italian, particularly in negative contexts to express **interdiction**: *Certe cose non si fanno* ('Certain things must not be done'), *Non si dimenticano i cari amici* ('Dear friends can't be forgotten'). The *si passivante* is also typical of the **commercial language** where the pronoun *si* regularly precedes the verb or attaches to it for purposes of conciseness: *Qui si vende/vendesi formaggio fresco* ('Fresh cheese is sold here'), *Si affittano/affitasi appartamenti* ('Apartments for rent'). As the second example shows, if we opt for the enclitic *si*, we have to keep in mind that *si* must always attach to the 3rd person sing. form of the verb (*affitasi*) even if the direct object is plural (*appartamenti*).

Usually, as shown in most of the examples above, with the *si passivante* construction, the direct object (equivalent to the subject of a passive sentence with the same meaning) follows the verb.

> **N.B.** When *si* + 3rd pers. of verb is not followed by a direct object (*Oggi si studia* 'We study today', *Si dice che Maria sia generosa* 'They say that Maria is generous'), the construction is not a *si passivante* construction but an impersonal one. For the impersonal *si* see 23.13.

23.4 The Reflexive Forms: Marco si alza presto; Io mi diverto

A verb is reflexive when the action performed by the subject refers back to the same subject either directly (*Marco si lava* 'Marco washes himself') or indirectly (*Marco si canta una canzone* 'Marco sings a song to himself'). Not all verbs have reflexive forms; only the transitive ones do. In order to make an Italian verb reflexive, the reflexive pronouns (see 13.13) must be placed directly before the conjugated forms in the indicative, subjunctive, and conditional tenses; on the contrary, they must attach to the ends of the imperative, participle, gerund, and infinitive forms of the verb. In the case of the infinitive, the final *-e* is dropped in front of the pronouns: *lavare > lavarmi, lavarti, lavarsi,* etc. All the **reflexive verbs take *essere* as auxiliary** in compound tenses, so their past participle always agrees in gender and number with the subject: *Lui si è lavato* 'He washed himself', *Lei si è lavata* 'She washed herself'.

Below are the forms of the reflexive *lavarsi* ('to wash oneself') used as a model. Verbs in *-ersi* and in *-irsi* make their reflexive forms in the same way, according respectively to the second (see 20.15) and third (see 20.23) conjugation.

Reflexive Forms (*lavarsi* 'to wash oneself')

INDICATIVE		SUBJUNCTIVE	
Present	**Present Perfect**	**Present**	**Past**
io mi lavo	*io mi sono lavato/a*	*io mi lavi*	*io mi sia lavato/a*
tu ti lavi	*tu ti sei lavato/a*	*tu ti lavi*	*tu ti sia lavato/a*
lui/lei/(Lei) si lava	*lui/lei/(Lei) si è lavato/a*	*lui/lei/(Lei) si lavi*	*lui/lei/(Lei) si sia lavato/a*
noi ci laviamo	*noi ci siamo lavati/e*	*noi ci laviamo*	*noi ci siamo lavati/e*
voi vi lavate	*voi vi siete lavati/e*	*voi vi laviate*	*voi vi siate lavati/e*
loro/(Loro) si lavano	*loro/(Loro) si sono lavati/e*	*loro/(Loro) si lavino*	*loro/(Loro) si siano lavati/e*
Imperfect	**Pluperfect**	**Imperfect**	**Pluperfect**
io mi lavavo	*io mi ero lavato/a*	*io mi lavassi*	*io mi fossi lavato/a*
tu ti lavavi	*tu ti eri lavato/a*	*tu ti lavassi*	*tu ti fossi lavato/a*
lui/lei/(Lei) si lavava	*lui/lei/(Lei) si era lavato/a*	*lui/lei/(Lei) si lavasse*	*lui/lei/(Lei) si fosse lavato/a*
noi ci lavavamo	*noi ci eravamo lavati/e*	*noi ci lavassimo*	*noi ci fossimo lavati/e*
voi vi lavavate	*voi vi eravate lavati/e*	*voi vi lavaste*	*voi vi foste lavati/e*
loro/(Loro) si lavavano	*loro/(Loro) si erano lavati/e*	*loro/(Loro) si lavassero*	*loro/(Loro) si fossero lavati/e*

		CONDITIONAL	
Preterite	**Preterite Perfect**	**Present**	**Past**
io mi lavai	io mi fui lavato/a	io mi laverei	io mi sarei lavato/a
tu ti lavasti	tu ti fosti lavato/a	tu ti laveresti	tu ti saresti lavato/a
lui/lei/(Lei) si lavò	lui/lei/(Lei) si fu lavato/a	lui/lei/(Lei) si laverebbe	lui/lei/(Lei) si sarebbe lavato/a
noi ci lavammo	noi ci fummo lavati/e	noi ci laveremmo	noi ci saremmo lavati/e
voi vi lavaste	voi vi foste lavati/e	voi vi lavereste	voi vi sareste lavati/e
loro/(Loro) si lavarono	loro/(Loro) si furono lavati/e	loro/(Loro) si laverebbero	loro/(Loro) si sarebbero lavati/e
		IMPERATIVE	
Future	**Future Perfect**	**Present**	
io mi laverò	io mi sarò lavato/a	lavati (tu)	
tu ti laverai	tu ti sarai lavato/a	laviamoci (noi)	
lui/lei/(Lei) si laverà	lui/lei/(Lei) si sarà lavato/a	lavatevi (voi)	
noi ci laveremo	noi ci saremo lavati/e		
voi vi laverete	voi vi sarete lavati/e	**N.B.** The 3rd sing. and pl. persons of the present subj. *si lavi* (Lei) and *si lavino* (Loro) are used to express formal commands.	
loro/(Loro) si laveranno	loro/(Loro) si saranno lavati/e		

INFINITIVE		PARTICIPLE		GERUND	
Present	**Past**	**Present**	**Past**	**Present**	**Past**
lavarsi	essersi lavato/a/i/e	lavantesi/lavantisi	lavatosi/tasi/tisi/tesi	lavandosi	essendosi lavato/a/i/e

23.5 Reciprocal Forms: Noi ci amiamo; Loro si sposano

A verb has a reciprocal meaning when the action performed by a compound subject is done reciprocally to each other: *Marco e Maria si abbracciano* ('Marco and Maria hug each other'), *Noi ci salutiamo* ('We say hello to each other'). Included in this category are the verbs *abbracciarsi* ('to hug each other'), *amarsi* ('to love each other'), *baciarsi* ('to kiss each other'), *incontrarsi* ('to meet each other'), *salutarsi* ('to greet each other'), and so on. They work exactly like the reflexive verbs (see 23.4) but are conjugated only in the three plural persons, so they are used only with the plural pronouns *ci*, *vi*, and *si* (see 13.15).

Below are the reciprocal forms of the verb *baciarsi* ('to kiss each other') used as a model. Verbs in *-ersi* and in *-irsi* make their reflexive forms in the same way, respectively according to the second (see 20.15) and third (see 20.23) conjugations.

Reciprical Forms (*baciarsi* 'to kiss each other')

INDICATIVE		SUBJUNCTIVE	
Present	**Present Perfect**	**Present**	**Past**
noi ci baciamo	*noi ci siamo baciati/e*	*noi ci baciamo*	*noi ci siamo baciati/e*
voi vi baciate	*voi vi siete baciati/e*	*voi vi baciate*	*voi vi siate baciati/e*
loro/(Loro) si baciano	*loro/(Loro) si sono baciati/e*	*loro/(Loro) si bacino*	*loro/(Loro) si siano baciati/e*
Imperfect	**Pluperfect**	**Imperfect**	**Pluperfect**
noi ci baciavamo	*noi ci eravamo baciati/e*	*noi ci baciassimo*	*noi ci fossimo baciati/e*
voi vi baciavate	*voi vi eravate baciati/e*	*voi vi baciaste*	*voi vi foste baciati/e*
loro/(Loro) si baciavano	*loro/(Loro) si erano baciati/e*	*loro/(Loro) si baciassero*	*loro/(Loro) si fossero baciati/e*
		CONDITIONAL	
Preterite	**Preterite Perfect**	**Present**	**Past**
noi ci baciammo	*noi ci fummo baciati/e*	*noi ci baceremmo*	*noi ci saremmo baciati/e*
voi vi baciaste	*voi vi foste baciati/e*	*voi vi bacereste*	*voi vi sareste baciati/e*
loro/(Loro) si baciarono	*loro/(Loro) si furono baciati/e*	*loro/(Loro) si bacerebbero*	*loro/(Loro) si sarebbero baciati/e*
		IMPERATIVE	
Future	**Future Perfect**	**Present**	
noi ci baceremo	*noi ci saremo baciati/e*	*baciamoci (noi)*	
voi vi bacerete	*voi vi sarete baciati/e*	*baciatevi (foi)*	
loro/(Loro) si baceranno	*loro(Loro) si saranno baciati/e*		
		N.B. The 3rd person pl. of the present subj. *si bacino* (*Loro*) is used to express formal commands.	

INFINITIVE		PARTICIPLE		GERUND	
Present	**Past**	**Present**	**Past**	**Present**	**Past**
baciarsi	*essersi baciati/e*	*baciantisi/tesi*	*baciatisi/tesi*	*baciandosi*	*essendosi baciati/e*

> **N.B.** Since reciprocal verb forms can only be plural, the roots of both participles are plural: *bacianti-* (< *baciante-*), *baciati-* (< *baciato-*).

23.6 *'Reflexive' Pronominal Verbs:* arrabbiarsi, sedersi, meravigliarsi, *etc.*

A verb can be said to be pronominal if it is accompanied by a reflexive pronoun (*mi, ti, si, ci,* and *vi*), and it has exactly the same forms as a reflexive verb, but it does not express a reflexive meaning. For example, in an expression like *mi arrabbio* ('I get angry'), the pronoun *mi* does not imply 'myself' at all, but is simply part of the verb. **Pronominal verbs all take *essere*** ('to be') **in compound tenses.**

Pronominal verbs can be divided into four groups:

- the **first group** comprises verbs such as *arrabbiarsi*, which **can't be conjugated without reflexive pronouns:** in fact, forms such *io arrabbio, tu arrabbi,* and so on do not exist.

Grouped with *arrabbiarsi* are common verbs such as *accorgersi* ('to realize'), *arrangiarsi* ('to manage'), *arrendersi* ('to surrender'), *congratularsi* ('to congratulate'), *fidarsi* ('to trust in'), *pentirsi* ('to regret'), *vergognarsi* ('to be ashamed');

- the **second group** includes pronominal verbs that **coexist with equivalent forms without pronouns and have exactly the same meaning.** For instance, 'I sit' can be equally translated in Italian with *sedersi* (*Io mi siedo* 'I sit') or simply with *sedere* (*Io siedo* 'I sit'). Together with *sedersi/sedere* are *approffittarsi/approfittare* ('to take advantage'), *dimenticarsi/dimenticare* ('to forget'), *ricordarsi/ricordare* ('to remember'), *sbagliarsi/sbagliare* ('to make a mistake');

- the **third group** is made up of pronominal verbs that also **coexist with equivalent forms without pronouns but convey a different meaning.** Note the difference between *annoiarsi* ('to get bored') and *annoiare* ('to bore'): *Mi annoio allo spettacolo* ('I am getting bored by the show'), *L'attore annoia gli spettatori* ('The actor is boring the audience'). Other verbs in this category are *addormentarsi/addormentare* ('to fall asleep'/'to put to sleep'), *lamentarsi/lamentare* ('to complain'/'to denounce'), *meravigliarsi/meravigliare* ('to be surprised'/'to surprise'), *trovarsi/trovare* ('to be situated'/'to find');

- the **fourth group** is composed of some verbs that **take a pronoun in the colloquial register, giving them confidential overtones.** The most common verbs in this group are *bersi* (*Beviamoci una birra* is equivalent to *Beviamo una birra* 'Let's have a beer'), *farsi* (*Ci facciamo una passeggiata?* is equivalent to *Facciamo una passeggiata?* 'Do we take a walk?'), and *prendersi* (*Mi prendo un minuto di pausa* is equivalent to *Prendo un minuto di pausa* 'I am taking a minute's rest').

23.7 Pronominal Verbs in -ci: capirci, volerci, starci, etc.

These verbs are particularly colorful and, because of their idiomatic meaning, are typical of the spoken language (see also 14.4). The most significant of them, together with some examples of their usage, are indicated below:

- **capirci** ('to understand something about something') is a very colloquial verb and is generally used in negative phrases accompanied by the word *niente* ('nothing'), or the colorful expressions *un accidente* or *un'acca* (both meaning 'a damn'): *Non ci capisco niente* ('I understand zilch about it');
- **crederci** ('to believe it'): *Davvero? Non ci credo!* ('Really? I do not believe it!');
- **entrarci** ('to have something to do with'): *Io non c'entro niente con questo e non ci sono mai entrato* ('I do not have anything to do with this, and I never did');
- **starci** ('to agree', 'to be part of something'): *Va bene, io ci sto* ('OK, I am in'). The verb *starci* can also be used in colloquial Italian with sexual overtones: *È una ragazza che ci sta facilmente* ('She's an easy girl');
- **tenerci** ('to care about'): *Lo sai, ci ho sempre tenuto ai miei voti* ('You know; I always cared about my grades');

- **volerci** ('to take' or 'to be required') is used in the third person singular and plural only. It takes *essere* in compound tenses and the past participle must agree with the subject: *C'è voluta molta pazienza* ('It took a lot of patience'), *Ci vogliono diversi permessi per entrare in molti paesi* ('Several permits are required to enter many countries'). It can also combine with a reflexive pronoun to make the action more personal: *Mi ci sono volute tre ore ad arrivare a Roma* ('It took me three hours to arrive in Rome');
- **metterci** ('to take') can be considered a synonym of *volerci* though it can be used only in reference to a certain amount of time. Unlike *volerci*, it admits all persons and takes *avere* in compound tenses: *Ci ho messo due ore a fare il dolce* ('It took me three hours to make the cake').

23.8 Pronominal Verbs in -ne: dirne, poterne, valerne, *etc.*

Like the above pronominal verbs in *-ci*, the verbs in *-ne* are quite colorful and more commonly used in spoken language because of their idiomatic meaning (see also 14.7). The most significant of them, together with some examples of their usage, are provided below:

- **dirne** is used only in a few expressions such as *dirne di tutti i colori* or *dirne di cotte e di crude*, which are roughly equivalent to the English 'call somebody every name under the sun': *Marco ne ha dette di cotte e di crude sul suo amico* ('Marco called his friend every name under the sun');
- **poterne** occurs only in the expression *non poterne più* ('to have had enough'): *Non ne posso più di lavorare giorno e notte* ('I have had enough working day and night');
- **valerne** is only used in the expression *valerne la pena* ('to be worth it'): *Studia bene, ne vale la pena* ('Study well; it's worth it');
- **volerne** ('to hold it against'): *Non ti preoccupare, non te ne voglio* ('Don't worry; I don't hold it against you').

23.9 Pronominal Verbs in -cela: avercela, farcela, *and* mettercela

These verbs also convey an idiomatic meaning typical of the spoken language; the most significant are given below, together with some examples of their usage:

- **avercela** ('to be mad at') takes *avere* in compound tenses, which makes its past participle *avuta* invariable because it agrees with *la*: *Non ce l'ho mai avuta con te* ('I have never been mad at you');
- **farcela**, followed by *a* + infinitive, can be considered synonymous with *riuscire* and means 'to be able to'. The past participle is always *fatta* because it agrees with *la*: *Scusami, non ce l'ho fatta a venire* ('Pardon me; I was not able to come');
- **mettercela** is only used in the expression *mettercela tutta* ('to do everything possible'). It takes *avere* in compound tenses and has an invariable past participle *messa* that agrees with *la*: *Loro ce l'hanno messa tutta per essere puntuali* ('They did everything they could to be on time').

23.10 Pronominal Verbs in -sela: cavarsela, passarsela, prendersela, *etc.*

Other verbs expressing an idiomatic meaning are verbs ending in *-sela*. The reflexive pronoun *se* changes according to the subject, while the pronoun *la* never varies (*io me la cavo, tu te la cavi,* etc.). All these verbs are conjugated with *essere* in compound tenses and have an invariable past participle in *-a* which agrees with the pronoun *la* (*io me la sono cavata, tu te la sei presa,* etc.). The most significant verbs of this kind are detailed below with examples of their usage:

- **cavarsela** ('to overcome a difficult situation' or 'to know how to do something well enough'): *L'esame era difficile, ma me la sono cavata* ('The exam was difficult, but I muddled through it');
- **passarsela** ('to be' or 'to live') usually occurs with adverbs such as *bene* ('well'), *male* ('badly'), *discretamente* ('not too bad') that describe the conditions in which one is or lives: *Al momento me la passo benissimo* ('At the moment I am very well');
- **prendersela** ('to be offended' or 'to get angry'): *Non te la prendere per così poco* ('Do not be offended by such a trifle');
- **sentirsela** followed by *di* + infinitive ('to feel up to doing something'): *Non me la sento di rischiare* ('I don't feel up to taking a risk');
- **vedersela** ('to deal with'): *Me la vedrò io con loro* ('I will deal with them'). When *vedersela* is followed by the word *brutta*, it means 'to find oneself in a dangerous or difficult situation': *Me la sono vista brutta con l'esame di matematica* ('I had a really hard time with the math exam').

23.11 Pronominal Verbs in -cene, -cisi, and -sene: volercene, mettercisi, andarsene, *etc.*

Similar to the above pronominal verbs, the following verbs are also decidedly colorful because of their idiomatic meaning and they are mostly used in spoken Italian:

- **volercene** ('to take a lot of') is similar to *volerci* (see 23.7) but unlike the latter, it implies the meaning of 'a lot of'. Note the difference between *Ce ne vuole di coraggio a dire questo* ('It takes a lot of courage to say something like that') and *Ci vuole coraggio a dire questo* ('It takes courage to say something like that'). The verb *volercene* uses *essere* in compound tenses, so its past participle agrees with the subject, which in this case is preceded by the preposition *di*: *Ce ne è voluta di pazienza a sopportarti così a lungo* ('It took a lot of patience to suffer you for so long');
- **mettercisi** ('to become involved in'): *In questa situazione così pericolosa io non mi ci metto* ('I am not becoming involved in such a dangerous situation');
- **andarsene** ('to go away', 'to leave'): *Vattene di qua* ('Go away from here'). The *se* in *andarsene* is a reflexive pronoun that must agree with the subject while the pronoun *ne* never changes. The verb takes *essere* in compound tenses and its past participle agrees with the subject: *Ieri sera ve ne siete andati presto* ('Yesterday night, you left early');
- **fregarsene** ('not to give a damn') has the same construction as *andarsene*: *Loro se ne sono fregati di noi* ('They didn't give a damn about us').

23.12 Impersonal Forms: piove, è bello, si gioca, *etc.*

Impersonal verbs do not change according to grammatical subjects, having only one form: the **third person singular.** While in English an impersonal verb takes the impersonal pronoun 'it', in Italian such a verb takes no subject at all (*piove* 'it rains', *nevica* 'it snows').

'Weather verbs' is a term sometimes used to refer to these forms because such weather-indicating verbs are impersonal. These verbs can use either *essere* ('to be') or *avere* ('to have') as auxiliary (see 20.11): *È piovuto/Ha piovuto* ('It rained'), *È nevicato/Ha nevicato* ('It snowed'). The phrases *Fa caldo/freddo/fresco/bello/brutto* ('It is hot/cold/cool/good/bad weather') and the forms *Fa giorno/buio* ('It is growing light/dark') can be considered part of this group. These forms with the verb *fare* can use only the auxiliary *avere*: *Ieri ha fatto brutto* ('Yesterday the weather was bad'), *Ha fatto buio presto* ('It grew dark early').

In addition to the above verbs, which allow only the impersonal form, there are others all conjugated with the auxiliary *essere* in the compound tenses that can be used impersonally as well as personally. These verbs or verbal phrases are:

- verbs indicating an **event** or an **occurrence** like *avvenire* and its synonyms *accadere, capitare, succedere*, all equivalent to the English 'to happen': *Accade sempre* ('It always happens'), *È successo a me di perdere la chiave* ('It happened that I have lost my key');
- verbs indicating a **necessity** like *bisognare* ('to be necessary'), *occorrere* ('to be needed'), *toccare* ('to have to'), or **convenience** like *convenire* ('to be convenient'): *Bisogna sempre ringraziare* ('It is always necessary to say thank you'), *È convenuto a tutti* ('It was convenient for everybody');
- verbs indicating an **appearance** like *sembrare* and the equivalent *parere* (both meaning 'to seem', 'to look like'): *Sembra che lei venga a trovarci* ('It seems she is coming to see us'), *È parso a tutti di volare* ('It looked to everybody like we were flying');
- verbs combined with the **impersonal *si*** (see 23.13): *Si vede che sei in buona forma* ('One can see you are in good shape'), *Si fa di tutto per andare in vacanza* ('One makes every effort to go on vacation');
- expressions formed with the third singular person of *essere* ('to be') indicating **interdiction** like *è vietato* and the equivalent *è proibito* (both meaning 'it is forbidden'), or **permission** like *è permesso* and the equivalent *è consentito* (both meaning 'it is allowed'): *È vietato fumare* ('No smoking'), *È consentito l'uso del cellulare* ('Cellular phones are allowed');
- expressions formed by the third singular person of *essere* ('to be') + adjective like *è vero* ('it is true'), *era falso* ('it was false'), *sarà giusto* ('it will be fair'), or *essere* + adverbs like *è bene* ('it is good'), *è male* ('it is bad'): *È vero che parli troppo* ('It is true that you speak too much'), *È bene dormire otto ore ogni notte* ('It is good to sleep eight hours every night').

Italian has two other ways of making a verb impersonal:

- using the **generic** subject **uno** ('one') or **qualcuno** ('someone'): *Uno non dice una parola quando è imbarazzato* ('One has a hard time uttering a word when one's embarassed'), *Qualcuno pagherà* ('Someone will pay');

- using the **third person plural of a verb indicating an unknown subject**: *Dicono che Boston sia una bella città* ('They say Boston is a beautiful city'), *Chiamano dalla strada* ('They are calling from the street').

23.13 The Impersonal *si*

In Italian all the verbs and all the tenses can be constructed in the impersonal form using ***si* + 3rd person singualar of the verb**. This structure corresponds to the English impersonal construction 'one', 'people', 'you', 'we', or 'they' plus the verb: *All'incrocio si gira a sinistra* ('At the intersection one turns left'), *Si vede che sei stanco* ('We can see you that are tired').

The impersonal *si* construction is commonly used in very generic expressions such as *si dice che ...* ('they say that ...'), *si pensa che ...* ('it is thought that ...'), *si crede che ...* ('it is believed that ...'), and so on. It is common in requesting information or permission: *Come si scrive 'Ciao'?* ('How do you write *'Ciao'*?) *Come si va in cantina?* ('How can one get to the basement?'), *Si può entrare?* ('Can we come in?').

The impersonal *si* construction **always uses *essere* as auxiliary.** If the verb is normally conjugated with the auxiliary *avere* (see 20.8), the past participle, in the impersonal *si* construction, always ends in -*o*: *Si è mangiato molto oggi* ('We have eaten a lot today'). If instead the verb normally uses *essere* as auxiliary (see 20.8), the past participle, in the impersonal *si* construction, can be either masculine plural (-*i*) or feminine plural (-*e*) when a feminine subject is implicit: *Si è arrivati puntuali* ('We arrived on time'), *Si è arrivate in ritardo* ('We [girls] arrived late').

In the impersonal construction ***si è* + adjective**, the adjective is always plural: *Si è stanchi* ('We are tired'), *Quando è festa si è felici* ('On holidays you feel happy'). When a feminine subject is implicit, the adjective is feminine: *Si è stimate* ('We [women] are appreciated').

23.14 Modal Verbs: dovere, potere, *and* volere

Dovere, potere, and *volere* are called modal verbs and are usually used with the infinitive form of a verb:

- ***dovere*** corresponds to the English 'must', 'to have to' and indicates **necessity** (*Marco deve studiare per passare l'esame* 'Marco must study to pass the exam') or **obligation** (*Tu devi essere puntuale* 'You must be on time'). *Dovere* can also sometimes mean 'to owe' both in a literal and in a figurative sense: *Ti devo 10 dollari* ('I owe you $10.00'), *Devo ai miei genitori il mio successo* ('I owe my parents my success');
- ***potere*** corresponds to the English 'can', 'may' and indicates **permission** (*Posso entrare?* 'May I come in?') or **ability** (*Posso nuotare per due ore senza fermarmi* 'I can swim for two hours without stopping'). Even if *potere* implies the idea of ability, it does not convey the idea of skill that 'can' does. The use of *sapere* (see 23.15) is in this case more accurate. When *potere* indicates **probability**, which it does at times, it becomes equivalent to adverbs such as *forse* ('maybe') or *probabilmente* ('probably'): *Posso non avere sentito bene* is equivalent to *Forse non ho sentito bene* ('Maybe I did not hear well');

- ***volere*** corresponds to the English 'to want', 'to wish' and indicates **will** (*Voglio partire* 'I want to leave') and **desire**, especially in the conditional mood (*Vorrei tu fossi qui* 'I wish you were here'). Unlike *dovere* and *potere*, it can be followed by a direct object (*Voglio un gelato* 'I want an ice cream') as well as by an infinitive verb (*Voglio mangiare* 'I want to eat'). *Volere* forms, with the word *bene*, the phrase *volere bene*, which corresponds to the English 'to love', 'to have affection for': *Mamma, ti voglio bene* ('Mom, I love you'). In this case *volere* must always use *avere* ('to have') as auxiliary: *Ti ho voluto tanto bene* ('I really loved you'). When it is combined with the particle *ci*, *volere* acquires an idiomatic meaning (see 23.7) and is equivalent to the English 'to take', 'to be necessary': *Ci vuole tanto lavoro* ('It takes a lot of work').

The verb *dovere*, *potere*, *volere* take the auxilary (see also 20.12) *avere* ('to have'), if the infinitive verb that follows itself requires *avere*: *Carla ha dovuto lavorare tutto il giorno* ('Carla had to work all day long'). On the contrary, they take the auxilary *essere* ('to be'), if the infinitive verb that follows itself requires *essere*: *Non sono potuti venire* ('They couldn't come'). If a modal verb is not followed by an infinitive, it must always take the auxiliary *avere*: *Non sono venuto perché non ho potuto* ('I did not come because I couldn't').

When such verbs are used with direct and indirect object pronouns (see also 21.47), the pronouns can be placed before *dovere*, *potere*, and *volere* (*Ti devo/posso/voglio telefonare* 'I must/can/want to call you') or they can attach to the end of any infinitive that follows them (*Devo/Posso/Voglio telefonarti* 'I must/can/want call you'), in which case the infinitive loses its final -*e*.

> **N.B.** The conditional of *potere* and *volere* is generally used to make polite requests (see also 21.29): *Potrei avere un bicchiere di acqua?* ('May I have a glass of water?'), *Vorrei un panino* ('I would like a sandwich').

23.15 Sapere *and* Conoscere

Although the verbs *sapere* and *conoscere* both can be translated into English with 'to know', they have different applications in Italian:

- ***sapere*** is used to express knowledge of facts and information (*So che non stai bene oggi* 'I know you are not well today') and the knowledge of how to do something or the ability to do something. In the latter case the verb *sapere* works as a modal verb followed by an infinitive verb: *So nuotare* ('I know how to swim');
- ***conoscere*** instead means 'to know' in the sense of 'being acquainted with' and is used for people, places, works of art, songs, and so on: *Conosco Pietro* ('I know Pietro'), *Conosco la città di New York* ('I am familiar with New York City'). In the past tenses the verb *conoscere* is always equivalent in meaning to the past tenses of 'to meet': *Ho conosciuto Carlo due anni fa* ('I met Carlo two years ago'), *Ci conoscemmo ad una festa* ('We met at a party').

23.16 Phrasal Verbs

A group of verbs (known as phrasal) form, when combined with infinitives or gerunds, unique verb predicates that differ in function from the verb used alone. Note the difference between *Io sto in montagna per due settimane* ('I am staying at the mountains for two weeks') where *stare* simply means 'to stay' and *Io sto per partire adesso* ('I am about to leave now') where *stare*, followed by the preposition *per* + infinitive (*partire*), expresses instead the idea of an impending action. Italian phrasal verbs can be divided into **five categories** explained in the next paragraphs (see 23.17–23.21).

23.17 Verbs Expressing a Progressive Action: stare, andare, *and* venire + Gerund

Progressive actions are in progress at the time of speaking or at a point in time in the past. In Italian these actions are usually espressed by using **stare + gerund** (see also 21.15): *Sto guardando la televisione* ('I am watching TV'), *Stavamo mangiando quando ci hai telefonato* ('We were eating when you called').

Progressive actions can also be expressed with the verbs **andare** or **venire + gerund,** especially to express repetitive actions: *Vai/Vieni dicendo continuamente le stesse cose* ('You are continually saying the same things'). However, these two forms are quite rare in contemporary Italian.

23.18 Verbs Expressing an Impending Action: stare per ..., essere in procinto di ..., *etc.*

An impending action is an action that is about to begin or to take place and can be expressed in Italian with special verbal phrases followed by an infinitive. All of these phrases can be translated into English with 'to be about to do something' or 'to be on the verge of doing something'. They are indicated in the table below with a sample of their use:

Verbal phrases	Examples
stare per + infinitive	*Sto per partire* ('I am about to leave')
essere sul punto di + infinitive	*Erano sul punto di mangiare* ('They were about to eat')
essere in procinto di + infinitive	*Sono in procinto di partire* ('I am on the verge of leaving')
essere lì lì per + infinitive	*Erano lì lì per svenire* ('They were on the verge of fainting')
accingersi a + infinitive	*Mi accingo a andare a letto* ('I am about to go to bed')
prepararsi a + infinitive	*Marco si prepara a cucinare* ('Marco is about to cook')

23.19 Verbs Expressing the Start of an Action: cominciare a ..., iniziare a ..., *etc.*

The start of an action is an action that started in the past, or an action that has just begun but has not yet progressed, or an action that is starting at the moment of speaking. It can be expressed in Italian with several verbal forms followed by an infinitive, all equivalent to the English 'to start/to begin'. They are indicated below with a sample of their use:

Verbal phrases	Examples
cominciare a + infinitive	*Ho appena cominciato a studiare* ('I have just started studying')
iniziare a + infinitive	*Iniziò a piovere* ('It began to rain')
mettersi a + infinitive	*Mi metto a lavorare* ('I start working')

All the above verbs when constructed with the prefix *ri-* (< *re-*) indicate the beginning of a repeated action: *Ricomincio a lavorare* ('I start working again'), *Rinizia a piovere* ('It is starting to rain again').

23.20 Verbs Expressing the Continuation of an Action: continuare a ..., seguitare a ..., etc.

A continuing action is an action that has begun and keeps on going. It can be expressed in Italian with *andare avanti a, continuare a, seguitare a,* followed by an infinitive. All of these expressions can be translated into English with the phrase 'to continue to do something' or 'to keep on doing something'. They are indicated below with a sample of their use:

Verbal phrases	Examples
andare avanti a + infinitive	*Vai avanti a studiare matematica* ('Keep studying math')
continuare a + infinitive	*Continua a lavorare bene* ('Continue to work well')
seguitare a + infinitive	*Non seguitare a telefonarmi* ('Do not keep calling me')

The phrases **insistere a/nel** and the equivalent **persistere a/nel** + infinitive ('to insist on', 'persist in doing something') also express the continuation of an action but both convey the idea of persistence, generally used with a negative nuance: *Perché insisti a/nel chiamarmi? Non voglio più avere a che fare con te* ('Why do you insist on calling me? I don't want to have anything to do with you anymore').

23.21 Verbs Expressing the End of an Action: finire di ..., smetterla di ..., etc.

Such verbs as *finire* ('to finish', 'to end'), *smettere* ('to stop'), and the rare *cessare* ('to cease', 'to stop') followed by *di* + infinitive indicate the end of an action. All of them can be formed with the pronoun *la* in a colloquial context to add more emphasis and insistence to the meaning as in the colloquial form *piantarla di* ('to stop'). They are indicated below with a sample of their use:

Verbal phrases	Examples
finire di or **finirla di** + infinitive	*Perché non la finisci di piangere?* ('Why don't you stop crying?')
smettere di or **smetterla di** + infinitive	*Smettete di parlare* ('Stop talking')
piantarla di + infinitive	*Piantala di darmi fastidio!* ('Stop bothering me, please!')

When the pronominal versions of the verbs (forms with *la*) are employed, the auxiliary *avere* ('to have') is used in compound tenses, and the past participle always ends in *-a* because it agrees with the feminine pronoun *la*: *Marco non l'ha smessa ancora, continua a piangere* ('Marco has not stopped yet; he is still crying').

23.22 The Causative Verb *fare*: Faccio preparare il pranzo

The verb **fare + infinitive** forms a causative construction equivalent to the English phrase 'to make someone do something': *Il professore fa leggere Giovanna* ('The professor is making Giovanna read'). Note that in Italian, contrary to English, the person being made to do something always comes after the verb.

When the causative sentence has two objects (whoever is doing something and the direct object of the infinitive verb), the same construction *fare* + infinitive is the equivalent of 'to have something done by someone'. In this case, the person being made to do something must be introduced by the preposition *a* or its articulated forms when necessary. If, for example, to the sentence *Il professore fa leggere Giovanna,* we add the direct object *libro* ('book'), *Giovanna* must be preceded by *a*: *Il professore fa leggere il libro a Giovanna* ('The professor is making Giovanna read the book').

The person being made to do something can be replaced by a direct object pronoun (see 13.6), if the direct object is not expressed: *Il professore la fa leggere* ('The professor is making her read'); if the direct object is expressed, the pronoun must be an indirect object pronoun (see 13.9): *Il professore le fa leggere il libro* ('The professor makes her read the book'). When both the person and the object are replaced by pronouns, a combined pronoun must be used (see 13.10): *Il professore glielo fa leggere* ('The professor is making her read it').

In case of ambiguity with an indirect object, the preposition *da*, or its articulated forms when necessary, is used instead of *a* in front of the person being made to do something. For example, the sentence *Ho fatto spedire la lettera a Giacomo* could have two meanings: 1) 'I had Giacomo send the letter' or 2) 'I had the letter sent to Giacomo'. If the first meaning is intended, then *da* must replace *a* to avoid any ambiguity: *Ho fatto spedire la lettera da Giacomo*.

> **N.B.** The pronominal form ***farsi*** can also be used as a causative verb: *Mi faccio tagliare i capelli dalla mamma* ('I am having my hair cut by my mom').

23.23 The Causative Verb *lasciare*: Lascia uscire il cane

Like *fare* (see 23.22), the verb *lasciare* can have a causative meaning. The two verb constructions are very similar, but while *fare* + infinitive means making someone do something, **lasciare + infinitive** is equivalent to the English phrase 'to allow someone to do something' or 'to let someone do something': *Il professore lascia leggere Marco* ('The professor lets Marco read'). Note that in Italian, not in English, the person who is allowed to do something always comes after the infinitive verb.

Like *fare*, *lasciare* can have two objects: whoever is allowed to do something and the direct object of the infinitive verb. When both are expressed, the person allowed to do something must be introduced by the preposition *a* or its articulated forms when necessary: *Il professore lascia leggere il libro a Marco* ('The professor lets Marco read the book').

The person allowed to do something can be replaced by a pronoun that must be a direct object pronoun (see 13.7), if the direct object is not expressed: *Il professore lo lascia leggere* ('The professor lets him read') or an indirect object pronoun (see 13.9) if the direct object is expressed: *Il professore gli lascia leggere il libro* ('The professor lets him read the book'). When pronouns substitute for both the person and the object, they must be a combined pronoun (see 13.10): *Il professore glielo lascia leggere* ('The professor lets him read it').

The construction **lasciare che** + **subjunctive** often replaces *lasciare* + infinitive, especially in more formal contexts: *Lasciate che io incontri il presidente questa sera* ('Let me meet with the president tonight').

23.24 Verbs of Perception with the Infinitive: ascoltare, guardare, sentire, *etc.*

Some Italian verbs of perception such as **ascoltare** ('to listen to'), **guardare** ('to watch'), and especially **sentire** ('to hear') and **vedere** ('to see') can be followed by the infinitive form of other verbs: *Ho visto Marco piangere* ('I saw Marco crying'), *Sento abbaiare un cane* ('I hear a dog barking'), *Ho visto crollare un muro* ('I saw a wall collapsing'). As the second and third examples show, the word order could differ from English. In Italian, in fact, the object of the main verb (the person, animal, or object 'doing something') must be placed in front of the infinitive only if another object follows the infinitive: *Ho sentito Giovanni cantare una canzone* ('I heard Giovanni singing a song'). Otherwise, the first object can occur before or after the infinitive: *Ho sentito Giovanni cantare* is equivalent to *Ho sentito cantare Giovanni* ('I heard Giovanni singing').

If the person, animal, or object 'doing something' is an unstressed pronoun (see 13.5), it precedes the main verb: *Ti ho visto piangere* ('I saw you crying'), *Li ho ascoltati parlare di calcio* ('I listened to them talk about soccer'). However, if the verb of perception is an imperative, an infinitive, or a gerund, the pronoun must attach to it: *Vederti soffrire mi fa male* ('Seeing you suffer pains me'), *Ascoltatelo suonare il piano* ('Listen to him playing the piano').

This typical infinitive after a verb of perception can be replaced by a **relative clause formed with *che* + conjugated verb**: *Ho sentito qualcuno che urlava* [= *urlare*] ('I heard someone who was screaming'), *Vedo un gatto che corre* [=*correre*] ('I see a cat that is running').

23.25 Defective Verbs: addirsi, solere, *and* urgere

Besides impersonal verbs (see 23.12), conjugated in the third person only, there is a class of verbs for which certain forms of conjugation do not exist. These are referred to as defective verbs because they have an incomplete conjugation and lack certain subjective forms, tenses, and moods. They are a small set and are typical of a very formal or literary context. Furthermore, most are not used in contemporary Italian anymore, so it is better to replace them by synonymous or comparable phrases. For this reason, only the most significant are indicated below:

- **addirsi** ('to fit') has only the third persons of the present (*si addice, si addicono*), imperfect (*si addiceva, si addicevano*), present subjunctive (*si addica, si addicano*), and imperfect subjunctive (*si addicesse, si addicessero*). The past participle *addetto* is used only as an adjective or noun meaning 'one who is in charge of': *L'operaio addetto all'imballaggio è assente* ('The worker in charge of packing is absent');
- **solere** ('to be accustomed to') has only a few forms of the present (*lui/lei suole, voi solete, loro solgono*) and the imperfect indicative (*io solevo, tu solevi*). It is preferably replaced by the phrases *essere solito*: *Lui è solito* [= *suole*] *essere in ritardo* ('He is accustomed to being late');
- **urgere** ('to be urgent') is conjugated in the third persons of the simple tenses (*urge, urgono, urgevano*) and the present gerund (*urgendo*). It is usually replaced by the phrase *essere urgente*: *È urgente* [= *Urge*] *un intervento chirurgico* ('A surgical procedure is urgently required').

23.26 Forms and Uses of piacere

The verb **piacere** ('to please') is used when referring to things or actions someone likes, but it functions differently from its English equivalent 'to like.' It is mostly used with the third person singular or plural, even if it admits all forms: *Tu mi piaci* ('I like you'), *Loro ci piacciono* ('We like them'), and so on.

In Italian, as opposed to English, the subject of the sentence is the person, thing, or action liked, while the person who likes is the indirect object, usually expressed by an indirect object pronoun (see 13.9): *Mi/A me piace molto tua sorella* ('I really like your sister'). In this example the pronoun *Mi* and *A me* are indirect objects, while *tua sorella* is the subject. The structure remains the same when a noun occurs instead of a pronoun; in this case the preposition *a*, or its articulated forms, when necessary, always precedes the noun: *A Carla piace il gelato* ('Carla likes ice cream'), *Ai giovani piace viaggiare* ('Young people like to travel').

When the verb *piacere* refers to a singular noun or to an infinitive verb, the **singular forms** *piace, piaceva, piacque,* and so on must be used: *Mi piace la musica* ('I like music'), *A Marta piacerà venire con noi* ('Marta would like to come with us'); when instead *piacere* refers to a plural noun, the **plural forms** *piacciono, piacevano, piacquero,* and so on are required: *Ci piacciono gli spaghetti* ('We like spaghetti'), *A tutti piacciono le vacanze* ('Everybody like vacations').

Piacere **is always conjugated with** *essere* in compound tenses, and so the past participle must agree in gender and number with the subject, in this case the noun that represents what is liked: *Mi è piaciuta la pasta* ('I liked pasta'), *A me sono piaciuti gli spaghetti* ('I liked spaghetti'). In case of an infinitive after *piacere,* the past participle always ends in -*o*: *Mi è piaciuto vedere quella commedia* ('I liked watching that comedy'), *Ci è piaciuto visitare il Vaticano* ('We liked to visit Vatican City').

The chart below indicates only the present tense forms of *piacere* and their English equivalents, all the other tenses functioning in the same way, according to the second conjugation rules (see 20.17, 20.19).

The verb *piacere*	English equivalent
mi (= *a me*) *piace/piacciono*	('I like')
ti (= *a te*) *piace/piacciono*	('you like')
gli (= *a lui*) *piace/piacciono*	('he likes')
le (= *a lei*) *piace/piacciono*	('she likes')
Le (= *a Lei*) *piace/piacciono*	('you like' sing. formal)
ci (= *a noi*) *piace/piacciono*	('we like')
vi (= *a voi*) *piace/piacciono*	('you like')
gli (= *a loro*) *piace/piacciono*	('they like')
Loro (= *a Loro*) *piace/piacciono*	('you like' plur. formal)

A clause formed by **che + subjunctive** must replace the infinitive if whoever is doing the action expressed by the verb following *piacere* is different from the person who likes doing the action. For example, in a sentence like *Mi piace andare in vacanza* ('I like to go on vacation') the person who 'likes' and the one who 'goes' are the same, while in *Mi piace che voi andiate in vacanza* ('I would like you to go on vacation'), they are not, so the construction *che* + subjunctive is necessary.

> **N.B.** To express **dislike** in Italian, it is necessary to add *non* in front of *piacere*: *Non mi è piaciuta la commedia* ('I did not like comedy'), *Non mi piace dormire* ('I do not like to sleep'). The Italian verb *dispiacere* means 'to be sorry' and must not be confused with 'to dislike' (*non piacere*).

23.27 Verbs Similar to piacere: bastare, interessare, *etc.*

There are some common verbs similar to *piacere* ('to like') in construction and function (for *piacere*, see 26.27). Below is a list of the most significant ones and a sample of their use:

Verbs like *piacere*	Examples
bastare ('to be sufficient')	*Ci basta questo* ('This is sufficient for us')
dispiacere ('to be sorry')	*Ti dispiace non essere qui?* ('Are you sorry not to be here?')
disgustare ('to disgust')	*Mi disgustano i vermi* ('Worms disgust me')
interessare ('to interest')	*A Leo interessano tutti gli sport* ('Leo is interested in all sports')
mancare ('to lack')	*Gli manca il coraggio* ('He lacks courage')
occorrere ('to need')	*Mi occorrono molti soldi* ('I need a lot of money')
servire ('to need')	*Mi serve dormire di più* ('I need to sleep more')
succedere ('to occur')	*Gli è successo qualcosa* ('Something occured to him')

23.28 The Case of "Computer" Verbs: chattare, bannare, zippare, *etc.*

With the arrival of the WEB and the amazing success of the Social Networks, English is having an incredible influence on Italian. Indeed, Italian has not only adopted a lot of English nouns into its vocabulary (see 3.11), accepting them in their original form (*mouse, hacker,* etc.), but it has also created a whole class of new verbs by taking English "computer" verbs and giving them an Italian form. A characteristic of these verbs is that they all acquire the first conjugation suffix *-are*, so they follow the first conjugation rules (see 20.14). Here is a short list of the most common of them, completely integrated into contemporary Italian (although their original English meaning and form are apparent): *bannare, bypassare, bloggare, cliccare, downloadare, flaggare, formattare, linkare, postare, resettare, spammare, taggare, twittare, uploadare, zippare.*

23.29 Hypothetical Constructions

Italian hypothetical constructions consist of two clauses: a dependent one, introduced by *se* ('if') that lays out the condition or hypothesis, and a main clause that gives the consequence or result of the condition or hypothesis: *Se arrivi in ritardo, trovi il negozio chiuso* ('If you are late, you will find the store closed'), *Se tu fossi con me, sarebbe bello* ('If you were with me, it would be nice').

Hypothetical situations can be presented by the writer or the speaker as 1) real or really probable, 2) as possible but improbable, and 3) as unreal or impossible. The three cases are presented in detail below.

1) Reality

It is possible to talk in the present, the past, or the future about something that is real, or likely to occur. In these cases Italian uses the indicative mood in the *se* clause (condition) and the indicative or the imperative in the main clause (consequence) according to the following table:

Condition (*se*-clause) >	Consequence
Se + **present**: *Se piove,* ('If it rains,') >	**present:** *non esci* ('you do not go out') **future:** *non uscirai* ('you won't go out') **imperative:** *non uscire* ('do not go out')
Se + **future**: *Se potrò,* ('If I can,') >	**future:** *ti chiamerò* ('I'll call you')
Se + **present perfect**: *Se hai sbagliato,* ('If you made a mistake',) > or *Se* + **preterite** (rarely): *Se sbagliasti,* ('If you made a mistake',) >	**present:** *paghi* ('you pay for it') **future:** *pagherai* ('you will pay for it') **present perfect:** *hai pagato* ('you paid for it') **imperative:** *paga* ('you pay for it')

2) Probability

To express a probable situation that can or cannot occur, the *se* clause (condition) is in the imperfect subjunctive and the main clause (consequence) is in the present or past conditional, according to the following table:

Condition (*se*-clause) >	Consequence
***Se* + imperfect subjective:** *Se lui fosse gentile,* ('If he were a nice person',) >	**present conditional:** *non risponderebbe così male* ('he would not answer so badly')
***Se* + imperfect subjunctive:** *Se lui fosse gentile,* ('Had he been a nice person',) >	**past conditional:** *non avrebbe risposto così male* ('he would not have answered so badly') **N.B.** The past conditional is possible only as a past consequence of a permanent condition, *essere gentile* ('to be nice') in this specific case.

Contrary to the indicative, the conjunction ***se* could be easily omitted** in front of the subjunctive without hindering comprehension of the sentence. In fact, the combination of subjunctive and conditional is in itself sufficient to make the meaning clear: all the examples above could be presented without *se* and be absolutely understandable for an Italian listener or reader.

***Se* + imperfect subjunctive alone** introduces a suggestion and corresponds to the English 'What about ...?', 'How about ...?': *Se uscissimo?* ('What about going out?'), *Se ti mettessi a studiare?* ('How about if you start studying?').

3) Impossibility

To express an unreal and impossible situation, since the past condition did not occur, the *se* clause is in the pluperfect subjunctive and the main clause (consequence) is in the past conditional, or sometimes in the present, according to the following table:

Condition (*se*-clause) >	Consequence
***Se* + pluperfect subjective:** *Se avessi fatto l'università,* ('If I had gone to college',) >	**present conditional:** *oggi avrei un lavoro migliore* ('I would have a better job, now') **N.B.** The present conditional is possible only as a present consequence of a past condition, *aver fatto l'università* ('having gone to college') in this specific case.
***Se* + pluperfect subjunctive:** *Se avessi fatto l'università,* ('If I had gone to college',) >	**past conditional:** *mio padre sarebbe stato felice* ('my father would have been happy')

As with the construction of probability, the conjunction ***se* could easily be omitted** in front of the subjunctive without adversely affecting the clarity of the sentence.

***Se* + pluperfect subjunctive alone** expresses regret: *Se avessi studiato!* ('If I had only studied!'), *Se tu avessi accettato quel lavoro!* ('If you had only accepted that job!'). Formulated as a question, the same construction can also indicate doubt. In this case *se* is generally preceded by the conjunction *e*: *E se fossero partiti?* ('What if they had left?'), *E se non andassi a lavoro* ('What if I do not go to work?').

In contemporary spoken Italian the **imperfect indicative** can occur simultaneously in the *se* clause (condition) and in the main clause (consequence). In fact the imperfect tends to replace respectively the more grammatical subjunctive and conditional when possible but improbable or impossible situations are presented: *Se ero ricco, compravo una bella macchina* ('If I had been rich, I would have bought a nice car'), *Se lo scorso anno vincevo il lotto, ora non lavoravo* (If I had won the lottery last year, I wouldn't have been working now'). In the first example what is presented as condition, is possible but improbable, therefore the sentence, according to the rules should be: *Se fossi ricco, comprerei una bella macchina*. The condition in the second example is definitely impossible since it is something that did not happen in the past, so the right form of it should be: *Se lo scorso anno avessi vinto il lotto, ora non lavorerei*. Even if this use of the imperfect indicative is quite common, it is still considered a sign of a less than adequate education. Consequently, it is always preferable to choose the appropriate construction with the subjunctive and conditional.

Bibliography

Adorno, Cecilia. *La grammatica italiana*. Milano: Mondadori, 2003.
Antonelli, Giuseppe. *L'italiano nella società della comunicazione*. Bologna: il Mulino, 2007.
Celi, Monica. *Grammatica d'uso della lingua italiana*. Milano: Hoelphi, 2010.
Chiuchiù, Angelo, Maria Cristina Fazi, and Maria Rosaria Bagianti. *Le preposizioni*. Perugia: Guerra, 1999.
Cinque, Guglielmo. *Italian Syntax and Universal Grammar*. Cambridge: Cambridge UP, 1996.
D'Achille, Paolo. *L'Italiano contemporaneo*. Bologna: Il Mulino, 2010.
D'Agostino, Mario. *Sociolinguistica dell'Italia contemporanea*. Bologna: il Mulino, 2007.
Dardano Maurizio. *Costruire parole. La morfologia derivativa dell'italiano*. Bologna: 2009.
___, and Gianluca Frenguelli, eds. *L'italiano di oggi. Fenomeni, problemi, prospettive*. Roma: Aracne, 2008.
De Mauro, Tullio, ed. *Grande dizionario italiano dell'uso*. Torino: UTET, 2005.
Di Natale, Francesco. *Andare oltre. Dubbi e problemi di grammatica italiana per stranieri*. Perugia: Guerra, 1997.
Fiorentino, Giuliana, ed. *Perché la grammatica? La didattica dell'italiano tra scuola e università*. Roma: Carocci, 2009.
Francesca, Travisi. "Morfosintassi dei pronomi relativi nell'uso giornalistico contemporaneo." *Studi di grammatica italiana* 19 (2000): 233–86.
Francesco, Bruni. *L'italiano nelle regioni. Testi e documenti*. Torino: UTET, 1997.
Kinder, John, and Vincenzo Savini. *Using Italian. A Guide to Contemporary Usage*. Cambridge: Cambridge UP, 2004.
Kolbjørn, Blücher. "Tempo e modo nelle frasi con riferimento temporale 'futuro nel passato' nell'italiano contemporaneo: un panorama sistemico, sintattico e stilistico." *Studi di grammatica italiana* 24 (2005): 231–92.
Leoni, Federico Albano, and Pietro Maturi. *Manuale di fonetica*. Roma: Carocci, 2002.
Lo Duca, Maria. *Esperimenti grammaticali. Riflessioni e proposte sull'insegnamento della grammatica dell'italiano*. Roma: Carrocci, 2004.
Lorenzetti, Luca. *L'italiano contemporaneo*. Roma: Carrocci, 2002.
Luciano, Canepari. *Dizionario di pronuncia italiana*. 1999. Bologna: Zanichelli, 2000.
___. *Manuale di pronuncia italiana*. 1999. Bologna: Zanichelli, 2004.
Maraschio, Nicoletta. "Grafia e ortografia: evoluzione e codificazione." *Storia della lingua italiana*. Vol. I: *I luoghi della codificazione*. Ed. Luca Serriani and Pietro Trifone. Torino: Einaudi, 1993. 139–227.
Maturi, Pietro. *I suoni delle lingue, i suoni dell'italiano*. Bologna: il Mulino, 2006.
Maurizio, Dardano. *La lingua della Nazione*. Roma: Laterza, 2011.
McIntosh, Colin. *Oxford Italian Grammar and Verbs*. Oxford: Oxford UP, 2002.
Mioni, Alberto. *Elementi di fonetica*. Padova: Unipress, 2001.
Moretti, Giovanni Battista. *Italiano come prima o seconda lingua nelle sue varietà scritte e parlate. Forme, strutture e usi*. Perugia: Guerra, 1992.
___. *L'italiano come prima o seconda lingua*. Perugia: Guerra, 2005.

Patota, Giuseppe. *Grammatica di riferimento della lingua italiana per stranieri*. Firenze: Le Monnier, 2003.

———. *Grammatica di riferimento dell'italiano contemporaneo*. Milano: Garzanti, 2006.

Peccianti, Maria Cristina. *Grammatica d'uso della lingua italiana per stranieri*. Firenze: Giunti, 1997.

Renzi, Lorenzo, Giampaolo Salvi, and Anna Cardinaletti, eds. *Grande grammatica italiana di consultazione*. Vol. I: La Frase. *I sintagmi nominale e preposizionale*. Vol. II: *I sintagmi verbale, aggettivale, avverbiale. La subordinazione*. Vol. III: *Tipi di frase, deissi, formazione delle parole*. Bologna: il Mulino, 2001.

Salvi, Giampaolo, and Laura Vannelli. *Nuova grammatica italiana*. Bologna: il Mulino, 2004.

Schena, Leo, Michele Prandi, and Marco Mazzoleni, eds. *Intorno al congiuntivo*. Bologna: CLUEB, 2002.

Serianni, Luca. *Grammatica italiana. Italiano comune e lingua letteraria*. Torino: UTET, 1988.

———. *Italiano*. Milano: Garzanti, 2000.

———. *Italiano. Grammatica, sintassi, dubbi*. Milano: Garzanti, 2000.

Simone, Raffaele. *Fondamenti di linguistica*. Roma: Laterza, 2008.

Stoppelli, Marina. *I verbi italiani*. Milano: Garzanti, 2004.

Tartaglione, Roberto, and Susanna Nocchi. *Grammatica avanzata della lingua italiana*. Firenze: Alma, 2006.

Urbani, Stefano. *Forme del verbo italiano*. Roma: Bonacci, 1990.

Index

A
a, 139–141
  pronunciation of, 21
  + article, 141, 146–147
  + infinitive, 207, 231, 240, 245–246
  + noun or pronoun, 229
a condizione che, 157
a meno che, 157, 159
a mo' di, 65
a momenti, 65
a parte, 159
a patto che, 157
a stento, 65
a volte, 66
a quanto, 159
per quel che, 159
abbastanza, 68
abbreviated nouns, see nouns
accents, 27
accingersi a + infinitive, 245
acciocché, 155
-acchione, 169
-accio, 169
acerrimo, 77
ad eccezione di/che, 159
adjectives
  agreement, 53–55
  as nouns, 61
  compound, 58
  degrees of, see comparatives and superlatives
  demonstrative 93–98
  descriptive, 53–61
  gender of, 46, 53–54
  in *-co*, *-go*, *-ca*, and *-ga*, 54

  indefinite, 100–106
  interrogative, 89–90
  invariable, 54–55
  numeral, see numbers
  position of, 59–60
  with prepositions, 61
  "BAGS" adjectives, 59–60
adverbs
  degrees of, 71–78
  exclamatory, 69
  gender of, 46
  in *-mente*, 62–63
  in *-oni*, 64
  interrogative, 90–91
  irregular, 64
  of affirmation, 69
  of manner, 65
  of place, 67
  of quantity, 68
  of time, 66
  position of, 70
  with double forms, 63–64
adverbial phrases, see adverbs
affatto, 69, 62, 162
affinché, 154–155
age, 112
agrodolce, 58
al contrario, 151
al fine di, 155
alcunché, 105
alcuni/e, as partitive, 138
alcuno, 101
all'infuori di/che, 159
all'inizio, 156

alla buona, 65
alla fine, 156
alla giornata, 65
alla maniera di, 65
allo stesso modo, 158
allora, 66, 152
alphabet, 21
alquanto, 106
alto, 59, 63, 76
altrimenti, 62, 151
altro, 102–103
altroché / altro che, 103
altrove, 68
altrui, 83
ammesso che, 157
anche, 149
anche se, 157–158
ancora, 66, 162
andare, 182
    as passive auxiliary, 234–235
    + gerund, 226
andare avanti a + infinitive, 246
andarsene, 241
antiaderente, 58
anzi, 151
apostrophe, 28
appena, 25, 65–66, 156, 201–202, 227
-are, 171–172, 180
articles
    definite, 33–35
    indefinite, 31–33
    omission of, 35
    partitive, 137–138
articulated prepositions, 146–147
assai, 68–69
-astro, 169–170
autosufficiente, 58
avanti, 67–68
avercela, 240
avere, 122, 132–133, 175–180

B
b, pronunciation of, 23

basso, 63, 76
bastare, 250
bell'e, 56
bello, 55–56, 59
benché, 157
bene, 64
bere, 187
bocconi, 64
bracci, braccia, 49
bravo, 59
brutto, 59
buono, 56–57, 59, 76

C
c, pronunciation of, 23
cadauno, see *ciascheduno*
capelli, 50
capirci, 239
capitalization, 30
capo-, 45, 50–51, 164
caro, 59
carponi, 64
cattivo, 64, 76
cavalcioni, 64
cavarsela, 241
celeberrimo, 77
centinaio, 48
cento, 109, 114
certamente, 63
certo, 59, 63, 101–102
certuni, 105
ch, pronunciation of, 23
che
    as conjunction, 153–154
    as indefinite pronoun, 105
    as interrogative, 89
    as relative pronoun, 84–86
    in comparisons, 72–74
    with subjunctive, 209–213
ché, 154
che cosa, 89
chi, 84, 86–87, 89
chiaro, 63

chicchesia, 105
chiunque, 103, 105, 214
ci
    as participle, 131–134
    as pronoun, 122, 126, 128–130
    in idiomatic expressions, 133133–134
    pronunciation of, 23
    with direct object pronouns, 132
    with *essere*, 133
ciascheduno, 105
ciascuno, 104
ciglia/cigli, 49
ciò, 87, 97
cioè, 151
ciondoloni, 64
codesto, 97
colui, 87, 97–98
come
    as adverb, 69, 90
    as comparative connective, 72, 74, 152, 160
    as modal connective, 158, 160
come se, 214
cominciare a + infinitive, 246
comparatives
    irregular, 76–77
    of equality, 72, 74
    of inequality, 72–74
comunque, 158
con, 145
conditional, 172, 213, 215–215
    as connective, see conjunctions
conjugations, see verbs
conjunctions
    adversative, 150–151
    causal, 154
    comparative, 160
    concessive, 157
    conclusive, 151–152
    conditional, 157
    copulative, 149–150
    correlative, 152
    declarative, 151
    disjunctive, 150

    gender of, 46
    modal, 158
    of exception, 159
    purpose, 155
    restrictive, 159–160
    time, 155–156
connectives, see conjunctions
conoscere, 190, 244
considerato che, 154
consonants, 23–24
continuare a + infinitive, 246
cosa, 89
così ... come, 72, 74, 152, 160
così così, 65
così, 26–27, 74, 142
crederci, 239
cui, 84–86

D

d, pronunciation of, 23
da, 142–143
    in the passive form, 233
    + article, 147, 233
    + infinitive, 175, 231, 235
    + present, 201
da che / dacché, 157
da quando, 155
dal momento che, 154
dappertutto, 68
dare, 182
dare fastidio a, 229
dare ragione/torto, 35
date, 111
davanti, 67, 129
dentro, 67, 148
di, 143–144
    in comparisons, 73–75, 77
    + article, 137, 147
    + possessor, 81
    + infinitive, 153, 157, 212, 219, 230–231, 241, 245–246
    + noun, 65, 95, 113, 229
    + pronoun, 113, 229

di conseguenza, 152
di quando in quando, 66
di quanto, 160
dietro, 67, 148
difatti, 151
diphthongs, 22
dirne, 240
dita/diti, 49
diverso, 59
dolceamaro, 58
dopo, 66–67, 147, 156
dopo che, 155–156, 202, 205, 227
doppio, 113
double consonants, 24
dove, 69, 90, 92
dovere, 179, 186, 223, 243–244
dovunque, 68
due, with idiomatic meaning, 114
dunque, 151

E
e, 149
    pronunciation of, 22
e ... e, 152
ebbene, 152
eccetto, 159, 214
ecco, 124, 135
egli, 116–117
elision, 28
ella, 116–117
-ello, 168
-entissimo, 77
entrarci, 239
eppure, 150
-ere, 171–172, 184
-errimo, 77
essere, 133, 174–180, 233, 236
essere di, 144,
essere in procinto di + infinitive, 245
essere lì lì per + infinitive, 245
essere pregato di, 219
essere sul punto di + infinitive, 245
esso/a, 116–117

-ettino, 168
-etto, 168

F
f, pronunciation of, 23
fare, 183
    + infinitive 247
farcela, 240
fare bene/male, 229
fare paura, 35
finalissima, 78
finché, 156
finire, 178, 196
finire di, 246
finirla di, 246
fino a che, 156
fino a quando, 156
fondamenta/fondamenti, 49
forte, 63
fra, 74, 87, 106, 144–145
fregarsene, 241
fuorché, 159, 214
fuori, 67, 148
future, see also verbs
    simple 201–202
    perfect, 202
    progressive, 202

G
g, pronunciation of, 23
gente, 50
gerund, 158, 173, 223–226
gesta/gesti, 49
gh, pronunciation of, 23
gi, pronunciation of, 23
giacché, 154
ginocchioni, 64
giù, 67–68, 148
giusto, 63
gli,
    as article, 33
    as pronoun, 124–126
    pronunciation of, 24

gn, pronunciation of, 24
grande, 57, 59, 76
group of letters, 23–24

H
h, pronunciation of, 23
hypothetical constructions, 251

I
i
    as article, 33
    pronunciation of, 22
-iccio, 169
-igno, 169–170
il, 33
il più, 74–75
il quale, 86
il meno, 74–75
imperative, 172, 218–220, see also verbs
imperfect, see also verbs
    indicative 203–204, 206
    progressive 204
    subjunctive, 211
impersonal *si*, 243
impossibility, see hypothetical constructions
in, 140–141
    + article 146–147
in altre parole, 151
in altri termini, 151
in effetti, 151
in maniera, see *in modo*
in modo, 65
in modo che, 155
in modo da, 155
in quanto, 154
in quel di, 96
in seguito, 156
indicative, 154–156, 158, 160, 172, 200, see also verbs
infatti, 151
inferiore, 76
infinitive, 155, 173, 220–223
    gender of, 46
    with prepositions, 61

iniziare a + infinitive, 246
-ino, 168
integerrimo, 77
invece, 150
io, 116–117, 172
iper-, 75, 165
-issimamente, 76
-issimo, 75, 77–78

L
l, pronunciation of, 23
l', see *lo* and *la*
l'un ... l'altro, 103
l'un e l'altro, 103
la
    as article, 33
    as pronoun, 121–123
là, 27, 68, 95
laggiù, 68, 98
lasciare + infinitive, 247–248
lasciare che + subjunctive, 248
lasciare di, 247–248
le
    as article, 33
    as pronoun, 121–123
lei, see *lui*
Lei, formal pronoun, 118–119
lì, see *là*
li
    as article, 33
    as pronoun, 121–123
lo
    as article, 33
    as pronoun, 121–123
lontano, 63, 67, 143, 148
loro, 116, 118, 121–125, 127
Loro, formal pronoun, 118–119
lui 116–118, 120, 122, 124, 127, 172

M
m, pronunciation of, 23
ma, 150
maggiore, 76

mai, 66, 91
male, 64
malgrado, 157, 213
me lo, 126
me stesso, 129
measurements, 112
meglio, 64, 74
membra/membri, 49
meno,
    in comparisons, 69, 71–75, 77, 160
    in time expressions, 112
-mente, 62
mentre, 150, 155–156, 225
mettercela, 240
metterci, 239
mettercisi, 241
mettersi a + infinitive, 246
mezzo, 58
mi ci, 132
mica, 162
migliaio, 48
migliore, 64, 76
-mila, 109
miliardo, 109
milione, 109, 114
mille, 109, 114
minore, 76
mio, 79
miserrimo, 77
molto, 60, 68–69, 75–77, 106, 135, 232
mura/muri, 49

N

n, pronunciation of, 23
ne, 134–136
né ... né, 152, 162
neanche, 150, 162
negative structures, 162–163
nel bel mezzo, 56
nemmeno, see *neanche*
neppure, see *neanche*
nient'altro, 103
niente, 69, 101, 104–105, 133, 162–163

no, 91, 163
noi, 116–117, 121–122, 124, 127, 172
non, 161–162
non poterne più, 136
non solo ... ma anche, 152
non vedere l'ora, 210
nonostante, 148, 157, 213, 225
notizie, 50
nouns
    abbreviated, 43
    changing meaning with gender, 43
    compound, 45–46, 50–52
    English integrated into Italian, 42
    feminine in *-o*, 37–38
    foreign, 41–42
    from masculine to feminine, 37
    from singular to plural, 46–49
    gender of, 36–46
    in *-i, -u*, 40
    in *-ista, -cida, -iatra, -arca*, 39–40
    in *-ore, -trice, -ione, -zione, -tudine, -ie*, 40
    Italian vs English, 50
    masculine in *-a* (including *-ma* and *-ta*), 38
    some spelling problems, 47–48
    with dual plurals and meanings, 49
    with same form and different meaning, 43
nulla, see *niente*
numbers
    cardinal, 107–111
    collective, 113–114
    expressing age, 112
    expressing measurements, 113
    expressing time, 112
    idiomatic uses of, 114–115
    in mathematics, 112
    multiplicative, 113
    ordinal, 110–111
    with dates, 111
nuovo, 59

O

o, 150
    pronunciation of, 22

o ... o, 152
o meglio, 151
-occio, 169
occasionissima, 78
ogni, 104
ogni [qual] volta, 156
ogni tanto, 66
-ognolo, 169
ognuno, 104
-one, 169
-oni, 64
oppure, 150
ora, 152
ossia, 151
-ottello, 168
ottimamente, 77
-otto, 168
ovunque, 68
ovvero, 151

P

p, pronunciation of, 23
paio, 48
parecchio, 68–69, 106
parimenti, 62
partitives, see articles
passarsela, 241
passive form, see verbs
past tenses, see also verbs
    conditional, 215
    gerund, 224
    infinitive, 220–221
    participle, 226–227
    subjunctive, 211
peggio, 64, 74
peggiore, 64, 76
per, 145–146
    + infinitive, 146, 155, 159, 245, 263
per altro, 103
per cui, 152
per il fatto che, 154
per quanto, 159
per quel che, 159

perché, 22, 46, 62, 69, 90–91, 149, 154–155, 213, 225, 227
perciò, 151
perfect, 206, see also verbs
però, 150
pertanto, 151
pessimamente, 77
piacere, 187, 149–150
piantarla di + infinitive, 246
piccolo, 59, 76
più
    in comparisons, 69, 71–75, 77, 160
    in time expressions, 112
piuttosto, 151
pluperfect, see also verbs
    indicative, 205
    subjunctive, 211
poco, 60, 65, 68, 77, 106, 135, 140, 143, 232
poi, 66, 156
poiché, 154
possessives
    agreement of, 80–81
    forms of, 79
    omission of, 82
    position of, 82
    with family members, 81
potere, 179, 187, 223, 243–244
poterne, 240
povero, 59
prefixes, 164–166
prendersela, 241
prepararsi a + infinitive, 245
prepositions, 139–148
present, see also verbs
    conditional, 215
    gerund, 224
    indicative, 200–201
    infinitive, 220–221
    participle, 226
    perfect, 204–206
    progressive, 201
    subjunctive, 211
preterite, 204–205, see also verbs

prima, 66–67
prima che, 155–156, 214
probability, see hypothetical constructions
pronouns
    demonstrative, 93–98
    direct object and past participle agreement, 123
    direct object, 120–124
    double object and past participle agreement, 127
    double object, 126–127
    indefinite, 99–106
    indirect object, 124–125
    interrogative, 89–90
    object prepositional, 127–128
    personal, 116–130
    reciprocal, 130
    reflexive, 128–130
    relative, 84–87
    subject, 116–120
proprio, 64, 83, 91
punctuation, 30
pur di, 155
purché, 157

Q

q, pronunciation of, 23
qu, pronunciation of, 23
qua, 25, 27, 67
quadruplo, 113
qual, 29
qualche, 100–101, 138
qualche volta, 66
qualcos'altro, 100
qualcosa / qualche cosa, 100
qualcuno, 100–101, 104
quale, 60, 89–90
qualora, 157
qualsiasi, see *qualunque*
qualsivoglia, 105
qualunque, 103, 104
quando, 46, 66, 69, 90–91, 149–150, 155–157, 201–202, 214, 227
quand'anche, 157

quanto
    as a relative, 87
    as interrogative, 60, 69, 70, 90–91
    in comparisons, 72, 74
    expressing a matter, 222
quasi, 69, 158
quasi che, 214
quasi quasi, 65
quattro, with idiomatic meaning, 114
quegli, as a singular subject pronoun, 97
quello, 93–98
questo, 93–98
questi, as a singular subject pronoun, 97
qui, see *qua*
quindi, 151

R

r, pronunciation of, 23
reality, see hypothetical constructions
reciprocal forms, see verbs
reflexive forms, see verbs
regolarmente, 62
relative pronouns, see pronouns
reflexive pronouns, see pronouns

S

s, pronunciation of, 23
saluberrimo, 77
salvo, 159
santo, 57–58
sapere, 188, 223, 244
sc, pronunciation of, 24
se, 91, 129, 157–158
se ... o, 152, 162
se non, 159
sé, 27, 121, 129
sebbene, 157, 213, 225
seguitare a + infinitive, 246
semmai, 157
sempre, 66, 95, 164
sempre che, 157
sentirsela, 241

senza, 65, 148–149, 230
senza che, 158, 214
si, 121, 129–130
si passivante, 235
sì, 69, 91–92
sia ... che, 152
siccome, 154
simile, 97
smettere /smetterla di + infinitive, 246
solo, 63
sopra, 25, 67
sotto, 67, 147–148
stare, 183
    + gerund, 207, 225
stare a, 223
stare per + infinitive, 245
starci, 239
stesso, 98, 129–130
sto, as demonstrative, 96
stra-, 75, 166
strasciconi, 64
stress, 25–27
su, 68, 146
subjunctive, 153'–160, 172, 202, 204, 208–214, 219, 250, see also verbs
succedere, 250
suffixes, 166–170
super-, 75, 165
superiore, 76
superlatives
    absolute, 75–77
    in *-errimo* and *-entissimo*, 77
    irregular, 76–77
    of nouns, 78
    relative, 74–75
syllabification, 25
syntactic doubling, 24–25

T

t, pronunciation of, 23
tale, 97
tale e quale, 102
taluni, 105
talvolta, 66
tanto, 66, 68–69, 72, 74, 106, 152
tanto che, 152
tanto ... quanto, 72, 152
tenerci, 239
tentoni, 64
time, 112
tra, see *fra*
tra l'altro, 103
tranne, 159
triphthongs, 22
triplo, 113
troppo, 60, 68–69, 106, 232
tu, 116–118, 172
tutt'altro, 103
tuttavia, 150, 158
tutto, 34–35, 106

U

u, pronunciation of, 22
-uccio, 169, 170
un, 31–32
un', 33–32
un certo, 101
un po', 138
una, see *uno*
uno
    as article 31–32
    as adjective, 98
    as indefinite pronoun, 98
    as number 107–108
-uplo, 113
uscire, 198

V

v, pronunciation of, 23
vale a dire, 151
valerne, 240
valerne la pena, 136
vario, 60
vecchio, 59

vedere, 189, 248
vedersela, 241
veloce, 63
venire, 199
    as passive auxilary, 234–235
    + gerund, 226
verbs
    and prepositions, 228–232
    causative, 247–248
    compound tense formation 179–180
    defective, 248
    impersonal forms, 242
    in - *cene*, -*cisi*, and -*sene*, 241
    in -*arre*, -*orre*, -*urre*, 191–195
    in -*care*, -*gare*, -*iare*, and -*are*, 181–182
    in -*ci*, 241
    in -*ne*, 240
    in -*sela*, 241
    intransitive, 173, 177–178
    irregular in -*are*, 182–184
    irregular in -*ere*, 185–191
    irregular in -*ire*, 197–199
    modal, 179, 223, 243–244
    of perception, 248
    passive form, 233–234
    phrasal, 245–247
    pronominal, 238–241
    reciprocal form, 237
    reflexive form, 236
    regular and irregular conjugations, 180–199
    regular in -*are*, 180–181
    regular in -*ere*, 184–185
    regular in -*ire*, 195–196
    transit, 173, 177–178
    uses of mood and tenses, 200–227
    weather-indicating, 242
    with -*isc*-, 196
    with double auxiliary, 178–179
    with prepositions, 228–232
vi, 122, 126, 128–130
    equivalent to *ci*, 134
viceversa, 151
vicino, 67, 143, 148
visto che, 154
voi, 116, 118–119, 122–123, 127–128
volercene, 241
volerci, 240
volere, 179, 189, 223, 243–244
volerne, 240
vowels, 21–22

Z

z, pronunciation of, 23
zoppiconi, 64

VIA FOLIOS
A refereed book series dedicated to the culture of Italian Americans in North America

FRED MISURELLA, *Only Sons,* Vol. 79, Fiction $17
JEFF JACKSON, ed., *The Portable Lentricchia,* Vol. 78, Fiction, $16
RICHARD VETERE, *The Other Colors in a Snowstorm,* Vol. 77, Fiction, $10
GARIBALDI LAPOLLA, Steven Belluscio, ed., *The Fire in the Flesh,* Vol. 76, Ethnic Studies, $25
GEORGE GUIDA, *The Pope Stories and Other Tales of Troubled Times,* Vol. 75, Fiction, $15
ROBERT VISCUSI, *ellis island,* Vol. 74, Poetry, $28
ELENA GIANINI BELOTTI, *The Bitter Taste of Strangers Bread,* Vol. 73, Fiction, $24
PINO APRILE, *Terroni: All That Has Been Done to Ensure That the Italians of the South Become "Southerners,"* Vol. 72, Ethnic/Cultural Studies, $20
EMANUEL DI PASQUALE, *Harvest,* Vol. 71, Poetry, $10
ROBERT ZWEIG, *Return to Naples,* Vol. 70, Memoir, $16
LETIZIA AIROS AND OTTORINO CAPELLI, eds., *Guido,* Vol. 69, Italian/American Studies, $12
FRED GARAPHÉ, *Moustche Pete Is Dead! Evviva Baffo Pietro! The Fra Noi Columns 1985–1988,* Vol. 67, Literature/Oral History, $12
PAOLO RUFFILLI, *Dark Room,* Vol. 66, Poetry, $10
HELEN BAROLINI, *Crossing the Alps,* Vol. 65, Fiction, $14
COSMO FERRARA, *Profiles of Italian Americans,* Vol. 64, Italian/American Studies, $16
GIL FAGIANI, *Chianti in Connecticut,* Vol. 63, Poetry, $10
PIERO BASSETTI, NICCOLÓ D'AQUINO, *Italic Lessons,* Vol. 62, Italian/American Studies $10
CAVALIERI AND PASCARELLI, eds., *The Poet's Cookbook,* Vol. 61, Poetry/Recipes, $12
EMANUEL DI PASQUALE, *Siciliana,* Vol. 60, Poetry, $8
NATALIA COSTA-ZALESSOW, ed., *Bufalini,* Vol. 59, Poetry, $18
RICHARD VETERE, *Baroque,* Vol. 58, Fiction, $18
LEWIS TURCO, *La Famiglia/The Family,* Vol. 57, Memoir, $15
NICK JAMES MILETI, *The Unscrupulous,* Vol. 56, Humanities, $20
BASSETTI, ACCOLLA, D'AQUINO, *Italici: An Encounter with Bassetti,* Vol. 55, Italian Studies, $8
GIOSE RIMANELLI, *The Three-Legged One,* Vol. 54, Fiction, $15
CHARLES KLOPP, *Bele Antiche Storie,* Vol. 53, Critiscism, $25
JOSEPH RICAPITO, *Second Wave,* Vol. 52, Poetry, $12
GARY MORMINO, *Italians in Florida,* Vol. 51, Italiana Americana/History, $15
GIANFRANCO ANGELUCCI, *Federico F,* Vol. 50, Fiction, $16
ANTHONY VALERIO, *The Little Sailor,* Vol. 49, Fiction, $8.
ROSS TALARICO, *The Reptilian Interludes,* Vol. 48, Poetry, $15
RACHAEL GUIDO DEVRIES, *Teeny Tiny Tino's Fishing Story,* Vol. 47, Children's Lit, $6
EMANUEL DI PASQUALE, *Writing Anew,* Vol. 46, Poetry, $15
MARIA FAMA, *Looking for Cover,* Vol. 45, Poetry, $15
ANTHONY VALERIO, *Toni Cade Bambara's One Sicilian Night,* Vol. 44, Poetry, $10.
EMANUEL CARNEVALI, Dennis Barone, ed., *Furnished Rooms,* Vol. 43, Poetry, $14
BRENT ADKINS, et al., eds. *Shifting Borders, Negotiating Places,* Vol. 42, Proceedings, $18
GEORGE GUIDA, *Low Italian,* Vol. 41, Poetry, $10
GARDAPHE, GIORDANO, TAMBURRI, *Introducing Italian Americana,* Vol. 40, Ital. Amer. Studies, $10
DANIELA GIOSEFFI, *Blood Autumn/Autunno di sangue,* Vol. 39, Poetry, $15/$25
FRED MISURELLA, *Lies to Live by,* Vol. 38, Stories, $15
STEVEN BELLUSCIO, *Constructing a Bibliography,* Vol. 37, Italian Americana, $15
ANTHONY J. TAMBURRI, ed., *Italian Cultural Studies 2002,* Vol. 36, Essays, $18
BEA TUSIANI, *con amore,* Vol. 35, Memoir, $19
FLAVIA BRIZIO-SKOV, ed., *Reconstructing Societies in the Aftermath of War,* Vol. 34, History, $30
TAMBURRI, et al, eds., *Italian Cultural Studies 2001,* Vol. 33, Essays, $18
ELIZABETH G. MESSINA, ed., *In Our Own Voices,* Vol. 32, Ital. Amer. Studies, $25
STANISLAO G. PUGLIESE, *Desperate Inscriptions,* Vol. 31, History, $12
HOSTERT AND TAMBURRI, eds., *Screening Ethnicity,* Vol. 30, Italian American Culture, $25
PARATI AND LAWTON, eds., *Italian Cultural Studies,* Vol. 29, Essays, $18
HELEN BAROLINI, *More Italian Hours,* Vol. 28, Fiction, $16
FRANCO NASI, ed., *Intorno alla Via Emilia,* Vol. 27, Culture, $16
ARTHUR L. CLEMENTS, *The Book of Madness & Love,* Vol. 26, Poetry, $10

VIA FOLIOS
A refereed book series dedicated to the culture of Italian Americans in North America

JOHN CASEY, et al., *Imagining Humanity,* Vol. 25, Interdisciplinary Studies, $18
ROBERT LIMA, *Sardinia/Sardegna,* Vol. 24, Poetry, $10
DANIELA GIOSEFFI, *Going On,* Vol. 23, Poetry, $10
ROSS TALARICO, *The Journey Home,* Vol. 22, Poetry, $12
EMANUEL DI PASQUALE, *The Silver Lake Love Poems,* Vol. 21, Poetry, $7
JOSEPH TUSIANI, *Ethnicity,* Vol. 20, Poetry, $12
JENNIFER LAGIER, *Second-Class Citizen,* Vol. 19, Poetry, $8
FELIX STEFANILE, *The Country of Absence,* Vol. 18, Poetry, $9
PHILIP CANNISTRARO, *Blackshirts,* Vol. 17, History, $12
LUIGI RUSTICHELLI, ed., *Seminario sul racconto,* Vol. 16, Narrative, $10
LEWIS TURCO, *Shaking the Family Tree,* Vol. 15, Memoirs, $9
LUIGI RUSTICHELLI, ed., *Seminario sulla drammaturgia,* Vol. 14, Theater/Essays, $10
FRED GARDAPHÈ, *Moustache Pete Is Dead! Long Live Moustache Pete!* Vol. 13, Oral Lit., $10
JONE GAILLARD CORSI, *Il libretto d'autore, 1860–1930,* Vol. 12, Criticism, $17
HELEN BAROLINI, *Chiaroscuro: Essays of Identity,* Vol. 11, Essays, $15
PICARAZZI AND FEINSTEIN, eds., *An African Harlequin in Milan,* Vol. 10, Theater/Essays, $15
JOSEPH RICAPITO, *Florentine Streets & Other Poems,* Vol. 9, Poetry, $9
FRED MISURELLA, *Short Time,* Vol. 8, Novella, $7
NED CONDINI, *Quartettsatz,* Vol. 7, Poetry, $7
ANTHONY TAMBURRI, ed., *Fuori: Essays by Italian/American Lesbians and Gays,* Vol. 6, Essays, $10
ANTONIO GRAMSCI, P. Verdicchio, Trans. & Introd., *The Southern Question,* Vol. 5, SocCrit., $5
DANIELA GIOSEFFI, *Word Wounds & Water Flowers,* Vol. 4, Poetry, $8
WILEY FEINSTEIN, *Humility's Deceit: Calvino Reading Ariosto Reading Calvino,* Vol. 3, Criticism, $10
PAOLO A. GIORDANO, ed., *Joseph Tusiani: Poet, Translator, Humanist,* Vol. 2, Criticism, $25
ROBERT VISCUSI, *Oration Upon the Most Recent Death of Christopher Columbus,* Vol. 1, Poetry, $3

Bordighera Press is an imprint of Bordighera, Incorcorpated, an independently owned not-for-profit scholarly organization that has no legal affiliation with the University of Central Florida or with The John D. Calandra Italian American Institute, Queen's College/CUNY.

www.ingramcontent.com/pod-product-compliance
Lightning Source LLC
Chambersburg PA
CBHW080428230426
43662CB00015B/2217